Information Technology for CSEC® Examinations

Third edition

Kelvin Skeete, Kyle Skeete

Information Technology for CSEC® Examinations is an independent publication and has not been authorised, sponsored, or otherwise approved by CXC.

CAMBRIDGE
UNIVERSITY PRESS

CAMBRIDGE
UNIVERSITY PRESS

University Printing House, Cambridge CB2 8BS, United Kingdom

One Liberty Plaza, 20th Floor, New York, NY 10006, USA

477 Williamstown Road, Port Melbourne, VIC 3207, Australia

314–321, 3rd Floor, Plot 3, Splendor Forum, Jasola District Centre, New Delhi – 110025, India

103 Penang Road, #05-06/07, Visioncrest Commercial, Singapore 238467

Cambridge University Press is part of the University of Cambridge.

It furthers the University's mission by disseminating knowledge in the pursuit of education, learning and research at the highest international levels of excellence.

www.cambridge.org
Information on this title: www.cambridge.org/9780521153270

© Cambridge University Press 2010

First published 2004
Second edition 2007
Third edition 2010

20 19 18 17 16 15 14 13 12 11 10 9

Printed in Great Britain by CPI Group (UK) Ltd, Croydon CR0 4YY

A catalogue record for this publication is available from the British Library

ISBN 978-0-521-15327-0 Paperback with CD-ROM for Windows and Mac

Contents

Introduction

Welcome to the third edition of Information Technology for CSEC®! This massive overhaul to the previous edition has two main goals:

1 to update the book so that it <u>completely</u> covers the new Information Technology Syllabus as described in CXC 30/G/SYLL 08;
2 to update the practical sections to the latest versions of Microsoft Office® (2003 and 2007).

The Caribbean Examinations Council (CXC) has made significant changes to the Information Technology Syllabus that take effect from the May/June 2010 examinations. In order to address these changes:

- new sections have been added to the book, covering Microsoft PowerPoint® and FrontPage®;
- much greater emphasis has been placed on problem solving (there is now a dedicated Problem Solving section);
- a section devoted to Pascal programming has been included;
- additional material has been added throughout the book, especially to the Theory section.

Since the last edition was published, Microsoft Office 2007 has increased in popularity as new computers are coming with it installed. Office 2007 has a new and improved interface that is a radical departure from previous versions. Unfortunately, many schools and businesses still use earlier previous versions, placing students in the unfortunate situation of being taught on one version but having to practise on another.

This edition has taken the ambitious step of covering <u>both</u> Office 2003 and 2007 in the practical sections. Where the two versions diverge, the differences are clearly highlighted. No longer will students have to struggle searching for commands in Office 2007. Just as importantly, the <u>similarities</u> between the two versions are emphasised, making it easy for students to take the skills learned in one version and transfer them to another.

But that isn't all we have done in this new edition. Traditionally, students struggle with Microsoft Excel® and Access®. We've simplified the most difficult topics such as Queries and Criteria Ranges to make them much easier to understand.

The book also includes a CD-ROM that installs any files required by the practical exercises. The exercise files are installed to the location of the student's choosing (usually the Desktop). They are grouped by the part of the book (Word, Excel, Access, PowerPoint) and the chapter. Using the exercise files provides the following benefits:

- all the files required to do an exercise are located in a folder of their own;
- exercises don't need to be done in order;
- mistakes made in previous exercises don't interfere with future exercises.

As you can see, a lot of effort went into producing the third edition of Information Technology for CSEC. We are quite pleased with what we have accomplished, and are confident that this will be the best edition yet!

Acknowledgements

The author and publishers are grateful for the permissions granted to reproduce copyright materials. While every effort has been made, it has not always been possible to identify the sources of all the materials used, or to trace all copyright holders. If any omissions are brought to our notice, we will be happy to include the appropriate acknowledgments on reprinting.

Microsoft product screen shots reprinted with permission from Microsoft Corporation

p. 4l Ramin Khojasteh/Shutterstock; p. 4r Alexander Sabilin/Shutterstock; p. 7 RYGER/Shutterstock; p. 10 Matzsoca/Shutterstock; p. 11 Smitry Sosenushkin/Shutterstock; p. 14l Popovici Ioan/ Shutterstock; p. 14r Pchemyan Georgiy/Shutterstock; p. 17l Stephen Leech/Shutterstock; p. 17r Bet Noire/ Shutterstock; p. 18 Craig Berhorst/Shutterstock; p. 19 Michael Ransburg/Shutterstock; p. 20 Spencer Grant, age fotostock, Photolibrary; p. 22t 0833379753/ Shutterstock; p. 22b Dimitar Janevski/Shutterstock; p. 23t Feng Yu/Shutterstock; p. 23b Dmitry Rukhlenko/Shutterstock; p. 24l Helene Rogers/Alamy; p. 24r Lena_Small/Shutterstock; p. 25 Utemov Alexey/ Shutterstock; p. 27 Marc Pinter/Alamy; p. 28t Marek Slusarczyk/Shutterstock; p. 28b robootb/Shutterstock; p. 47 Helen Shorey/Shutterstock; p. 48 Aleksi Markku/ Shutterstock; p. 53 Konstantin Yolshin/Shutterstock; p. 59 Corey K. Graham; p. 67 M_G/Shutterstock; p. 72 Patrick Eden/Alamy; pp.76, 251 image courtesy of Tesco Stores Ltd, Cheshunt, Herts; p. 253 BBC Learning – 'Dance Mat Typing'; p. 261 AridOcean/ Shutterstock; p. 271 McMay Steeve/ABACA/Press Association Images

l = left, r = right, t = top, b = bottom

Part 1

Theory

1. The basic components of computers

What is a computer?

Many people see a computer as a sort of magical grey box that you get from Compaq or IBM which you use to run programs (and the occasional game when your boss or parents aren't watching). However, the formal definition of a computer is somewhat broader. Simply put, a computer is an electronic device that can accept data and instructions, process them or store them for later retrieval, and sometimes generate output (usually based on the processing) (see Figure 1.1). As you would expect, this definition includes more than the PC (personal computer) that you have at home or at school. For example, most new models of cars come with a computer to manage their fuel injection systems.

Advantages of using computers

Computers obviously wouldn't be as popular as they are now if they did not offer advantages over doing tasks manually. Some of these advantages are:

- Computers can perform calculations much more quickly and accurately than humans. For example, modern computers can perform hundreds of millions of calculations per second.

- Large amounts of data can be stored in a small amount of space. For example, hundreds of pages worth of text can be stored on a flash drive.
- Computers can work continuously and perform repetitive tasks well. Unlike their human counterparts, computers do not get bored or tired.
- Computers can simulate things that would take too long, be too dangerous or simply be impossible for humans to attempt.

Drawbacks of using computers

What? There are disadvantages to using computers? As hard as it is to believe, computers do have their drawbacks. These include:

- The introduction of computers can cause redundancy in the workplace. Employees may lose their jobs if a computer can do a job more efficiently and ultimately more cheaply.
- Computers make it easy for people to misuse information. Computers make it easy to store large amounts of information about people. In some cases this information can be freely and easily accessed and used for purposes for which it was not originally intended.

- Downtime happens when a computer breaks down or data becomes corrupted. Businesses often rely so much on technology that when computers fail they have no back-up manual systems and are temporarily rendered helpless as a result.
- The introduction of computer systems in the workplace is expensive. The cost is not only due to the purchasing of the equipment; in some companies, the time it takes to train the staff to use the system causes several thousands of dollars of lost productivity.
- There are health risks associated with excessive or improper use of computers. The glare from the screen can cause eyestrain and inadequate support for the wrists when typing can cause carpal-tunnel syndrome.

However, most people see these disadvantages as minor (especially when compared with the tremendous benefits); hence the popularity of computers today.

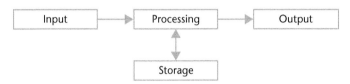

Figure 1.1 *A diagram outlining how the typical computer system functions*

Types of computer

Ask the average person what types of computer he/she knows and the response will probably be, 'That's easy! Dell, Gateway, Compaq, IBM …'. However, these are merely <u>brands</u> of computers. The types of computer are (roughly in order of size and speed): supercomputers, mainframes, minicomputers and microcomputers.

Supercomputer
'Supercomputer' is the general term given to the fastest computers in the world. These computers are very large and may take up several rooms. Because of their tremendous processing power, supercomputers are used in fields that require vast amounts of complex mathematical calculations, such as weather simulation and nuclear research.

Did you know?

The fastest computer in the world (at the time of writing) is IBM's Roadrunner supercomputer. It is over 20 000 times as fast as the most powerful desktop computer. It cost US $133 million to build and takes up over 6000 square feet.

Mainframe
Like supercomputers, mainframes are very fast large-scale computer systems. Mainframes have a large number of terminals and peripheral devices because they are used simultaneously by hundreds (or even thousands) of persons. As a result, mainframes may be even larger than supercomputers. To meet the demands of the large number of users, they have a large memory and large storage capacity.

Three applications of the use of a mainframe computer are:

- in banks for processing customer accounts
- by utility companies for processing telephone, water and electricity bills
- by airlines for making flight arrangements

What is the difference between a supercomputer and a mainframe?

If mainframes and supercomputers are both very large and fast computers, what is the difference between them? The mainframe divides its processing power among several users and programs at the same time (multiprocessing). A supercomputer, on the other hand, runs very few programs at the same time, so that those programs are run as quickly as possible.

Minicomputer
A minicomputer is a multiprocessing computer system that is smaller and slower than a mainframe. The term 'mini' is a bit misleading, though, because minicomputers are still a lot larger than the PCs people have in their homes. Minicomputers support fewer users than mainframes (200 is the limit used in some definitions).

If you are beginning to think that you do not see much of a difference between a mainframe and a minicomputer, don't worry. The distinction between the two is becoming increasingly blurred and is based mainly on the size and number of users.

Two examples of the applications of a minicomputer are:

- in networking, the operations in an automobile sales and service outlet
- in manufacturing, for inventory control, accounts and process control

Microcomputer

'Microcomputer' is a term used to refer to computers that contain a microprocessor. You know this type of computer by its more familiar name – the PC. This is the type of computer that you are most likely to use. As the name suggests, a microprocessor is a very small processor. This is in the form of a silicon chip like the Pentium processor.

Since they use smaller processors, microprocessors are much smaller than other forms of computers. Note that for this same reason, microprocessors are nowhere near as powerful as other types of computer. Microcomputers come in different types and sizes:

- The desktop, which is the most popular type, is usually supplied with separate units such as the tower, a monitor, keyboard, mouse and external speakers.
- The laptops or notebooks are small portable computers. These machines come with the monitor, keyboard and CPU assembled as a single unit.

Figure 1.2 *A notebook computer*

Three examples of the application of a microcomputer are:

- in homes for recreation
- in an office for producing documents and processing data, such as payroll, inventory and billing
- for communication through the use of Internet services

Computer systems

A computer system is the combination of **hardware** and **software.** The hardware consists of the physical components of the computer, such as the monitor or the keyboard. In other words, the parts of the computer that you can touch are all hardware. 'Software' is the term that is used to refer to the programs that run on the hardware. Neither one is much use without the other, since without hardware you would not be able to run software and without software you would just have an expensive piece of equipment that does nothing.

The two main types of software are the operating system and the application programs that run on top of the operating system.

Categories of computer hardware

There are four main categories of computer hardware:

1 the Central Processing Unit (CPU)
2 input devices, which allow data to be entered into the computer
3 output devices, which are used for outputting ('sending out') data from the computer
4 storage devices, both primary and backing

The Central Processing Unit (CPU)

As its name suggests, the Central Processing Unit (CPU) is the part of the computer that does the processing. It also controls the transfer of data between memory and the other devices that make up the computer system. The CPU consists of:

- the Control Unit (CU)
- the Arithmetic/Logic Unit (ALU)
- small, very fast areas of memory. The smallest and fastest memory is in the form of registers. There is also cache, which is larger and slower than the registers but is still much faster than RAM (you do not have to worry too much about these terms)

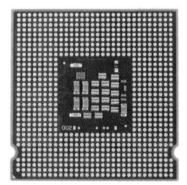

Figure 1.3 *A CPU chip*

The Control Unit (CU)

The Control Unit (CU) is the part of the CPU which, as you may be able to guess, controls the operations of the CPU. It is used:

- to direct the operation of the internal processor components (components that process the data)
- to control the flow of programs and data in and out of the primary memory (main memory)
- to read and interpret program instructions (instructions that allow the computer to perform various tasks)
- to control the flow of information to and from all the components of the computer, eg input and output devices (I/O devices), disk drives and printers

The Arithmetic/Logic Unit (ALU)

This is the part of the CPU that does the following:

- performs arithmetic operations. These operations include addition, subtraction, division, multiplication, etc.
- performs logical operations. These operations include reasoning and performing the comparisons necessary to make decisions.

Storage devices

A computer would not be a very useful device if it did not have the ability to store data or to allow instructions to be loaded at a later time (even if the 'later time' is a few seconds later). Imagine having to enter the same instructions and data every time you wanted the computer to perform a common task – or if the computer could not remember anything that it had done before!

Technology certainly would not have progressed as much as it has today. For this reason, computers come with storage devices. There are two types: primary and secondary.

Primary storage (main memory/immediate access storage)

There are two types of primary storage (note that both use chips):

1 **Random Access Memory (RAM).** The contents in this type of memory are temporary and are lost when

the computer is turned off (the data is volatile). RAM is used to store the instructions and data for currently running programs and the operating system.

2 **Read Only Memory (ROM).** This type of memory is permanent (usually) and the data stored in it is not lost when the computer is turned off (the data is non-volatile). As a result, ROM is used to store data that must not be lost even when the computer is turned off, such as the commands which start up (boot up) the computer. These instructions are programmed into the ROM chips by the manufacturers.

Secondary storage (backing storage/auxiliary storage devices)

Unlike primary storage, secondary storage is not done on chips. Some examples of secondary storage devices are:

- hard disks
- magnetic tape
- floppy disks
- microfilm
- CDs
- DVDs

These devices are used to store programs, as well as data that is not being processed, for later retrieval.

Peripheral devices

In order to understand what a peripheral device is, it is important to first become familiar with a few terms. The CPU is located on the main processor board (also known as the **motherboard**). The motherboard is found inside the **tower** (the rectangular 'box' to which most other components that make up the computer system are attached). The term '**peripheral device**' refers to those devices that make up the computer system apart from the motherboard, its associated electronics and main memory.

Some examples of peripheral devices are:

- input devices – keyboard, mouse, joystick, OMR (Optical Mark Reader), OCR (Optical Character Reader), MICR (Magnetic Ink Character Reader)
- storage devices – magnetic tape drive, hard drive, floppy drive
- output devices – dot matrix, laser and ink-jet printers, VDU (Visual Display Unit: monitor), speakers

Tips

In order to be able to give a list of peripheral devices, rather than commit a long list to memory, many students simply remember that all devices that are part of the computer system and are outside the tower (external devices) are peripheral devices. However, note that even if a device is <u>not</u> outside the tower, it can still be a peripheral device, for example the hard drive.

Exercise 1

1 Explain why a computer is so beneficial to a business or a home user.
2 What are the functions of a typical computer system?
3 Name one type of computer and give three applications for which it can be used.
4 Give the meanings of the following abbreviations and state one function of each:
   a ALU
   b CU
   c ROM
   d RAM
5 What is a peripheral device? Give four examples of peripheral devices.
6 State two limitations of computers.
7 State two advantages of computers.
8 At lunch Mary met with her two friends at a popular restaurant. They were discussing the growing need for computers within their various work institutions to assist with their tasks. However, the type of computer needed for each task is different. Mary is a secretary at a local insurance company and her company *needs a computer for her to type letters and store important records.* Suzy, on the other hand, is a data entry clerk at a telephone company and her company *needs a computer for the data entry staff to use simultaneously to process telephone bills.* John is a scientist and his company *needs a very fast computer to perform complex mathematical calculations.*
   State the type of computer that is best suited for each company.
9 **a** Explain why it is necessary for a computer to be equipped with secondary storage.
   b Give three examples of secondary storage devices.
10 Explain the difference between hardware and software.

2. Primary storage devices and media

In Chapter 1, there was a brief mention of primary storage devices. Here we will look at these in greater detail.

As was mentioned earlier, there are two types of primary storage (main memory): Random Access Memory (RAM) and Read Only Memory (ROM). These are made from silicon chips consisting of many electronic circuits.

Random Access Memory (RAM)

When people talk about memory, they are normally referring to RAM. As you can probably guess, the contents of RAM can be randomly accessed. This means that data from any location in RAM can be accessed when needed instead of having to go through each location in order until you get to the one you want. What is not apparent from its name, however, is the fact that not only can the contents of RAM be read – they can also be written to. This is (generally) not the case for the other type of primary storage, ROM.

The fact that the contents of RAM can be changed proves very useful indeed when it comes to running programs. First of all, when the computer boots up, the operating system (which is itself a program) is loaded from the disk into RAM. Then, when an application program is run, its instructions that will be executed are loaded into RAM (a separate part, of course). In addition, any data used by the program is also stored in RAM. This data can therefore be changed when the program runs.

The contents of RAM are lost when the computer is turned off. It is for this reason that if the electricity goes off or the power cord gets unplugged when the computer is in use, you 'lose your work'.

Read Only Memory (ROM)

The contents of ROM cannot be changed when the ROM is being used by the computer. They can only be read; hence the term **read only**. The contents of ROM are usually programmed by the manufacturers. This is one of the two main differences between ROM and RAM. The other is the fact that the contents of ROM are not lost when the computer is turned off. As a result, ROM is used to store the commands and data that are executed each time the computer is turned on. Like RAM, the contents of ROM can be accessed randomly.

ROM is not only found in typical computers though. It is also found in most devices with electronic components, such as videos, microwaves, cell phones, video games and even missiles. In these devices it is used to store commands that define how the device in question operates.

Other types of ROM

Programmable Read Only Memory (PROM)
This type of ROM can be programmed with a special machine as opposed to using the expensive masks needed to produce large volumes of ROM chips. Once a PROM is programmed, however, its contents cannot be changed.

Erasable Programmable Read Only Memory (EPROM)
This type of ROM is designed so that its contents can be erased using ultraviolet light. Then the chip can be reprogrammed. This can be done several times (as opposed to PROM, which can be programmed only once). One of the disadvantages of EPROM is that its contents do not last as long as those of other types of ROM. Also, because sunlight contains ultraviolet rays, you must protect EPROM chips from exposure to sunlight.

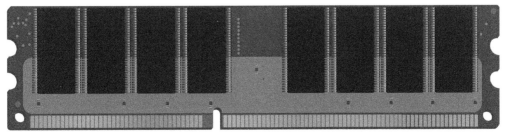

Figure 2.1 *A Random Access Memory (RAM) chip*

A comparison between RAM and ROM

The table below compares the features of RAM and ROM.

RAM	ROM
data can be both read and written	read only
volatile	non-volatile
contents modified by programs on the computer in question	contents modified by manufacturer
use chips	
data can be randomly accessed	

Technical terms used with the storage of data

You are probably familiar with the fact that the tremendous amounts of data that computers manipulate are stored in base two (binary). You have probably also heard of bytes, kilobytes, and so on. But in case you are still not entirely certain what these terms mean, here is a list of technical terms you will come across when talking about data storage.

A **bit** is a unit of storage that has two possible values, 0 and 1. It is the smallest unit.

A **byte** is a group of eight bits.

Did you know?

A group of four bits is known as a **nibble**. Therefore a byte consists of two nibbles. After saying this aloud a few times, one has to wonder what the person who came up with these terms was thinking when he did so!

Most people think of a **kilobyte** as one thousand bytes. Strictly speaking, the term actually means 2^{10} (1024) bytes. Similarly, the actual numbers of bytes referred to by the terms **megabyte**, **gigabyte**, and

terabyte are a bit different from what most people believe. Below is a table that shows the differences. A person using one of these terms is generally referring to the approximate figure. Programs that display file sizes use the actual sizes to give accurate results. The approximate and actual values are shown in the table.

Did you know?

When PC manufacturers, for example Dell, give the size of a hard drive, they usually are using the approximate figures. In order to avoid confusion (and probably for legal reasons too), they now have a footnote next to the symbol saying something like '1 GB = 1 billion bytes'.

It is not surprising if you are confused by this. But chances are that when you are asked what one of the afore mentioned terms means, you are expected to give the approximate number of bytes.

There are a few more data storage terms that you may not know the meaning of:

- **word** – the size of the data (or instruction) that the CPU can handle in a single cycle
- **word-length/word-size** – the number of bits in a word
- **address** – the identification of a particular location in the memory where a data item or an instruction is stored
- **address content** – the data or instruction that is stored in a given address
- **character** – any digit, letter or symbol

Tip

Be careful when using your symbols! kB (which means kilobytes) is different from kb (which means kilobits). However, many people use these interchangeably.

Term	Symbol	Number of bytes		Actual
		Approximate		
kilobyte	kB	1000	1 thousand	2^{10} (1024)
megabyte	MB	1000000	1 million	2^{20} (1048576)
gigabytc	GB	1000000000	1 billion	2^{30} (1073741824)
terabyte	TB	1000000000000	1 trillion	2^{40} (1099511627776)

Bistable devices

You have probably never heard of bistable devices but these are the foundation of digital electronics. A bistable device is a device that can exist in one of two possible states. It can be compared to an on/off switch. You will recall that you have already come across something that exists in two states – a bit. In fact, a bit is a bistable device. Another example of a bistable device is a key on a keyboard – it can be either up or down.

Exercise 2

1 State two similarities and two differences between RAM and ROM.
2 Name three devices other than the typical computer where ROM may be used.
3 Give the two types of ROM and state the difference between the two.
4 Define the following terms:
   a bit
   b byte
   c nibble
   d kilobyte
   e megabyte
   f gigabyte
   g terabyte
   h word
   i word-size/word-length
   j address
   k address content
   l character
5 Explain why a bistable device is said to function like an off/on switch and give an example of this type of device.
6 You were typing a document on the computer and the power to the computer was interrupted momentarily. When the computer was restarted, the document was no longer in memory.
   a Explain why the document was not still in memory.
   b Give one precaution that can be employed to ensure that a document is not completely lost in the event of a power failure.
7 Which type of memory stores commands and data that are used for starting the computer?
8 The technician who was making repairs to a video inadvertently left the video in the midday sun with its EPROM exposed. He later discovered that the video had developed additional problems as a result of being exposed to the sunlight. Explain what could have caused the problem.

3. Secondary storage devices and media

From magnetic tape and hard disks to CD-ROMs and DVD-ROMs, several secondary storage devices are available – each with a slightly different use. What all have in common is that each is used to store programs and data so that they can be retrieved at a later time.

Magnetic tape

Magnetic tape is used for storing large amounts of data. It is especially suitable for this purpose since it is very cheap. Magnetic tape comes in the form of a reel or cartridge and is made of plastic that is coated with a metal oxide. The tape is divided into parallel rows known as **tracks**. The most common tape is one with nine tracks. Tracks one to eight each store a bit in a byte (remember that a byte is made up of eight bits). Track nine is called the **parity track**. It is used as a method of checking the accuracy of the data. Each group of nine bits (one on each track) is known as a **frame** (see Figure 3.1).

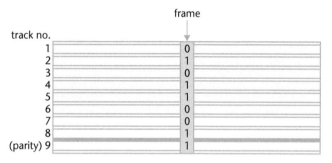

Figure 3.1 *The structure of magnetic tape*

There are two types of parity: odd parity and even parity. Both are quite simple. If data is stored using odd parity, then the number of ones in each frame should always be odd. So when each byte is being recorded, the computer checks the number of ones. If it was even, the corresponding bit in the parity track is set to one, therefore making the number of ones odd. If it was odd, the parity track is set to zero. Therefore, when the computer is reading the tape and it comes across a group of bits with an even number of ones, it will know that something is wrong. Even parity works in a similar manner. Some examples of even and odd parity are shown in the table below.

Original byte	Odd parity	Even parity
11001010	111001010	011001010
11101001	011101001	111101001

Magnetic tape is high density, high speed and has a large capacity. It is read using a **magnetic tape drive**. Data is accessed <u>sequentially</u>, which means that the data is accessed in the order in which it was stored. As you can imagine, this method of accessing data would be particularly slow if you required the records in a random (haphazard) manner. Magnetic tape is used for:

- backing up the hard disk
- data entry using a key-to-tape device
- archiving data

Floppy disk

Despite the name, **floppy disks** are made of hard plastic. They are 3½ inches in diameter and are read by **floppy disk drives**.

Figure 3.2 *Floppy disks*

If you were to remove the square plastic case (something that you are not advised to do), you would see what the data is actually stored on. It is a flat, round, plastic disk coated with magnetic material. Like magnetic tape, this is divided into tracks. However, these tracks are in the form of concentric circles (as shown in Figure 3.3).

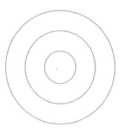

Figure 3.3 *Concentric circles*

Like all disks, a floppy disk must be **formatted** before it can be used for storing data. This is the process of preparing the disk for use in the computer. Note that when you format a disk you erase all the information on the disk. Data can be accessed sequentially (like with magnetic tape) or directly. With **direct access** (random access) you can jump straight to data at a particular location instead of going through all the locations before that one. Examples of the use/application of floppy disks are:

- storing small programs
- backing up data files
- storing small documents

Precautions needed with floppy disks

Even though floppy disks are very cheap, you should still take care of the ones that you have. You would also want to make sure that you do not lose data that you have on disk. Here are some precautions needed with floppy disks:

- Don't place the disk on a device that has or generates a magnetic field (e.g. a speaker).
- Don't bend the disk.
- Don't place the disk in hot or wet places.
- Only write on the disk with a soft-tip pen.
- Don't remove the disk from the drive when the disk drive's light is on.

Determining the storage capacity of a floppy disk

A floppy disk has two surfaces. There are usually 80 tracks on each. Each track on a disk is divided into wedge-shaped sections known as **sectors**. There are, on average, 18 sectors per track. The average amount of data that can be stored on one of these sectors is 0.5 kB. In order to determine the storage on <u>any</u> disk, you use the following formula:

Storage capacity = number of surfaces × number of tracks × number of sectors per track × number of bytes per sector.
  So, for a floppy disk:
The number of bytes per track = number of sectors per track × number of bytes per sector
    $= 18 \times 0.5\,kB = 9\,kB$
The number of bytes per side = number of bytes per track × number of tracks per side
    $= 9\,kB \times 80 = 720\,kB$
The number of bytes on the disk = number of bytes per side × number of sides
    $= 720\,kB \times 2 = 1440\,kB$ or $1.44\,MB$
(Note that a floppy disk has two surfaces – one on each side.)

Hard disk (fixed)

A hard disk is a large capacity, rigid magnetic disk that is used for storing data. Data is read from or written to a hard disk using an arm-like device known as a read/write head. This is a device that is used to write data to the disk (store it on the disk) and to read data from the disk.

Data may be read from/written to a hard disk using either a moving read/write head or a fixed head. A moving read/write head moves to the track that corresponds to the data while the disk is spinning. A fixed read/write head, as you may expect, does not move. Instead, there is a fixed head for each track. This gives the fixed-head system the advantage of having a faster access time.

The **access time** is the time it takes for the data to be accessed. This faster access time is because of the faster **seek time** (the time it takes the read/write head to get to a specific position on the disk). The fixed-head system is more expensive than the moving-head system. The term 'hard drive' refers to a collection of hard disks and read/write heads. Each disk (or **platter**) surface can have its own read/write head(s) in order to allow the quicker transfer of data. Like a floppy disk, this data can be accessed either sequentially or directly. However, a hard drive is much faster than a floppy disk drive. Each surface also has a much larger capacity than a floppy disk. It is also much more expensive.

Figure 3.4 *The top and bottom of a hard drive*

Because of its enormous capacity (up to several gigabytes), a hard drive is used for storing a wide variety of things such as:

- operating systems
- office programs
- multimedia programs
- games
- images, songs
- databases

Precautions needed with the hard disk

Just because it is called a 'hard disk' doesn't mean that you do not need to take precautions in order to protect it. Some of these precautions are:

- Don't turn the power off without shutting the computer down through the normal shut-down procedure. Failure to shut down the computer correctly can lead to corruption of data.
- Don't subject the computer to severe vibrations or jerks or move the computer if the power is turned on. This could cause physical damage to the hard drive.

External hard drives

Although hard drives are normally built into the computer, external hard drives are increasing in popularity. These drives are put in special enclosures to help protect them and can be attached to the computer via a USB port.

Optical disk

Magnetic techniques are not the only methods used to store data on various types of media. Data is also stored on optical disks. These are disks that are read using laser beams. Chances are that you will be familiar with two types of optical disk: CDs and DVDs. CDs and DVDs have different capacities and use slightly different optical technology. However, looking at them you'd never guess. CDs and DVDs look the same; they are both disk-shaped objects with a hole in the middle and a reflective surface. Both types of disk use the same method to read the data. A low-powered laser uses a lens to focus the laser beam on a part of the disk. Under the plastic layer on the reflective side there are areas that reflect light differently. The drive can detect these differences and converts these differences into ones and zeros that can be interpreted by the computer.

Like other types of storage media, optical disks store data in tracks. However, an optical disk has only one track spiralling from the inside of the disk (the hole in the middle) to the outside of the disk.

CDs

Compact Disks (CDs) have taken the world by storm, and for good reason. CDs are not much bigger than floppy disks, yet a single CD can hold the same amount of data as hundreds of floppy disks (typically 650 or 700 MB). Despite their tremendous storage capacities, CDs are pretty cheap. CDs are also fairly durable and may still function after mild scratches and the occasional fingerprint on the reflective surface. We will look at three types of CD commonly used in the computer industry and the technology involved.

CD-ROM

As you may suspect, the 'ROM' in CD-ROM means that CD-ROMs are 'read only'. Most software manufacturers distribute their programs on CD-ROM because modern programs are quite large and can take up hundreds of floppy disks. Manufacturers distribute the programs on CD-ROM as opposed to the other types of CD because it is the only type of CD found in the computer industry that is really suited for mass production. Large numbers of CD-ROMs can be created in a manner similar to printing a book. The original CD-ROM is created by using a laser to burn it. From this master, thousands of identical copies are created using **CD-ROM makers**. A CD-ROM maker is very expensive and not suitable for casual use.

The reflective surface of a CD-ROM has combinations of **pits** (bumps) and **lands** (the flat areas with no bumps) that are used to represent data (see Figure 3.5). Just like the audio CDs found in most homes, a CD-ROM can be used to store songs. Such CD-ROMs can be read in many CD players. However, they can also be used to store files that can be recognised by the computer. These files are commonly used to store things like large programs, multimedia encyclopedias, and so on. As you would expect, CD-ROMs can be read by CD-ROM drives. However, you may be surprised to hear that CD-ROMs can also be read in CD-R and CD-RW drives. If you do not know what these terms mean, don't worry – you will in a few minutes.

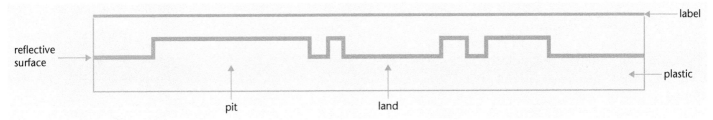

Figure 3.5 *A cross-section of a CD-ROM (not drawn to scale)*

CD-R

As was mentioned earlier, a CD-ROM maker is very expensive and not suitable for the average computer user. However, the introduction of the CD-R and the CD-R drive provided small businesses and home users with the ability to create CDs. A CD-R (Compact Disk – Recordable) is a WORM storage media. This acronym stands for Write Once Read Many. It means that a user can record on a blank CD-R but once he/she has finished recording, the CD-R can only be read. In other words, after you have finished burning a CD-R once, it becomes like a CD-ROM. A CD-R has a special layer of transparent dye on top of the reflective layer.

When the CD-R is being recorded (burned), the CD-R writer heats up certain parts of the dye. This makes them opaque. Devices that read CD-Rs can detect the difference between the transparent parts and the opaque parts. CD-Rs can be read in most CD-ROM drives, as well as in both CD-R and CD-RW drives. They are used to store a wide variety of things such as MP3s, digital photographs and custom-written software. One final thing to note, however, is that CD-Rs do not last as long as CD-ROMs.

Tip

Do not leave a CD-R in sunlight for prolonged periods of time. The sunlight may heat up the dye in the same way as the laser in a CD-R drive, causing data to be lost and ultimately rendering the CD-R unreadable.

How do I recognise a CD-R?

The reflective surface of a CD-R is coloured (usually green or blue). This is because of the type of dye used. For CD-ROMs and CD-RWs it is usually silver.

CD-RW

A CD-RW (Compact Disk – Rewriteable) is a type of CD that allows data to be recorded and erased several times. Like a CD-R, it has a dye layer. However, this dye layer is more advanced. When heated at one temperature it becomes transparent; at another it becomes opaque.

CD-RWs are burned and read by **CD-RW drives**. Such drives can also read CD-Rs and CD-ROMs and burn CD-Rs. CD-RWs are often used to store things that you would put on CD-Rs, such as digital photographs and MP3s. However, because they can be erased and burned again, they can be used to back up files. CD-RWs are more expensive than CD-Rs and, like CD-Rs, they do not last as long as CD-ROMs. They also cannot be read in older CD-ROM drives.

DVDs

A DVD is the next generation optical disk. It has a larger capacity than a CD and has features intended to reduce piracy. For example, a DVD encoded for the North American region can only be played in equipment bought in that region. Also, DVDs need to be decoded before they can be read. The large capacity of a DVD means it can be used to store high-quality movies (the movies actually have a higher quality than those on video tape). However, we will focus on the type of DVD most important to the computer industry – DVD-ROM.

DVD-ROM

Like a CD-ROM, a DVD-ROM is a read-only optical disk. DVD-ROMs are manufactured and read in a similar fashion to CD-ROMs. In fact, apart from the additional features, the only major difference is that DVD-ROMs store data more efficiently, therefore increasing the capacity. An increasing number of manufacturers are taking advantage of this larger capacity and are offering the options of buying a program on one DVD-ROM rather than on multiple CD-ROMs. A DVD-ROM is read in a **DVD-ROM drive**. Such drives can also read all types of CD-ROM.

Figure 3.7 *USB drive*

Flash memory

Flash memory is a form of secondary storage which utilises solid state electronics. Although it can hold a lot of information (up to a few gigabytes), it is very small, making it ideal for use in portable devices such as digital cameras and MP3 players.

When used in such devices, it is in the form of a tiny card. To copy data from the card, you remove it from the slot and put it in a card reader which you then connect to your computer.

Device interfaces

There are three main device interfaces that are used to connect secondary storage devices to the motherboard: IDE, SCSI and SATA.

IDE

IDE stands for Integrated Drive Electronics. Up until a few years ago, this was the default interface for hard drives and CD-ROM drives.

SCSI

Pronounced 'scuzzy', SCSI stands for Small Computer System Interface. Despite the name, up until recently, the fastest drives out there were SCSI drives. Drives that use the SCSI interface are more expensive than their IDE counterparts and spin at higher RPM. SCSI is an intelligent interface that has a processor built into the controller. It is normally used for high-performance hard drives and tape drives.

SATA

SATA is an acronym for Serial Advanced Technology Attachment. SATA was designed as a replacement for IDE and therefore allows for much higher transfer speeds. Newer computers come with SATA hard drives and DVD drives instead of IDE.

Figure 3.6 *Compact flash memory*

USB drives

A USB drive is a tiny portable drive (about the size of a person's thumb) that can plug directly into your computer's USB port. Because they use flash memory, USB drives are also referred to as flash drives. The flash memory is built into the USB drive so it can't be removed.

USB drives are much more reliable than floppy disks and can hold a lot more information. For that reason they are making floppy disks obsolete.

Secondary storage terms

Here are some terms that you will come across when reading about secondary storage devices. You have already been informally introduced to some of these earlier in the chapter. Needless to say, you are expected to be familiar with these terms.

A **sector** is a pie-shaped section of a disk that contains the amount of data that can be read at one time by the drive.

A **track** is:

- one of the concentric rings on a magnetic disk in which the data is stored
- the spiral on a CD or DVD in which the data is stored
- one of the parallel rows on a magnetic tape in which the data is stored

A **cylinder** is the parallel set of tracks in a hard drive that are accessible from one position of the read/write heads (see Figure 3.8).

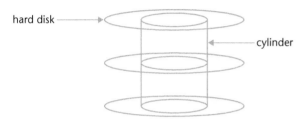

hard disk

cylinder

Figure 3.8 *A cylinder*

A **buffer** is an intermediate storage location where data is temporarily stored until it is ready to be used. This is necessary because different parts of the computer system operate at different speeds, eg the printer and the CPU.

Access time is the amount of time it takes to complete a request for data to be retrieved from storage.

Direct access is a way of accessing data by going to the exact location and reading only the required data, thereby avoiding data that came before or after. Disk drives generally access data in this way.

Serial access refers to accessing data in the order in which it was stored. This method is slower than direct access but is used by magnetic tape drives. If it turns out that the data was stored in a particular order, eg alphabetical or chronological order, we say that the data was accessed **sequentially**.

Comparison of storage devices and media

Storage devices and media are compared in the table below.

Storage device	Capacity	Technology	Portable	Direct access?
floppy disk	1.44 MB	magnetic	yes	yes
CD-ROM	700 MB	optical	yes	yes
DVD-ROM	4.7 GB	optical	yes	yes
USB drive	a few GB	flash	yes	yes
hard drive	hundreds of GB	magnetic	external only	yes
magnetic tape	hundreds of GB	magnetic	yes	no – sequential only

Exercise 3

1. Each frame on a tape includes a parity track.
   a. State the purpose of the parity track.
   b. What are the two types of parity?
   c. Explain each type of parity.
2. a. What technique is used to store data to a magnetic tape?
   b. Give a storage device which:
      i. reads or writes data sequentially
      ii. reads or writes data directly or sequentially.
3. What is the purpose of formatting a disk?
4. a. What is sequential access?
   b. Give a storage medium that is accessed sequentially.
5. Explain the terms:
   a. track
   b. sector
   c. cylinder
6. Give three precautions that are necessary when handling floppy disks.
7. a. What is a buffer?
   b. Give an example where a buffer may be used.
8. CDs and DVDs use the same kind of technology. State the major difference between them.
9. Explain the difference between the following:
   a. CD-ROM
   b. CD-R
   c. CD-RW
10. A company has a 50 MB file to back up. Select a storage medium that is best suited for backing up the file and explain your choice of this medium.
11. A software development company has decided to distribute its software on CDs instead of disks. Give two advantages of the use of CDs for distributing software over the use of disks.
12. What advantages do USB drives have over floppy drives?
13. What type of secondary storage is used in portable devices like digital cameras and MP3 players?
14. What are the three main types of secondary device interfaces?

4. Input devices and media

In order for a computer to do anything it must be told what to do. Commands and data may be entered into the computer using what are known as input devices. Several input devices are available and each has its own application, advantages and disadvantages. Some of these input devices are described below.

The keyboard

The keyboard is the most common input device available. Nearly every computer comes with one. It has a series of keys similar to a typewriter. Each key has a letter, number, symbol or word on it. The user presses the key (or combination of keys) desired, causing a special code to be added to the keyboard buffer. This code (known as an **ASCII code**) remains in the buffer until the CPU is ready for it. It is then decoded and the computer takes the appropriate action – displaying a character, moving the cursor, and so on. Keyboards are best suited for data entry or typing text documents, even though they can be used for several other things.

Figure 4.1 *A computer keyboard*

The mouse

A mouse is a hand-held device that is moved on the surface of the desk or on a mouse pad. Older mice have a ball underneath to track movement whereas newer ones use a laser beam. As the mouse moves, the pointer on the screen moves as well. When the pointer is over the item that the user wishes to select, he or she clicks one of the mouse buttons.

A mouse is commonly used:

- for selecting a menu command or 'pressing' a button on the screen
- for highlighting icons and text
- as a pointing device

Disadvantages of the mouse

- It is limited to items on the screen.
- If the mouse uses a ball, it may move erratically when it needs cleaning.
- Mice are not ideal for drawing.

Figure 4.2 *A computer mouse*

The joystick

A joystick is a device with a stick perpendicular to its base, as well as buttons on the stick and/or the base. The joystick is used as a computer input device and is often designed to resemble those used in fighter jets in order for it to feel more realistic. It is primarily used in playing computer games or in virtual reality. The user moves the stick, causing an object on the screen to be moved. When the user presses one of the buttons it usually triggers some appropriate action in the game or simulation, such as firing missiles.

Advantages

- It gives the user the feeling of a more realistic action.
- It moves objects in any direction.

Disadvantages

- It is limited to certain applications. A program must be specially written in order for a joystick to be used. Also, the nature of a joystick means that it does not suit most applications so games designers are usually the only ones who bother to design their programs to support joysticks.

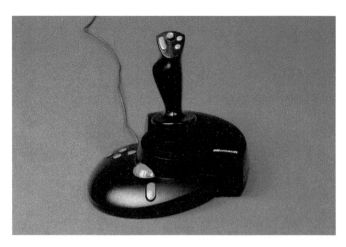

Figure 4.3 *A computer joystick*

The Optical Mark Reader (OMR)

An Optical Mark Reader (OMR) is a device that senses the presence of pencil and pen marks that are made on special forms. Such forms usually have several options with circles next to them. A person is asked to fill out the form by shading the circles for the correct options. This is an especially fast method of data entry for situations where a person is asked to choose various options such as in questionnaires, multiple-choice exams or registration forms.

Advantages

- Reduced cost of inputting large volumes of data
- Fast method of inputting data
- Less labour needed to input the data

Disadvantages

- If options are not shaded properly the machine may misread selections.
- Forms that are creased jam the machine, causing down time.
- Badly damaged forms have to be rewritten or keyed in manually.

The Optical Character Reader (OCR)

An Optical Character Reader (OCR) is a device that senses the presence of text by recognising the characters. When the document is scanned, a photo-electric device reads the characters, which are then converted to electrical signals. The signals represent patterns that give an indication of the characters involved. As you may expect, it is a fast method of data entry for documents that have already been typed/written. However, the accuracy of the input is dependent on the quality of the formation of characters.

An OCR is used for:

- capturing data from airline tickets
- reading postal codes
- capturing data from telephone and electricity bills

Advantages

- Reduced cost of inputting large volumes of data
- Quick method of inputting data
- Less labour needed to input the data

Disadvantages

- The OCR may misread characters that are not formed properly.

The scanner

A scanner is a device that is used to scan images and text into the computer. There are two types – flatbed and hand-held. With the hand-held version, the scanner is dragged over the image or text in order to scan it. For a flatbed scanner, the document is placed on the flat surface of the scanner. In both cases, when the document is scanned, it is imported into special software as an image (even if the document is plain text). A scanner is used:

- for scanning text
- for scanning photographs
- in desktop publishing

Advantages

- It is a quick, accurate method of entering existing images into the computer.

Disadvantages

- Some scanned files require a large amount of space. High-quality scans require a lot of space.
- Text is scanned as images. This prevents the text from immediately being used in word processors and also takes up a lot more space on disk than if the text were stored as a text file.

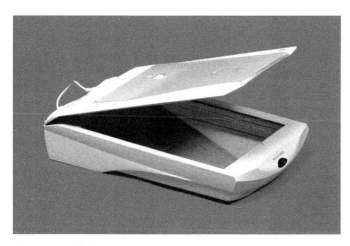

Figure 4.4 *A flatbed scanner*

Did you know?

The functionality of a scanner is significantly increased when it is used in conjunction with other hardware and software. For example, a scanner can be used with a printer as a copier, and character recognition software can convert the text in scanned documents to text files.

Bar code scanners

Almost every item you purchase has on it a small label with a group of parallel black lines of varying thickness. Each group is known as a **bar code**. It serves as a means of identifying the type and brand of a particular item. Even though humans cannot make sense of the codes, there is a type of scanner that can interpret these codes in order to determine the item number. This device is called a bar code scanner. The bar code is placed over the scanner (or vice versa) and a beep sounds if the scanner recognises the code. The item number is used in conjunction with a database in order to determine the price of the item and/or to update stock figures. Bar code scanners are used in libraries, supermarkets and retail stores.

Advantages

- Instant update. When an item is scanned, the system automatically notes that there is one less of that particular item in stock.
- Accuracy of transaction. You do not have to worry about a cashier entering the wrong price.
- Speed of transaction. It is faster than keying in the price manually.

Disadvantages

- The system is expensive to set up.
- It is limited to items that have a bar code.

The Point of Sale (POS) Terminal

There are terminals, to which online input devices like bar code scanners are connected, that process transactions as soon as the data is read, that is at the 'point of sale'. Such a terminal is known as a **Point of Sale (POS) Terminal**. It is connected to a database that allows it to retrieve and update information about a product. Note that devices such as cash registers can be Point of Sale Terminals. For example, when a bar code scanner converts the bar code of an item to an item number, the Point of Sale Terminal retrieves the price of the item. It then updates the total price of the customer's items. It can then update the database to which it is connected to note that there is one less of that particular item in stock. If the quantity of that item has fallen below a certain level, the terminal can even notify the main computer that it is necessary to order more of that item.

Point of Sale Terminals are used:

- at the checkout counter of supermarkets, retail stores, etc.
- in bank transactions

Advantages

- Instant updating of transactions
- Accuracy of transaction
- Speed of transaction

Disadvantages

- Cost of setting up the system

Is a bar code scanner a POS Terminal?

No. The term 'POS Terminal' refers to the terminal that does processing where the transactions are being made, along with the input device that is used to get the information about the transaction into the terminal. A bar code scanner is just an input device that is part of many POS Terminals.

The Magnetic Ink Character Reader (MICR)

Certain documents – especially cheques – have strange-looking combinations of numbers and markings printed in magnetic ink. Even though these characters can be read by humans, there is a special device that also serves this purpose. It is known as a Magnetic Ink Character Reader (MICR). When a document containing these characters is passed through the MICR, the MICR detects the presence of the magnetic ink and interprets the characters. Like a bar code scanner, it is used along with databases, since these characters are used to represent things such as bank numbers and cheque numbers. It is most commonly used by banks and is very fast and accurate.

Advantages

- It is a fast, accurate way of inputting large volumes of data that is in the required format.
- Less labour is needed to input the data.

Disadvantages

- It is very expensive.
- Cheques that are badly damaged have to be keyed manually.

The light pen

A light pen is a light-sensitive device that looks like a pen. When the light pen is moved across the screen, its position can be detected. A user can 'write' on the screen in the same way that he/she writes on a piece of paper so it feels very natural. It is therefore very well suited for drawing images or for signatures. It can also be used to make a selection from a menu that is displayed on the screen.

The touch screen/terminal

A touch screen/terminal is a touch-sensitive screen that can detect when a person touches it, as well as the area of the screen that has been touched. Various options are displayed on the screen and the user presses the one he or she wants. When the person's finger touches the screen it blocks out the light from the area of the screen that is touched. The system uses the location of the area that is pressed to determine the correct option. It is very easy to use, and as a result, users do not require training. This makes it especially suitable for airports, fast-food outlets, theatre booking offices, for example. It is also quicker than having a user type in the information.

Advantages

- The user can select the option very quickly.
- The user does not require any training to use it.

Disadvantages

- The system is expensive.
- It is limited to certain applications.

The microphone

A microphone is a device that functions in much the same way as the microphones you see used on stage. However, it does not usually look the same because it is designed so that the user does not have to hold it while he or she is speaking. Whenever you talk to the computer, either to give it a command or to input information, you use some sort of microphone. When you talk, your sound waves cause a diaphragm to vibrate. These vibrations are converted into electrical impulses that are then transmitted to the computer. One application for which a microphone is used is in Voice Data Entry (VDE).

Figure 4.5 *A computer microphone*

Voice Data Entry (VDE)

Voice Data Entry (VDE) is the process by which a person speaks to the computer through a microphone as a means of entering data. A speech recognition program converts the spoken words into text.

This technology is still in its infancy and as a result each word must be followed by a short period of silence in order for the computer to be able to separate the words. Also, as you may expect, the programs used have limited vocabularies.

Although VDE is often used as an input method when both hands are already being used, its main use is in computer systems used by physically handicapped persons.

Advantages

- It does not require vision or the use of the hand.
- It enhances productivity by supplementing other data entry methods.

Disadvantages

- It is limited by its vocabulary.
- A pause is required after each word.
- It gets confused by homonyms. For example, the computer might mistake 'roll' for 'role', even though a human being would be able to tell which one is suited to the context.

Graphics pads and tablets

Graphics pads and tablets are flat pressure-sensitive surfaces that are commonly used in Computer-Aided Design (CAD). The user draws on the graphics tablet with a pen-like device known as a **stylus**. The drawing appears on the monitor inside a program designed for this method of input. Another device that can be used with a graphics tablet is called a **puck**. It somewhat resembles a mouse but does not rely on a ball. Rather, the graphics tablet keeps track of its position. It can do so even if the puck is not on the surface of the tablet. Graphics pads and tablets are used for tracing drawings and in engineering and art designs.

Key-to-disk system

With computers capable of doing billions of calculations per second, it is no surprise that it is impossible to type in data as quickly as the computer can process it. If a high-speed computer had to spend almost all of its time simply waiting for someone to type in large amounts of information, then the whole process would be very inefficient indeed. A **key-to-disk** system is one method of getting around this problem. It consists of a keyboard, a screen and a disk drive, as well as a processor to verify and validate the data. A data entry clerk types in (keys in) the data using the keyboard. The data may then be typed in a second time in order to verify it (to make sure that it was entered correctly). The data is then saved on disk.

The data from the disk can then be transferred to the high-speed computer in an entire batch. This is a form of batch data entry.

Advantages

- Valuable processing units are not tied up when doing data entry.
- It is cost effective.

Disadvantages

- Data cannot be processed as soon as it is keyed in.

The digital camera

Like a conventional camera, a digital camera is a device that utilises a lens in order to take photographs by capturing light on some sort of media. What distinguishes a digital camera from a conventional camera is the media on which the image is stored. Whereas an ordinary camera stores images on film, a digital camera uses digital methods to capture and store images. Digital cameras generally use tiny light-sensitive diodes that convert the light into electrical charges. The light from the object passes through filters that separate it into its red, green and blue components. The intensity of each component is measured using the diodes. The data is then stored on a flash memory card.

Each digital camera has a particular resolution (given in megapixels) that determines the quality of image that can be stored. A **pixel** is basically a dot in an image, whether the image is on a screen or on printer paper. The term '**resolution**' refers to the number of pixels that a device can produce, display or store in a particular area. The higher the resolution, the greater the number of pixels that can be used to provide fine details in images.

Figure 4.6 *A digital camera*

Advantages

- It is a convenient method of capturing images for computer applications such as web pages. Since images are stored in a digital format it is simply a matter of transferring the images to the computer via a cable.
- Photographs can be viewed as soon as they are taken so that if you do not like one, you can delete it and take it again.

Disadvantages

- The quality of the images is not as high as for those stored on film.
- High-quality images take up a lot of space.
- Digital cameras use up batteries very quickly.

Webcams

A webcam is a small camera that you use to send live video over the Internet. The video quality isn't usually very good, but that's OK since you don't use webcams to do professional videos. Instead, webcams are normally used so you can see the people you are videoconferencing or chatting with.

Figure 4.7 *A webcam*

Exercise 4

1 State two input devices that allow data to be read directly from the source document. For each device, give two applications for which the device can be used.

2 Explain the benefits of using a mouse over a keyboard.

3 Explain how a touch screen functions and give two advantages of using a touch screen over a mouse.

4 A small retail outlet is in the process of installing a computer system for its checkout counter. One option is to use a bar code system. Explain two advantages and two disadvantages of using a bar code system.

5 An Examination Body uses registration forms that are read by an Optical Mark Reader. Occasionally, the machine does not accept some of the forms. Give two possible causes of rejection of the forms.

6 State two advantages of Voice Data Entry.

7 Explain two benefits of using the following:
   a an optical character reader
   b a key-to-disk system

8 The Principal of your school is considering setting up a database of students' information. He would like to store their photos in the database as well. Suggest two devices other than the keyboard and the mouse that can be used to facilitate this task.

9 Give an application of the use of a light pen.

10 You have a friend in New York who has an Internet connection. You too have an Internet connection. Give one device that can be used for speech communication between you and your friend via the computer. State how the selected device operates.

11 What are webcams used for?

5. Output devices and media

A computer obviously would not be much use unless it had some way of giving us some sort of feedback. It does so through what are known as **output devices**. There are two types of output. **Hard copy** (permanent copy) is a permanent form of output that is tangible (you can touch it), for example data printed on paper. **Soft copy** (temporary copy) is temporary output, such as displays on a screen or speech from a speech synthesiser. Some output devices and their functions are described below.

The monitor

Figure 5.1 *LCD and CRT monitors*

The monitor is the part of the computer that people refer to as the screen. There are two main types:

- Liquid Crystal Display (LCD)
- Cathode Ray Tube (CRT)

LCD
This is the type of monitor that new computers come with. These monitors are much thinner and lighter than the bulkier CRT monitors. They also use a lot less energy. LCD monitors used to be very expensive but prices have fallen drastically in the last few years.

CRT
CRT monitors are bulky monitors that look like old-fashioned TVs. That is because they use the same technology. Up until recently, they were much cheaper and had much better image quality than LCD monitors. Now that LCD prices have fallen and their image quality has increased, there's no longer a real reason to buy a CRT monitor.

The printer

Another popular output device is the printer. A printer is a device used to output text and images from the computer onto paper. Therefore, unlike monitors, printers can produce hard copy. Printers can be placed into two categories: impact printers and non-impact printers.

Impact printers
Impact printers are printers that transfer data onto paper by hitting the paper with some part of the printer in a similar way to a typewriter. As you can expect, impact printers tend to be very noisy. The characters to be printed are pressed against an inked ribbon onto the paper. After a while the ribbon becomes worn or faded and must be changed. Multiple copies of documents can be printed using carbon paper.

There are two types of impact printers: line printers and character printers. Both types of impact printers print on perforated paper.

Line printers
Line printers are printers that can use multiple print hammers to print an entire line of text at one time (or at least fast enough so that it appears so). A line printer accomplishes this using one of two methods:

- using a drum that rotates an entire line of the same character under the print hammers which strike when the appropriate character is under them

- using a chain containing multiple sets of characters that are rotated across the current row, allowing different characters to be under the print hammers at the same time.

Although a line printer can print text at a very fast rate, it has some disadvantages. First of all, it cannot print graphics, and secondly the text that it prints isn't of very high quality.

Character (serial) printers

Character (serial) printers are printers that print a character at a time. It is no surprise, therefore, that these are slower than line printers. The two main types of character printers are daisy wheel and dot matrix printers.

Daisy wheel printers use a wheel containing characters that rotates until the right character is facing the paper. A hammer is then used to force the character into the ink ribbon onto the paper. Although it prints high-quality text, it cannot print graphics. Printing different fonts (types of writing) on the same document is impracticable, since you have to change the wheel in order to get a different font.

Dot matrix printers have a print head capable of firing tiny pins arranged in a matrix. As the print head moves back and forth, these pins strike the ribbon causing dots to be made on the paper. These dots can be arranged to form characters, but what sets dot matrix printers apart from other impact printers is that these same dots can be used to print graphics. Some dot matrix printers can also print in colour.

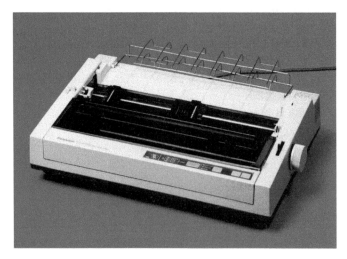

Figure 5.2 *A dot matrix printer*

Although impact printers are not as common these days, they are usually used to:

- print bills or forms that require carbon copies
- print special reports that require large continuous sheets (some payroll and accounting reports)

Non-impact printers

Non-impact printers are printers that print using methods that do not involve striking the paper or an ink ribbon. They are generally faster than most impact printers and a lot quieter. Some types are also much more expensive. Non-impact printers do not use perforated paper.

Inkjet printers

Inkjet printers are printers that squirt very small drops of ink on the paper in order to produce text and images. This is the most popular type of printer (especially in the home) since, although it produces high-quality output at a relatively high speed, it is still fairly cheap. Actually, you'll probably end up spending much more money on ink and paper than you will on the printer itself.

A print head moves back and forth while the paper passes through the printer. The print head contains several nozzles through which the drops of ink are squirted. This is done in two ways:

1 vaporising the ink in order to create bubbles that force a small amount of ink out of the nozzle – printers that use this method are known as bubble-jet printers
2 causing tiny crystals at the back of each nozzle to vibrate, forcing drops of ink out of the nozzles.

These printers can print in colour by mixing inks in the same manner that artists mix paints to get a desired colour.

Figure 5.3 *A bubble-jet printer*

Laser printers

A laser printer is a very fast printer that utilises a laser beam along with toner and a photoconductive rotating drum in order to produce very high-quality output. The printing process is very complicated indeed. The drum is first given a positive charge. Then the laser is used to precisely discharge parts of the drum to form the images and text to be printed. The positively charged toner is attracted to the discharged parts of the drum but not to the rest (remember that similar charges repel and opposites attract). The paper, after it has been made more negatively charged than the drum, passes over the drum, pulling the toner from the drum onto itself. The paper is discharged as soon as it picks up the toner and then heated so that the toner becomes fused with the paper.

Although most laser printers are black and white, some can print in colour. Laser printers are faster than inkjet printers, so fast in fact that they are called **page printers** because it appears that they print an entire page at one time. However, expensive prices mean that laser printer use is usually limited to office environments. Home users who want high quality usually stick to the cheaper inkjet printers.

Thermal printers

Thermal printers are printers that print by using heat. Some thermal printers use special heat-sensitive paper. Heat is then applied to the paper to form text and graphics. This type of printer has low maintenance cost since you do not have to buy new ink, toner or print ribbon. Some fax machines print faxes using this principle.

Graphics plotters

Like printers, graphics plotters are devices that can produce output on paper. However, they operate using a different principle. Instead of producing images and text using print heads, inked ribbons or lasers, they use something a bit more low-tech – pens. The principle is quite simple – why not draw images in the same way an architect would? There are several types of plotters: flatbed, rotating drum and turtle-type plotters. Although each is unique, all work by moving pens across the surface of the paper in order to produce continuous lines that may vary in thickness or colour.

These plotters produce very precise high-quality diagrams at a very fast speed and are therefore perfect for engineering applications. However, they aren't suitable for just anyone since they can be quite large and expensive.

Computer Output on Microfilm (COM)

Have you ever looked at the film from which photographs are produced? A frame of film is much smaller than the photograph that is produced from it. COM uses the same principle. The data to be stored is loaded in a **microfilm recorder** that displays the output on a screen for it to be photographed by a high-speed camera. The recording process is very quick indeed. The photograph may be stored on **microfilm, microfiche** or **ultrafiche**.

Microfilm is a roll of 16 mm film. Microfiche is a rectangular card made of the same material as film. Many frames corresponding to the various screens can be stored on a single microfiche sheet. Ultrafiche is similar to microfiche except that several times as many frames can be stored on a single sheet.

Since a frame is much smaller than the screen of which it was taken, output stored on microfilm takes up a lot less space than if the same data was printed out. It is therefore very useful for storing archival data or bulky data. Because frames are so tiny, the images and text are not readable by humans. Therefore, when a person wants to view the data, the appropriate microfilm/microfiche is selected and placed in a microfilm reader. Each frame can then be displayed on a screen so that it can be read.

Speakers

Sound is a form of output even though most people do not think of it in this way. The output device that is used to produce sounds is the speaker. The computer speaker is not much different from those found in stereo systems. It operates using the same principle – electrical current causes a diaphragm to vibrate. These vibrations produce sound.

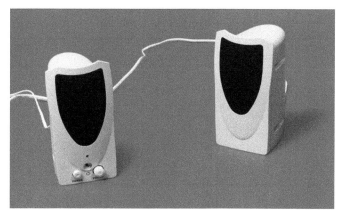

Figure 5.4 *Computer speakers*

Exercise 5

1. Explain the difference between a hard copy and a soft copy.
2. Give two examples each of devices that produce hard copy and soft copy data.
3. Give two categories of printer and explain the differences between them.
4. State briefly how each of the following types of printer works, and for each, give one advantage of using that kind of printer.
   a. dot matrix
   b. thermal
   c. inkjet
5. a. What are pixels?
   b. What important part do pixels play in the quality of the screen display?
6. Give two advantages of storing information on microfilm or microfiche.
7. A computer store has computer software that generates invoices. The invoices are to be printed in triplicate using carbon paper. Recommend a printer that is best suited for this application and state why this printer is recommended.
8. What do the acronyms CRT and LCD stand for?
9. Give an application in which a graph plotter is used. Explain why a plotter is used instead of a printer.
10. a. What is attached to a monitor to reduce eyestrain?
    b. Explain why a monitor is pivoted.

6. Hardware specifications

If you've ever purchased a computer – or tried to choose one – you no doubt found yourself bombarded with all sorts of specifications. This chapter will show you how to interpret these specifications. The main things to consider when choosing a computer are:

- the type of CPU and its speed
- the size of the hard drive
- how much RAM the computer has

CPU

The two CPU manufacturers, Intel and AMD, have several processors to choose from, as you can see in the table below.

Intel	AMD
Celeron	Semron
Pentium E	Athlon 64 X2
Core 2 Duo	Phenom
Core 2 Quad	Phenom II
Core i7	

More powerful

Once you have chosen the type of CPU, the next thing to consider is its clock speed, which is measured in gigahertz (GHz). At the time of writing, a midrange CPU has a speed of 2.6 GHz whereas a top-end CPU may be over 3.33 GHz.

Word size
Occasionally the CPU specification will also mention the word size of the CPU. In older processors this will be 32 bits but modern CPUs are 64-bit.

RAM

A typical RAM specification has the following format:
4GB **DDR2** SDRAM at **1333 MHz** (**2 DIMMs**).
  1   **2**   **3**   **4**

1 <u>Size</u> Common RAM sizes are 512 MB, 1 GB, 2 GB and 4 GB. The bigger the better.
2 <u>Type</u> The three main types of memory are DDR, DDR2 (the most common) and DDR3.
3 <u>Speed</u> Some specifications may include the RAM speed. Common speeds are 667, 800, 1066 and 1333 MHz.
4 <u>Number of RAM modules</u> The specification may tell you how many DIMMS (RAM modules) there

are. In the example above, the 4 GB are split into two memory modules.

Hard drive

The two main factors you must consider when purchasing a hard drive are:

1 the size (measured in gigabytes or terabytes); typical sizes are 500 GB, 750 GB, and 1.5 TB
2 the interface type (IDE, SATA or SCSI)

Expansion slots

Motherboards have slots where you can plug in expansion cards such as video cards or sound cards. As you can probably guess, these slots are called **expansion slots**. There are three main types that you may encounter: PCI, AGP and PCI Express.

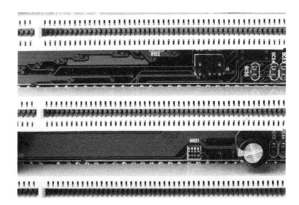

Figure 6.1 *Expansion slots on a motherboard*

PCI
PCI stands for **Peripheral Component Interconnect**. Although it was introduced in 1993, most motherboards still come with multiple PCI slots. Traditional PCI is too slow for modern graphics cards. Instead it is used for devices such as internal modems, network cards and sound cards which don't require as much bandwidth.

AGP
AGP is an abbreviation for **Accelerated Graphics Port**. The word 'graphics' here is very important since AGP can only be used for graphics cards. In recent years it has been replaced by the faster, more flexible PCI Express.

Figure 6.2 *PCI Express Graphics Card*

PCI Express

At the time of writing, the fastest type of expansion slot is PCI Express (abbreviated as PCIe). The latest graphics cards require PCI Express since the other types of slots just aren't fast enough. Fortunately all modern motherboards come with at least 1 PCI Express slot.

Ports

At the back of your computer tower (and sometimes at the front) you'll find several ports where you can plug in external peripheral devices. Each type of port has a specific shape so that you can't plug in a device in the wrong place. Here are <u>some</u> of the ports you'll encounter.

PS/2

These are small, round ports that allow you to connect older mice and keyboards. These are being phased out in favour of USB ports.

USB

Universal Serial Bus (USB) is by far the most common type of port, allowing you to connect almost any type of device. Mice, keyboards, flash drives, joysticks, printers, digital cameras and webcams all come with USB connectors.

VGA

For years, the Video Graphics Array (VGA) port has been the standard means of connecting a monitor to the computer tower. However, these are slowly being replaced by DVI ports.

FireWire

Don't feel bad if you've never heard of FireWire (or its official name, IEEE 1394). The average computer does not come with a FireWire port – this luxury is typically reserved for the high-end computers. The main use of FireWire is to transfer data from digital camcorders.

PS/2 port (mouse)

PS/2 port (keyboard)

USB ports

Figure 6.3 *Computer ports*

Exercise 6

1 List three types of expansion slot as well as what they are used for.
2 Name three different kinds of ports.
3 Suppose you were given these specifications for a computer:
   - Dell Studio One 19 (Solid Pure White)
   - Genuine Windows Vista® Home Premium SP1
   - 18.5" LCD Monitor, 16:9 Aspect Ratio, WXGA (1366×768)
   - 3.0 GHz Intel® Core™ 2 Duo Processor E8400 (64-bit)
   - 4 GB Dual Channel DDR2 SDRAM at 800 MHz (2 DIMMs)
   - Western Digital 7200 rpm 1 GB SATA Hard Drive
   - Slot load CD/DVD burner (DVD+/–RW) w/double layer write capability
   - Dell USB Keyboard and Mouse
   - Built-in webcam
   - Stereo speakers

   a List two output devices, three input devices and two storage devices.
   b What type of CPU does it have? How fast is it?
   c What is the CPU's word size?
   d What is the capacity of the hard drive?
   e What interface does the hard drive use?
   f What is the resolution of the monitor?
   g How much RAM does the computer have? What type of RAM is it?
   h How many sticks of RAM are there?
4 Write some specs for your dream computer. Be sure to specify what type of CPU, how much RAM and how much disk space you want.

7. How data is stored in the computer

Discrete and continuous data

Data can be put into two broad categories: discrete and continuous. It is hard to appreciate the difference between the two without looking at an example. That is why we will look at a few.

Imagine a friend trying to describe people to you. One of the things that might be mentioned is each person's height. Your friend may decide a person may be tall, medium or short. These are three discrete (clear-cut) values. If you were to get a list of heights in this form (i.e. consisting of discrete values), it would be **discrete data**. You may prefer to be given the heights in centimetres. The friend may give you the following heights: 175.2 cm, 180.3 cm and 181.0 cm. These are figures from a continuous range of values. There is nothing to say that you couldn't be given 176.189 356 335 cm as a height. Therefore the data is **continuous**.

It is important to note that the terms 'discrete' and 'continuous' do not refer to the accuracy of the data. If you measure a 7 ft person to be 3 ft 1.123131 inches tall, you'd be better off referring to the person as 'tall'.

You generally cannot tell whether or not data is discrete or continuous simply by looking at the data. What determines whether it is discrete or continuous is the range of possible values. Discrete data can only come from a limited set of values. There may be two possible values or a million, but the set of values is still limited. What makes data continuous is not how many numbers are after a decimal point, but rather the fact that each figure may be <u>any</u> one of a continuous range of values.

You may have heard of the expression 'not everything is either black or white', meaning things aren't always clear-cut. In a world where everything is 'black' or 'white', each individual thing is one of two discrete values. You can compare continuous data to the 'shades of grey'.

Digital data is discrete. Analogue data is continuous.

Human-readable and machine-readable data

Just because something makes sense to you does not mean that it makes sense to the computer. Conversely, anyone who has tried to read the contents of data files will know that humans cannot usually understand things that a computer can. Data that can be understood by humans is called **human-readable data**, whereas data that can be understood by computers is known as **machine-readable data**. Printers and monitors produce human-readable copies, whereas disk drives and tape drives produce machine-readable copies.

We as humans are used to one number system – the **decimal number system** (base 10 or **denary**). However, the computer uses an entirely different system called **binary** (base 2). Therefore, in order for the computer to be able to process any data we give it (whether it is in the form of numbers, text, images, sounds, etc.), it must first convert the data into binary. While describing how the computer converts multimedia into binary is beyond the scope of this book, we must take a close look at how the computer converts decimal numbers to binary and also look briefly at how computers represent text.

Types of number

Before we go any further with this chapter it is time for a short refresher course in mathematics to make sure you are familiar with a few terms that you may encounter later in the chapter.

- **Natural numbers** are numbers such as 1, 2, 3, 4, 5, … The set of **whole numbers** consists of 0 along with all the natural numbers.
- **Integers** are numbers such as … –10, –9, –8, …, 0, 1, 2, 3, 4, 5, … that have no fractional parts.
- **Real numbers** are numbers with a decimal point like 5.25, 1.0. Although this is not the precise mathematical definition, it is suitable enough for our needs.
- The **magnitude** of a number refers to how large a number is. It does not depend on the sign of the number. For example, the magnitude of both 10 and –10 is 10.

Number systems

If n is a whole number such as 2, 3, 4, …, 10, then the digits in a base n number go from 0 to $n - 1$. For example, a base 10 number can only have digits from 0 to 9. Similarly a base 2 number can only consist of 0s and 1s.

What happens with bases larger than 10?

You cannot use numbers such as 10 or 15 as digits. Instead, letters are used to represent these numbers. For example, in hexadecimal (base 16) the letters A–F are used to represent 10–15.

Each digit in a number has a place value that depends on its position and the base of the number. At the far right of the number, regardless of the base, are the units, which have a place value of 1. As you go from right to left by one digit, the place value in a base n number increases by a factor n. For example, let's take a look at the base 10 number 18 432, which may also be written as $18\,432_{10}$.

As shown in Table 7.1, as you go from right to left, the place value of the digits increases by a factor of 10.

Table 7.1 Increase by factor of 10

Place value (in base 10)	10 000 (10^4)	1000 (10^3)	100 (10^2)	10 (10^1)	1 (10^0)
Digit (in base 10)	1	8	4	3	2

How do you know the base of a number?

The base of a number is usually denoted by a subscript to the right of the number. For example, the '10' in '$18\,432_{10}$' tells you that the number is in base 10. If no subscript is given, you may assume that the number is in base 10.

Binary number system

As mentioned above, the digits in a binary number can be either 0 or 1. Each digit in binary is known as a **bit**.

As you go from the right-most bit (called the least significant bit) to the left-most bit (called the most significant bit), the place value increases by a factor of 2.

Converting a number from base 2 to base 10

A table similar to Table 7.1 for base 10 can be used to convert a binary number into a decimal number. For example, let us convert the number 10111_2 to base 10. To do so you must follow a few simple steps:

- Write down the binary number with the digits well spaced.
- Above each digit, write its place value in base 10. You should end up with something looking like Table 7.2.
- Multiply each digit by its place value and add the results together.

Thus:

$$10111_2 = (1 \times 16) + (0 \times 8) + (1 \times 4) + (1 \times 2) + (1 \times 1)$$
$$= 16 + 0 + 4 + 2 + 1$$
$$= 23_{10}$$

Table 7.2 Increase by factor of 2

Place value (in base 10)	16 (2^4)	8 (2^3)	4 (2^2)	2 (2^1)	1 (2^0)
Digit (in base 2)	1	0	1	1	1

A similar method can be used to convert from any other base to base 10.

Converting a number from base 10 to base 2

Unfortunately, the method for converting from base 10 to base 2 is not as simple as the method given above.

- Divide the decimal number by 2. Write down the quotient and the remainder.
- On the next row of the division, divide the quotient from the previous row by 2. Write down the new quotient and the remainder.
- Continue the process until the quotient is 0.
- Use the remainders (going from bottom to top) to write down the binary digits (going from left to right).

Let us use this method to convert 103_{10} into binary (see Table 7.3). This gives us $103_{10} = 1100111_2$.

You should check the binary number by converting it back to base 10 and seeing if you get the original number.

Table 7.3 Successive division by 2 to find the binary number

2	103	
2	51	R1
2	25	R1
2	12	R1
2	6	R0
2	3	R0
2	1	R1
	0	R1

Write down the remainders in this direction

Addition

In order to understand how binary addition works, we must first compare it with decimal addition. An important thing to note is what happens when the total for a column is not less than the base.

For example, when you add 4 to 3 the total, 7, is less than 10 (which is the base).

```
    4
 +  3
    7
```

However, when you add 8 to 7 you get 15, which is clearly not less than 10. Anyone who has done even the most basic arithmetic knows what you do in a situation like this. Obviously you cannot write '15' in the units column. However, we know that 15 is equivalent to $(1 * 10) + 5$.

We also know that the place value of the column to the immediate left is ten times that of the one you are summing. So what you do is 'carry' a 1 to the column on the immediate left to indicate one group of 10. You then include the 1 in the sum of that column.

```
      8
 +    7
  1   5
```

1 ⟵ Carry 1

Binary addition works in the same way. Since it is base 2 you cannot have anything that is not less than 2 in any column. Therefore if the sum of a column is 2 or greater a carry is involved. For example, in binary:

```
     0          1          0
 +   0      +   0      +   1
     0          1          1
```

However:

```
      1          1
 +    1      +   1
  1   0      1   1
```

1   **1** ⟵ This 1 stands for 1 group of 2.

In binary, the place value of the column to which you are carrying is twice that of the one you are adding. So the 1 you carry stands for '1 group of 2'.

What do you do for a case like the one shown below?

```
      1
      1
      1
      1
 +    1
 ─────────
```

The total for the units column is 5. This is the equivalent to $(2 \times 2) + 1$ or '2 groups of 2 with remainder of 1'. This may be a bit confusing at first, but consider the following:

1 Because 5 is definitely not less than 2, a carry is involved.

2 The place value of the column to the immediate left (i.e. the one to which you are carrying) is twice that of the column you are totalling. Therefore, you need to find out how many groups of 2 are in 5. The answer is 2 so you will place a 2 at the bottom of the column on the left.

3 You then have to determine how much remains. Since $2 \times 2 = 4$, the remainder is $5 - 4 = 1$. So you leave a 1 in the column you were totalling.

```
      1
      1
      1
      1
 +    1
 ─────────
      1
 2
```

You cannot have a 2 in any column for the answer so another carry is required. The final result is:

```
        1
        1
        1
        1
    +   1
 ───────────
 1  0   1
```

1   2

If you feel uncomfortable with adding more than two rows don't worry – there is another (easier to understand) method you can use:

1 Add two rows at a time.
2 Add the result to the subsequent row.
3 Repeat the process until all the rows are added.

For example, let us add the binary numbers 01110, 11101 and 10111.

First add the first two rows.

```
        0    1    1    1    0
  +     1    1    1    0    1
  1     0    1    0    1    1
  1     1    1
```

Then add the result to the third row.

```
        1    0    1    0    1    1
  +          1    0    1    1    1
  1     0    0    0    0    1    0
  1     1    1    1    1    1
```

Subtraction

We will examine binary subtraction by again considering how the decimal equivalent works. As with the addition, we are only concerned with the exceptional cases. For example, consider what happens when we subtract 28 from 95.

```
        9    5
  -     2    8
```

We have a problem because 8 is larger than 5. To get around this we 'borrow' 10 and add it to the 5 to make it 15. We get this 10 from the column on the immediate left. Since 8 is not larger than 15 the only problem we would have with the subtraction process is that we have to 'pay back' the 10 we borrowed. To do this we simply add 1 to the 2 to make 3. This additional 1 is equivalent to the 10 we added to the 5 (because of its place value).

```
        9   ¹⁵5̸
  -    ³2̸    8
        6    7
```

In binary, the same principle applies. Subtracting 10_2 from 11_2 does not require borrowing so you can subtract right away.

```
        1    1
  -     1    0
             1
```

However, this is not the case when you try to subtract 1_2 from 10_2.

```
        1    0
  -     0    1
```

Since the 1 in the units column is larger than the 0 from which you are trying to subtract it, you have to borrow from the column on the immediate left. You add 2 to the 0 (in the top row) to make it 2. Since you have borrowed one group of two, you must pay it back by adding a 1 (which represents the 1 group of 2) to the 0 in the bottom row.

```
        1      ²0̸
  -        ¹0̸    1
           0      1
```

Now take a look at a more difficult example. Subtract 1101_2 from 11010_2.

```
        1    ³1̸   ²0̸   1    ²0̸
  -        ¹0̸  ²1̸    1   ¹0̸    1
               1    1    0    1
```

Representation of integers

So far we have looked at binary numbers in a very general and limited manner. In fact, we have acted as if negative binary numbers do not exist at all. Obviously this is not the case since a computer that could not work with negative numbers would not be of much use at all!

However, now that we have covered some of the basics of binary, we will look at the systems that are used to represent integers (both positive and negative) in binary.

Each of these systems has the following in common:

1 Negative numbers start with a 1 whereas non-negative numbers start with a 0.
2 You must be told the maximum number of bits that will be used to store an integer. This also tells you the range of numbers that can be stored.
3 In order to convert a negative base 10 number to binary you must first convert the magnitude of the number into binary and then modify it. For example, to convert –20 to binary you first have to convert 20 to binary.
4 All these systems represent each positive integer the same way.

To highlight the differences among the various systems, we will see how the decimal number –45 is represented in each of the systems. However, the first step in representing any negative number, regardless of the system, is to represent the magnitude of the number using the specified number of bits. When you are told to use one of the systems, but not given the number of bits, you can assume it is 8, which is what we will do in this case.

How do we represent positive integers?

The magnitude of any number is always positive. Therefore, in order to represent negative integers, we have to learn how positive integers are represented. In each of the systems that will be discussed, in order to represent a positive base 10 number using n bits:

1 Convert the base 10 number to binary in the usual manner.
2 Add 0s to the front of the binary number until you have $n - 1$ bits in total.
3 Put a 0 in front of the $n - 1$ bits to show that the number is positive.

You may be wondering why we did not combine steps **2** and **3**. Remember that the left-most bit is used to show whether or not a number is negative. Therefore, you only have $n - 1$ bits that can be used to represent the number. As a result, you cannot use any of the systems to store any integers with magnitudes that take up more than $n - 1$ bits.

In our example −45, we have 7 (8 − 1) bits in which to store the magnitude, 45. The binary for 45 is 101101_2, which is 6 bits. Therefore, we have to add an additional zero so that the magnitude is 7 bits. We put the zero in front so that the value of the magnitude is not changed and we get 0101101. We then put a zero in front of that to show that the number is positive. Therefore, in all the systems that will be mentioned, positive 45 is 00101101_2.

Is zero positive or negative?

Neither, actually. Although it is possible in some systems to represent 0 as negative, it is customary to represent 0_{10} using 0s for all the bits. For example, no matter what system is being used, using 8 bits, 0_{10} is 00000000_2.

Since each positive integer is represented in the same way, we will concentrate on how negative integers are stored.

Signs and magnitude

This is the simplest system of the lot. It is also the easiest to understand since it is very similar to the way we represent decimal numbers. The left-most bit is used as the sign bit. All the other bits represent the magnitude of the number. So in our example (where we use 8 bits in total), 7 bits will be used to store the magnitude of the number. We

have already established that positive 45 will be stored as **0**0101101.

sign bit   magnitude

How do we represent −45 using 8 bits? All we have to do is to change the sign bit of the 8-bit representation for 45 from 0 to 1. Therefore, −45 is represented by **1**0101101. So to represent a negative base 10 number in binary with sign and magnitude using n bits:

1 Write down the binary for the magnitude as a positive number using n bits.
2 Change the sign bit (the bit at the front) from 0 to 1.

Now that you know how the sign and magnitude system works, you should be able to convert a binary number that contains both sign and magnitude into base 10. For example:

> The following binary numbers use 10 bits to store sign and magnitude. What are their equivalents in base 10?
>
> **a** 1100100010
> **b** 0100000111
> **c** 0001110101
> **d** 1011011000

The numbers are shown with their place value in Table 7.4.

Table 7.4

Place value (in base 10)	Sign	256	128	64	32	16	8	4	2	1
Digit (in base 2)	1	1	0	0	1	0	0	0	1	0
	0	1	0	0	0	0	0	1	1	1
	0	0	0	1	1	1	0	1	0	1
	1	0	1	1	0	1	1	0	0	0

Simply by inspection, we can tell that the numbers in **a** and **d** are negative, whereas those in **b** and **c** are positive. Let us now calculate the magnitude of each item:

a 256 + 32 + 2 = 290
b 256 + 4 + 2 + 1 = 263
c 64 + 32 + 16 + 4 + 1 = 117
d 128 + 64 + 16 + 8 = 216

So, when 10 bits are used to store sign and magnitude, the numbers represent:

a $1100100010_2 = -290$
b $0100000111_2 = 263$
c $0001110101_2 = 117$
d $1011011000_2 = -216$

Ones complement

It is almost guaranteed that you will be asked to find the ones complement of a binary number. And since this is perhaps the easiest thing an examiner can ask you to do, it should almost be guaranteed that you would get it right. Doing so is a simple one-step process:

Going from left to right (or right to left) simply change all the 1s to 0s and 0s to 1s.

For example, the ones complement of $\mathbf{11101011_2}$ is $\mathbf{00010100_2}$. Also note that the reverse is true; that is, the ones complement of $\mathbf{00010100_2}$ is $\mathbf{11101011_2}$.

The ones complement system can also be used to represent positive and negative numbers. Since all the systems that are mentioned in this section represent positive numbers in the same way, we will focus on how you represent negative numbers. Using n bits, the process is as follows:

1 Write down the binary for the magnitude as a positive number using n bits.
2 Find the ones complement of those n bits.

For example, let us represent −45 in this system using 8 bits.

We already know that the magnitude of −45 is 45 and that it is represented as a positive number using 8 bits as 00101101. We then change all the 0s to 1s and vice versa and end up with 11010010. Note that this starts with '1', so it correctly shows that this sequence of bits represents a negative number. Also note that this is different from 10101101, which is how −45 was represented using 8-bit sign and magnitude.

What is the base 10 number that is represented, using ones complement, by the following?

a 011111010_2
b 111111010_2

Note that the only difference between the two binary numbers given is the left-most bit. However, the method used to solve part **a** is considerably different from the one used to solve part **b**.

Let's take a look at part **a**. Since it starts with a '0', the number is non-negative. Therefore you can simply convert from binary to the decimal system in the usual manner (Table 7.5).

Table 7.5

Place value (in base 10)		128	64	32	16	8	4	2	1
Digit (in base 2)	0	1	1	1	1	1	0	1	0

So the answer for part **a** is:

$$128 + 64 + 32 + 16 + 8 + 2 = 250$$

The set of bits given in part **b** starts with a '1'. This changes things completely since it means that the number is negative. Since it is negative, all the bits are inverted. You must first invert the bits again (i.e. find their ones complement) in order to get back the magnitude of the number. When we do this, we see that the magnitude is represented by 000000101_2. Therefore, the magnitude (in base 10) is $4 + 1 = 5$. So the answer to part **b** is −5.

Twos complement

To find the twos complement of a binary number is almost as easy as finding the ones complement. In fact, it is exactly the same with the exception of one additional step. The steps are:

1 Find the ones complement of the binary number.
2 Add 1.

So the twos complement of $\mathbf{10010101_2}$ is $\mathbf{01101010_2} + 1_2 = 01101011_2$. Note that like for ones complement the reverse is also true. So the twos complement of 01101011_2 is $10010100_2 + 1_2 = 10010101_2$.

What is the twos complement of 00000000_2?

Well, we first invert all the bits so we end up with 11111111. Then we have to add 1.

```
  1 1 1 1 1 1 1 1
+               1
  0 0 0 0 0 0 0 0
1 1 1 1 1 1 1 1
```

What do we do with this additional carry?

If, when dealing with twos complement you end up getting a carry that would require you to have an additional bit (what we shall call an additional carry), you discard it. So the twos complement of 00000000_2 is 00000000_2.

Like the ones complement, the twos complement system can be used to represent positive and negative numbers. In order to represent a negative number using n bits:

1 Convert the magnitude to binary. This magnitude may be as large as 2^{n-1}. If the binary uses less than n bits, add 0s to the left of the bit sequence until you have a total of n bits. Note that unless the magnitude is 2^{n-1}, this gives you the same sequence of bits as the positive representation of the magnitude using n bits.

2 Find the twos complement of those n bits.

Note that the first step in this method is slightly different than the one for the ones complement system. The reason for this is illustrated in the Table 7.6. As you can see, the ones complement system has a slight problem; it has two different ways to represent zero (all 0s or all 1s). Not only is this inefficient, it would also make it more difficult for the computer to check to see if a number is 0. Twos complement, because of the way it was designed, in essence 'pushes' the values after the largest positive number (7 in this case) down a row in the table. Therefore there is only one representation of zero. This gives us the added benefit of having a bit sequence (1000 in this case) that you can use to represent an additional number. This additional number is -2^{n-1}.

For example, using 8 bits we can represent -128 (which we could not do with the same number of bits using the ones complement system). Note that -128 is $-2^7 = 2^{8-1}$. The process is as follows:

1 The magnitude of -128 is 128. The binary for this is 10000000_2, which as you can see is 8 bits so we do not need to add any extra 0s to the left.

2 The twos complement of these bits is $01111111_2 + 1_2 = 10000000_2$.

If you were the least bit observant, you would have realised that this is the same binary number that we started out with. This is not a mistake! Actually, as a shortcut you can represent -2^{n-1} in the twos complement system as '1' followed by $(n-1)$ 0s. The reason why we went through the (relatively) long process was to show that you could use the given method to represent any decimal integer in the specified range.

What is the range of numbers that can be represented?

In ones complement you can only represent base 10 numbers with a magnitude that is less than 2^{n-1}. In the twos complement system you can represent the number -2^{n-1} in addition to these numbers. Therefore, in mathematical terms, you can represent any integer x such that: $-2^{n-1} \le x < 2^{n-1}$.

Table 7.6

Binary	Decimal equivalent if the binary system is 4-bit	
	Ones complement	Twos complement
0000	0	0
0001	1	1
0010	2	2
0011	3	3
0100	4	4
0101	5	5
0110	6	6
0111	7	7
1000	-7	-8
1001	-6	-7
1010	-5	-6
1011	-4	-5
1100	-3	-4
1101	-2	-3
1110	-1	-2
1111	0	-1

To represent -45 using 8 bits, we have to find the twos complement of 00101101_2. Note that this is the same as the 8-bit representation of positive 45. The ones complement of 00101101_2 is 11010010_2. When we add 1 to this we get 11010011_2, which is the twos complement representation of -45 using 8 bits.

Although the system seems rather more complicated than the ones complement, determining what decimal number a sequence of bits represents is surprisingly similar.

For example:

What is the base 10 number that is represented, using twos complement, by 11111010_2?

Since the left-most bit is a '1' we know that the number is negative. Therefore we must find out what the original magnitude was before twos complement was applied. How do we do this? Well, remember that if the twos complement of **a** is **b**, then the twos complement of **b** is **a**. What we have, 111111010_2, is like **b**. Therefore, in order to get the magnitude, **a**, we simply have to find the twos complement of 111111010_2.

Magnitude = $000000101_2 + 1_2 = 000000110_2$. This is the binary for $4 + 2 = 6_{10}$. Therefore the number that is being represented is -6.

Why not use (the simpler) sign and magnitude for all negative numbers?

Representing integers using the twos complement system involves more steps than the much simpler sign and magnitude system. However, the twos complement system has its benefits, one of which is described below.

Consider the following:

$30 - 14$	(1)
$= 30 + (-14)$	(2)
$= 16$	

Although you may be wondering why we bothered to insert line (2), you will know that the above statements make perfect mathematical sense. After all, subtracting one number, **b**, from another number, **a**, is the same thing as adding $-$**b** to **a**. Well, at least this is the case in base 10. Is it the case in base 2?

Consider the following:

$30_{10} = 00011110_2$
$14_{10} = 00001110_2$
$-14_{10} = 1000111_2$ using 8-bit sign and magnitude
$-14_{10} = 11110010_2$ using 8-bit twos complement

```
    0 0 0 1 1 1 1 0
  - 0 0 0 0 1 1 1 0
    0 0 0 1 0 0 0 0
```

When we add the 8-bit sign and magnitude representation for -14 to the binary for 30 we get:

```
    0 0 0 1 1 1 1 0
  + 1 0 0 0 1 1 1 0
    1 0 1 0 1 1 0 0
        1 1 1 1
```

This is clearly not -16_{10}. Now let's add the 8-bit twos complement representation of -14 to the binary for 30. We get:

```
    0 0 0 1 1 1 1 0
  + 1 1 1 1 0 0 1 0
    0 0 0 1 0 0 0 0
  1 1 1 1 1 1 1
```

Additional carry

As is the case when finding the twos complement of a binary number, we discard the additional carry. So we end up with 00010000_2 which is 16 as we expected. Therefore you can subtract a number, **b**, from a number, **a**, by simply adding the twos complement of **b** to the binary for **a** (using the correct number of bits of course). Note that this is not the case when using sign and magnitude.

Binary Coded Decimal (BCD)

Wouldn't life be a lot simpler if a base 10 number were represented using the binary for each digit? Well, it turns out that there already is such a system. It is known as Binary Coded Decimal (BCD). Each digit is represented in binary by a 4-bit binary code. For your convenience these codes are shown in Table 7.7.

Table 7.7

Digit (base 10)	Binary code
0	0000
1	0001
2	0010
3	0011
4	0100
5	0101
6	0110
7	0111
8	1000
9	1001

As you have probably noticed, each code is simply the 4-bit binary for the particular digit. A negative sign is represented by 1011. For example, the BCD for 250 is 0010 0101 0000.

This system is used in certain electronic devices such as calculators and microwaves, since it makes it easier to display individual digits on the LCD displays that such devices use.

Why don't all devices use BCD?

The problem with BCD is that even when you use four bits for each digit there are some combinations of bits that do not represent any digits. Therefore it is not a very efficient means of storage. Also, BCD makes arithmetic more difficult.

ASCII codes

All the data that the computer works with is stored in binary, even text. Sentences of text are made up of individual characters and each character has a binary code associated with it. Although a variety of systems are used, the most popular, especially with PCs, is the set of ASCII codes. The American Standard Code for Information Interchange is the standard that PCs use when representing data. You are not required to commit the codes to memory. However, you may be tested to see if you understand how it works. In addition to letters and numbers, there are codes for a number of symbols, as well as for commands such as Delete and Backspace, for example.

Each code takes up 1 byte (8 bits). Capital letters are represented by the binary for 65–90, lowercase letters by 97–122, and the digits zero to nine by 49–57. You are not expected to remember all of this but you may be given questions like the following:

> The ASCII code for D is 01000100_2. What is the binary for the ASCII code for W?

D is the 4th letter of the alphabet and W is the 23rd. Therefore, in order to get the ASCII code for W you have to add 19 (23 − 4) to the ASCII code for D. Obviously you cannot just add a binary number to a base 10 number. Therefore you have to convert one of them. Since you have been asked to give the ASCII code for W in binary, it is easier to convert 19 to binary and to add it to 01000100_2. The binary for 19 is 00010011_2.

```
   0 1 0 0 0 1 0 0
 + 0 0 0 1 0 0 1 1
   0 1 0 1 0 1 1 1
```

So W is represented in ASCII by 01010111_2 (which is binary for 87).

> If the ASCII code for K is 01001011_2, what letter is represented by 01001111?

We first subtract the ASCII code for K from the ASCII code for the unknown letter since the code for the unknown letter is larger.

```
   0 1 0 0 1 1 1 1
 − 0 1 0 0 1 0 1 1
   0 0 0 0 0 1 0 0
```

This is the binary for 4_{10}. Therefore the unknown letter is four letters after the letter K. So the letter is O.

Other numbers systems used in computing

Although computers only understand binary, there are two other number systems commonly used in computing – octal (base 8) and hexadecimal (base 16). These systems are used because of their close relationship to binary.

Octal

Octal was originally used in mainframes and can still be seen today in Unix. Like hexadecimal, it is closely related to binary but unlike hexadecimal it doesn't require letters to represent digits. Since octal is base 8, the largest digit you can have is 7.

Converting octal to decimal

You can convert from octal to decimal (base 10) by using a similar table to the one we used for binary (see Table 7.8). The main difference is that the columns are powers of 8.

For example, let us convert 154_8 to base 10.

Table 7.8

Place value (in base 10)	512 (8^3)	64 (8^2)	8 (8^1)	1 (8^0)
Octal digit		1	5	4

$154_8 = (1 \times 64) + (8 \times 5) + (1 \times 4) = 108_{10}$

Converting octal to binary

To convert from octal to binary, write the three-digit binary equivalent of each digit. Table 7.9 shows the relationship between the octal and binary digits.

Table 7.9

Octal digit	Corresponding binary digits
0	000
1	001
2	010
3	011
4	100
5	101
6	110
7	111

For example:

Convert 530_8 to binary.

Find the binary number corresponding to each digit of the octal number:

$$5 \quad\quad 3 \quad\quad 0$$
$$101 \quad 011 \quad 000$$

So 530_8 is 101011000_2.

Note

You can't do this for all number systems. This is only possible because of the close relationship that octal has to binary.

Converting binary to octal

Table 7.9 can also be used to convert from binary to octal. To convert from binary to octal:

- Group the binary numbers into groups of 3, starting from the <u>right</u>.
- Write the corresponding octal digit for each group.

For example:

Convert 10010101110010110_2 to octal.

When we group the digits, we get:

$$10 \quad 010 \quad 101 \quad 110 \quad 010 \quad 110$$

In order to make the left-most group three digits, we put a 0 in front. So we get:

$$010 \quad 010 \quad 101 \quad 110 \quad 010 \quad 110$$
$$2 \quad\quad 2 \quad\quad 5 \quad\quad 6 \quad\quad 2 \quad\quad 6$$

Hexadecimal

Hexadecimal (base 16) has a lot of the same useful properties as octal. And even better, it allows you to represent a byte using two digits. Since hexadecimal is base 16, a single digit must be able to take any value between 0 and 15. But obviously you can't put a 15 in a column. Instead, the letters A to F are used as shown in Table 7.10.

Table 7.10

Hexadecimal digit	Decimal value	Corresponding binary digits
0	0	0000
1	1	0001
2	2	0010
3	3	0011
4	4	0100
5	5	0101
6	6	0110
7	7	0111
8	8	1000
9	9	1001
A	10	1010
B	11	1011
C	12	1100
D	13	1101
E	14	1110
F	15	1111

In order to show that a number is hexadecimal you either:

- use 16 as a subscript, for example $9AF_{16}$

Or

- put 0x in front, for example 0x9AF

Converting hexadecimal to decimal

To convert from hexadecimal to decimal multiply the decimal value of each digit by its place value. For example:

Convert 0x7FE to decimal.

Table 7.11

Place value (in base 10)	256 (16^2)	16 (16^1)	1 (16^0)
Hexadecimal digit	7	F	E
Decimal value	7	15	14

You multiply the first row by the last row, so:

$$0x7FE = (256 \times 7) + (16 \times 15) + (1 \times 14)$$
$$= 1792 + 240 + 14$$
$$= 204\,610$$

Converting hexadecimal to binary

You convert hexadecimal to binary in a similar manner as with octal, but this time you write the 4-digit binary equivalent of each digit.

Suppose we had to convert 0xABC to binary. Looking at Table 7.10 (which is pretty easy to construct), we get:

```
A      B      C
1010   1011   1100
```

So 0×ABC is 101010111100_2.

Converting binary to hexadecimal

Table 7.10 can also be used to convert binary to hexadecimal. The procedure is as follows:

- Starting from the <u>right</u>, group the binary numbers into groups of 4.
- Write the corresponding hexadecimal digit for each group.

For example, convert 101010010100_2 to hexadecimal. When we group the digits we get:

```
1010   1001   0100
A      9      4
```

Exercise 7

1 State the two categories of data and give an example of each.

2 **a** Name a device that produces
   i human-readable copies
   ii machine-readable copies
   b Name an input device that can accept data in human-readable form.

3 Convert the following binary numbers to decimal:

   a 10101000_2
   b 1111_2
   c 1110011_2
   d 0010011_2
   e 11111111_2
   f 11001110_2

4 Convert the following decimal numbers to binary:

   a 45_{10}
   b 25_{10}
   c 10_{10}
   d 18_{10}
   e 75_{10}
   f 30_{10}

5 Add the following binary numbers:

   a 00 + 11
   b 10 + 10 + 11
   c 11011 + 1011 + 111
   d 11111 + 11111
   e 0011 + 001100
   f 11001010 + 10001

6 Subtract the following binary numbers:

   a 1100100 – 110010
   b 100011 – 11001
   c 101011110 – 100010011
   d 11001000 – 11000110
   e 1011001 – 100011
   f 1001011000 – 110010000

7 What is the BCD representation of the following?

   a -59_{10}
   b 25_{10}
   c 1245_{10}
   d -35_{10}
   e 75_{10}
   f -100_{10}

8 Convert the following BCD representations to decimal:

   a 1011001101001001
   b 1010001100000000
   c 101001010000
   d 101101100000111
   e 1010001010101010000
   f 1011000100000000000000000

9 Convert the following sign and magnitude numbers to their decimal values:

   a 100001111
   b 000011100
   c 1100011011
   d 0111111111
   e 110100111
   f 010011111

10 Convert the following decimal values to sign and magnitude numbers:

a −60

b 95

c 108

d −97

e 64

f −38

11 Find the ones complement of following numbers:

a 01010101

b 11101111

c 101010111001

d 00000001

e 1001110001

f 010010010010

12 Find the ones complement of the following decimal numbers:

a 75

b 88

c 100

d −50

e −10

f −68

13 Find the twos complement of the following numbers:

a 101011100

b 101011011

c 0100110100

d 0110101010

e 0100000111

f 1111101010

14 Find the twos complement of the following decimal numbers:

a 25

b 98

c −14

d −33

e −911

f 89

15 In a certain character coding system, each character occupies 7 bits and the letters of the alphabet are assigned consecutive codes. If 'M' is represented by 1010001, what is the representation of 'H'?

16 The ASCII code for the letter 'V' has a decimal equivalent of 86. What is the ASCII code for the letter 'Z'?

17 What is the value of X in the following equations?

a $100011 - X_2 = 001010_2$

b $X_2 + 11001 = 75_{10}$

18 Convert the following octal numbers to decimal and binary.

a 10

b 47

c 156

d 747

19 Convert the following hexadecimal numbers to decimal and binary.

a 0x10

b 0xFF

c 0x123

d 0xDEF

20 Convert the following binary numbers to octal and hexadecimal.

a 111100001111

b 101010101010

c 100010011001

d 1010111100100

8. Types of programs, interfaces and processing

Operating system (OS)

Although the typical computer system has several programs on it, the most important piece of software on any computer is, without a doubt, the Operating System (OS). An operating system is a set of programs that controls all the hardware and application programs that make up the computer system. Many people only know about Microsoft Windows, but several other operating systems are available, such as DOS, UNIX and Linux. Even though operating systems may differ in areas such as appearance and the type of interface, the typical OS can perform the following functions:

- It executes programs and prematurely terminates those that are not working properly.
- It allocates and schedules the resources of a computer. The OS controls which program has access to which resource at a particular time. These resources include CPU time and input/output/ storage devices.
- It manages memory. The OS loads programs into memory and removes them when they are not being used. It also loads data into memory when a program requires it and it restricts the areas of memory a program has access to.
- It manages files. An OS can create, modify, rename, move or erase files. It also keeps track of the physical location of files on storage media and allows them to be logically grouped into directories (folders).
- It provides utilities to keep the computer system in good working order. Most operating systems provide utilities to do things such as backing up files or checking the disk for errors.
- It provides an interface with which a user can interact. An OS allows the user to enter commands using an input device such as the keyboard or mouse. It also provides feedback to the user via output devices.

User interface

A user interface can be thought of as a link between user and computer. It allows the user and the computer to communicate with each other. The goal of a user interface is to be easy to use while allowing tasks to be performed efficiently. Unfortunately these goals are usually mutually exclusive so that in most cases a compromise has to be reached. The two <u>main</u> types of user interfaces are the command-line interface and the graphical user interface.

Command-line interface

A command-line interface does not have the fancy buttons or graphics found in a graphical user interface. Rather, it is a simple text-based interface where a user types in commands via the keyboard, usually one line at a time (Figure 8.1). After a command is executed, the computer may display text, indicating things like a listing of files or whether or not the operation was successful. Each command has a particular structure or syntax. In order to execute a command, the user must not only remember what commands exist; he or she must also remember the syntax. This is the main drawback with this type of interface. However, once a user has taken the time to learn the various commands, the command-line interface is a very powerful way to get tasks done. DOS and UNIX are two operating systems that use a command-line interface.

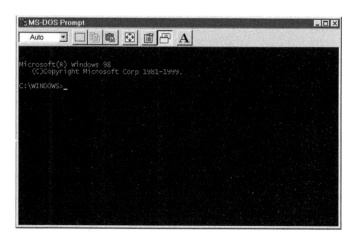

Figure 8.1 *A screen-shot of a command-line interface*

Graphical User Interface (GUI)

Instead of requiring a user to memorise and then type in commands, a graphical user interface displays all the available options by taking advantage of the graphical capabilities of the screen. The user can use the mouse (and sometimes the keyboard) to select the various items.

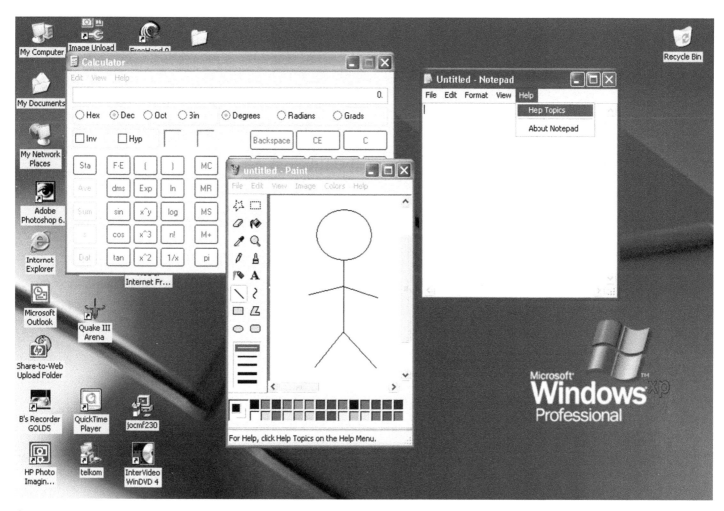

Figure 8.2 *A screen-shot of a graphical user interface (Windows XP)*

GUIs display the various commands and options using menus, buttons and icons (tiny pictures that are used to indicate what a particular item represents). Items that cannot be selected at the current time are displayed in a different manner in order to show that they are disabled. Groups of similar items may be displayed in **windows**.

A GUI is a much more intuitive interface than its command-line counterpart. By using icons, it is easy for a user to tell what an item does. Since a GUI displays all the available options, and also indicates those that are not applicable, a user does not have to worry as much about memorising commands and their syntax. Also, the use of the mouse makes certain tasks a lot easier, such as selecting multiple items or dragging an item from one location to another. However, GUIs tend to be less powerful than command-line interfaces.

Although a GUI makes heavy use of the mouse, the keyboard is still used a lot, especially to enter text. One OS that uses a GUI is Microsoft Windows XP (see Figure 8.2).

Menus

In the same way that a menu in a restaurant allows you to select from among the available meals, a menu displays the various commands that a program offers. When the mouse moves over a menu or menu item it is usually highlighted. Clicking a menu item may cause another menu to be displayed. That menu is called a **submenu**. Two types of menus commonly used are:

- **pull-down menus.** Such menus are usually found on the rectangular bar going across the top of the screen called the **Menu Bar**. When the menu is clicked, a list of its menu items is 'pulled down'. When an item is selected, the list disappears.
- **pop-up (context) menus.** These are menus that 'pop up' as if out of nowhere when a particular mouse button (usually the one on the right) is clicked when the mouse pointer is over a particular object. The menu items displayed depend on the object and certain items may be disabled if the object does not support them.

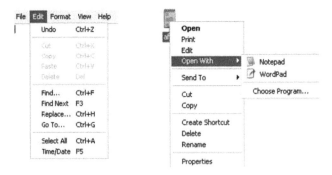

Figure 8.3 *A pull-down menu and a pop-up menu*

Buttons

Buttons are usually small rectangular areas on the screen drawn so as to resemble the buttons that you find on electronic devices. When the button is clicked, an action is usually triggered.

Windows

A window, not to be confused with the operating system, is a rectangular area on the screen that contains objects that are related to each other. It is an integral part of a GUI. When a program is run, it is usually displayed in a separate window, which may be resized, moved or closed.

Figure 8.4 *A screen-shot of a window (in Windows XP)*

Other types of interfaces

Command-line and graphical user interfaces are examples of <u>software</u> interfaces. In addition there are <u>hardware</u> interfaces such as:

- touch screens – like the ones you see on CNN
- Braille keyboards – which allow blind users to use the computer
- sensors

Application programs

An application program is a program that is used to perform tasks other than the operation and management of the computer system. These programs run on the OS for which they are designed and extend the capabilities of that OS. An application program performs a variety of related tasks.

Some examples of application programs are:

- word processing, spreadsheet and database management software
- accounting software
- graphics editors
- games

Application software can be classified as one or more of the following:

- general-purpose
- customized
- custom-written
- specialised
- integrated software package

General-purpose software

General-purpose software is not specific to a particular type of organisation and can perform a wide range of tasks. General-purpose software is mass-produced and is therefore relatively cheap. Most of the software you are familiar with is general-purpose software, for example database, spreadsheet and word processing software.

Customised software

Sometimes a general-purpose program fulfils most, but not all, of the tasks a person or a company requires. It may be slightly modified so that it better suits the purpose of the client. Such software is said to be customised. Most general-purpose software provides facilities for customisation through writing code or recording macros.

Microsoft Access, Dbase and Microsoft Excel are examples of general-purpose software that can be customised.

Custom-written software

Custom-written software is software that is written entirely to the specifications of the owner. As you might expect, it is more expensive than general-purpose software. However, since the program would only have the features that the owner requires, it is usually more efficient than general-purpose software.

The very nature of custom-written software suggests that it is not limited to any particular industry or application. Also, it is very unlikely that a custom-written program will have a name (or at least one that many people will be familiar with). So it usually does not make any sense to try to give a list of custom-written programs.

Specialised software

Specialised software is software that is designed to perform tasks specific to a particular application. Therefore it does not have as wide a range of features as general-purpose software and is not usually suitable for the average person. However, by just focusing on a specific application, a specialised program can be very efficient at what it does. Specialised software is common in non-computer-related fields such as accounting and manufacturing. Examples of specialised software are ACCPAC, which is an accounting software package, airline reservations software, payroll programs and CAD software.

Integrated software packages

Sometimes multiple pieces of software are bundled as an **integrated package**. For instance, the Microsoft Office suite consists of Word, Excel, Access, PowerPoint and more.

Integrated packages make it very easy to share data. Also, the package costs less than if you were to buy its components individually. Unfortunately, such packages are very large and you often get functionality you don't need.

How computers run multiple tasks 'simultaneously'

What if you were told that a processor can only do one task at any given time? 'Nonsense!' you might say, 'I can listen to music, while surfing the net and chatting to my friends on MSN … all at the same time.' But what is _really_ happening is that the computer is using a variety of techniques to give the _illusion_ that these programs are running simultaneously. Let's look at some of these techniques now.

Multiprogramming

Multiprogramming was a technique where a program was allowed to run until it needed a resource, at which point another program in the batch took its place.

By submitting a batch of programs and using multiprogramming, expensive CPU time could be efficiently utilised. However, one big drawback of this approach was that some programs would have to wait a very long time for their 'turn'.

Multitasking

Multitasking is the concurrent execution of two or more tasks. Each task is given a slice of the CPU's time and they take turns until they are done. A turn is so short that the CPU can switch between tasks several times a second. This happens so quickly that it _appears_ that the tasks are being done at the same time.

Although multitasking is a very old technique, it is still the foundation of the operating systems we use today. And it doesn't look as if it's going to be replaced in the near future.

Multiprocessing

If _one_ processor can only do one task at a given moment, why not get two or more processors? This is the approach that multiprocessing takes. The formal definition of multiprocessing is 'the simultaneous processing by two or more CPUs'.

If your computer has two processors, then it really can run two programs at one time. Alternatively, a single program can use both processors at the same time so it can run faster.

If you purchased your computer in the last couple of years, you may have heard about dual-core or quad-core CPUs. These are CPUs with two or four processors respectively (the term 'core' is refers to a processor). These modern computers are capable of true multiprocessing.

Processing

Processing is the manipulation of data to produce information. Although the two terms are often used interchangeably, consider the following: What would you do if someone told you 'I want 20'. You'd probably ask, 'Twenty? Twenty what?' If the person tells you 'I want 20 floppy disks' then you would know what he or she was referring to. The difference between the two requests is that the second has structure since it puts the '20' into context. Data is like the first request, lacking structure. Information is data with structure, as in the second request.

There are three types of processing: batch (or off-line) processing, on-line processing and real-time processing.

Batch processing

Batch processing is the processing of a number of jobs simultaneously from start to finish without user intervention. This allows the processor to be utilised efficiently, thereby increasing the productivity of the computer. Data is gathered, stored in batches and processed later. Immediate information is not possible.

Examples of batch processing are:

- processing hand-written receipts
- inventory control
- accounts receivable where invoices are hand-written

On-line processing

As efficient as batch processing is, it is not always suitable since there are many occasions where data needs to be processed quickly or to be shared among users. In on-line processing, when a transaction is made, the processing may or may not be done during the transaction. An input device is connected to the computer, which allows data to be entered during the transaction. The data is stored and may be processed shortly after.

Examples of on-line processing systems are:

- ATMs
- Point of Sale Terminals at the checkout counter of a supermarket

Real-time processing

There are cases where even on-line processing is not fast enough, where a delay of even a few seconds is unacceptable. For example, in an airline reservation system, where people are calling every second to make or cancel reservations on various flights, the operators need to know the instant when all the seats are booked or when a seat becomes available. Or in a nuclear power plant, various settings must be monitored in order to know the instant something goes wrong. Such systems use real-time processing. In real-time processing, the data is processed immediately, thus making information current and readily available.

Exercise 8

1. Why is the operating system program important to the computer?
2. MS-DOS is a popular operating system; name two others.
3. State two roles the operating system plays as part of the computer system.
4. What is an interface? Explain the different types.
5. What is an icon?
6. List two types of menus.
7. **a** What is the purpose of an application program?
   b Give two examples.
8. Mary completed a computer maintenance course four months ago. She decided that since she had money she would apply her knowledge gained at the course and build a computer. After she had assembled the computer she remembered that the hardware she assembled would be of no use unless she purchased *software to manage the resources of the computer*, as well as *software for her particular processing needs*. Mary had a choice of purchasing software with a command-driven interface, or one that provides *screen listings with options from which the user can select appropriate functions*. Mary preferred the latter interface because it also contains *small graphical images that can be selected when the function they represent is required*.
   State the terms for the four phrases in italics in the passage above.
9. State two advantages of general-purpose software.
10. Explain the following and give two applications of each:
    a batch processing
    b on-line processing
    c real-time processing
11. What are the advantage and disadvantages of using integrated software packages over using individual programs?
12. Explain what each of the following terms mean:
    a Multiprogramming
    b Multitasking
    c Multiprocessing

9. Data communication

Data communication is the transmission of data from one location to the other in order to enable communication between the locations. In modern civilisation, effective data communication is absolutely critical. It is achieved through the use of computers, transmission cables, satellites and wireless technology.

The data is transmitted via data communication channels. These channels are categorised according to their **bandwidth** (volume of data that can be transmitted through the channel each second). There are three categories of channels. These are:

- **narrow-band.** Data is transmitted at a slow speed (just over 10 characters per second), for example telegraphed transmission.
- **voice-band.** Telephone lines are utilised, allowing data to be transmitted at rates up to 8000 characters per second.
- **broad-band.** Broad-band uses fibre-optic cables, microwave and satellite transmissions to allow very fast transmission of data (hundreds of thousands of characters per second).

There are various types of communication systems that vary according to the directions in which data can be transmitted. These are:

- **simplex.** Data can be transmitted in only one direction.
- **half duplex.** Data can be transmitted in both directions, but not at the same time.
- **duplex (full duplex).** Data can be transmitted in both directions at the same time and independent of each other.

Protocol

Every second millions of transmissions take place. These transmissions are often sent between devices that function in different ways. Imagine the confusion that would result if there were not rules to tell these devices how to transmit and receive data. You would end up with devices that could not communicate with devices made by different manufacturers. Obviously this is not the case. To ensure that transmissions are coordinated with minimal interference, protocols were developed. These are sets of rules and procedures governing the transmission and receiving of data. Some international protocols with which you may be familiar are: HTTP, PPP, TCP/IP and FTP.

Networks

A network is a group of computers and peripheral devices that are connected to each other by cables or wireless electronics. Networks reduce costs and increase efficiency by allowing the sharing of programs, data and peripheral devices. In some cases there are special computers called servers that are dedicated to the managing of particular resources. For example, a **file server** is a computer with a large storage capacity that is used to store and manage files that are used by the various computers on the network. It is also responsible for file security. A **print server** may be connected to a printer in order to manage the print jobs coming from computers all across the network.

Local Area Networks (LANs)

A Local Area Network (LAN) is made up of two or more computers connected to each other within the same geographical area but not necessarily within the same building. LANs are usually used by small and medium sized businesses.

Figure 9.1 *A Local Area Network (LAN) card*

LANs are usually connected using **twisted pair cables** or **coaxial cables**. Twisted pair cables are cheap but are relatively slow so they are usually used where the volume of data transmitted is small or where speed is not critical. Coaxial cables are faster but more expensive. They are used when voice and video transmissions are necessary or when large amounts of data are to be transmitted.

Wireless technology is becoming popular within LANs. As the name suggests, wireless technology does not use cables. Instead it uses radio and microwave signals to transmit and receive data. It is used in situations where cables are inconvenient.

Wide Area Network (WAN)

A Wide Area Network (WAN) is a network that covers a wide geographical area. Obviously you would not link the computers in a WAN using twisted pair cables or coaxial cables. Instead WANs use a combination of fibre-optic cables and telephone lines, as well as satellite and microwave technology, to transmit data.

Fibre-optic cables are extremely thin cables through which light, which is used to transmit data, passes. Fibre-optic cables allow extremely fast and accurate transmission of large volumes of data and have become very popular in the telecommunications industry.

Disadvantages of networking

Although networking offers tremendous advantages, there are some disadvantages associated with it that should be considered.

- Networks are expensive to set up. Servers, routers, cables and network cards may be required in order for a network to be set up. In addition, configuring a network is a very complex process that may require an additional employee – a network administrator.
- Security problems. People may be able to access shared information that they are not supposed to see by hacking into computers on the network.

Modem (modulator/demodulator)

A **modem** is a device that can convert digital signals into analogue and vice versa. A modem at one computer converts the digital signals produced by the computer to analogue signals for transmission along a telephone line. The modem at the receiving computer converts the analogue signals back to digital signals to be interpreted by that computer.

Figure 9.2 *A computer modem*

The speed of the modem is measured in bits per second (bps). The speed at which a modem can transmit or receive data is limited by the line over which the data is to be transmitted.

Transmission media

Transmission media (what data travels via) can be divided into two broad categories: wired media and wireless media.

The following are all wired media:

- twisted pair cables
- coaxial cables
- telephone lines
- fibre-optic cables

Examples of <u>wireless</u> media are:

- satellite transmissions
- microwave
- infra-red

Wireless technology

Wireless networking has seen exponential growth in the last few years because of the convenience it offers. You aren't restricted by how far a cable can reach and don't have to worry about tangled wires. There are wireless mice, wireless headsets, and even wireless modems. The two main wireless technologies are Bluetooth and Wi-Fi. In the near future, there will be another called WiMAX.

Bluetooth

IEEE 802.15.1, also known as **Bluetooth**, is a low power wireless protocol for exchanging data over short distances (e.g. a few metres). Bluetooth can be found in several devices including cell phones, mice, keyboards and printers. It automates the process of connecting these devices and allows them to provide services for each other.

It is commonly used for:

- wireless headsets
- wireless input and output devices such as mice, keyboard and printers
- transferring files between cell phones

Wi-Fi

The other big name when it comes to wireless is IEEE 802.1, also known as **Wi-Fi**. This technology allows wireless LANs to be set up. It is more powerful than Bluetooth as it is faster and has a longer range.

However, it is more difficult to set up. A wide range of devices support Wi-Fi including laptops, cell phones, wireless modems, gaming consoles and printers.

Note

Desktop computers usually don't come with built-in Wi-Fi. So if you want to connect a desktop PC to a Wi-Fi network you'll have to buy a wireless adapter. In contrast, every laptop made within the last few years (in particular the Centrino branded laptops) is Wi-Fi enabled out of the box.

Wireless access points (WAPs) are the glue that hold Wi-Fi networks together. They allow Wi-Fi enabled devices that are within range to connect to the wireless network. For single room, a single WAP is usually enough, but office setups typically require multiple WAPs.

When a Wi-Fi enabled device such as a laptop comes within range of a WAP, it automatically detects the wireless network and gives you the option of connecting to it. Wireless networks may be secured via passwords to prevent unauthorised people from gaining access.

Although it is possible for an entire network to be wireless, what usually happens is that at least one WAP is plugged into existing wired infrastructure. This is done for two main reasons:

1 to connect the wireless network to the Internet
2 because wireless components are slower and more expensive than their wired counterparts

Note

Wireless modems are also wireless access points.

Wi-Fi isn't only used in a home or office setting. Many places such as universities, hotels, airports and cafés provide Wi-Fi hotspots. A **hotspot** is a public venue (containing one or more WAPs) that provides Wi-Fi access to the Internet.

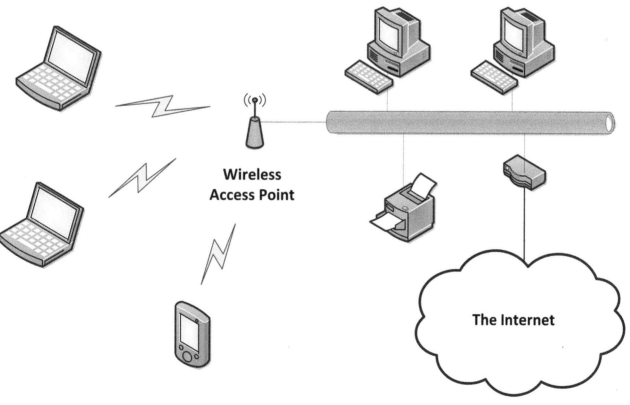

Figure 9.3 *Typical wireless network setup*

Terms associated with data communications

Upload. This is the process by which one computer, the host, sends a file to a remote computer via communication channels.

Download. This is the process by which a computer obtains a file from a host computer via communications channels.

Point-to-point transmission. This is the process by which data is sent from one location to another.

Broadcast transmission. This is the process by which data is transmitted in such a way that any person with the correct equipment can receive it. This means that it is difficult to control who receives the data.

Bulletin board. This is a centralised computerised location to which remote computers can connect (usually via a telephone line). Once connected, a user can upload messages and files or download those posted by other users.

Exercise 9

1   What is data communication?
2   Name the three categories of data communication and explain each category.
3   Name the various types of communication systems in which data can be transmitted and give examples of each.
4   Why is there a need for protocol in today's technological age?
5   Explain the following terms:
    a upload
    b Wide Area Network
    c half duplex
6   Give a similarity and a difference between e-mail and bulletin board.
7   What is a network? Give one advantage and one disadvantage of using a network.
8   Why is bandwidth important in the transmitting and receiving of data?
9   Cables are usually used in connecting computers in a network. What other technology can be used where cables are not involved? What signals are used in this technology?
10 A modem is a very important device in networking.
    a What are the meaning of and the purpose of the modem?
    b What is the speed of the modem measured in?
11 Give three examples of wired media and three examples of wireless media.
12 What are the two main types of wireless technology? Compare the two.
13 What is a hotspot?

10. Hardware and software applications

Various industries have differing needs when it comes to computer hardware and software. What is suited for one industry may not be suited for another. In this chapter we will take a look at the hardware and software used in various industries.

Electronic office

The use of Information Technology in the office is widespread. A number of tasks are now computerised, leading to what is known as the **electronic office**. Computers are used to:

* create and edit documents
* store records
* communicate via e-mail
* send and receive faxes

Hardware

* Microcomputers in a local network or standalone PCs
* Inkjet or laser printers (to print out documents)
* Fax machine

Software

* Office software – word processor, spreadsheet and database programs
* Accounting software
* Web browser, e-mail client

Banking

Computers are used in banking for:

* processing customer transactions (deposits and withdrawals, loans)
* cheque clearing (processing cheques written by the bank's customers)
* electronic fund transfer (transferring of money using electronic means)

Hardware

* Mainframe computer networked with terminals at each employee's workstation
* Line printers that are used for printing reports and customer statements
* Character printers for printing transactions in passbooks

* ATM machines
* Magnetic Ink Character Reader

Software

* Accounting software for managing customer accounts and the financial records of the bank
* Word-processing software used for preparing correspondence
* WAN software

Retail outlet

A retail outlet is a shop that sells commodities to consumers. A supermarket is an example of a retail outlet. Computers may be used in a retail outlet for:

* billing (invoicing)
* inventory control
* marketing
* point of sale systems (at the checkout counter)
* accounting

Hardware

* Mainframe or minicomputer networked with terminals and cash registers (in larger retail stores)
* Bar code scanner
* Line printers that are used for printing reports and statements
* Character printers for printing letters and memos

Software

* Inventory and accounting software
* Word processing software
* Videotext software (for marketing items)
* Payroll software

Manufacturing

Computers are used extensively in the manufacturing industry. In fact, many employees have been made redundant because computers are doing their jobs faster and more efficiently. The computers are used for a variety of applications, including:

* assembly line operations – computers can direct the operations of the machines used along the assembly line.

- performing simulations – computers can simulate things like car crashes that would be too expensive or dangerous to do in real life
- underlined process control – computers are used for controlling temperature, pressure, flow, viscosity, etc.

Computer-Aided Manufacturing (CAM)

Computer-Aided Manufacturing (CAM) is the process by which computers control aspects of the manufacturing process. In CAM, computers directly control the machinery, which offers certain advantages such as:

- improved consistency of physical characteristics of the product
- higher quality and faster throughput of product
- optimisation of raw material usage

CAM is often used in association with CAD.

Hardware

- Robots
- Process controls, e.g. temperature regulator, flow meter and viscometer
- Mainframe, minicomputers and microcomputers
- Graphics plotters

Robots

Computer-controlled mechanical devices known as robots are used for performing certain functions in industry. Robots, however, are not limited to industrial environments. Robots are used in the manufacturing industry in:

- vehicle manufacture for welding, assembling parts and packaging parts
- mining, cutting and cleaning of coal
- hazardous jobs
- repetitive, boring jobs

Robots offer the benefits of reduced labour cost (in the long run) and higher productivity.

Software

- Computer-Aided Design (CAD) software
- Specialised software to control machinery

Science and technology

Computers play an extremely important role in science and technology. They are used for a wide variety of applications, such as weather forecasting, telecommunications and aiding scientific research. Various fields in science and technology utilise knowledge-based systems. An important example of

this is the use of **expert systems** for making medical diagnoses or in a variety of applications in geological exploration and the construction industry.

Expert systems

Consider what happens when you go to the doctor. The doctor asks you a few questions and runs a few tests and uses the information obtained from these to make a diagnosis. Doctors can do this because their minds act as a sort of database that has information about which symptoms correspond to which illnesses.

An expert system is software that imitates experts such as doctors by comparing responses to certain questions to those in a database in order to make a diagnosis or recommendation. Expert systems have the advantage of not making biased decisions or incorrect decisions caused by stress and fatigue. They make decisions based only on the information supplied. However, this same characteristic means that an expert system is incapable of making moral judgements. They are limited to certain areas of expertise and cannot adapt as a human would in light of new medical developments (without first being reprogrammed). An expert system is therefore no substitute for human intelligence.

Hardware

- Sensors
- Process controls

Software

- Simulation software
- Software for the expert systems

Education

Computers are playing an increasingly important role in educational institutions. In addition to being used while teaching subjects, computers are used in the following ways:

- simulation of laboratory experiments in subjects such as chemistry and physics
- Computer-Assisted Instruction (CAI)
- Computer-Assisted Learning (CAL)
- maintaining student records
- research purposes – resources such as multimedia CD-ROMs, as well as the Internet, are used to research information

Computer-Assisted Instruction (CAI)

Computer-Assisted Instruction (CAI) employs the use of the computer to facilitate the process of learning. It uses activities based on the drill-and-practice principle, making it very useful in committing things to memory.

Exercises may be given in the form of educational games to make learning more fun, especially for younger students.

Hardware

- PCs (as well as a few mainframes or minicomputers in universities)
- Voice synthesisers for teaching people with speech and hearing disabilities
- Laser and inkjet printers (as well as the occasional character printer)

Software

- Word processors – to prepare letters, type tests or assignments
- Spreadsheet software – for calculating students' grades, as well as to display other statistics such as the maximum and minimum scores
- Database software – to keep track of each student's personal and academic records
- Simulation software – to simulate experiments too dangerous or costly to do in real life
- Tutorial packages for the various subjects

Law enforcement

The use of computers in law enforcement has helped various agencies to quickly solve many cases that would have been either impossible to solve or that would have taken much longer. Computers are used to maintain databases of criminals and the crimes that have been committed. A lot of the technology mentioned in movies is used extensively in forensic science, for example DNA and fingerprint matching. Computers are also used in the electronic office to improve efficiency in the various agencies and police departments.

Did you know?

Computers are not only used to investigate crimes; they are also used to prevent them. For example, in some places of the world, computers monitor telephone conversations, 'listening' for certain key words that would indicate that someone is planning a major crime (such as an assassination).

Hardware

- Mainframes, microcomputers to store the massive databases
- PCs

- Scanners for scanning photographs of criminals
- Printers
- Fax machines to send information from one department to another

Software

- Database management software
- Software for scanning photos
- Software that can match photographs, voice samples, DNA and fingerprints with those stored in databases in order to identify people
- Programs to 'listen' for certain key words

Recreation and entertainment

The entertainment industry is a multibillion-dollar industry. Computer technology is an integral part of this technology. Whether in the games industry or the recording industry, computers play an important role.

Games

Games have come a long way since Pacman. Current games use the latest technology to create an experience that looks and sounds realistic. There are computer games that simulate sports, combat, driving and flying, along with the arcade-type games that are meant to be pure fun. Just because a game isn't played on a PC doesn't mean that there is not a computer involved. Even games consoles such as the Playstation or XBox are types of computers.

Hardware

- PCs (usually with 3D cards)
- Speakers
- Game consoles
- Joystick, game-pad or steering wheel

Figure 10.1 *A gaming console*

Software

- The games themselves
- 3D renderers – to generate the 3D shaded images that are found in most games (Figure 10.2)
- Game editors – that allow the users to create additional levels for certain games

Entertainment industry

Nowadays it is difficult to imagine what the entertainment industry would be like without computers. In fact, some people are starting to complain about songs and movies looking and sounding <u>too</u> computer enhanced.

In the music business, computers are used:

- in the recording studios
- to synthesise and edit music
- to add special effects to the music

Most modern movies, especially the blockbusters, are produced using computers. Before the actual shooting occurs, animation software is used to create moving storyboards in order for the crew and cast to get a good idea of what a scene will look like. Computers are also used to generate scenes and characters in some movies. Movies such as *The Matrix*, *The Mummy Returns* and the recent episodes of *Star Wars* use what is known as Computer-Generated Imagery (CGI) to produce jaw-dropping special effects that could never be shot in real life.

Many movie makers use specialised, custom-written software to produce special effects for movies. For example, for the movie *Deep Blue Sea*, a special program was created that could generate a photo-realistic sea.

Figure 10.2 *Image from a 3D rendering program*

Did you know?

The movie *The Matrix* uses computers in an effect known as **bullet-time photography**. This is where you see a slow-motion sequence while the camera angle is changing. The computer is used to control the path of the camera, as well as to make the slow-motion sequence move more smoothly.

In addition to the animation, graphics and special effects software, devices such as light pens and graphics tablets may be used within the movie and television industry.

Engineering and design

Once upon a time, all engineering drawings were done using pencils and paper. Nowadays, most are done on computer. Along with the obvious advantage of neater looking documents, this has many other benefits.

Engineers make heavy use of CAD software when they design buildings, bridges, roadways, etc.

Computer-Aided Design (CAD)

Computer-Aided Design (CAD) is the use of computers to help design three-dimensional technical drawings. This is achieved through the use of special software. CAD drawings consist of shapes and objects that may easily be moved and resized. This offers a considerable advantage over the pencil and paper equivalent, since you would not have to erase or redraw any lines in order to accomplish this. Also, it is easy to undo any changes that you do make; simply click the Undo button.

The use of CAD software offers another considerable advantage – libraries of commonly drawn objects. So instead of having to draw such an object from scratch all you would have to do is import the object from the library and make some minute changes. This saves lots of work, time, and by extension, money. Since each library is simply a database of parts, it can be used in conjunction with other databases to get information about the parts such as the price.

Computer-Aided Design and Drafting (CADD) is similar to CAD, except that it can be used to produce detailed two-dimensional pictures of objects in addition to the technical drawings produced through CAD. Unlike the technical drawings, these 2D drafts are not used as blueprints for the creation of physical objects.

Computer-Aided Engineering (CAE)

Computer-Aided Engineering (CAE) is the use of computers to analyse engineering designs and to simulate complex electrical and mechanical systems. It is often used to see if technical designs created through CAD are practicable. This is so common that many CAD programs have basic CAE features.

Software

- CAD and CAE software

Hardware

- PCs (workstations) connected to a minicomputer or mainframe
- High-resolution monitors, which are needed because of the fine details that may be found in the drawings
- Flatbed or drum graphics plotter
- Inkjet or laser printers

Exercise 10

1 List two ways in which computers can be used in the home.

2 State at least three ways in which information can be used to assist medical personnel.

3 Various fields in science and technology utilise knowledge-based systems. An important example of this is the use of expert systems.
   a What is an expert system?
   b How would expert systems be used in the medical profession?
   c State one advantage and one disadvantage of the use of expert systems in the medical profession.

4 State four ways in which the police may use IT in their jobs.

5 a State two uses of computers in banking.
   b State two services that banks now provide because of computers, which they could not provide before.
   c State two advantages that the bank can now cite because of the services in part **b.**

6 State two applications where the following software packages can be used at school:
   a word processing
   b spreadsheet
   c database

7 a State the purpose of CAD.
   b State two advantages which CAD has over using conventional pencil and paper to draw.

8 Robots have been introduced in a local car manufacturing company.
   a Give one application that a robot could be used for in this company.
   b State two advantages that the company could cite because of the use of robots.
   c Give one disadvantage of robots for the workforce.
   d State one disadvantage of robots for the company.

9 State one advantage of Computer-Aided Manufacturing.

11. The Internet and intranets

The Internet

The world's biggest network, the Internet, is actually a collection of smaller networks located all over the world. The Internet can be used for a variety of purposes, such as checking e-mail, chatting, downloading files, searching for information, listening to music, making business transactions and viewing video clips. With so many features, it is no small wonder that every day millions of people around the world use the Internet and increasing numbers are rushing to sign up for it.

Gaining access to the Internet

In order to gain access to the vast resources found on the Internet you must first become part of one of the networks which it comprise it. The networks of several large companies and universities are directly connected to the Internet, so if you are part of one of these networks and you have the appropriate network privileges, you can access the Internet.

The average person, however, gains access through a local **Internet Service Provider (ISP)**. An ISP is a company with a direct connection to the Internet that grants subscribers access to various Internet services. Subscribers connect using one of two methods:

- **dial-up connection.** The user's modem dials the ISP. The user is required to enter his or her username and password before access is granted to the Internet.
- **broad-band cable or Digital Subscriber Line (DSL) connection.** The user is permanently connected to the Internet (i.e. does not have to dial).

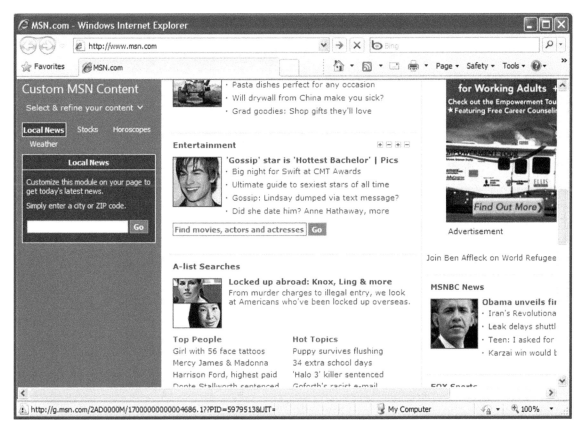

Figure 11.1 *A web page*

The World Wide Web

The best-known (and most commonly used) aspect of the Internet is the World Wide Web (WWW). It is basically a collection of text and multimedia documents called **web pages**, some of which are linked. Web pages are usually encoded in a special language called **Hypertext Markup Language (HTML)** that allows one web page to provide links to several others. These web pages are stored on computers dedicated to storing web pages called, surprisingly enough, **web servers**. A group of related web pages on the same web server is known as a **website**. Each web page and website has an address called a **Uniform Resource Locator (URL)**; for example, the URL for the main page of the Microsoft website is http://www.microsoft.com.

Web pages are viewed using special software called **web browsers** such as Internet Explorer, Firefox, Safari or Opera. These web pages may contain a wealth of information in the form of text, images, animations, sounds and videos. The URL tells the browser which web page to download and load. The transmission of web pages is governed by a protocol known as **Hypertext Transfer Protocol (HTTP)**.

How do you find a web page?

There are literally billions of web pages on the Internet. Obviously you cannot remember the URLs of all of them. And even if you could, how would you find out the URL in the first place? Fortunately, there are ways to do this. You can find web pages containing certain words by using a search engine such as Google (http://www.google.com). You can also browse a web directory such as Yahoo (http://www.yahoo.com). Web directories have various websites listed by category but have fewer web pages listed than a search engine.

E-mail

Another buzzword that people associate with the Internet is **e-mail**. Short for electronic mail, e-mail is mail that is sent and received electronically over a network. It is a service that is provided by most ISPs, as well as by some network administrators.

Let us compare e-mail with normal mail. In the same way a person has his or her own mailing address, each person using e-mail must have an e-mail address, usually in the form <name>@<someplace.com>, for example johndoe@hotmail.com. The e-mail service provider (usually the ISP) has a special server to handle the e-mail for its customers. This is called the **mail server** and can be compared with the post office. Each person has a mailbox for his or her e-mail address. Incoming mail is sent here and outgoing mail is sent from here.

E-mails are mainly text messages that may (but do not usually) have some formatting similar to a word processing document. However, e-mail may also be used to send files. These files are attached to the e-mail message and are therefore called **attachments**. Programs such as Microsoft Outlook Express and Eudora are used to compose and read e-mails. When you are sending e-mail you have to specify the e-mail address(es) of the recipient(s). A person is usually notified of new e-mail by the e-mail program. Before mail is read, it is downloaded from the mail server to the user's computer.

Advantages

- It is faster than standard post. Whereas normal mail takes days to reach its destination, e-mails reach anywhere in the world in a few minutes or even seconds.
- It is cheaper and more convenient. Once you have an Internet connection and a computer, e-mails are free. You do not have to worry about stamps, envelopes or anything like that.
- It is very easy to send files.
- The same message can be quickly and easily sent to several people.

Disadvantages

- It obviously cannot be used to send parcels.
- You cannot send e-mail to people who do not have an e-mail account.
- E-mail makes it very easy for computer viruses to be spread.

Tip

If you have access to the Internet but do not have an e-mail address, you can sign up for one for free from one of several websites. The most popular of these are Yahoo and Hotmail.

Internet Relay Chat (IRC) and Instant Messaging

E-mail is not the only way that the Internet can be used to communicate with other people. Internet Relay Chat (IRC) is another way of doing so. People with IRC client programs, such as MIRC, can take part in one of several discussions on an IRC server. When you type a message, it is sent to the server and then relayed to the IRC clients of the other people in the discussion. In this way, several people can take part in a discussion at one time.

Instant Messaging is a fast-growing part of Internet culture. Instant Messaging programs such as ICQ and MSN Messenger allow people to send and receive messages. As the name suggests, this messaging is more or less instant so it is well suited to having conversations. A conversation normally consists of two or three people, although it may be larger. A fast typist may even take part in several conversations simultaneously. Each conversation usually takes place in a separate window.

Each person who uses Instant Messaging has an account that is used to identify him or her. When a person signs on, this account is mapped to the location of his/her computer on the Internet (or network). This allows messages to reach the intended destination. A person can add the account IDs of his or her friends or acquaintances to a 'buddy list'. The person is then notified whenever one of the people from the 'buddy list' goes online or offline.

Blogs

What is a blog?

A **blog** (or web log) is an online journal that an individual can use to post his or her thoughts and have people comment on them. Posting to a blog is called **blogging** and the person doing the posting is called a **blogger**.

A blog is just another kind of website, so anything posted on your blog is usually public. What makes blogs special is that although they are very easy to set up, even the most basic blog comes with several features. For example, whenever you make a post, the date is automatically displayed. Posts can also be organised by date or by category.

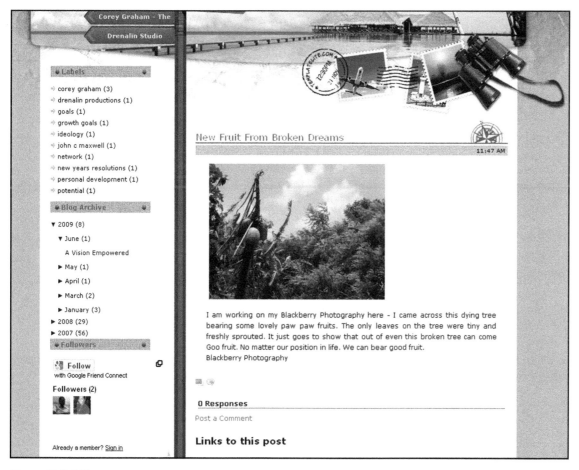

Figure 11.2 *A blog*

Some of the ways blogs are used are:

- as diaries
- to publish news
- to give minute by minute accounts of live events
- to provide social commentary

How to get your own blog

Several sites allow you to create a blog absolutely free. The most popular ones are:

- WordPress (www.wordpress.com)
- Blogger (www.blogger.com)
- Windows Live Spaces (spaces.live.com)

Podcasts

The word 'podcast' comes from 'iPod' and 'broadcast', since it originally referred to audio broadcasts that could be downloaded to people's iPods. But the term quickly evolved to mean 'a pre-recorded audio/video broadcast that is stored in a digital form for users to download'.

You can easily find podcasts of:

- radio shows
- interviews
- transcripts of written articles
- lectures

Users can subscribe so that they are notified when new podcasts are available. They can also opt to have the podcasts downloaded automatically.

Other aspects of the Internet

There's much more to the Internet than what we have covered so far. In this section we'll look at some of the lesser known aspects of the Internet.

File Transfer Protocol (FTP)

File Transfer Protocol (FTP) is a set of rules used to govern the sending and receiving of files on the Internet.

Many websites have associated FTP sites from which files can be downloaded. Actually, you may have downloaded from FTP sites without knowing it since some web pages link directly to the files. People with the necessary access privileges may also upload files to the FTP sites.

Telnet

Telnet is one of the ways that a person can access a remote computer over a network such as the Internet. It is often used by network administrators to remotely control and/or troubleshoot the operation of a web server. Telnet programs act as if your computer is a terminal that is connected to the remote computer. This is called **terminal emulation**. People or companies can limit the privileges of people who are logging onto their computer(s) via telnet.

Newsgroups

A good way to have access to a wealth of information about a particular topic is by joining a newsgroup. An Internet newsgroup consists of people who are interested in or knowledgeable about a particular topic. You can post messages on a newsgroup so that people can respond to them. You can read messages from a newsgroup by using a program known as a **newsgroup reader**. Messages are stored on several news servers. The length of time that a message is kept on the server depends on the server.

Newsgroups are periodically synchronised so that a message that is sent to one server can be found on another.

Intranets

Various concepts that people associate with the Internet such as web pages and e-mail are actually not limited to the Internet. There are other networks that use the same network protocol as the Internet, TCP/IP, that have these features. One such type of network that belongs to, and is used exclusively by, a particular company, is called an intranet.

An intranet allows for greater control of access to resources but as you may expect does not have as many resources as the Internet.

Extranets

An extranet is an extension to a company's intranet that allows its clients and business partners to share its information. Although it can be accessed by people outside the company, it is not open to the general public.

Exercise 11

1. What is the Internet?
2. What is an ISP? Give two examples of local ISPs.
3. What does WWW stand for? Explain the term.
4. What is a group of related web pages on the same web server called?
5. What is the address of each web page and website called? Give an example.
6. What is the software used to view web pages called? Give two examples.
7. What does the acronym HTTP mean? What part does it play in the World Wide Web?
8. How does e-mail differ from the bulletin board?
9. What is a newsgroup?
10. What is a blog and what features do blogs normally have?
11. What is a podcast?
12. What is the difference between the Internet, an intranet and an extranet?

12. Information processing

Data versus information

Data
Data is raw facts and figures. For example, suppose that in an exam the marks obtained by ten students were 88, 72, 40, 55, 17, 100, 93, 61, 38, 79. These figures have very little meaning in this raw state. Some teacher probably just jotted these figures down in her mark book. This is an example of data.

Information
Since data has very little meaning, it must be worked on to transform it into something that is meaningful. The act of working on data is known as **processing**. This may involve sorting, calculating, or compiling. The processed data is known as **information**.

Figure 12.1 *The relationship between data and information*

The data in the example above may be processed to give information such as:

- The maximum mark is 100.
- The minimum mark is 17.
- The average mark is 64.3.
- Seven students passed but three failed.

What is information processing?

Information processing covers the full gamut of things you'd want to do with data. According to the Encyclopedia Britannica, it is the 'acquisition, recording, organization, retrieval, display, and dissemination of information'.

Forms of information processing

Information processing occurs in a variety of forms as shown below.

Automation
Automation is the act of using computers and machines instead of human labour. Many businesses and organisations automate the handling of information such as correspondence, inventory tracking, invoicing and accounts receivable, record keeping, data analysis and sharing of information.

Automation has several benefits including enhanced speed of processing and printing, higher accuracy and reliability, and the professional presentation of information.

Despite the benefits, automation has negative social implications since it has a tendency to create job redundancy.

Process control
A **process** is an operation or an action that is performed in doing something. Special-purpose computers are used for controlling processes to optimise their efficiency. Examples of systems that are controlled are: temperature, pressure, humidity, automatic doors, flow of liquids and traffic lights. Figure 12.2 represents a system for controlling the temperature of a liquid.

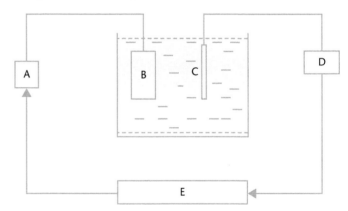

Figure 12.2 *System for controlling the temperature of a liquid: A, switch, turns heating element on or off; B, heating element, heats the liquid; C, analogue thermometer measures the temperature and sends out an analogue signal; D, analogue-to-digital converter; E, computer regulates the switch based on the desired temperature.*

To begin with, the computer is set to the desired temperature. The thermometer measures the temperature and sends out an analogue signal. The signal is converted to a digital signal by the analogue-to-digital converter so that it may be accepted by the computer. If the liquid is below the desired temperature, the computer turns on the switch to the heater and the liquid is heated. If the temperature is above the desired temperature, the computer turns off the switch to the heater, causing the liquid to cool.

Commercial data processing
Many businesses depend on computers to run critical aspects of the business. By doing so information is readily available to management, thereby

empowering them to make timely decisions. A variety of data is processed including accounting data and data relating to the ordering and selling of goods. The information that is produced from an accounting system gives a good indication of the financial status of the organisation, what monies are owed to it and what is owed by the organisation to its suppliers for goods and services.

Sourcing and ordering goods is done on-line by the use of the Internet. When the goods are received by the purchaser, the inventory is updated, providing management with vital information about the amount of money that is invested in stock.

When a sale of goods is being made, the items are scanned causing the stock to be updated and the accounts receivable is also updated for credit customers. The system also provides the customer with a receipt which shows the items that were purchased, the amount for each item and the total bill.

Industrial data processing

In industries such as the manufacturing industry, a significant portion of the data has to do with the physical properties of equipment and materials. For example, data may be collected about the x-, y- and z-coordinates of a robotic arm or the pressure in a tank. Embedded systems such as programmable logic controllers can use this data to automate the machinery. Meanwhile statistics about yields and efficiency rates can be compiled.

Scientific data processing

With scientific data processing, the data comes from a variety of instruments and sensors. In some cases the data is manually keyed into the computers, but this is obviously time consuming and error prone. It is preferable to hook up the sensors to computers and have them record the data directly. Depending on the type of instrument, this may require the use of an analogue-to-digital converter.

A good example of scientific data processing is the production of weather maps. Raw data about temperature, wind speed and humidity is collected from a variety of locations. This data is combined and processed to generate information about expected weather conditions. Furthermore, this information is presented to viewers in an attractive, colour-coded graphical way.

Information retrieval

Information retrieval (IR) is the process of finding information within documents, databases and web pages. The best known example of IR is the Google search engine, but universities and libraries have their own IR systems as well. Such systems are necessary to sift through the vast quantities of information being produced and stored on a daily basis.

Despite tremendous advances in this technology, information retrieval systems are not perfect

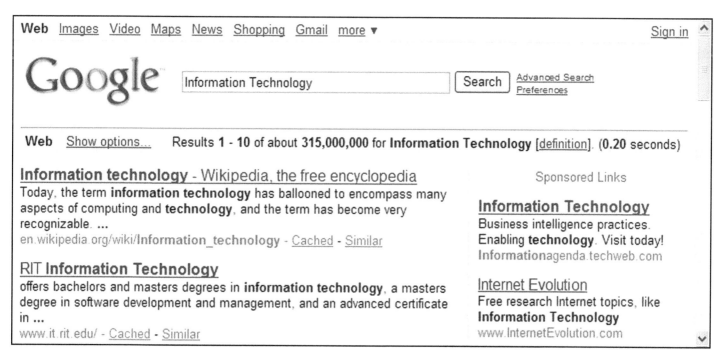

Figure 12.3 *Google, the quintessential information retrieval system*

since computers do not actually <u>understand</u> the information they are searching through. Instead they rely on clever techniques such as counting the number of times a phrase occurs in a document to judge its relevance.

Source documents

Some kinds of data are taken from documents to be processed. These documents are known as **source documents** since they are the sources that supply the data. Examples of source documents are airline tickets, prescription invoices, medical record cards, multiple choice sheets, banking deposit and withdrawal slips and payroll time cards.

The data from source documents may be keyed in manually or it may be scanned into the computer using appropriate hardware and software.

Turnaround documents

A **turnaround document** is a document that has been output by a computer, filled out and then used as a source document. Examples include completed forms that are scanned into the computer and meter cards used to collect readings.

Human-readable versus machine-readable documents

As you would imagine, **human-readable documents** are documents that are in a form for humans to read. With advances in natural language processing, computers are better able to recognise text in such documents but they still make mistakes (especially if the text is handwritten).

A **machine-readable document** is one where the data is encoded in a way that can easily be read by computers. The entire document doesn't have to be machine-readable. Usually such documents have a <u>portion</u> that is machine-readable in addition to the human-readable part. Examples include modern passports, items with barcodes and cheques (which have magnetic ink).

Validation and verification

When entering data into the computer from source documents it is very possible to input erroneous data. Errors should be kept to a minimum to reduce the negative impact that may be caused. Verification and validation techniques are used to minimise errors.

Verification

Verification is the process of confirming that the data that is entered into the computer is the same as what was written on the source documents. For example, when you top up your mobile phone, most retailers ask you to write the cell number in a book and also read the number aloud to confirm that it is correct. This is a form of verification.

Another method of verifying data is the **double entry process** where two persons key the same document. The computer compares the two versions and any differences are highlighted. These differences are then checked against the source document and corrected.

Verification helps guard against various typographical errors, including transposition errors. A **transposition error** is when two or more characters in the data are accidentally rearranged, for example typing 'teh' instead of 'the'.

Validation

Just because you key in exactly what is on the source document doesn't mean that there are no errors. For instance, you might correctly key in the age someone put on a form – but that person might have put his age as 650. This is why you need to validate the data. **Validation** is the process by which data is checked to ensure that it is reasonable and complete. In order to validate data, you can perform:

- range checks
- reasonableness checks
- data type checks
- inconsistency checks

Note

Although these are validation checks, <u>some</u> of the errors they detect might actually be due to the data being keyed incorrectly. For example, the typist might type a date as 2009/01/82 instead of 2009/01/28, causing it to be flagged as an invalid date.

Difference between verification and validation

The difference between verification and validation can be summed up as this: verification checks to see if data was keyed in correctly whereas validation checks whether the correct kind of data was entered.

Range checks

A **range check** makes sure that values fall between specified minimum and maximum values. Imagine that you are keying the ages of students who attend secondary school. The ages should fall within a particular range (e.g. 11–18). The data entry software can be set to reject data that does not fall within that range.

Reasonableness checks

Reasonableness checks determine whether values are reasonable by making sure that they don't deviate too much from established norms. For example, if someone puts the height of a 2-year-old as 5 ft, it should be flagged as being unreasonable since toddlers aren't that tall.

Unlike range checks, the accepted values for reasonableness checks may vary depending on the circumstances. For instance, it wouldn't be unreasonable for a 14-year-old to be 5 ft. The computer would make the decision based on historical averages for the different ages.

Data type checks

A **data type check** ensures that the values keyed in are the correct types, for example numeric, date, yes/no. When processing data, it must be of the correct data type for it to be processed. For example, if text is keyed in when the value is supposed to be numeric, calculations can't be performed on that value.

To prevent problems like this, the data entry software should be designed to validate the data type. If a database table is used for storing the data, the data type for each field can be set when making the table structure. If the user tries to enter a value that isn't the correct data type, it is rejected and the user is notified.

Inconsistency checks

An **inconsistency check** is a test to see if there are any conflicts between related data items. Here are some examples of the types of conflicts an inconsistency check could be used to detect:

- the ending date of a course being before the starting date
- a discount being more than the original price of an item

File organisation

As you know, data is stored in files. But there are a number of ways that data can be organised within the files. Some file organisations are not appropriate for certain applications so if you choose the wrong one, there may be a <u>huge</u> performance penalty. Three types of file organisation are:

1 sequential
2 random
3 indexed sequential

Regardless of the file organisation, the records in a file may be accessed sequentially (in a particular order) or directly.

Sequential organisation

This is when the records are <u>physically</u> stored in the same order as they are <u>logically</u> organised, for example alphabetically or chronologically. As you can imagine, this type of organisation is very fast when you want to access the records in sequence. However, it is slow when you need to access records randomly.

Another drawback of sequential organisation is that it takes a lot of effort (and time) to maintain the sequential order. Every time a record is added, the computer has to:

1 determine where the record is to be inserted
2 move around the existing records to make space for the new one (see Figure 12.4 below).

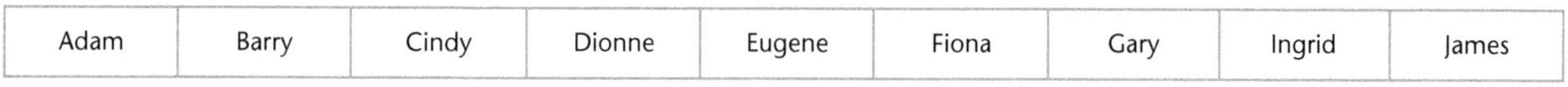

Adam	Barry	Cindy	Dionne	Eugene	Fiona	Gary	Ingrid	James

Figure 12.4a *Records stored in sequential order*

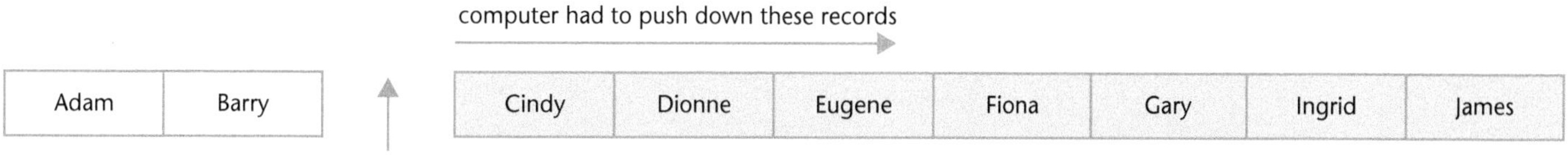

computer had to push down these records

Adam	Barry		Cindy	Dionne	Eugene	Fiona	Gary	Ingrid	James

Figure 12.4b *Inserting Bob's record*

Random organisation

With random (or direct) file organisation, the computer calculates where each record should be stored. That way, when a particular record has to be accessed, the computer can figure out exactly where to look and jump directly to that location. However, sequential access is very slow since the records aren't stored in any particular order.

Indexed sequential organisation

An indexed sequential file is a sequential file which is indexed as well so that records can be accessed directly. This means that records can be quickly accessed both sequentially <u>and</u> directly. However, this convenience comes at a price. It is even more work to maintain than a regular sequential file because you need to keep the index up-to-date as well.

Choosing the appropriate file organisation

When you want to organise your files for a particular application, you need to consider:

1 how the records will usually be accessed
2 how often they are going to be updated
3 how often new records will be added

Example 1 – Employee payrolls

The records are usually accessed sequentially. Individual records don't have to be updated very often since people's names and salaries hardly change. Furthermore, employees aren't hired or fired very often. Therefore the data should be organised sequentially.

Example 2 – Store prices

The cashier must be able to directly retrieve the price of a particular item. Updating prices is very common; adding new items is less so. The constant need to directly access items is the deciding factor, so the files should be randomly organised.

As you can see, different applications require different approaches.

Exercise 12

1 What is the difference between data and information? Give an example.
2 What is information processing?
3 Describe four forms of information processing.
4 What is information retrieval?
5 Define the following terms and give an example of each:
   a source document
   b turnaround document
   c human-readable document
   d machine-readable document
6 What is the difference between validation and verification?
7 What is a transposition error? Give an example.
8 Describe how the double-entry process works.
9 Describe four types of validation checking and come up with your own example of each.
10 Explain the three different ways that files can be organised. What are the advantages and disadvantages of each?
11 LEMON is developing a yellow pages application. They've asked you, a highly paid IT consultant, how they should organise their files. What would you recommend and why?

13. Protecting and securing information

After going to such great lengths to acquire information, the last thing a company wants is for something to happen to it. Since information is so valuable, considerable effort is spent protecting it from theft, fire, viruses, hackers, data loss and data corruption. Numerous methods are used to protect and secure information. The most widely used of these methods are:

- using passwords
- file encryption
- physical access restriction
- software access restriction
- using firewalls
- back-up and recovery
- using fireproof cabinets
- archiving
- virus protection

Passwords

A password is a combination of characters used to prevent unauthorised computer access. A person wishing to secure a computer or individual files on the computer can set a password. In order for access to be granted, the correct password must be entered. Obviously the password should be given only to people who can be trusted and it should not be easy to guess the password.

Encryption

Encryption is the process of securing information by encoding it so that it bears no similarity to the original. Files are encrypted using a **key** provided by the person who wants to encrypt the information. This key is a combination of characters that is used to tell an **encoding algorithm** how to encrypt the information. The encoding algorithm uses a kind of mathematical formula in the conversion process. Someone looking at the encrypted information would then not be able to guess what the original information was. Therefore, by encryption, sensitive information can be protected from prying eyes.

In order to read encrypted information, it must first be **decrypted**. This is the process of decoding encrypted information in order to obtain the original information. A key is required to do so; the same key that was used to encrypt the information. If the

wrong key is entered, the file(s) cannot be decrypted. As with a password, the encryption (and decryption) key should be given only to people you want to give access to your data.

Physical access restriction

Obviously you do not have to worry about the security of your data if no one can get to it. Physical access restrictions are used to do just that – prevent unauthorised persons from gaining physical access to stored information.

The information that is to be protected may be found on a computer or on removable storage or in manual files. Two methods of physical access restriction are:

- housing the computer or the removable storage in a dedicated room or building. This area would be secured using locks and a combination of surveillance cameras, alarms and security guards
- locking manual files or removable storage in a cabinet or vault

Biometrics

A very secure form of physical access restriction can be achieved through **biometrics**. Biometrics is the use of a person's body characteristics to uniquely identify him or her. You will have seen movie scenes where a person has to get an iris scan or use his handprint to gain access to a top secret location – these are both examples of biometric locks.

Figure 13.1 *A fingerprint scanner*

Biometric technology is becoming increasing prevalent. It is quite common nowadays to see laptops coming with fingerprint scanners. Users can login into these laptops by sliding their fingers over the scanner.

Software access restrictions

This is quite simply the process of restricting access to software. This may be done using passwords or encryption; however, there is another method that is fairly popular. Chances are that if you have installed recent commercial software you have been prompted to enter a serial number (installation key) before the actual installation starts. When you buy the software you are given a key, which is usually several characters long. If a correct key is not entered, the installation will not continue. This is done in an attempt to cut down on **software piracy** (the unlawful copying of computer software).

What is the difference between an installation key and a password?

An installation key is generated using a kind of mathematical formula that is also used to see if the key is correct. As a result, multiple keys may be deemed correct, whereas with a password there is only one correct answer.

Virus protection

A **virus** is a malicious program that is designed to corrupt the files on a person's computer and/or prevent the computer from working properly. Like a biological virus, a computer virus can spread from one infected file or computer to another. Viruses may cause damage to programs and data. The way this damage is done and the method of transmission depends on the virus. People create viruses for electronic vandalism, revenge or mischief. Computers may be protected from viruses by avoiding using computers or disks that are suspected of having a virus and by using up-to-date anti-virus software.

E-mail viruses

An increasing number of viruses are being spread by the attachments to e-mail messages. When you open the attachment your computer becomes infected. Some of these viruses can even take advantage of the capabilities of e-mail and send themselves to everyone in an e-mail address book. If someone sends you an infected file as an attachment, and you do not scan the file before you open it, your computer will most likely become infected.

Anti-virus software

An **anti-virus program** (or virus-guard) is a special type of software that tries to detect and remove viruses that are on a computer or removable storage media. New viruses come out every day, so virus-guards need to be kept up-to-date. Many anti-virus programs allow you to download new **virus definitions** (information about how to recognise particular viruses). Advanced anti-virus programs, such as Norton Antivirus, also try to detect viruses for which there aren't yet virus definitions by observing programs for suspicious, virus-like activity.

Fireproof cabinets

All the fancy security in the world cannot protect your data from natural disasters or fire. Fortunately, there is a very simple (although low-tech) way to protect manual files and those on removable storage from fire. A fireproof cabinet is a cabinet that is designed to withstand the high temperatures of a fire. When things that would ordinarily burn (or melt) very easily, for example paper or disks, are placed inside one of these, they also are protected from fire.

Firewalls

As was mentioned earlier, any file on a network is vulnerable to hackers. However, there are ways to protect computers that are on a network from hackers. A **firewall** (in computer terms) is a program that identifies certain weaknesses in networked computers and tries to prevent them from being exploited. This makes it much more difficult (but not impossible) for hackers to gain unauthorised access to the computer. Therefore firewalls help to keep the data on these computers secure.

Firewalls are often installed on computers that access the Internet, especially those that have a permanent connection through cable modems and DSL. Since computers that use dial-up connections are not always connected to the Internet, hackers do not target them as often.

Computer hackers

Almost everyone has heard of computer hackers. Although many people aren't quite sure what they do, hackers are seen as people to be feared by anyone who has a computer or who regularly uses the Internet.

Simply put, a hacker is a person who tries to gain access to areas on networks that he/she is not supposed to have access to. Hackers may try to:

- pretend to be someone who has legitimate access to certain areas or files
- use brute force attacks (trying thousands of passwords until the right one is found)
- find weaknesses in the network (known as backdoors) and try to exploit them
- put Trojan Horses on computers in the network so that they can gain easy access to restricted areas
- corrupt or delete the files being shared

Back-up and recovery

Sometimes, instead of securing data from people who have malicious intent, you have to protect it from your own carelessness. This is what back-up and recovery are for. Backing up data is the process of making a copy of the data and storing it on another storage medium. The storage media most commonly used for this process are: CD-RW, magnetic tape, diskettes and **zip disks** (disks that are roughly the size of a floppy disk but have a capacity of around 250 MB).

If the original data is lost, misplaced or destroyed, it can be **recovered** by copying the back-up onto the computer. Data should be backed up on a regular basis and should be placed in a fireproof cabinet and/or a copy should be kept at a different site.

Archiving

When data has remained unchanged for a long time and is not accessed on a regular basis, it is said to be **inactive**. If this data is taking up valuable space (which is very likely), you might want to store it in a separate location instead. This is what is known as **archiving** the data. The term is also used to refer to the process by which a second back-up of a file is kept separately from the working back-up copy.

Data corruption

When something causes data to become lost or damaged, this data is said to be **corrupted**. Data may be corrupted by:

- a computer virus
- wilful acts of employees

- computer malfunction
- power surges or outages
- poor methods for updating data

Obviously you do not want your data to become corrupted. Fortunately there are ways of reducing the risk of data corruption, such as:

- minimising the risk of computer malfunction by performing periodic computer maintenance and keeping the computer in a cool room away from smoke and dust
- using surge protectors and uninterrupted power supply units
- performing quality control audits to minimise wilful corruption
- installing anti-virus software

Exercise 13

1. State two ways in which data is corrupted and explain how each can be avoided.
2. Identify five measures that can be taken to secure data.
3. a What is encryption?
   b What is 'decrypting' as it relates to encryption?
4. a What is a computer virus?
   b How can viruses be avoided?
   c Name two types of anti-virus software.
5. In order to secure its data, a company uses the following method for encrypting text: each letter is replaced by the letter five letters later in alphabetical order. For example, the letter 'A' is replaced by 'F', 'B' is replaced by 'G', and so on. Note that the letter 'A' is considered to follow the letter 'Z'.
   a What would the word 'technology' be stored as?
   b What is the meaning of the following text? H T W W J H Y
6. What is meant by the term 'archiving'?
7. What is the purpose of a password?
8. State three problems that would arise if a company had private information about its staff stored in a central location to which various departments had access.
9. What is a firewall?
10. What is a hacker?
11. What does the word 'biometrics' mean?

14. Measures to reduce information misuse

Information misuse

Since computers make it so easy to collect, store and share information, they also make it easy to misuse it. It is not an exaggeration to say that everyone is at risk of being the victim of information misuse. For example, information is collected on people who use the Internet, whether they know it or not. However, just because a person has never used the Internet (or even a computer) does not mean that his or her personal information has not been misused.

Information may be misused in the following ways:

- by collecting information about people without their permission
- by vengeful employees or employers who want to spread propaganda on unsuspecting persons
- by (wilfully or unwittingly) storing incorrect information on an innocent person that may be available to the public
- when unauthorised persons are able to view and/ or change information
- by using information for purposes other than those for which it was intended

Storage of incorrect information

Whenever data is kept, the owner should ensure that it is accurate and correct. Storage of inaccurate data could result in negative effects on the individuals and the organisations on which the data is stored. For example, in a credit rating system, if incorrect data on a consumer is stored it could be damaging to the consumer, since it might prevent him or her from obtaining credit.

Unauthorised collection of information

A lot of information that is collected is done so without the permission of the people involved. Some examples of unauthorised collection of information are industrial espionage, electronic eavesdropping, and surveillance.

Industrial espionage

Industrial espionage is when secret information is obtained by spying on competitors or opponents. Needless to say, this is illegal.

Electronic eavesdropping

Electronic eavesdropping is the tapping into a communication channel to retrieve information. Data may be encrypted before it is transmitted to prevent eavesdropping on that data. Hackers commonly use electronic eavesdropping. For example, skilled hackers can collect information that you type at websites, such as your credit card number, passwords or personal details.

If a hacker is able to obtain your credit card number, he or she will be able to order items online and charge them to your account. This is known as **credit card fraud**.

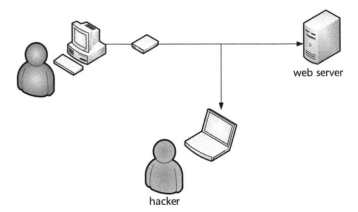

Figure 14.1 *Electronic eavesdropping*

Surveillance

The computer-related activities of many people are kept under surveillance. The information gathered through this surveillance may be used to develop profiles of these people. What is not always appreciated is how common this is. The fact is that the monitoring of a person's computer activities happens so often that many people have come to accept it as a way of life.

Surveillance is not only done by law enforcement personnel. Many websites keep you under surveillance.

Cookie trouble

Many websites keep track of your activities without your knowledge. Some websites store small text files known as **cookies** on your computer that contain a variety of information about you – such as who you are, your location and your activities on their website. Very few cookies are used for malicious purposes, although these have become such a concern that new versions of web browsers have features to prevent cookies from being stored on your computer.

Unauthorised distribution of information

It is quite common for information that has been collected on an individual or organisation to be distributed without permission. In fact, chances are that it has happened to you. For example, many people receive junk mail (regular or via e-mail) because a company has given information about you, such as your name, address and interests, to another. The Internet has made the unauthorised distribution of information very easy since many databases can be accessed online by anyone with an Internet connection. For example, there are online directories of e-mail addresses.

Identity theft

Identity theft is a type of fraud where someone deliberately takes on another person's identity without his or her knowledge. Someone who is able to obtain proof of your identity, for example your credit card number, national registration number, account password or PIN code, can 'steal' your identity. To the electronic systems, that person <u>is</u> you.

This is why it is extremely important to guard your personal information and <u>immediately</u> notify authorities if your purse or wallet is stolen.

Ways to reduce misuse of information

Information is misused all of the time – that is a fact. The good news is that there are several ways to reduce the misuse of information. Some of these are:

- Enforcing data protection laws
- Utilising security systems
- Keeping information accurate and up to date
- Having severe penalties for when employees and employers divulge private information

Data protection laws

Every person has fundamental rights when it comes to his or her personal information. In recognition of these rights, such as information privacy, many countries have passed data protection laws. These laws are designed to protect individuals and organisations – something that has become increasingly important because the storage of data on computers makes it easier than ever for information to be misused.

Data protection laws generally state that personal data must:

- be obtained and processed fairly and lawfully
- be held for specified purposes
- not be used for any reason incompatible with its original purpose
- be relevant and adequate

- be accurate and up-to-date
- not be kept longer than necessary
- be made available to the individual concerned and provision made for corrections
- be kept secure

Piracy

Software piracy is the copying of programs without the consent of the owner. It has become a huge problem for software manufacturers because it causes loss of revenue and jobs.

Some measures have been put in place to reduce software piracy such as:

- use of registration keys that are only available with purchase of the software
- severe penalties such as heavy fines and/or imprisonment for anyone found selling or knowingly using pirated software

Unfortunately these measures have limited success because it is so easy to copy software. Therefore it is quite common to see people selling pirated software.

Exercise 14

1 What is the purpose of the data protection laws?
2 a What is software piracy?
  b Give a measure to reduce software piracy.
3 a What is unauthorised collection of information?
  b List two ways of obtaining unauthorised information.
4 Explain in your own words the following:
  a industrial espionage
  b electronic eavesdropping
  c surveillance
5 What is the purpose of a cookie?
6 List two ways to reduce misuse of information.
7 Why is it necessary for governments to implement data protection laws?
8 A friend purchased a very exciting game and was going to give it to you to make a copy for your computer. The software was protected by copyright law. What are the implications of you making a copy?
10 Explain what identity theft is and how to reduce the chances of having your identity stolen.

15. Information technology: job skills and careers

Job skills

As information technology (IT) is introduced in the workplace, employees are being required to learn new skills. Some of these new skills that are recommended or required for various professions are given below.

Office employees

Employees in the computerised workplace should be able to:

- prepare and edit documents using a word processor
- calculate and analyse numerical data using a spreadsheet program
- store, edit, retrieve and query records in a database
- use computerised accounts for processing customer and company accounts
- send and receive faxes
- use web browsers and know how to send and read e-mail

Teachers

Most teachers are expected to use computers to prepare and supplement their lessons. Such teachers should be able to:

- use word processors to prepare exercises and notes
- use presentation software to make demonstrations
- use the Internet for research purposes and teach students how to do so
- teach students how to use the multimedia, simulation or tutorial software designed to aid learning

Figure 15.1 *Using an electronic whiteboard*

It is also useful if teachers can:

- use spreadsheet applications to record and calculate students' marks
- assemble the main parts of a computer and do simple troubleshooting

Engineers

Nowadays, with the use of computers so prevalent in the field of engineering, engineers should be able to:

- use CAD software, simulation software and in some cases graphics plotters
- design computer-based process control systems

Medical personnel

It is useful if medical personnel are able to:

- use computer-controlled devices to monitor a patient's condition
- use expert systems for the diagnosis and treatment of illnesses
- store, edit and retrieve a patient's record using database management software
- use specialised equipment for performing operations

Musicians

As was mentioned in Chapter 10, computers are used extensively in the music industry. It is not surprising if a musician (especially one who works behind the scenes) knows how to use computers to:

- sample sounds
- record sounds
- synthesise music
- edit songs and add special effects

Movie industry personnel

Many people in the movie industry, such as graphic artists and editors, have to know how to use computers. Some of the things they need to be able to do are:

- use animation software
- use graphics editors
- use custom-written special effects software
- operate robots (such as those used to imitate dangerous animals)

Mass media personnel

People in the business of mass media, for example reporters and editors, rely almost entirely on computers. Therefore they need to know how to:

- use a word processor to produce and edit articles
- scan photos with a scanner
- use desktop publishing to design advertisements
- use the Internet for research and communication
- take photographs with a digital camera

Law enforcement personnel

People who work in law enforcement should have a working knowledge of computers. The recommended computer skills, depending on the person's job description, include some of the following:

- using a scanner to scan photographs of criminals
- using computers for fingerprint matching and DNA analysis
- using database management software to store data on criminals and retrieve it at a later date
- using statistical analysis software

Retraining

In order for employees to acquire the new skills required as a result of the introduction of IT, they need to be retrained. Retraining is necessary on a fairly regular basis in order to keep up with the rapid changes that are taking place in IT. Such training may be done in the schools and tertiary institutions that conduct courses in IT. Training is also done through correspondence courses and on-the-job training. Although retraining an employee allows him or her to eventually develop the necessary additional skills, it is expensive and results in lost productivity.

Loss of jobs

Computers and computerised robots can do many tasks more quickly and efficiently than their human counterparts. In fact, computers actually put some people out of a job. For example, in manufacturing, people performing dangerous and repetitive tasks are replaced by robots. In banks, some tellers are replaced by ATMs.

When IT is introduced in a workplace, some employees also lose their jobs because they are replaced by people doing similar jobs but who are more computer literate. For example, an ordinary typist may be replaced by one who can use a word processing program.

Creation of jobs

Although the introduction of IT may cause many people to lose their jobs, it creates some as well. Job titles such as Programmer, Database Administrator, Network Administrator, Computer Engineer, Computer Technician and Computer Operator would never even exist were it not for IT.

Roles of personnel in computer-related professions

Data-processing department

As you have most likely guessed, the data-processing department is the department that handles the tasks associated with the processing of data. Since data processing is such an important function, quite a number of personnel are assigned to it. Below is a list of the tasks done by various personnel who may be found in a data-processing department.

Programmers

- Write applications programs or systems programs
- Test and debug programs
- Prepare the installation of CD-ROMs
- Maintain programs

Systems programmers

- Design systems programs
- Write systems programs
- Test and debug programs

Systems analysts and designers

- Interview users who need information for a computer system
- Review the manual or computerised system to find a solution
- Define and design the computer hardware and software system
- Inform management on the status of a project
- Work with the programmers to develop and test the system
- Assist in documenting the system and the training of users

Managers

- Make sure jobs in the department are done correctly, on time and within the budget
- Prepare budgets for the department
- Manage the human resources within the department

Database administrators

- Design and develop database applications
- Control access to the data
- Keep the data up-to-date

Network administrators

- Set up the network
- Develop and/or install the software that is used on the network
- Grant access privileges
- Monitor the use of the network and its resources

Data-entry operators

- Transfer data from source documents onto machine readable media or directly into the computer
- Verify previously entered data

Computer operators

- Start up and shut down the computer equipment
- Supervise data-entry operators
- Back up data files on a regular basis
- Mount tapes, load printer paper, change ribbons, etc.

Librarians

- File, store and distribute data files, tapes, CD-ROMs, DVDs, etc.
- File archived material
- File and distribute hard copies
- File documentation for programs

Technicians

- Assemble and service computer equipment
- Find and fix computer problems

Computer engineers

- Design computer configurations
- Determine the network cabling requirements and layout
- Determine the power requirements for the computer department
- Design computer chips
- Design and develop processes for the manufacturing of computer parts

Webmasters

- Maintain websites
- Ensure that the web servers are working correctly

Web developers

- Create, modify and maintain web applications
- Handle any programming tasks required by the website

Service and support industries

Below is a list of the tasks done by various personnel in service and support industries.

Consultants

- Advise clients on solutions to their problems
- Identify the best source for procurement of hardware and software

Data communication specialists

- Determine the requirements associated with data communication using WANs and/or LANs
- Set up the teleconferencing system

Computer trainers

- Train people to use computer hardware and software
- Develop training manuals
- Examine and mark examination scripts

Electronic data-processing auditors (EDP)

The main responsibility of an electronic data-processing auditor (EDP) is to monitor and assess the compliance of all aspects of the information system and to report and issue corrective action requests for non-compliance with standard operating procedures. Other duties are to:

- determine the accuracy of processed data
- inspect methods to ensure that procedures and routines are adhered to

Salespersons

- Sell computer services (hardware, software, training, etc.)

Exercise 15

1 What is the impact of IT in today's workplace?
2 How would a reporter use IT in his or her job?
3 List three new jobs that have been created as a result of computerisation.
4 List two functions of each of the following:
   a systems programmer
   b database administrator
   c computer operator
   d network administrator
   e webmasters
   f web developers
5 You are about to apply for a job as a teacher. What are some of the IT skills that would be useful in your job?

16. Current trends in technology

Telecommuting

In larger countries it is not unusual for an employee to have to travel several miles in order to get to his or her workplace. However, since many of these jobs may be done at almost any location, travelling to work every day is just a formality. There are many jobs that are done exclusively on the computer; the only thing that forces the employee to travel to the workplace is the fact that the job entails working with files on the office network. However, with today's technology a person can work with files on a remote network.

Telecommuting takes advantage of this technology to reduce unnecessary commuting to and from the office. It is the term used to refer to when an employee works off-site (usually at home) using a computer and a communications channel to communicate with the office network/computer. The reduced commuting means reduced costs, less stress (from not having to put up with rush-hour traffic) and is more convenient for the employee. All that is required is a connection to the office network via a communications channel. The most common method of doing this is with a modem, telephone line and remote networking software.

There are a few disadvantages associated with telecommuting. The employee may have to absorb resulting additional telephone and electricity costs. There is also the initial cost of setting up the computer systems, both at home and at the office, to support telecommuting. However, the most serious disadvantage is the lack of supervision. Since the employee can work when he or she wishes, and may be distracted by things such as telephone calls and television, there may be a loss of productivity. Also, there may be the problem of reduced social interaction between employees.

Videoconferencing and teleconferencing

Both videoconferencing and teleconferencing use the same principle as telecommuting – they use computer technology and telecommunications channels so that businessmen and businesswomen can reduce the need to travel.

Videoconferencing is the use of computer, video, audio and communications technology to enable people in different locations to see and talk to one another. It is used by organisations to conduct meetings involving individuals who work at various locations in the world. All that is needed are computers with microphones and digital video cameras (or webcams) and a communications channel from each location to the next. The communications channel is usually established using a modem and a telephone line.

Videoconferencing offers people the advantages of convenience, productivity gains and reduced travel time and costs. However, it leads to increased telecommunications costs and a loss of personal contact. Also, if the connections are slow, the video and audio may not be of very high quality.

Teleconferencing is similar to videoconferencing except that there is no video.

Electronic commerce (e-commerce)

Figure 16.1 *An example of an e-commerce site.*

Electronic commerce, or **e-commerce**, is the buying and selling of goods and services using electronic means to conduct the transactions. However, the term is commonly used to refer to the process by which commerce is done over the Internet.

Tip

A good example of e-commerce in action is Amazon.com. You are encouraged to visit its website at URL http://www.amazon.com and to take a look around to get an idea of how one form of e-commerce works.

E-commerce generally takes place as follows. A person goes to the website belonging to the individual or company offering the desired goods or services. On that site he or she is able to browse through the various products and see descriptions of them. There may also be additional features, such as links to similar products to the one in which he or she is interested. Once the product(s) are selected, the customer chooses between two main purchasing options:

1 paying via traditional methods such as cheque or money order
2 paying with a credit card, by entering his or her credit card number when prompted to

Once the payment has been cleared, the product is sent to the customer. This may be done in a variety of ways, depending on the nature of the product, such as:

- The selected items are shipped to the customer. In this case the customer obviously has to enter the address to which the items are going to be shipped.
- The customer is granted access to additional areas of the website. For example, a company might have an online database to which paying persons are granted access.
- The customer is allowed to download software or multimedia. It is generally cheaper to get software this way as opposed to buying it in a store, since the manufacturer does not have to pay for packaging.
- The client is given the desired service.

Benefits

The rising number of people and companies conducting e-commerce is a testament to the fact that e-commerce offers tremendous benefits. Customers enjoy increased convenience since they can complete transactions from the comfort of their homes. This has the added benefit that people can buy products from all over the world and therefore have a wider range to choose from. It is also very easy to compare prices from various companies' websites. In many cases these prices are lower than if the product or service were bought in the traditional way because of the elimination of an intermediary.

E-commerce also offers features that aren't offered in most stores. Many large retailers have thousands of products available so they provide a search feature that allows you to simply type in what you are searching for. The results may be sorted by a variety of criteria such as price or manufacturer. There may also be statistics showing how popular a particular item is. At some sites, potential customers can read reviews of products from people who purchased them. Other sites allow you to download clips from songs on music CDs so you can decide if you like the CD.

These benefits are not limited to consumers, however, or businesses would not feel too inclined to get involved in e-commerce. The most obvious advantage is that businesses of all sizes can tap into the worldwide market of Internet users. There are also a number of not so obvious ones. By having the information about items and transactions in databases it is easy to keep track of stock levels and know when items have to be re-ordered. Also, these same databases can be used to compile statistics about users that can be used for marketing purposes. For example, many sites keep track of a user's purchases to recommend items that he or she may be interested in. This can generate a lot of additional business. Lastly, there are many cases where e-commerce can lower production costs, for example in the case of software manufacturers.

Drawbacks

There are some drawbacks that you should strongly consider before engaging in e-commerce. The first thing a consumer should worry about is fraud. It is fairly easy for a person to create a website and pretend to be a legitimate company. Then people may make purchases only to find out that the person has ripped them off. Even making purchases at legitimate companies has some risk. Internet companies have a tendency to shut down without warning so you may pay money but still not get your product. Also, a skilled hacker may steal your credit card number when you type it in at a website. The hacker could then use your credit card number to make several purchases before you discover that something is wrong. Fortunately, most large companies have measures put in place to address these issues.

There are also some slight drawbacks associated with making purchases at home. It is difficult to judge the quality of many products without going to the store and holding or touching the item. There is also a reduction in social interaction (even though some people wouldn't see this as a disadvantage!). You also do not get immediate customer service.

In many cases, setting up a company for e-commerce takes a lot of work. Network and data storage facilities have to be set up or upgraded. Staff may need to be retrained and some jobs may be made redundant. Measures need to be put in place to protect users from fraud and to deal with laws pertaining to taxation and litigation.

Natural Language Processing (NLP)

It is not a well-known fact that computers have tremendous difficulty understanding data and instructions (either oral or typed) that are given to it in natural languages such as English. However, a gradually increasing number of programs enable computers to do Natural Language Processing. This is the field in artificial intelligence that deals with the processing and analysing of written or spoken natural language.

It can be used for a variety of purposes such as:

- checking spelling and grammar in documents, a feature which is found in most modern word processors
- interpreting spoken commands
- retrieving answers to a user's questions (spoken or typed)
- summarising documents

All of this is achieved by utilising a database of words and expressions.

Voice synthesis

Voice synthesis is the process by which an electronic device, such as a computer, imitates the human voice. You may have come across examples such as the 'talking' clock or a bathroom scale that 'tells' you your weight. These work by linking together the stored sounds of a few key words or phrases such as 'one', 'two', 'three', 'the time is' or 'your weight is'.

Not all forms of voice synthesis are quite as simple as this. Special programs are available which, when used with speakers, allow a computer to 'say' almost anything. Obviously it would not be practical to store every single word in a particular language. Voice synthesis programs take advantage of the fact that all words are made up of a combination of sounds called **phonemes**. These sounds are the basic building blocks of speech. Any program that is capable of getting the computer to produce all the phonemes for a language can 'speak' anything in that language. Text-to-speech programs work with libraries of phonemes to allow a computer to 'read aloud'. They do so by breaking down text into individual phonemes that are 'said' one at a time.

Desktop publishing

A lot of people have heard of **desktop publishing** but few people actually know what it is. Desktop publishing is the use of computers to produce professional-looking documents such as newsletters, booklets and fliers, which are to be distributed. This is usually done on a system consisting of a PC with a high-quality printer and maybe a scanner or digital camera. Desktop publishing programs have features that allow you to create text art, insert graphics, adjust the page layout and much more.

Although there is software that is specially designed for desktop publishing, most word processors can be used for desktop publishing (with a little extra work).

Voice over Internet Protocol

Voice over Internet Protocol (VoIP) is a technology that allows the Internet infrastructure to be used to transmit telephone calls. Making overseas telephone calls using VoIP is often much cheaper than using the regular telephone networks. For this reason, many businesses (especially offshore companies) rely very heavily on VoIP.

Hardware and software requirements

In order to use VoIP you need an Internet connection and either:

- a dedicated VoIP telephone

or

- a computer with a headset and special software such as Skype installed

Laser technology

Lasers are used extensively in information technology. They are used as part of the CD and DVD recording process. These same discs are read using lasers of a different intensity. Laser printers, as you would imagine, also utilise lasers.

Exercise 16

1. A local business institution has decided to give employees the opportunity to telecommute.
   a. What is telecommuting?
   b. Give two reasons why an employee would prefer to telecommute.
   c. Give one drawback of telecommuting.
   d. List two items an employee would need to have if he or she were to work from home.
2. What kind of software is likely to be used by graphic artists at a newspaper publishing company? State one reason why the software is likely to be used.
3. State one advantage to an employee of telecommuting.
4. State one disadvantage to an employee of telecommuting.
5. What is videoconferencing? List two pieces of equipment needed.
6. What does 'e' in 'e-commerce' stand for?
7. What is the purpose of e-commerce?
8. List two benefits of using e-commerce.
9. List two drawbacks of using e-commerce.
10. What does NLP stand for? Explain the purpose of NLP.
11. Explain what VoIP is and give an advantage of using VoIP over traditional telephone networks.

Part 2

Problem Solving

1. Introduction to problem solving

In this section and the next, you will learn how to design <u>simple</u> computer programs (so don't expect to be designing the next version of Microsoft Word).

What is a computer program?

A **computer program** is a set of computer instructions, which are used for solving a problem. The program directs the computer to perform the actions that are needed to arrive at a solution.

The number of instructions required to solve a problem depends on the complexity of the problem. These instructions may range from a few to many hundreds or thousands.

A computer programmer writes the instructions that are used for solving the problem. In many instances the user of the computer program does not see the programming instructions. These instructions are stored in files, which are accessed by the computer when the program is run or executed.

The user of the program in some instances performs certain tasks as directed by the program. These tasks may include data entry, performing updates, printing reports, and setting up files for storing data and querying databases.

What do we mean by 'problem'?

A computer program is meant to solve a problem, but what do we mean by 'problem'? Think of a programming problem in the same light as you would think of a mathematical problem. It's not something <u>bad</u> (though some people may say otherwise). Rather, it is something that needs to be solved or a task that needs to be accomplished.

The problems that you will be asked to solve at this level won't be too difficult. They will normally involve getting the computer to perform simple calculations and display the results on the screen. For example, you may have to get the computer to calculate the total bill for some groceries.

How should you design programs?

Whenever you are designing programs, there are two main phases:

1 the <u>problem-solving phase</u> (which we will cover in this section). Ideally you shouldn't touch the computer during this phase.

2 the implementation phase (which will be covered in the next section). This is where you take the designs you came up with during the problem-solving phase and implement them on the computer.

The five main problem-solving steps

Whenever you attempt to solve a problem, there are certain steps you should follow.

1 Define the problem.
2 Propose and evaluate solutions.
3 Determine the most efficient solution.
4 Represent the most efficient solution in the form of an algorithm.
5 Test the algorithm.

What is an algorithm?

By this point you are probably wondering 'What are these algorithms they keep talking about?' An **algorithm** is a formal sequence of instructions that defines _a_ solution to a problem. The word 'a' is emphasized because a problem may have more than one solution. In a sense, an algorithm is sort of like a recipe – but for computers.

You will learn a number of ways to represent algorithms, but whatever method you use there are certain characteristics that are required.

Defining the problem

In order for you to come up with an algorithm to solve a problem, you must first have a clear understanding of what the problem is.

The first thing you have to do is to obtain a **problem statement** (a clear definition of the problem that needs to be solved). At this level it will usually be provided for you, but in the real world the programmer would have to work with his client to come up with one.

Here are some (very simple) examples of problem statements:

- The program must read two numbers and print the larger of the two.
- Write a program that reads three numbers and displays their average.

Determining the input, output, processing and storage

The next step in defining the problem is to break it down into its main components:

1 **Inputs** – the data you are provided with or have to obtain from the user. Some words that help you to identify the inputs are: read, input, enter, given, accept
2 **Outputs** – the results that should be produced
3 **Processing** – the tasks that must be performed, i.e. what must be done with the inputs to get the outputs
4 **Storage** – the data that must be stored

Defining diagrams

One way of illustrating the main components of a problem is by using a **defining diagram**. A defining diagram is a table with three columns: 'Input', 'Processing' and 'Output'.

Consider the following problem statement:

> Write a program that reads two numbers and prints the total.

Even this simple statement requires some detective work to figure out the input, output and especially the processing.

Input
The word 'read' tells us that the inputs will be in the form of two numbers. For reasons that will be explained later, it's helpful to give the inputs names, so we'll call them num1 and num2.

Output
The desired result is the total, so we'll call the output 'total'.

Processing
Each task that must be performed counts as processing. Reading the two numbers is processing and so is printing the total. But is that everything? The total doesn't magically appear. You have to do something to the inputs to obtain the total. So there is an in-between step that is implied – calculating the total.

Therefore, the defining diagram would look like this:

Input	Processing	Output
two numbers, say num1, num2	1 Read two numbers. 2 Calculate the total. 3 Print the total.	total

Let's look at a more complicated example:

> Read the price of an item and its type. A 5% discount is to be given on all books. If the item is a CD then there will be a 10% discount. All other items are to get a 2% discount. Calculate and print both the discount as well as the discounted price.

Even though it looks complicated, the defining diagram isn't too complex.

Input	Processing	Output
item, type	1 Read the item and its type. 2 Calculate the discount. 3 Calculate the discounted price. 4 Print the discount and discounted price.	discount discounted price

The key thing to note is the line 'calculate the discount'. We don't actually have to specify how we calculate the discount. So although half the problem statement is spent saying what percentage discount should be given on what type of item, there is no mention of percentages in the diagram.

However, the fact that so much information is left out of the defining diagram raises an important issue:

Note

The processing steps are not a solution to a problem.

1 Explain what each of these terms means:
  a computer program
  b problem
  c problem statement
  d algorithm
2 What are the two main phases of program design?
3 There are four main components of a problem. The first two are inputs and outputs. What are the other two?
4 What are the five main problem-solving steps?
5 Construct defining diagrams for the following
  a The program should accept the ages of two students and print the age difference between the two.
  b Write a program to print the larger of two numbers.
  c Create a program that reads two numbers and prints their sum, difference and product.
  d Write a program that reads an employee's hourly rate as well as the number of hours he or she worked during the week. Print the wages of the employee.
  e Employees are paid one and a half times the hourly rate for each hour over 40 hours that they work. Read the number of hours an employee worked as well as his or her hourly rate. Print the total wages for the employee (including overtime).

2. Types of data

So far we haven't given much consideration to the data we are working with. We haven't worried too much about the type of data, what to call it or where it should be stored. In this chapter, you'll learn all about variables and the various data types.

Data types

The types of data can be divided into three broad categories – textual, numerical and Boolean.

Textual data
Textual data is data that may include a combination of letters, symbols and numbers. It can be in the form of a single **character**, or a group of characters known as a **string**. Because it can contain things other than numbers, you don't perform calculations on textual data.

Numerical data
When it comes to programming there are two main types of numbers:

- **Integers** are numbers that <u>don't</u> have a decimal point, for example 5, 18, –20, 0, 100 000.
- **Real numbers** are numbers with a decimal point, for example 10.25, –5.75, 350.0.

Boolean data
While you would've been accustomed to working with text and numbers, chances are that you don't know what Boolean data is. Boolean data is data that must either be true or false, for example whether or not a person is married.

Examples
The following table gives some examples of the various data types.

Data	Type
the grade a student got in a course, e.g. A, B, C, D, F	character
the time Usain Bolt takes to run a 100 m race (in seconds)	real number
the number of books in a person's bag	integer
whether or not a piece of luggage is overweight	Boolean
the cost of an item in a store	real number
a person's name	string

Constants and variables

In order to illustrate the difference between constants and variables, let us look at another problem statement.

> Write a program that allows the user to enter the radius of a circle. It should then calculate and display the area of the circle and its circumference. (The area of a circle is <u>pi * radius^2</u>. The circumference of a circle is <u>2 * pi * radius</u>.)

The defining diagram for this problem is given below:

Input	Processing	Output
radius	1 Read the radius of the circle. 2 Calculate the area. 3 Calculate the circumference. 4 Print the area and circumference.	area circumference

Constants
Looking at the problem statement, you can see that both formulae use the value pi. The value of pi (as a fraction) has always been 22/7 and will always be 22/7. It doesn't change. Data which doesn't change (such as pi) are called **constants**. Some other examples are:

- the speed of light in a vacuum
- the number of months in a year
- the number of inches in a foot

Variables
Data that can change or take on other values are called **variables**. In our example there are several variables:

- the radius of the circle
- the area of the circle
- the circumference of the circle

The radius is changed according to what value the user enters and the area and circumference depend on the radius.

This raises an important question – where would the computer store this information? The computer must store the radius that the user enters so that it can be referred to later. The computer must also store, at least temporarily, the results of the calculations.

The programmer must tell the computer how and when to use variables. The computer associates each variable with a particular location in memory. Suppose that user enters a radius of 7. The computer would store it in the memory location allocated to the radius. Then when it needs the radius for the calculations, it would refer back to that memory location.

Below is an illustration of how variables are stored in memory (RAM).

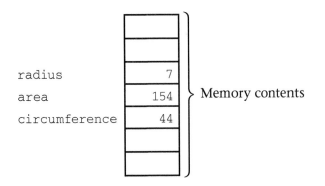

Exercise 2

1 What are the three categories of data?
2 What is a string?
3 Why can't you perform calculations on textual data?
4 What is the difference between a real number and an integer?
5 What is the difference between a constant and a variable? Give five examples of each.

Note

A variable can only hold one value at a time. When you give a variable a new value, the old one is lost.

Naming variables

Variables are given names to make it easier to refer to them. Some variables practically name themselves, like those in the above example. Others require a bit more thought. Here are some rules you should follow while thinking of a variable name:

- The name of the variable should reveal what it does.
- It should only contain letters, numbers and underscores.
- It should begin with a letter.
- It must not contain any spaces. If you want to use a space, use an underscore instead.

Most programming languages have similar rules, so if you follow them now you shouldn't run into any trouble later down the road.

Here are some examples of variable names.

- If you wanted to store the monthly salary of an employee, you would name the variable `salary` or `monthly_salary`.
- If you had to store the weights of two patients, you could name the variables `weight1` and `weight2`.

3. Finding the best solution

As was mentioned in Chapter 1, processing steps in a defining diagram do not give the solution to a problem. They state what must be done but not how to do it. In this chapter, we will look at finding solutions to problems and ultimately choosing the best one.

Ask yourself how you would solve the problem manually

The surest way to figure out what steps a computer should take to solve a problem is to ask yourself how <u>you</u> would solve the problem. Just pick some <u>sensible</u> numbers and try working out the problem on your own. Then make a note of what you did, even the things that seem really obvious.

Let's look at a couple of examples.

Example 1

Write a program that reads the price of an item as well as the quantity purchased, and displays the total cost.

Here is the defining diagram. It uses three variables: price, quantity and cost.

Input	Processing	Output
price quantity	1 Read the price and the quantity. 2 Calculate the cost. 3 Print the cost.	cost

The defining diagram says that we have to calculate the cost, but it doesn't tell us <u>how</u>. Well, how would <u>you</u> calculate the cost? If the price of one shirt was $30.00 and you bought four, how would you work out the cost? You'd take the $30.00 and multiply it by 4.

Now let's forget about the numbers and generalise the method so that it works in <u>all</u> cases. What you did was to take the price of one item and multiply it by the quantity in order to get the cost.

Now we have to write our solution as a list of instructions. Notice the use of variables (which have been underlined).

- Read the <u>price</u> and the <u>quantity</u>.
- Multiply <u>price</u> by <u>quantity</u> and store the result in <u>cost</u>.
- Print <u>cost</u>.

Example 2

Write a program that takes the marks of 20 students and prints the highest mark.

The defining diagram is shown below:

Input	Processing	Output
marks of 20 students	1 Read the list of marks. 2 Determine the highest mark. 3 Print the highest mark.	highest mark

How would <u>we</u> solve this problem? Let's try an example. Twenty marks is a lot of marks to work with, so let's try it with five and see if we can get a general method that works.

Here are five randomly chosen marks: 40, 90, 80, 99, and 70. How do we determine the highest mark?

- We start with the first number, 40.
- Then we look at the next number, 90. It's more than 40. We have a new maximum.
- Then we look at 80. It's not more than the highest mark we've seen so far, 90.
- But we then we come to 99. It is the highest mark we've seen so far.
- The last mark, 70, is not bigger than 99, so 99 is the highest mark overall.

This solution is formally described below:

- Read the list of marks.
- Set the first mark as the maximum (for the time being).
- For each of the remaining marks:
  - Compare it to current maximum.
  - If it is the larger, make it the new maximum.
- Print maximum.

Finding a more efficient solution

Recall that when you are solving a problem, you are supposed to evaluate the solutions and determine the most efficient one. The first solution you come up with might not necessarily be the best one. Let's look at an example where the initial solution can be improved upon.

Example 3

Write a program that reads an even number, *N*, which is larger than 2, and prints the even numbers that are less than *N*.

Input	Processing	Output
N	**1** Read *N*. **2** Determine the even numbers less than *N*. **3** Print the even numbers less than *N*.	the even numbers that are less than *N*

We go through the usual process of asking ourselves how we would solve the problem. Let's suppose *N* is 10. The most obvious way is to look at all the numbers that are less than 10, see which ones are even and print those. The number 1 isn't even so don't print that; 2 is even so print it, and so on. The number 9 is the last value we check since we only want the even numbers that are <u>less</u> than 10.

This leads to the following solution:

- Read *N*.
- Go from 1 to the largest number that is less than *N*.
  - If it is divisible by 2, print it.

It isn't hard to see how we can improve on this solution. For starters, it doesn't make any sense starting from 1, since 2 is the smallest even number. But more importantly, it doesn't make sense checking each number to see if it is even. To get the next even number, you just add 2 to the previous one.

So our new, much more efficient solution is:

- Read *N*
- Set num to 2.
- As long as num is less than *N*:
  - Print num.
  - Add 2 to num.

Making the solution more robust

Even the most efficient solutions can be undone by user error. Let's conclude the chapter by looking at how to make solutions more robust.

The following example <u>looks</u> straightforward.

Example 4

Write a program that reads two numbers and prints the quotient.

Input	Processing	Output
num1, num2	**1** Read num1 and num2. **2** Calculate the quotient. **3** Print the quotient.	quotient

To find the quotient we divide the first number by the second one. So, for example, if the two numbers were 10 and 5, the quotient would be 2. The solution couldn't be more straightforward:

- Read num1 and num2.
- Divide num1 by num2 and store the result in quotient.
- Print quotient.

But what happens if the user enters 0 for the second number? The program is <u>guaranteed</u> to crash since you can't divide by zero. We can make it more robust by checking to see if the second number is 0.

The new, improved solution follows.

- Read num1 and num2.
- <u>If num2 is zero, tell the user that you can't divide by zero and stop</u>.
- Otherwise, divide the first number by the second and store the result in quotient.
- Print quotient.

Exercise 3

1 Come up with a solution to the salary problem given in Exercise 1, question **5 e**.

2 List the steps needed to find the minimum mark from a list of 30 marks.

3 Find a solution for the following problem: Read a list containing the number of goals scored by FC Barcelona in each match of the season. A season consists of 30 matches. Calculate the total number of goals scored.

4 List the steps needed to solve the problem below. Then try to improve your solution. Read the number of games won, lost and drawn by Real Madrid then calculate the overall number of points that Madrid amassed. A win is worth 3 points, a draw 1 point and a loss is 0 points.

4. Introduction to algorithms

Once you have found the best solution, the next step is to convert it to an algorithm. Recall that an algorithm is a formal sequence of instructions that defines a solution to a problem. Thus to create an algorithm, we need to take the solution and formalise it.

Characteristics an algorithm should have

Every algorithm should have the following characteristics.

1 <u>It must be precise.</u> For instance, instead of saying to repeat a step 'several times', it should specify how many times the step should be repeated.
2 <u>It must be unambiguous.</u> An algorithm shouldn't include statements that may be interpreted multiple ways. No required information should be missing.
3 <u>It must terminate after a finite number of steps</u>. Algorithms should not go on forever.
4 <u>The instructions must be in a logical sequence.</u> An algorithm should clearly state what order the steps must be completed in.
5 <u>It should always give the correct solution.</u>

Algorithms can be represented in several ways. You will learn two of them – **pseudocode** and **flowcharts**. We will look at pseudocode below. Flowcharts are covered in more detail in Chapter 15.

Pseudocode

We'll look at pseudocode first of all. Pseudocode is a special language used to write algorithms that has less stringent rules than programming languages do.

Why do you need pseudocode?

Each programming language has its own peculiarities. A symbol that means one thing in one language may mean something completely different in another one. Pseudocode is sufficiently generalised that any programmer can understand it, regardless of what programming language he or she uses.

Although the rules of pseudocode are more relaxed than those for programming languages, pseudocode is still formal enough to precisely describe the solution to a problem. So it is ideal for writing algorithms.

How do you write pseudocode?

There is no 'right' way to write pseudocode. What is important is that you are consistent. The next few chapters will teach you one way to write pseudocode. There are other slightly different ways but they are all equivalent.

Exercise 4

1 List the five characteristics an algorithm should have.
2 Give two ways that algorithms can be represented.
3 What is pseudocode and why do you need it?

5. Data input and storage

The input instruction

Data to be processed must be entered into the computer and stored. Such data may be entered from the keyboard.

As the data is entered into the computer, it is stored in the computer's memory in variables or it may be stored in tables so that it can be accessed when needed for processing. During processing, some results are also stored in the memory of the computer. Data can also be stored in a statement in the form of constants.

When developing the pseudocodes for solving a problem, the commands that are used to permit the input of data are the words **READ** or **INPUT**. This is followed by one or more variable names to represent the data that is being entered and stored. When more than one variable is used, place the comma between each variable.

The syntax is: READ <variable name>, <variable name>

For example:

> Write an instruction to input the quantity and price of an item.

> Solution: READ QUANTITY, PRICE

> Write an instruction to read three scores.

> Solution: READ SCORE1, SCORE2, SCORE3

Note

Do not read a constant as input!

The data input for a problem may not be stated. However, if such input is needed to arrive at a solution, then it is necessary to use READ to input the data.

Validation

The accuracy and completeness of data that is entered into the computer is of paramount importance. Hence, wherever possible, data entry checks are written into the program to ensure the accuracy and completeness of data. The process of checking the data entry for accuracy and completeness is called **validation**.

For example, suppose that data is being entered that includes the parishes in Barbados. The programmer would have included instructions so that each time the parish is entered, a check is made which compares the entered data with a list of all the parishes. If the comparison is false, a message is displayed on the screen informing the user that the parish was entered incorrectly. The computer does not accept the entry if it is inaccurate.

Prompts

While entering data, messages may appear on the screen notifying the user of what data is to be entered. These messages are called **prompts** or **captions**. It is good programming practice to include a prompt or a caption for each input.

Prompt statements begin with the command **PRINT**, followed by the message enclosed in quotation marks. All messages should be proper messages which are written in English. Meaningful abbreviations may be used.

For example:

```
PRINT 'Enter the name'
```

A READ statement usually follows the prompt statement to facilitate the entry of data corresponding to the prompt.

Exercise 5

1. Write an instruction to input a number.
2. Write an instruction to read the name of a student.
3. Write an instruction to input two numbers.
4. Write an instruction to read the name and age of a student.
5. Write an instruction to read the names of four students.
6. Write an instruction to input the name, age and height of a student.
7. Write an instruction to read the name of a form, the number of students in the form and the subject being taught.
8. Write an instruction to read the make, colour and price of a car.
9. Write an instruction to read the name of a student, his or her address and telephone number.
10. Write an instruction to enter the birth date, height, weight and complexion of a student.

6. Displaying information

The output instruction

Output is needed in most programs. Output can be sent to the screen or the printer. When developing the pseudocodes for solving a problem, the command that is used to produce the output is the word **PRINT**.

PRINT can be used to output the value of a variable or to output the data that is a constant.

Outputting the value of a variable

The syntax is: PRINT <variable name>

For example:

```
PRINT SUM
```

When a variable is printed, the content of the variable is printed and not the name of the variable. The computer locates the segment of memory with the name of the variable and prints the information that is stored in that segment.

For example:

```
A = 10
PRINT A
```

In this example, the variable A is given a value 10 as in the first instruction. The second instruction causes 10 to be printed and not the letter A.

Variables used with the PRINT instruction must not be new variables that are being introduced in this instruction, but should be variables that have been executed in an instruction prior to the PRINT instruction. Hence, it is necessary to refer to prior instructions to ensure that this rule is enforced.

Outputting a constant

The syntax is: PRINT <string>

For example:

```
PRINT 'Name'
```

In this example, the word 'Name' is printed without the quotation marks. When outputting a constant, the data should be enclosed in quotation marks.

Outputting a constant and a variable at the same time

This is necessary in order to give a description of the value of the variable that is being printed.

The syntax is: PRINT <string>, <variable>

For example:

```
PRINT 'Cost', COST
```

In this example 'Cost' is a constant and COST is a variable. The word 'Cost' is printed, as well as the value that is stored in the variable COST.

In the following algorithm 20.00 is stored in the variable PRICE and 'Price of item:' is a constant.

```
PRICE = 20.00
PRINT 'Price of item:', PRICE
```

Hence, 'Price of item:20.00' is printed.

Exercise 6

1 Write an instruction to print 'Today is Monday'.
2 Write an instruction to print 'Total ='.
3 Write an instruction to output 'Enter your name'.
4 Write an instruction to read a name and one to output it.
5 Write an instruction to read two scores and one to output them.
6 Write a structured algorithm to prompt the user to enter his or her name, store it and output the name.
7 Write a structured algorithm which requests the user to input the price of an item. The algorithm should also allow the user to enter the price and output it with a suitable label.
8 Write a structured algorithm that displays a message asking the user to enter the name of a book and its author. It should also allow the user to input the required data and output the information appropriately labelled.
9 Write a structured algorithm to read the licence plate number of a bus, the route it will be travelling and the number of passengers it contains. Output the information appropriately labelled.
10 Write a structured algorithm to prompt the user to enter a tune, its composer and the year it was released. The algorithm should allow the user to input the data and output it using suitable labels.

7. Performing calculations

Calculations used for processing data

Data that is to be processed could involve performing calculations. Calculations can be done by using the mathematical operators for addition, subtraction, multiplication or division, for example '+', '−', '*', '/'. When calculations are to be performed, numeric variables or numeric constants must be used. The result of the calculation must be stored in a variable for future use, such as for printing or use in subsequent calculations.

The syntax for a calculation instruction is: <variable> = <what is being calculated>.

For example:

- `AMTDUE = PRICE * QUANTITY`
- `INCHES = FEET * 12`
- `SUM = FIRSTNO + SECONDNO`

The result of the calculation is stored in the variable to the left of '='. This variable is therefore assigned the result of the calculation. Any statement that assigns a value to a variable is called an **assignment statement**. The value being assigned could be a constant or a variable or a calculation.

For example:

- `SUM = 0 or STORE 0 TO SUM`
- `A = B or STORE B TO A`
- `GRADE = 'A' or STORE 'A' TO GRADE`
- `TOTAL = A+B+C or STORE A+B+C TO TOTAL`

Each assignment statement must begin with:

1 a variable, followed by the equal sign, then either a variable, a constant or a calculation

or

2 the word `STORE`, followed by a variable, a constant or a calculation, then the word `TO` and a variable.

It is incorrect to write an assignment statement in the following manner with the calculation to the left of the equal sign:

```
DEPOSITS + SHARES + INTEREST = TOTAL
```

The variable, which begins an assignment statement, should not be a variable that was read as input if the input is to be printed.

Variables used in the formula for calculating must be variables that were used in executed statements prior to the calculation instruction and not new variables.

For example, the following instructions are executed in the given order:

```
A = 1
B = 2
C = A + B
```

Here `C` is given the value of the total of `A` and `B`, i.e.

```
C = 1 + 2
  = 3
```

However, in this example, if either of the first two instructions with `A` or `B` were not executed, then reference to `A` or `B` in the third instruction would be incorrect and the computer would be unable to calculate `A + B` and assign the result to `C`.

Simple arithmetic

Writing statements to do arithmetic calculations isn't difficult. The hardest thing is remembering when to do what. The table below should help you to work this out.

If you hear the word...	Then you have to...	Example
sum, total	add	sum = num1 + num2
difference	subtract	difference = num1 − num2
product	multiply	product = num1 * num2
quotient	divide	quotient = num1 / num

Calculating percentages

A common programming problem is to calculate a person's percentage score in a test or exam, if you are given his or her score as well as the maximum mark.

Tip

To calculate the percentage, divide by the total (or maximum) and multiply by 100.
For instance, if the maximum mark for a test is 20, the percentage is calculated as follows:

- `PERCENT = SCORE / 20 * 100`

Finding a percentage of a number

Supposed you are asked to calculate the VAT on an item (VAT = 15%). In this case, you don't have to calculate the percentage – you were given it! Instead you have to find 15% of the item's price.

Tip

To find a percentage of a number, divide it by 100 and multiply by the percentage.

Here's how you would calculate the VAT:

- `VAT = PRICE / 100 * 15`

Increasing and decreasing

Writing a statement to increase or decrease a variable is very easy once you get the hang of it.

Let's look at a few examples:

- `COUNT = COUNT + 1`
- `NUM_LEFT = NUM_LEFT - 5`

When you increase or decrease the value of a variable, that variable appears on both sides of the assignment statement. Some people find this confusing.

Let's look in more detail at what's going on in the first example. Assume that COUNT currently has a value of 3.

1 The computer works out the expression on the right-hand side.

   a First it retrieves the <u>current</u> value of COUNT (3).
   b Then it adds 1 to it, getting 4.

2 Then it stores the new value 4 into the variable COUNT.
3 So the variable COUNT has increased by 1.

Increasing a variable by a percentage is slightly more complicated. Here's how you would increase a price by 5%.

`PRICE = PRICE + (PRICE * 5 / 100)`

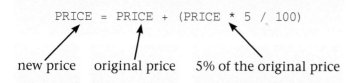

new price   original price   5% of the original price

The following examples show <u>equivalent</u> statements that all increase the variable SALARY by 2%:

- `SALARY = SALARY + (SALARY * 2 / 100)`
- `SALARY = SALARY + (SALARY * 0.02)`
- `SALARY = SALARY * (1.02)`

The following examples <u>decrease</u> the variable SALARY by 2%:

- `SALARY = SALARY - (SALARY * 2 / 100)`
- `SALARY = SALARY - (SALARY * 0.02)`
- `SALARY := SALARY * (0.98)`

Exercise 7

1. Write a structured algorithm that prompts the user to input two numbers. The algorithm should calculate and print the sum of the two numbers.

2. Write a structured algorithm that prompts the user to input the number of days in a month. Calculate and print the number of hours in the month appropriately labelled.

3. Write a structured algorithm that prompts the user to input the name and price of an item and the quantity purchased. It should print the name, price, quantity and amount due with appropriate labels.

4. Write a structured algorithm to prompt the user to enter the side length of a square. Calculate the area of the square and output it with a suitable label.

5. Write a structured algorithm to request the user to input two numbers which are stored in variables A and B. The algorithm should subtract B from A and output the answer with the message 'Answer is:'.

6. Write a pseudocode algorithm to ask the user to input the radius of a circle. Calculate the diameter and print it with a suitable label.

7. Write a structured algorithm to input the name of a video tape, the date it was borrowed, the rental fee charged and the amount of money paid in. Compute the amount of money due back to the borrower and output it with a suitable label.

8. Write a structured algorithm to prompt the user to input the ages of four of your friends. The algorithm should allow the user to input these ages, find their average and print it with a suitable label.

9. Write a structured algorithm to prompt the user to enter the prices for two different pay-per-view movies. Calculate the amount due and output it with the following message: 'Amount due BCC Television Ltd.'.

10. Write a pseudocode algorithm to ask the user to input the name of a student, the marks he or she received in a test and the maximum number of marks in the test. Calculate the percentage mark the student received. Print the information with suitable labels.

8. Selection statements

Forming conditions

When a program is executed, each instruction is processed in the sequence listed in the program, unless specific instructions direct it to deviate and select other instructions. An instruction containing the command IF allows deviation and selection to take place. Making a comparison based on a condition and acting on the result achieves this requirement.

Given criteria are used to form conditions. Imagine that you want to purchase a pair of blue, strapped shoes with 4-inch heels that cost less than $75.00. These criteria must be used to form appropriate conditions.

A condition is made up of three parts. The first part is a variable that was carried out before. The second part is a **relational operator**, and the third part is a variable that was carried out before or a constant. The relational operators are: =, ≠, <>, >, <, >=, <=.

Operators have the meanings shown in the table below:

Operator	Meaning
=	equal to
≠	not equal to
<>	not equal
>	greater than
<	less than
>=	greater than or equal to
<=	less than or equal to

Conditions may involve data of different data types. When the data of the condition is the character data type, the data should be enclosed in quotation marks.

The following conditions were formed based on the criteria listed above:

```
Colour = 'blue'
Style = 'straps'
Heel = '4-inch'
Cost < $75
```

In the next example the value that is stored in a variable MARK is being compared with 60 and the value that is stored in a variable ATTENDANCE is being compared with 'A':

```
MARK >= 60
ATTENDANCE = 'A'
```

A condition is evaluated when the instruction containing it is carried out. When the condition is met, the condition is said to be **true**; if the condition is not met, then the condition is said to be **false**.

When using the command IF, the instructions forming the condition and selection are called a construct. A **construct** is a series of instructions that forms a specific system based on a particular command in order for the command to work. Other constructs are also used, which will be introduced later.

Choosing the correct IF construct to solve the problem

A number of IF constructs are available for use in programming. Each construct will perform differently; hence it is very important to know what results you are trying to accomplish in order to choose the appropriate construct.

When one option is available and a selection may or may not be made, use the **IF-THEN** construct. For example:

In an examination out of 100, output the message 'Excellent!' for all students who received a score of 100. Many students could have received a score of 100.

Here there is only one option for performing the required action and that is pertaining to the score of 100.

When two options are available and a selection must be made, use the **IF-THEN-ELSE** construct. For example, in an examination a student may pass or fail. Hence, one of the two options must be selected.

When two or more options are available and a selection may or may not be made, use the **IF-THEN-ELSE-IF** construct. For example: In an examination which has four grades, select the grade a student received based on the mark received.

The IF-THEN construct

The IF-THEN construct is made up as follows:

```
IF <condition> THEN
<one or more instructions which will be carried out
if the condition is true>
ENDIF
```

IF marks the beginning and ENDIF the end of the construct. In this construct, the instructions between IF-THEN and ENDIF are executed only if the condition is true. If the comparison is false, the instructions between the IF-THEN and ENDIF are ignored.

For example:

> Read the time. If the time is 11.00, output 'Ring the bell'.

Solution:
```
PRINT 'Enter the time'
READ TIME
IF TIME = 11 THEN
PRINT 'Ring the bell'
ENDIF
```

> Read a number N. If N is greater than 100, add 10 to the number. Print the number.

Solution:
```
PRINT 'Enter a number''
READ N
IF N > 100 THEN
N = N + 10
ENDIF
PRINT 'Number', N
```

A common mistake is to include within the IF-THEN-ENDIF construct, instructions which should really be outside the ENDIF.

The following solution to the previous example is incorrect since N would be printed only if a number greater than 100 is read.

```
PRINT 'Enter a number''
READ N
IF N > 100 THEN
RESULT = N + 10
PRINT 'Number', N
ENDIF
```

The correct solution requires that N should be printed no matter what number is read because printing N is not based on the outcome of the condition.

The IF-THEN-ELSE construct

This construct is made up as follows:

```
IF <condition> THEN
<one or more instructions which will be carried out
if the condition is true>
ELSE
<one or more instructions which will be carried out
if the condition is false>
ENDIF
```

This construct provides two paths, the THEN path and the ELSE path, one of which must be selected.

The THEN path is made up of the instructions between the word THEN and the word ELSE.

The ELSE path is made up of instructions between the word ELSE and the word ENDIF. ENDIF marks the end of the last path.

For example:

> Input the age of a person. If the age is greater than 35, output 'old person' otherwise output 'young person'.

Solution:
```
PRINT 'Enter the age'
READ AGE
IF AGE > 35 THEN
PRINT 'old person'
ELSE
PRINT 'young person'
ENDIF
```

When developing the algorithm, it may appear that the IF-THEN construct should be used instead of the IF-THEN-ELSE construct. This confusion arises because it might not be realised that instructions used after the ENDIF refer to variables which were used within the IF-THEN path.

In such cases, if the condition of the IF statement is false, the variables within the IF-THEN path will not be encountered. As a result, reference to the variables in subsequent instructions after ENDIF, whether in calculations, conditions or printing, will cause errors.

To avoid this problem, use the IF-THEN-ELSE construct and include within both paths the variables which are to be referred to by subsequent instructions after the ENDIF.

For example:

A student is given a 5% discount off the fees for a course if the fees are paid before 30 days. Read a fee and the number of days. Output the fee, discount amount and fee less the discount amount.

Solution:
```
PRINT 'Enter the fee and the number of days'
READ FEE, DAYS
IF DAYS < 30 THEN
DISCOUNTAMT = FEE * 5/100
ELSE
DISCOUNTAMT = 0
ENDIF
AMTDUE = FEE - DISCOUNTAMT
PRINT 'Fee', FEE
PRINT 'Discount amount', DISCOUNTAMT
PRINT 'Fee less discount amount', AMTDUE
```

The IF-THEN-ELSE-IF construct
This construct is made up as follows:

```
IF <condition> THEN
<one or more instructions>
ELSE
IF <condition> THEN
<one or more instructions>
ENDIF
ENDIF
```

A number of paths are permitted in programming. Additional IF, THEN, ELSE and ENDIF instructions may be used to set up the required paths.

In this construct, when the first IF instruction is carried out, the condition in that instruction is evaluated. If the evaluation is true, the instructions between IF and ELSE are carried out. If it is false, the next IF instruction is carried out. The condition in that instruction is evaluated. If it is true, the instructions between that IF and ELSE/ENDIF are carried out. If the last path is an ELSE path, the instructions in this path are carried out if a true condition is not encountered.

For example:

A stadium has four stands, A, B, C and D. The admission fee for stand A is $2.00, stand B is $2.50, stand C is $4.00 and stand D is $5.00. Read a stand and the number of spectators in the stand. Calculate and print the revenue for the stand.

Solution:
```
PRINT 'Enter a stand and the number of
spectators'
READ STAND, SPECTATORS
IF STAND = 'A' THEN
REVENUE = SPECTATORS * 2.00
ELSE
IF STAND = 'B' THEN
REVENUE = SPECTATORS * 2.50
ELSE
IF STAND = 'C' THEN
REVENUE = SPECTATORS * 4.00
ELSE
IF STAND = 'D' THEN
REVENUE = SPECTATORS * 5.00
ENDIF
ENDIF
ENDIF
ENDIF
PRINT 'Stand', STAND
PRINT 'Revenue', REVENUE
```

Note that, for every IF statement, there must be a corresponding ENDIF.

Making a selection based on two or more conditions

The selection to be chosen could depend on two or more conditions. When this is required, logical operators AND and/or OR are used.

When AND is used, all of the conditions in the instruction work together as a unit. AND is also used to limit values to a particular range. A range has two values, i.e. a beginning value and an ending value. All of the conditions must be true for the THEN path to be selected. When OR is used, the conditions work independently. If either condition is true, the THEN path is selected.

For example:

Read the name of a day. If the name is 'Monday' or 'Tuesday' print 'Correct day''.

Solution:
```
PRINT 'Enter the day'
READ DAY
IF DAY = 'Monday' or DAY = 'Tuesday'
PRINT 'Correct day'
ENDIF
```

Employees are given a salary increase as follows:

- 6% of the salary if the salary is more than $3000.00
- 8% of the salary if the salary is more than $2000.00 but less than or equal to $3000.00
- 10% of the salary if the salary is less than or equal to $2000.00

Read a salary. Output the increase amount and the new salary.

Solution:

```
PRINT 'Enter the salary'
READ SALARY
IF SALARY > 3000 THEN
INCREASE = SALARY * 6/100
ELSE
IF SALARY > 2000 AND SALARY <= 3000 THEN
INCREASE = SALARY * 8/100
ELSE
IF SALARY <= 2000 THEN
INCREASE = SALARY * 10/100
ENDIF
ENDIF
ENDIF
NEWSALARY = SALARY + INCREASE
PRINT 'Increase amount', INCREASE
PRINT 'New salary', NEWSALARY
```

Two or more selection systems

The solution may require more than one selection system. Each selection system must be independent with its own IF-THEN-ENDIF or IF-THEN-ELSE-ENDIF instructions. End the first system with ENDIF before beginning the second system.

For example:

A student is given a 10% discount if the cost of a subject exceeds $100.00. 5% of the cost is refunded if the student receives grade 'A' in the examination. Read the cost and a grade. Output the discount amount and the amount refunded.

Solution:

```
PRINT 'Enter the cost and the grade'
READ COST, GRADE
IF COST > 100 THEN
DISCOUNT = COST * 10/100
ELSE
DISCOUNT = 0
ENDIF
IF GRADE = 'A' THEN
REFUND = COST * 5/100
ELSE
REFUND = 0
ENDIF
PRINT 'Discount', DISCOUNT
PRINT 'Refund', REFUND
```

Writing pseudocode algorithms that involve input, calculations and selection only

When analysing the problem ask the following questions:

- Is a prompt statement required?
- How many input variables are required?
- What should the input variables be called?
- Are calculations required?
- If calculations are required then what kind: addition, subtraction, division, multiplication, percentages or a combination?
- Is a selection required?
- If a selection is required, how many options are available?
- Which selection construct is required?
- Is the IF-THEN construct required?
- Is the IF-THEN-ELSE construct required?
- Is the IF-THEN-ELSE-IF construct required?
- Is it necessary to combine conditions?

After analysing the problem, observe if the sequence for solving the problem is stated, otherwise visualise the sequence for arriving at a solution. Use proper assignment statements to perform the calculation.

If selection(s) are required that are dependent on previous calculations then perform those calculations before making the selection.

If calculations are required within the selection(s), perform the calculations within the selection.

If output is required within the selection(s) print within the selection otherwise print after ending the selection.

After writing the algorithm, test it with test data by tracing the data through the algorithm. Correct any errors that are observed.

Exercise 8

1. Write a structured algorithm to prompt the user to input the mark a student received in a test. If the mark is less than 60, output the word 'Fail', otherwise output the word 'Pass'.

2. Write a structured algorithm that prompts the user to input the pass mark and the mark a student received in a test. Output the word 'Fail' or 'Pass' accordingly.

3. Write a structured algorithm that prompts the user to input two unequal values that are stored in variables A and B. It should print the higher value.

4. Write a structured algorithm that prompts the user to input two unequal values that are stored in variables A and B. It should print the lower value.

5. Write a structured algorithm that prompts the user to input the mass of a person. If the mass is greater than 75 kg, it should prompt the user to input the name and age, and it should also print the person's name and age.

6. Write a structured algorithm that instructs the user to input the price and quantity of an item. Calculate the discount amount at 10% of the total if the total is greater than or equal to $1000.00. Otherwise calculate the discount amount at 5% of the total. Output the total and the discount amount.

7. Write a structured algorithm that requests the user to input a positive number which is stored in a variable N. If N is less than 2000, it should subtract 20 from N. Print the result.

8. Write a structured algorithm to input the ages of three students. The algorithm should compare the ages and print the age of the oldest student.

9. Write a structured algorithm to input the maximum and minimum temperature of a day. If the maximum temperature is greater than 30 °C, output the message 'It was a hot day!'. It should also output the difference in the temperature.

10. A credit union pays 4% interest on shares that are greater than $25 000.00 and 3% on all other shares. No interest is paid on deposits. Write a structured algorithm that prompts the user to input a share and a deposit. The algorithm should calculate and output the interest amount and the total savings (Total savings = shares + deposit + interest amount).

9. Loops

Introduction to loops

Suppose you wanted to print the message 'Hi there' four times. You could simply say:

```
PRINT 'Hi there'
PRINT 'Hi there'
PRINT 'Hi there'
PRINT 'Hi there'
```

This is very repetitive. And what would happen if you had to print it one hundred times? Or one thousand? It would be nice if you could tell the computer: 'Repeat these lines a hundred times'. That's exactly what loops are for.

A **loop** is a programming construct that repeats instructions placed inside it. They are especially useful when you have to perform the same task multiple times.

Types of loops

There are two main types of loops:

1 **FOR** loops repeat instructions a predetermined number of times, for example 10 times or 100 times. The example above is exactly the sort of thing you would use a FOR loop to do.
2 **WHILE** loops repeat instructions as long as some condition is true. This type of loop is often programmed to stop when the user enters some value, for example 'quit' or '999'.

FOR loops

Looping for a definite number of times (the FOR construct)

The FOR construct consists of:

```
FOR <variable> = <beginning> TO <ending> STEP
<increment> DO
<instructions which are to be repeated>
ENDFOR
```

FOR is the beginning and ENDFOR the end of the loop. The loop variable is used to count the number of times the loop is executed. The value of this variable starts at the beginning value and is increased by one each time the loop is executed unless otherwise directed by the STEP clause.

The STEP clause indicates how much the loop variable is to be increased or decreased by each time the loop is executed. The STEP clause is not necessary if the increment is one. Use the minus (–) sign with the increment value to decrease the loop variable value.

When the end value is reached, the loop terminates and the instruction following ENDFOR is then executed.

The beginning, ending and increment values can be constants or variables. Variables give greater flexibility for altering the number of times for repeating the loop. When variables are used the said variables must be read as input before the FOR instruction is encountered.

Here is an example of how you would use a FOR loop:

```
FOR num = 2 TO 5 DO
      PRINT num
ENDFOR
```

This would cause the computer to display:

```
2
3
4
5
```

Here is an example that uses the STEP clause:

```
FOR i = 10 to 0 step -2 DO
      PRINT i
ENDFOR
```

Because we have a step value of –2, each time around the loop, the computer will decrease the value by –2. So this example would print:

```
10
8
6
4
2
0
```

How to construct a FOR loop

Whenever you are constructing a FOR loop, you should follow these steps:

1 Develop the algorithm assuming that only one cycle is involved.
2 Determine what instructions are to be repeated. Place the FOR statement at the top of these

instructions and `ENDFOR` at the bottom of the said instructions.

3 Use a new variable as the loop variable. The loop variable is followed by the = sign. Add the start value or variable then the word `TO`. This is followed by the end value or variable. If the step value is a value other than 1, add the `STEP` clause and the step value or variable. Complete the `FOR` instruction with the word `DO`.

For example:

> Write an algorithm to calculate and print the average score for each student in a class of 25. Each student was given three tests.

Solution:
Step 1
```
READ A, B, C
SUM = A + B + C
AVERAGE = SUM / 3
PRINT 'Average', AVERAGE
```

Step 2
```
FOR
READ A, B, C
SUM = A + B + C
AVERAGE = SUM / 3
PRINT 'Average', AVERAGE
ENDFOR
```

Step 3
```
FOR S = 1 TO 25 DO
READ A, B, C
SUM = A + B + C
AVERAGE = SUM / 3
PRINT 'Average', AVERAGE
ENDFOR
```

Special case – reading N values
Sometimes, instead of telling you how many numbers to read, a problem says N numbers. For example;

> Write an algorithm that reads N ages and for those that are more than 65 say 'Senior citizen'.

If it had said to read 10 ages we could've done a `FOR` loop from 1 to 10. But instead of a number we have this N. This actually isn't a problem, as we can easily do a `FOR` loop from 1 to N. But how does the computer know the value of N? Easy, we get it from the user.

So our solution would look something like this:
```
READ N
FOR i = 1 to N DO
    READ age
    IF age > 65 THEN
        PRINT 'Senior citizen'
    ENDIF
ENDFOR
```

While loops
The `WHILE` construct consists of:

```
<an initial value for the condition>
WHILE <condition> DO
<instructions which are to be repeated>
ENDWHILE
```

The initial value for the condition can be stored in a variable which is read or it can be a value which is assigned to the variable.

For example:

```
READ A
A = 1
```

This initial value is necessary so that the comparison for the condition can be made when the `WHILE` instruction is executed the first time.

The condition is made up of the said variable which stores the initial value called the **loop variable**, an operator >, <, >=, <= or <> and a termination constant. The termination constant is known as the **dummy value**. A dummy value is not a real value for the problem being solved. For example, 999 could be the dummy value for terminating the entry of ages of individuals, as an age of 999 years is not real. The variable chosen to form part of the condition must match the data type of the dummy constant.

For example:

- `WHILE A <> 999 DO` (numeric constant)
- `WHILE A < 20 DO` (numeric constant)
- `WHILE NAME <> 'END' DO` (character constant)

The instruction which contains the WHILE statement is to be interpreted to mean the following:

> Repeat the instructions that fall between WHILE and ENDWHILE as long as the condition is true. When the condition becomes false, the repetition ceases and any instructions following the ENDWHILE statement are then executed.

Instructions that are written before the WHILE instruction are carried out once. Those that are written between WHILE and ENDWHILE may be repeated and those written after ENDWHILE are done once after the loop is terminated.

An essential requirement when using the WHILE construct is that within the WHILE-ENDWHILE statements, an instruction which changes the value of the loop variable must be present. This instruction causes the loop to be terminated. If the instruction is not present, the instructions of the loop will be repeated forever.

The instruction for changing the value of the loop variable could be either an input statement or an instruction within the loop which assigns a value to the loop variable.

Selecting the correct operator for the condition

1 Use = if all values except a particular value can cause the loop to be terminated.
For example:

```
WHILE NO = 0 DO
```

The loop is repeated once if NO = 0, otherwise it is terminated.

2 Use <> if only one value is to be used for terminating the loop.
For example:

```
WHILE SCORE <> 999 DO
```

3 Use <= or < if the values to terminate the loop are greater than the dummy value or greater than or equal to the dummy value respectively.

4 Use >= or > if the values to terminate the loop are less than the dummy value or less than or equal to the dummy value respectively.

How to construct a **WHILE** loop

Here is the recommended method for constructing a WHILE loop. This method involves writing the algorithm for one cycle and then upgrading it for several cycles.

Step by step, the method is as follows:

1 Develop the algorithm assuming that only one cycle is involved.
2 Determine what instructions are to be repeated. Place the WHILE statement at the top of these instructions and ENDWHILE at the bottom of the said instructions.
3 Set the condition for the WHILE statement based on the dummy value supplied and a variable which was read. Select the appropriate operator to complete the condition. Complete the WHILE instruction with the word DO.
4 Copy the READ statement that is within the loop to a position before the WHILE statement so that the loop variable is given an initial value. This READ statement is used for entering data for the first set of attributes.
5 Move the READ statement which is within the loop to a new position just before the ENDWHILE statement. This READ statement is used for entering data for subsequent cycles.

For example:

> Write an algorithm to calculate and print the average of three (3) scores for a number of students terminated by 999.

Solution:
Step 1
```
READ A, B, C
SUM = A + B + C
AVERAGE = SUM / 3
PRINT 'Average', AVERAGE
```

Step 2
```
WHILE
READ A, B, C
SUM = A + B + C
AVERAGE = SUM / 3
PRINT 'Average', AVERAGE
ENDWHILE
```

Step 3

```
WHILE A <> 999 DO
READ A, B, C
SUM = A + B + C
AVERAGE = SUM / 3
PRINT 'Average', AVERAGE
ENDWHILE
```

Step 4

```
READ A, B, C
WHILE A <> 999 DO
READ A, B, C
SUM = A + B + C
AVERAGE = SUM / 3
PRINT 'Average', AVERAGE
ENDWHILE
```

Step 5

```
READ A, B, C
WHILE A <> 999 DO
SUM = A + B + C
AVERAGE = SUM / 3
PRINT 'Average', AVERAGE
READ A, B, C
ENDWHILE
```

Exercise 9

1 Write a structured algorithm that prints the message 'Are we there yet' 100 times.
2 Write an algorithm that prints the even numbers between 2 and 20.
3 Write a structured algorithm that reads the marks obtained by 30 students in a test, and for each mark prints whether the person passed or failed.
4 Write a structured algorithm that reads the number of children and adults that travel on a minibus for each day in January. Print the revenue for each day, if the bus fare for children is $1 and adults pay $1.50.
5 Write an algorithm that reads a series of numbers, terminated by 999, and prints the square of each number.
6 Write a structured algorithm that keeps prompting a person to enter her name until she enters the word 'quit'. Every time a person enters her name, the computer should greet them. For instance, if the person entered her name as Mary, the computer should say 'Hi, Mary'.
7 Write an algorithm that reads a series of marks, terminated by 999, and prints whether the student passed or failed.

10. Generating tables

What is a table?

A **table** is a list of information that is displayed in columns and rows.

Below is an example of a table.

Pounds (lb)	Kilograms (kg)
1	0.45
2	0.90
3	1.35
4	1.80

Each column has a title, which describes the information in the column. Tables are developed using the FOR loop.

Data entry that is needed to generate the table must be read prior to printing the column titles, and column titles must be printed before starting the FOR loop. This is necessary to avoid having the data entry or column titles printed within the table information.

Column titles and table information can be printed in columns by using a comma to separate each column.

Method for developing the algorithm for printing a table

1 Determine if the beginning, ending or increment values for the FOR statement have to be read.
2 If the values have to be read, then read them.
3 Print the column titles using adequate spacing.
4 Start the FOR loop. Use an appropriate loop variable and set the beginning, ending and increment values or variables.
5 Perform the required calculations for the table. The loop variable forms part of the calculation. Do not assign the result of the calculation back to the loop variable.
6 Print the loop variable and the result of the calculation in the correct order.
7 End the loop with ENDFOR.

For example:

Print a table of numbers that runs from 1 to 10 and the corresponding square for each number.

Solution:
```
PRINT 'Number', 'Square'
FOR N = 1 TO 10 DO
S = N * N
PRINT N, S
ENDFOR
```

Print a table that converts yards to feet and to inches. The table runs from 10 yards to 100 yards in steps of 5 yards.

Solution:
```
PRINT 'Yards', 'Feet', 'Inches'
FOR Y = 10 TO 100 STEP 5 DO
F = Y * 3
I = Y * 36
PRINT Y, F, I
ENDFOR
```

Print a table that converts minutes to hours. The table runs from X minutes to Y minutes in steps of 15 minutes.

Solution:
```
READ X, Y
PRINT 'Minutes', 'Hours'
FOR M = X TO Y STEP 15 DO
H = M / 60
PRINT M, H
ENDFOR
```

Print a tax table that runs from a salary of $250.00 to $600.00 in steps of $10.00. Tax is 5% of the salary if the salary is less than $400.00 and 6% of the salary if the salary is greater than or equal to $400.00.

Solution:
```
PRINT 'Salary', 'Tax'
FOR SALARY = 250 TO 600 STEP 10 DO
IF SALARY < 400 THEN
TAX = SALARY * 5/100
ELSE
TAX = SALARY * 6/100
ENDIF
PRINT SALARY, TAX
ENDFOR
```

The loop variable always represents the first column to be printed and all calculations are based on that variable.

Exercise 10

Write structured algorithms to solve the following problems.

1. Print a conversion table from Barbados currency to US currency. The table ranges from $20 BDS to $200 BDS in steps of $5. ($2 BDS = $1 US.)

2. Print a conversion table from Celsius to Fahrenheit. The table ranges from 10 °C to 50 °C (°F = 32 + (9 * °C)/5).

3. Print a conversion table from yards to metres. The table ranges from N yards to M yards in steps of P yards (1 yd = 0.91 m).

4. Print a conversion table from miles to kilometres. The table ranges from 1 mile to 25 miles (1 mile = 1.61 km).

5. Print a conversion table from lb to kg. The table ranges from 1 lb to X lb (1 lb = 0.45 kg).

6. Print a table that shows 3% and 5% of numbers ranging from 100 to 500 in steps of 10.

11. Totalling and counting

Totalling

Suppose you were given the following problem:

> Write an algorithm that reads 10 numbers and prints their total.

How would you go about it? The most obvious way to go about it is something like this:

```
READ num1, num2…num10
TOTAL = num1 + num2 + … + num10
```

Clearly this method doesn't scale well. What would we do if we had to add 100 numbers? Fortunately, we can solve this problem quite elegantly by using loops. Instead of trying to add all the numbers in one step, we can add one at a time and keep a running total.

Here's what our solution would look like (in English form):

1   Repeat the following steps 10 times:

    a   Read num

    b   Add num to the total.

2   Print the total.

There is one minor problem with this solution. The total has not been assigned an initial value. So when the computer gets to line **1 b**, it has no idea how much it must add to num. We can get around this problem by setting total to zero at the beginning.

This leads us to the following, correct algorithm:

```
total = 0
FOR i = 1 to 10 DO
    READ num
    total = total + num
ENDFOR
PRINT total
```

Note

Whenever you are finding the total, you must initialise the total first by setting it to 0.

Finding the total of an unknown quantity of numbers

Sometimes you don't know ahead of time how many numbers there will be. Instead, you keep reading

numbers until the user tells you to stop by entering a dummy value. In these cases you would use a WHILE loop.

For example:

> Write an algorithm that finds the total of a series of numbers, terminated by 999.

The resulting algorithm follows.

```
total = 0
READ num
WHILE num <> 999 DO
    total = total + num
    READ num
ENDFOR
PRINT total
```

Remember that you have to read the number before the while loop and at the bottom of the WHILE loop.

Counting

Another common problem is getting the computer to count. For instance you might be using a WHILE loop to read a series of numbers and want to know how many numbers a user entered. The principle is similar to totalling:

* Give a variable an initial value of zero (e.g. count = 0).
* Each time around the loop, increase the variable by 1.

This is illustrated by the algorithm below which reads a series of numbers and counts how many numbers were entered. The dummy value (or sentinel) is –1.

```
count = 0
READ num
WHILE num <> -1 DO
    count = count + 1
    READ num
ENDWHILE
PRINT 'Numbers entered = ', count
```

Averages

A related problem is finding the average of an unknown quantity of numbers. Remember that to find the average, you divide the total by how many numbers were added up. Sometimes you don't know ahead of time what the total is or how many numbers there will be – you have to calculate them.

Consider the following example.

Write an algorithm that reads a series of numbers, terminated by 999, and finds their average.

You would solve this problem is as follows:

```
count = 0
total = 0
READ num
WHILE num <> 999 DO
        count = count + 1
        total = total + num
        READ num
ENDWHILE
IF count > 0 THEN
        average = total / count
ENDIF
```

The most important parts are shown in bold. You have to remember to initialise both the count and the total. Then, inside the loop, you have to remember to update their values.

The last three lines may come as a surprise. They make the algorithm more robust by making sure you can't divide by zero (which would cause the program to crash). As an exercise for the reader, find out under what circumstances the count would be zero at the end of the WHILE loop.

Conditional counting

Sometimes you don't want to count <u>every</u> number – just the ones that meet certain criteria. In those cases, you only increment the counter if the criteria are met.

For example:

Write an algorithm that reads the scores obtained by rolling a die, terminated by –1. Print the numbers of 1s and 6s.

In this case we'll need two counters which we will call ones and sixes. The algorithm is listed below:

```
ones = 0
sixes = 0
READ score
WHILE score <> -1 DO
        IF score = 1 THEN
                ones = ones + 1
        ELSE
        IF score = 6 THEN
                sixes = sixes + 1
        ENDIF
        ENDIF
        READ score
ENDWHILE
```

Exercise 11

1. Write an algorithm that reads the prices of a set of items, terminated by –1, as well as the quantities. Print the total bill.
2. Write a structured algorithm that allows the user to input the amount of rainfall over a period of days. Calculate and print the average rainfall. The data is terminated by 999.
3. Write a structured algorithm that reads the scores for a number of batsmen who played in a cricket match as well as the number of extras made by the team as a whole. Print the total runs made by the team as well as the number of batsmen who scored ducks.
4. A school has two sets A and B. Write a structured algorithm to read the name of the set and the number of points that set got, for a series of races. The data is terminated by entering 'C'. Print the total number of points each set got. Below is an example of how the data would be entered.

A	5
B	3
B	1
B	5
A	3
B	1
C	0

12. Maximum and minimum

Finding the maximum from a series of positive integers

When finding the maximum value from a series of positive values, a loop must be used. A variable (let's call it MAX) should be initialised and set to a low value which is lower than the values being entered. The initial value of the variable could be set to 0.

A comparison must be made between the MAX variable and the input variable. If the input value is greater than the MAX variable, this value is assigned to the MAX variable.

For example:

Find the largest of a series of integers terminated by 0.

Solution:
```
MAX = 0
READ NO
WHILE NO <> 0 DO
    IF NO > MAX THEN
            MAX = NO
    ENDIF
    READ NO
ENDWHILE
PRINT 'Largest', MAX
```

If other information is required about the maximum, then another variable must be used to store that information.

This variable must be assigned the required information from the correct input variable. The assignment statement for performing this task must be within the selection system which determines the maximum.

For example:

Write an algorithm to input the name and age of 30 students. Determine the name of the oldest student and output it.

```
MAX = 0
FOR A = 1 TO 30 DO
    READ NAME, AGE
    IF AGE > MAX THEN
            MAX = AGE
            OLDNAME = NAME
    ENDIF
ENDFOR
PRINT 'Name of oldest student', OLDNAME
```

Finding the minimum from a series of positive integers

When finding the minimum value from a series of positive values, a loop must be used. A variable (let's call it MIN) should be initialised and set to a high value which is higher than the values being entered. The initial value of the variable could be set to 9999999.

A comparison must be made between the MIN variable and the input variable. If the input value is smaller than the MIN variable, this value is assigned to the MIN variable.

For example:

Find the smallest of a series of integers terminated by 0.

```
MIN = 9999999
READ NO
WHILE NO <> 0 DO
    IF NO < MIN THEN
            MIN = NO
    ENDIF
    READ NO
ENDWHILE
PRINT 'Smallest', MIN
```

If other information is required about the minimum, then another variable must be used to store that information.

This variable must be assigned the required information from the correct input variable. The assignment statement for performing this task must be within the selection system which determines the minimum.

For example:

Write an algorithm to input the name and age of 30 students. Determine the name of the youngest student and output it.

```
MIN = 999
FOR A = 1 TO 30 DO
    READ NAME, AGE
    IF AGE < MIN THEN
            MIN = AGE
            YOUNGNAME = NAME
    ENDIF
ENDFOR
PRINT 'Name of youngest student', YOUNGNAME
```

Exercise 12

1 Write a structured algorithm to read the name and population of a number of countries in the Caribbean terminated by 0. Print the name of the country with the highest population.

2 Write a structured algorithm to input the name and weight of a number of students in a class terminated by END. Print the name and weight of the lightest student as well as the average weight of the class.

3 Write a structured algorithm that requests that the user enter the scores for 30 students in a class. It should find the highest score and output it with a suitable label.

4 Write a structured algorithm that reads the temperature for each day in a month terminated by 999. Find the average temperature and the lowest temperature and print them with suitable labels.

5 Write a structured algorithm that prompts the user to input the name and amount of money collected by each student in a class of 20. Find the name of the student who collected the most money and output it together with 10% of the amount the student collected.

13. Trace tables

What is a trace table?

A **trace table** is a table that is completed by tracing the instructions in an algorithm with given data to arrive at solutions. Completing a trace table is a useful tool for testing your skills in understanding how the IF, WHILE and FOR constructs operate.

It is recommended that a table be drawn for each algorithm that is being traced as this allows the data to be better organised. In designing the table, draw a column for each variable used in the algorithm and draw enough rows to form the cells to store the values.

Start tracing from the top of the algorithm and write the appropriate value in the first vacant cell for the variable which is currently being assigned a value. One important fact to remember when calculating the values is that a variable can store only one item of data at a given time and that the current value is the value to be entered in the vacant cell.

If the values of variables are to be printed, write these values on your answer sheet as soon as the values are obtained rather than on completion of the entire table.

When printing is required within a loop, several values may have to be printed for the same variable depending on the number of times the print instruction was carried out. If printing is required only outside a loop, all of the values within the loop for the variable to be printed may not have to be printed.

For example:

Complete the trace table for the following algorithm:
```
A = 2
B = 3
C = 1
WHILE B < 45 DO
A = A + B
B = B + A
C = C + B
ENDWHILE
```

A	B	C
2	3	1

Solution:

A	B	C
2	3	1
5	8	9
13	21	30
34	55	85

What is printed in the following algorithm?
```
FOR N = 1 TO 5 DO
PRINT N
ENDFOR
```

Solution: 1, 2, 3, 4, 5

What is printed in the following algorithm?
```
C = 1
FOR N = 1 TO 5 DO
C = C + 1
ENDFOR
PRINT N, C
```

Solution: N = 5, C = 6

What is printed in the following algorithm?
```
FOR N = 5 TO 1 STEP -1 DO
PRINT N
ENDFOR
```

Solution: 5, 4, 3, 2, 1

What is printed in the following algorithm?
```
C = 1
D = 3
WHILE D < 22 DO
C = D * C
D = D + C
PRINT C, D
D = D + 1
ENDWHILE
PRINT D
```

Solution:
C = 3, 21
D = 6, 28, 29

Exercise 13a

What is printed in the following algorithms?

1
```
A = 5
B = 6
C = 4
D = A
E = B
F = C
A = F
B = D
C = E
PRINT A, B, C
```
2
```
T = 3
P = 2
IF T > 3 OR P > 3 THEN
N = 5
ELSE
N = 4
ENDIF
S = (N + P) * T
PRINT S
```
3
```
TOTAL = 0
FOR J = 1 TO 4 DO
IF J < 3 THEN
TOTAL = TOTAL + 2
ELSE
TOTAL = TOTAL + 3
ENDIF
PRINT TOTAL
ENDFOR
```
4
```
N = 3
K = 5
WHILE K > 1 DO
S = N * K
PRINT S
K = K - 1
ENDWHILE
IF N < 2 THEN
N = N + 4
PRINT N
ELSE
N = N + 5
PRINT N
ENDIF
```
5
```
N = 5
G = 2
IF N < 2 THEN
K = 2
ELSE
```
```
K = 6
ENDIF
T = K * G
PRINT T
```
6
```
X = 0
WHILE X < 6 DO
X = X + 1
PRINT X
ENDWHILE
```
7
```
X = 0
Y = 2
WHILE X < 15 DO
X = X + Y
Y = Y + 1
PRINT X, Y
ENDWHILE
```
8
```
X = 0
Y = 1
WHILE X < 6 DO
X = X + 1
Y = Y + 1
PRINT X, Y
ENDWHILE
```
9
```
X = 2
FOR J = 1 TO 4 DO
X = X + 2
PRINT J, X
ENDFOR
```
10
```
FOR N = 1 TO 3 DO
PRINT N
ENDFOR
FOR N = 3 TO 1 STEP -1 DO
PRINT N
ENDFOR
```

Complete the following trace tables:

11
```
CUM = 0
READ QTY, PRICE
WHILE QTY <> 0 DO
TOTAL = QTY * PRICE
CUM = CUM + TOTAL
READ QTY, PRICE
ENDWHILE
```

QTY	PRICE	TOTAL	CUM
			0
5	1.20		
2	0.50		
4	0.25		
0			

12
```
READ N
FOR J = 1 TO N DO
IF J < 5
S = (N + J) * 2
ELSE
S = (N - J) * 2
ENDIF
ENDFOR
```

N	J	S
6		
6		
6		
6		
6		
6		

13
```
TOT = 0
READ S
FOR P = 1 TO S DO
READ T
IF T > 5 THEN
Q = P * T
ELSE
IF T <= 5 AND T > 3 THEN
Q = P * T + 2
ELSE
Q = P * 4
ENDIF
ENDIF
TOT = TOT + T
ENDFOR
```

S	T	Q	TOT
			0
4	4		
4	6		
4	3		
4	5		

14
```
M = 1
N = 2
P = 1
WHILE M < 30 DO
N = M * 2
P = N + 1
M = P + 2
ENDWHILE
```

M	N	P
	2	1
5		

Exercise 13b

1 Write a structured algorithm that prompts the user to input a positive number that is less than 4. This number represents the month number in the year. It should print the name of the month.

2 Write a structured algorithm that prompts the user to input an integer N. The algorithm should multiply N by 2, then subtract 1 from the result and add 10 to store the final answer in Q. Print the final answer.

3 Write a structured algorithm that reads the name, birth date and telephone number of each student in your class terminated by END. Print a list which shows the name, birth date and telephone number for each student. All information for the same student must be on the same printed line. The algorithm should print labels at the top as follows: 'Student name', 'Birth date', 'Telephone number'.

4 A technician charges fees based on the number of hours worked as follows:
 • two hours or less, a fee of $90.00 per hour
 • up to six hours, a fee of $75.00 per hour
 • more than six hours, a fee of $60.00 per hour
 Write a structured algorithm to input the hours worked. The algorithm should output the hours worked and the fee charged.

5 You are required to produce a printout of the names of each student in your class. This printout should have a title 'List of students' on the first line followed by the class name and the current date on the second line. Write a structured algorithm to input the current date, name of the class and the name of each student in the class terminated by END. It should print the required information.

6   Write a structured algorithm to input three students' scores. The algorithm should calculate and print the average of the three scores.

7   Write a structured algorithm that prompts the user to input the name and price of an item. The algorithm should calculate the VAT at 15% of the price and the new price after VAT is added, and print the name of the item, the amount of VAT and the new price.

8   A bank calculates the average amount deposited each day by its customers. Write a structured algorithm that prompts the user to input the amount deposited by a number of customers terminated by 0. Output the average appropriately labelled.

9   Write a structured algorithm that prompts the user to input two numbers. The algorithm should multiply both numbers and then prompt the user to enter the answer. The algorithm should compare the answer entered with that calculated and output 'correct answer' or 'incorrect answer' accordingly. At the start, input how many sums will be done.

10 Write an algorithm to print a conversion table from metres to feet and inches. The algorithm should read a value N and it runs from 1 metre to N metres (1 metre = 3.28 ft, 1 metre = 39.37 inches).

14. Arrays

Introduction to arrays

Suppose a user typed in a list of 15 values and wanted to store the <u>entire</u> list in <u>memory at the same time</u>. You might decide to do it like this:

```
READ num1, num2... num15
```

Now suppose you wanted to print out those values. You could write:

```
PRINT num1, num2... num15
```

By now you should know what we're going to say next. What would happen if there were 100 values? Surely, there must be a better way! There is, and it uses a programming concept called an array.

An **array** is an indexed collection of values, all of which have the same data type. Suppose you have an array called `numList` that can hold 10 values.

- You can access the first value like this: `numList[1]`.
- The second would be `numList[2]`.
- And the last would be `numList[10]`.

Suppose the array was used to store the following list of values: 23, 10, 5, 14, 99, 55, 42, 78, 4, 1000. These values would be stored as shown in the table.

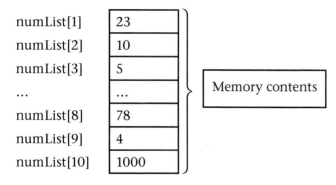

The individual array elements work the same way as regular variables. So, in our example:

- `PRINT numList[1]` would display the number 23.
- `numList[8] = 3` would change the value of `numList[8]` from 78 to 3.
- `numList[3] = numList[3] + 1` would increase the value of `numList[3]` to 6.

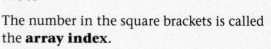

Note

The number in the square brackets is called the **array index**.

Using variables as indexes

A nice feature that arrays have is that you can use variables as array indexes. Using our example, the following code would print '10'.

```
index = 2
PRINT numList[index]
```

Before the computer prints the number, it first checks to see what value is stored in `index`. So to the computer, the process is exactly the same as if you had said `PRINT numList[2]`.

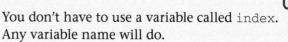

Note

You don't have to use a variable called `index`. Any variable name will do.

Using arrays with loops

Only when you use arrays with loops can you really appreciate how powerful they are. Remember our initial example? The one where we wanted to read 15 numbers? Well, here is how you would do it using arrays.

```
FOR i = 1 to 15 DO
      READ numList[i]
ENDFOR
```

The trick is that the loop variable is used as the array index. Each time around, the FOR loop increments `i`. So the first time around, the computer reads `numList[1]`, the next time it reads `numList[2]` and so on.

Note

The loop variable that is used to index into an array is traditionally called i. However, you could just as easily use a more descriptive name such as index.

Similarly, you could use a loop to print the values in the array.

```
FOR i = 1 to 15 DO
     PRINT numList[i]
ENDFOR
```

Exercise 14

1 Write an algorithm that prompts the user to enter 10 numbers, then stores them in an array.
2 Write an algorithm that first asks the user how many numbers he or she is going to enter, and then stores the entire list in an array.
3 Write an algorithm that reads a list of 10 numbers then prints them back out in reverse order.

15. Flowcharts

In the last few chapters we've done our algorithms in pseudocode. But this isn't the only way to represent an algorithm. Another common way is to use a flowchart, which is a pictorial representation of the algorithm. Some people find it easier to understand what is going on when they can actually <u>see</u> it.

Symbols

Below is a list of the various flowchart symbols and explanations of what each one is for.

Terminator

A terminator marks the beginning or the end of the algorithm. The symbol for a terminator is a rounded rectangle with the word 'Start' or 'Stop' inside.

Processing

Processing statements such as calculations or assignment statements are placed in rectangles. For example:

Input / Output

Input and output statements are illustrated as follows:

Decision

When the computer has to check a condition, for example in an `IF` statement or a loop, you place the condition in a diamond as follows:

Arrows

Arrows connect the various other symbols together, with the direction of the arrow indicating the flow of control.

Constructs

The following examples illustrate how you put these building blocks together to represent common programming constructs.

IF-THEN construct

In the following flowchart, the highlighted sections illustrate how you would represent an `IF-THEN` statement.

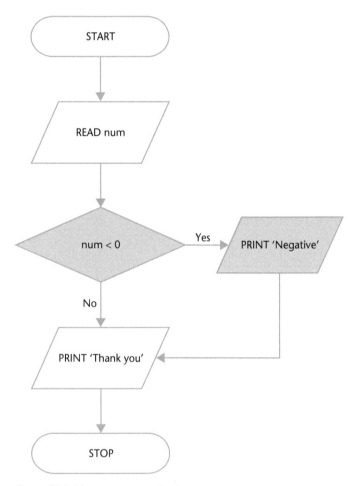

Figure 15.1 *The* `IF-THEN` *construct*

This is equivalent to:

```
READ num
IF num < 0 THEN
      PRINT 'Negative'
ENDIF
PRINT 'Thank you'
```

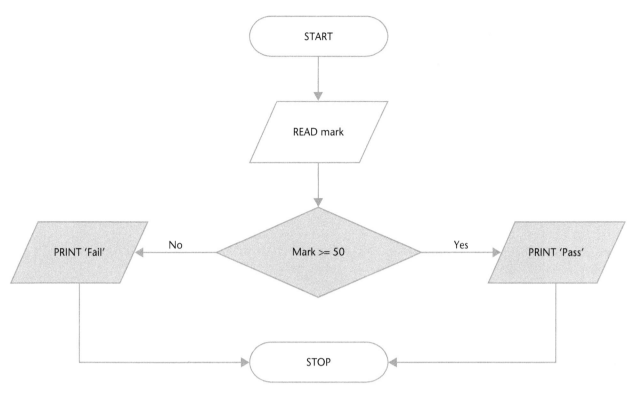

Figure 15.2 *The* IF-THEN-ELSE *construct*

IF-THEN-ELSE construct

In the flowchart in Figure 15.2, the IF-THEN-ELSE construct is highlighted.

This is the same as:

```
READ mark
IF mark >= 50 THEN
    PRINT 'Pass'
ELSE
    PRINT 'Fail'
ENDIF
```

WHILE loop

A WHILE loop can be represented as shown in Figure 15.3.

This flowchart is the same as:

```
READ num
WHILE num <> 999 DO
    PRINT num
    READ num
ENDWHILE
```

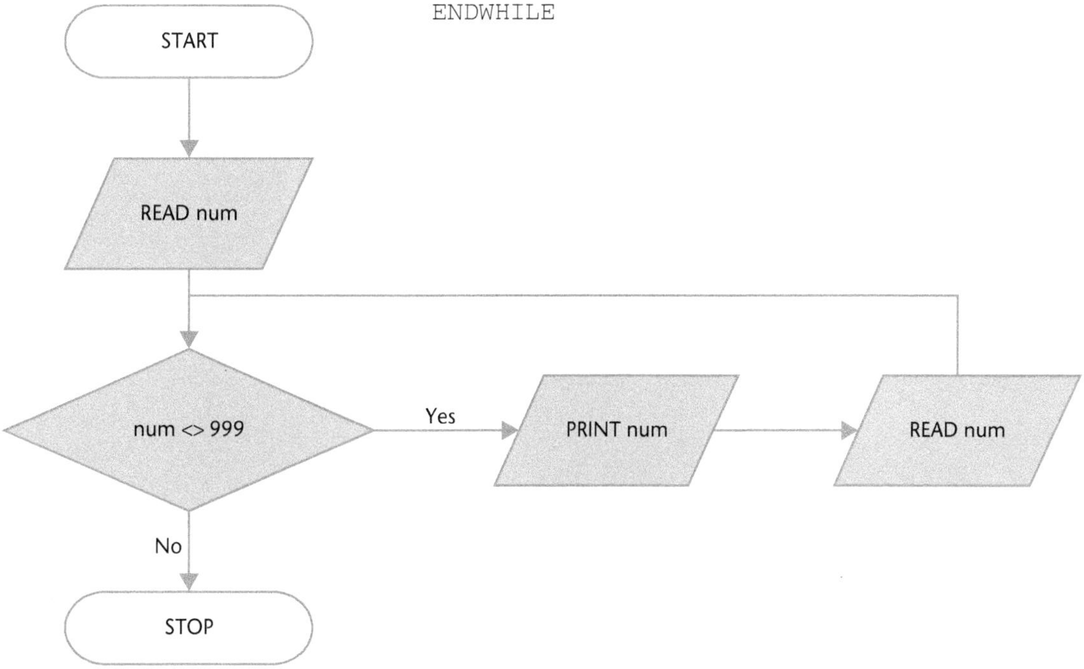

Figure 15.3 WHILE *loop*

FOR loop

The flowchart for a FOR loop (see Figure 15.4) doesn't look very different from one for a WHILE loop.

The equivalent pseudocode is:

```
FOR i = 1 to 5 DO
      PRINT num
ENDFOR
```

Example flowchart

Suppose you are asked to write a program that reads a set of marks for an exam, terminated by –1, and for each mark, indicates whether the person passed or failed (the pass mark is 50).

The pseudocode is given below:

```
READ mark
WHILE mark <> -1 DO
      IF mark >= 50 THEN
            PRINT 'Pass'
      ELSE
            PRINT 'Fail'
      ENDIF
      READ mark
ENDWHILE
```

The flowchart for this would look like Figure 15.5.

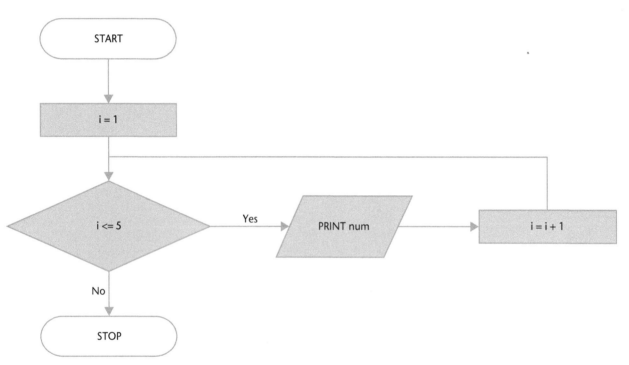

Figure 15.4 FOR *loop*

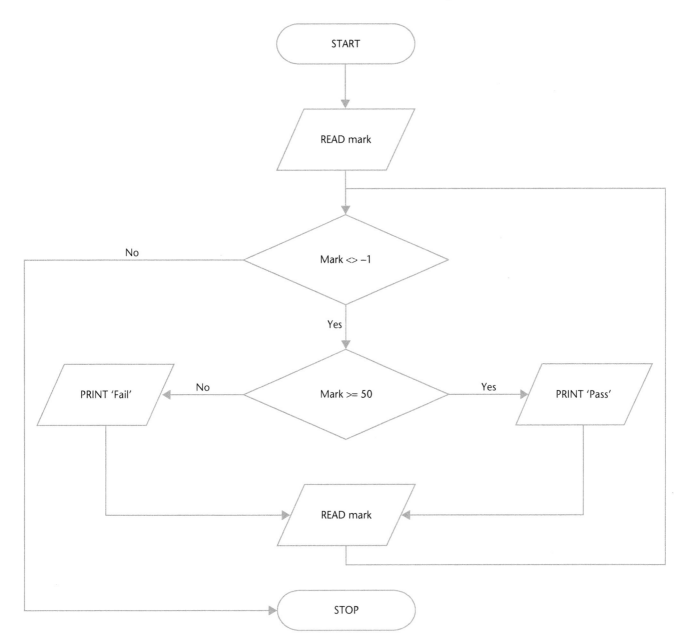

Figure 15.5 *Example flowchart*

Exercise 15

Construct flowcharts for each of the algorithms in Exercise 13a.

16. Top-down design

Top-down design or **stepwise refinement** is the process of doing a complicated task by breaking it down into smaller and smaller tasks.

Let's look at an example:

> Write a program that reads 10 positive numbers, stores them in an array, then prints the average and the maximum number.

This is a fairly complex problem. You have to:

1 Read the numbers and store them in an array.
2 Calculate and print the average.
3 Find the maximum number and print it.

Each of these subtasks is simpler than the original task. Furthermore, each of them is something that you already know how to do. So we have divided a complex task into simpler, more manageable subtasks. If you do this enough, you eventually end up with the steps needed to solve overall task. That is the essence of top-down design.

Hierarchical charts

In order to illustrate how a larger problem is broken down into subtasks you use a type of diagram called a **hierarchical chart**. Figure 16.1 is a hierarchical chart for our example.

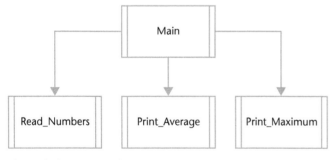

Figure 16.1 *Top-down design*

In the diagram, each box represents what is known as a **module**. The main module (which is trying to solve the overall problem) calls on the other modules to do their part. Each of the other modules is trying to solve a subtask. In a way, a module is like its own mini-program.

Representing modules in pseudocode
The following is the pseudocode for our example:

```
Call Read_Numbers
Call Print_Average
Call Print_Maximum

Sub_Algorithm Read_Numbers
FOR i = 1 to 10 DO
      READ numList[i]
ENDFOR
RETURN

Sub_Algorithm Print_Average
total = 0
FOR i = 1 to 10 DO
      total = total + numList[i]
ENDFOR
avg = total / 10
PRINT avg
RETURN

Sub_Algorithm Print_Maximum
max = 0
FOR i = 1 to 10 DO
      IF numList[i] > max THEN
            max = numList[i]
      ENDIF
ENDFOR
PRINT max
RETURN
```

There are a few things to note:

- In order for a module to call another module it uses the CALL statement.
- Each sub-algorithm is given a name so that the other modules can refer to it.
- At the end of each sub-algorithm is the word RETURN which tells the computer to return to where it left off in the module that called it.

Representing modules using flowcharts

If you need to represent modules using flowcharts:

1 Have a flowchart for each module.
2 Represent any calls to a module by putting the name of the module in a subprocess box (as shown below).

```
Read_Numbers
```

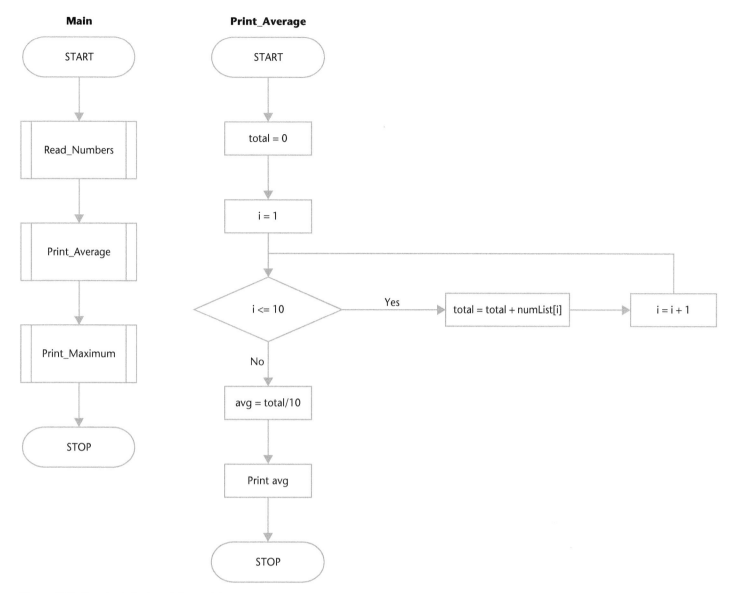

Figure 16.2 *Flowcharts for two of the modules*

Sharing the data

When working with modular solutions, the different modules need to be able to share data and communicate with each other. The recommended way to do so is via parameters and return values, but that is beyond the scope of this course.

Instead, the way we will do it is by global variables. A **global variable** is a variable that can be accessed by any module. In our example we are assuming that numList is a global variable.

So when the Read_Numbers module is called, it will store the numbers it reads into the numList array. Since it is global, the Print_Average and Print_Maximum modules can refer to it in order to access the numbers that were read.

17. Testing and debugging

Types of errors

Despite the best of intentions, algorithms (and programs) often contain errors. There are three main types of errors:

1. **Syntax errors.** These are errors where the rules of the programming language are broken. Common examples are forgetting semicolons, typing instructions in plain English, using the wrong variable types and putting spaces in variable names.

   It is usually pretty easy to tell when a program has a syntax error. The compiler will usually notify you of syntax errors when you try to run the program. The hardest part is often figuring out what the particular error message means.

2. **Logic errors.** A logic error occurs when the programmer fails to think through the solution correctly. As a result, the program doesn't work as it should. For example, the programmer may type something like:

   ```
   Read num1, num2
   Sum = num1 - num2
   ```

   In this case, the programmer is trying to calculate the sum of two numbers by subtracting them, instead of adding them like he is supposed to. Not all logic errors are this easy to spot, however. They are often only detected when the user realises that the problem isn't being solved correctly.

3. **Runtime errors.** These are due to unexpected behaviour (either on the part of the user or the program) while the program is being executed. This is the type of error that causes program crashes, blue screens and messages about 'illegal operations'. The classic example of a runtime error is dividing by zero.

Testing

There are two main types of testing you can do – manual tracing and computer testing. Computer testing is when you run the program with various test data, making sure it works correctly. Obviously you won't be doing computer testing during the problem solving phase (since you aren't supposed to be on the computer at this point).

Instead we will focus on manual tracing. A manual trace, also known as a **dry run**, is when you go through the logic of the algorithm line by line, trying to figure out if it is correct. Trace tables are extremely useful when you are doing this.

Choosing test data

When you are testing an algorithm, it is important to choose appropriate test data to use as inputs. The test data should be chosen in such a way that **every** line of the program gets tested. For example, consider the following algorithm:

```
READ A, B
IF A = B THEN
    PRINT 'Numbers are equal'
ELSE IF A > B THEN
    PRINT 'Higher value', A
ELSE
    PRINT 'Higher value', B
ENDIF
ENDIF
```

What test data should be used for A and B? Well, we want to make sure that all the branches of the IF statement are tested. Here are test values that you could use:

- 4, 4: these test the instructions when the two numbers are equal.
- 5, 2: these test the instructions when A is larger than B.
- 3, 7: these test the instructions when B is larger than A.

Note

You can't just use one pair of values. You have to use **all three pairs** in order to test this program thoroughly

Debugging

Debugging is just a fancy word for 'finding and removing errors from a program'. As you can imagine, testing and debugging go hand in hand. Modern programming languages have tools called **debuggers** to aid in debugging.

Exercise 17

Correct the mistakes in the following algorithms:

1
```
READ COST, QTY OF ITEMS
COST * QTY = TOTAL
IF AMT > 200 THEN
    DISCOUNT = 200 * 2 / 100
ENDIF
PRINT 'Discount', DISCOUNT
```

2
```
FOR J = 1 TO K DO
READ B
SUM = SUM + B
PRINT SUM
```

3
```
READ S
WHILE S <> 999 DO
IF A < 5 THEN
    TOTAL = TOTAL + S
ELSE
    TOTAL = TOTAL - S
ENDIF
ENDWHILE
PRINT TOTAL
```

4
```
READ A, B, C
TOTAL = A+B+C+D
IF TOTAL > 600 THEN
    E = TOTAL - 200
ELSE
    E IS TOTAL + 50
ENDIF
PRINT E
```

5 Explain the following terms:

  a dry run
  b syntax error
  c logic error
  d runtime error
  e debugging

6 Give examples of data that can be used to test the following algorithm:

```
READ amount
IF amount > 1000 THEN
    discount = amount * 5 / 100
ELSE
    discount = 0
ENDIF
PRINT discount
```

Solutions to pseudocode questions

Exercise 5

```
1   READ A
2   READ NAME
3   READ A, B
4   READ NAME, AGE
5   READ NAME1, NAME2, NAME3, NAME4
6   READ NAME, AGE, HEIGHT
7   READ FORM, NUM, SUBJECT
8   READ MAKE, COLOUR, PRICE
9   READ NAME, ADDRESS, TEL
10  READ BIRTHDATE, HEIGHT, WEIGHT, COMPLEX
```

Exercise 6

```
1   PRINT 'Today is Monday'
2   PRINT 'Total ='
3   PRINT 'Enter your name'
4   READ NAME
    PRINT NAME
5   READ A, B
    PRINT A, B
6   PRINT 'Enter your name'
    READ NAME
    PRINT NAME
7   PRINT 'Enter the price'
    READ PRICE
    PRINT 'Price', PRICE
8   PRINT 'Enter the name of a book and
    its author'
    READ NAME, AUTHOR
    PRINT 'Name of book', NAME
    PRINT 'Author', AUTHOR
9   READ NUM, ROUTE, PASS
    PRINT 'Bus number', NUM
    PRINT 'Route', ROUTE
    PRINT 'No. of passengers', PASS
10  PRINT 'Enter a tune, its composer
    and year released'
    READ TUNE, COMPOSER, YEAR
    PRINT 'Tune', TUNE
    PRINT 'Composer', COMPOSER
    PRINT 'Year released', YEAR
```

Exercise 7

```
1   PRINT 'Enter two numbers'
    INPUT A, B
    SUM = A + B
    PRINT 'Sum', SUM
2   PRINT 'Enter the days in the month'
    READ DAYS
    HOURS = DAYS * 24
    PRINT 'No. of hours in month', HOURS
3   PRINT 'Enter item name, price and
    quantity'
    READ NAME, PRICE, QTY
    AMTDUE = PRICE * QTY
    PRINT 'Name of item', NAME
    PRINT 'Price', PRICE
    PRINT 'Quantity', QTY
    PRINT 'Amount due', AMTDUE
4   PRINT 'Enter the side length of a
    square'
    READ LENGTH
    AREA = LENGTH * LENGTH
    PRINT 'Area of square', AREA
5   PRINT 'Enter two numbers'
    READ A, B
    C = A - B
    PRINT 'Answer is:', C
6   PRINT 'Enter the radius of a circle'
    READ RADIUS
    DIAMETER = RADIUS * 2
    PRINT 'Diameter', DIAMETER
7   READ NAME, DATE, FEE, AMT
    AMTDUE = AMT - FEE
    PRINT 'Amount due to borrower', AMTDUE
8   PRINT 'Enter the ages of four of your
    friends'
    READ AGE1, AGE2, AGE3, AGE4
    SUM = AGE1 + AGE2 + AGE3 + AGE4
    AVG = SUM / 4
    PRINT 'Average age', AVG
9   PRINT 'Enter the prices for two pay
    per view movies'
    READ PRICE1, PRICE2
    SUM = PRICE1 + PRICE2
    PRINT 'Amount due BCC Television Ltd.',
    SUM
```

```
10   PRINT 'Enter name, mark and maximum
     score of test'
     READ NAME, MARK, MAX
     PER = MARK / MAX * 100
     PRINT 'Name', NAME
     PRINT 'Mark', MARK
     PRINT 'Maximum mark', MAX
     PRINT 'Percentage', PER
```

Exercise 8

```
1   PRINT 'Enter a mark'
    READ MARK
    IF MARK < 60 THEN
    PRINT 'FAIL'
    ELSE
    PRINT 'PASS'
    ENDIF
2   PRINT 'Enter the pass mark and a
    student's mark'
    READ PASSMARK, MARK
    IF MARK < PASSMARK THEN
    PRINT 'FAIL'
    ELSE
    PRINT 'PASS'
    ENDIF
3   PRINT 'Enter two unequal values'
    READ A, B
    IF A > B THEN
    HIGHVAL = A
    ELSE
    HIGHVAL = B
    ENDIF
    PRINT HIGHVAL
4   PRINT 'Enter two unequal values'
    READ A, B
    IF A < B THEN
    LOWERVAL = A
    ELSE
    LOWERVAL = B
    ENDIF
    PRINT LOWERVAL
5   PRINT 'Enter the mass in kg'
    READ MASS
    IF MASS > 75 THEN
    PRINT 'Enter the name and age'
    READ NAME, AGE
    PRINT NAME, AGE
    ENDIF
```

```
6   PRINT 'Enter the price and quantity'
    READ PRICE, QTY
    TOTAL = PRICE * QTY
    IF TOTAL >= 1000 THEN
    DISCOUNT = TOTAL * 10/100
    ELSE
    DISCOUNT = TOTAL * 5/100
    ENDIF
    PRINT TOTAL, DISCOUNT
7   PRINT 'Enter a positive number'
    READ N
    IF N < 2000
    R = N - 20
    ELSE
    R = N
    ENDIF
    PRINT R
8   READ AGE1, AGE2, AGE3
    IF AGE1 > AGE2 AND AGE1> AGE3 THEN
    OLDEST = AGE1
    ELSE
    IF AGE2 > AGE1 AND AGE2 > AGE3 THEN
    OLDEST = AGE2
    ELSE
    IF AGE3 > AGE1 AND AGE3 > AGE2 THEN
    OLDEST = AGE3
    ENDIF
    ENDIF
    ENDIF
    PRINT 'Oldest', OLDEST
9   READ MAX, MIN
    IF MAX > 30 THEN
    PRINT 'It was a hot day!'
    ENDIF
    DIFF = MAX - MIN
    PRINT DIFF
10  PRINT 'Enter the share and deposit'
    READ SHARE, DEPOSIT
    IF SHARE > 25000 THEN
    INTEREST = SHARE * 4/100
    ELSE
    INTEREST = SHARE * 3/100
    ENDIF
    TOTSAVINGS = SHARE + DEPOSIT +
    INTEREST
    PRINT INTEREST, TOTSAVINGS
```

Exercise 9

1
```
FOR I = 1 to 100 DO
PRINT 'Are we there yet?'
ENDFOR
```
2
```
FOR NUM = 2 to 20 STEP 2 DO
PRINT NUM
ENDFOR
```
3
```
FOR I = 1 to 30 DO
READ MARK
IF MARK >= 50 THEN
PRINT 'PASS'
ELSE
PRINT 'FAIL'
ENDIF
ENDFOR
```
4
```
FOR DAY = 1 TO 31 DO
READ CHILDREN, ADULTS
REVENUE = CHILDREN + (ADULTS * 1.50)
PRINT REVENUE
ENDFOR
```
5
```
READ NUM
WHILE NUM <> 999 DO
SQUARE = NUM * NUM
PRINT SQUARE
READ NUM
ENDWHILE
```
6
```
PRINT 'ENTER YOUR NAME'
READ NAME
WHILE NAME <> 'QUIT' DO
PRINT 'Hi, ', NAME
PRINT 'ENTER YOUR NAME'
READ NAME
ENDWHILE
```
7
```
READ MARK
WHILE MARK <> 999 DO
IF MARK >= 50 THEN
PRINT 'PASS'
ELSE
PRINT 'FAIL'
ENDIF
ENDWHILE
```

Exercise 10

1
```
PRINT 'BDS', 'US'
FOR BDS = 20 TO 200 step 5 DO
US = BDS / 2
PRINT BDS, US
ENDFOR
```
2
```
PRINT 'Celsius', 'Fahrenheit'
FOR C = 10 TO 50 DO
F = 32 + (9 * C)/5
PRINT C, F
ENDFOR
```
3
```
READ N, M, P
PRINT 'Yards', 'Metres'
FOR YDS = N TO M STEP P DO
METRES = YDS * .91
PRINT YDS, METRES
ENDFOR
```
4
```
PRINT 'Miles', 'Kilometres'
FOR M = 1 TO 25 DO
KM = M * 1.61
PRINT M, KM
ENDFOR
```
5
```
READ X
PRINT 'lb', 'kg'
FOR LBS = 1 TO X DO
KGS = LBS * .45
PRINT LBS, KGS
ENDFOR
```
6
```
PRINT 'No', '3%', '5%'
FOR NO = 100 TO 500 STEP 10 DO
THREE = NO * 3/100
FIVE = NO * 5/100
PRINT NO, THREE, FIVE
ENDFOR
```

Exercise 11

1
```
TOTAL = 0
READ PRICE, QTY
WHILE PRICE <> -1 DO
TOTAL = TOTAL + (PRICE * QTY)
READ PRICE, QTY
ENDWHILE
PRINT 'The total bill is $', TOTAL
```
2
```
TOTAL = 0
DAYS = 0
READ RAINFALL
```

```
WHILE RAINFALL <> 999 DO
  DAYS = DAYS + 1
  TOTAL = TOTAL + RAINFALL
  READ RAINFALL
ENDWHILE
IF DAYS > 0 THEN
  AVERAGE = TOTAL / DAYS
  PRINT AVERAGE
ENDIF
```

3
```
TOTAL = 0
DUCKS = 0
READ RUNS
WHILE RUNS <> -1 DO
  TOTAL = TOTAL + RUNS
  IF RUNS = 0 THEN
    DUCKS = DUCKS + 1
  ENDIF
  READ RUNS
ENDWHILE
READ EXTRAS
TOTAL = TOTAL + EXTRAS
PRINT 'Total runs = ', TOTAL
PRINT 'Ducks = ', DUCKS
```

4
```
A = 0
B = 0
READ SET, POINTS
WHILE SET <> 'C' DO
  IF SET = 'A' THEN
    A = A + POINTS
  ELSE IF SET = 'B' THEN
    B = B + POINTS
  ENDIF
ENDIF
  READ SET, POINTS
ENDWHILE
PRINT 'Set A got ', A, 'points'
PRINT 'Set B got ', B, 'points'
```

Exercise 12

1
```
MAX = 0
READ NAME, POP
WHILE POP <> 0 DO
  IF POP > MAX THEN
    MAX = POP
    NAM = NAME
  ENDIF
  READ NAME, POP
```

```
ENDWHILE
PRINT NAM
```

2
```
TOTAL = 0
NUM = 0
MIN = 999
READ NAME, WT
WHILE NAME <> 'END' DO
  IF WT < MIN THEN
    MIN = WT
    NAM = NAME
  ENDIF
  TOTAL = TOTAL + WT
  NUM = NUM + 1
  READ NAME, WT
ENDWHILE
AVG = TOTAL/NUM
PRINT NAM, MIN, AVG
```

3
```
MAX = 0
FOR S = 1 TO 30 DO
  PRINT 'Enter a score'
  READ SCORE
  IF SCORE > MAX THEN
    MAX = SCORE
  ENDIF
ENDFOR
PRINT 'Highest score', MAX
```

4
```
MIN = 999
TOTAL = 0
DAYS = 0
READ TEMP
WHILE TEMP <> 999 DO
  DAYS = DAYS + 1
  TOTAL = TOTAL + TEMP
  IF TEMP < MIN THEN
    MIN = TEMP
  ENDIF
  READ TEMP
ENDWHILE
AVG = TOTAL / DAYS
PRINT 'Average temperature', AVG
PRINT 'Lowest temperature', MIN
```

5
```
MAX = 0
FOR S = 1 TO 20 DO
  PRINT 'Enter the name and amount
  collected'
  READ NAME, AMT
  IF AMT > MAX THEN
    MAX = AMT
    NAM = NAME
  ENDIF
ENDFOR
```

```
PER = MAX * 10/100
PRINT 'Name of student', NAM
PRINT '10%', PER
```

Exercise 13a

1 A = 4, B = 5, C = 6
2 S = 18
3 TOTAL = 2, 4, 7, 10
4 S = 15, 12, 9, 6. N = 8
5 T = 12
6 X = 1, 2, 3, 4, 5
7 X = 2, 5, 9, 14
   Y = 3, 4, 5, 6
8 X = 1, 2, 3, 4, 5
   Y = 2, 3, 4, 5, 6
9 J = 1, 2, 3, 4
   X = 4, 6, 8, 10
10 N = 1, 2, 3
    N = 3, 2, 1
11

QTY	PRICE	TOTAL	CUM
			0
5	1.20	6.00	6.00
2	0.50	1.00	7.00
4	0.25	1.00	8.00
0			

12

N	J	S
6	1	14
6	2	16
6	3	18
6	4	20
6	5	2
6	6	0

13

S	T	Q	TOT
			0
4	4	6	4
4	6	12	10
4	3	12	13
4	5	22	18

14

M	N	P
1	2	1
5	2	3
13	10	11
29	26	27
61	58	59

Exercise 13b

1
```
PRINT 'Enter a number between 0 and 4'
READ N
IF N = 1 THEN
MONTH = 'January'
ELSE
IF N = 2 THEN
MONTH = 'February'
ELSE
MONTH = 'March'
ENDIF
ENDIF
PRINT MONTH
```
2
```
PRINT 'Enter a whole number'
READ N
A = N * 2
Q = A - 1 + 10
PRINT Q
```
3
```
PRINT 'Student name', 'Birth date',
'Telephone number'
READ NAME, BIRTHDATE, TELE
WHILE NAME <> 'END' DO
PRINT NAME, BIRTHDATE, TELE
READ NAME, BIRTHDATE, TELE
ENDWHILE
```
4
```
READ HOURS
IF HOURS <= 2 THEN
FEE = HOURS * 90
ELSE
IF HOURS > 2 AND HOURS <= 6 THEN
FEE = HOURS * 75
ELSE
FEE = HOURS * 60
ENDIF
ENDIF
PRINT HOURS, FEE
```

5
```
PRINT 'List of students'
READ CLASS, DATE
PRINT CLASS, DATE
READ NAME
WHILE NAME <> 'END' DO
PRINT NAME
READ NAME
ENDWHILE
```
6
```
READ A, B, C
SUM = A + B + C
AVG = SUM / 3
PRINT SUM
```
7
```
PRINT 'Enter item name and its price'
READ NAME, PRICE
VAT = PRICE * 15/100
NEWPRICE = PRICE + VAT
PRINT NAME, VAT, NEWPRICE
```
8
```
TOTAL = 0
NUM = 0
PRINT 'Enter amount'
READ AMT
WHILE AMT <> 0 DO
TOTAL = TOTAL + AMT
NUM = NUM + 1
READ AMT
ENDWHILE
AVG = TOTAL / NUM
PRINT 'Average', AVG
```
9
```
PRINT 'How many sums?'
READ N
FOR SUMS = 1 TO N DO
PRINT 'Enter two numbers'
READ A, B
C = A * B
PRINT 'Enter the answer'
READ D
IF D = C THEN
PRINT 'Correct answer'
ELSE
PRINT 'Incorrect answer'
ENDIF
ENDFOR
```
10
```
READ N
PRINT 'Metres', 'Feet', 'Inches'
FOR M = 1 TO N DO
FT = M * 3.28
IN = M * 39.37
PRINT M, FT, IN
ENDFOR
```

Exercise 14

1
```
PRINT 'ENTER 10 NUMBERS'
FOR I = 1 TO 10 DO
READ LIST[I]
ENDFOR
```
2
```
PRINT 'How many numbers?'
READ N
FOR I = 1 TO N DO
READ LIST[I]
ENDFOR
```
3
```
FOR I = 1 TO 10 DO
READ LIST[I]
ENDFOR
FOR I = 10 TO 1 STEP -1 DO
PRINT LIST[I]
ENDFOR
```

Part 3

Programming

1. Introduction to programming

Recall that there are two main phases to designing a program – the problem-solving phase and the implementation phase. In this part of the book we will look at the implementation phase. During this phase, you:

- Take the algorithm you designed in the problem-solving phase and write it in your favourite programming language (we'll be using Pascal).
- Produce an executable program.
- Document the program.
- Maintain the program, i.e. update it and fix any problems that crop up.

Before we go on to Pascal, let us take a brief look at the generations of programming languages.

Generations of languages

Computer programs are written in accordance with the rules and statements of a particular programming language. Many programming languages have been developed throughout the years. These languages are classified into different generations.

First generation

Programs written in the first-generation language consist of a series of 0s and 1s. Such programs are referred to as **machine-language programs**. This language is the lowest computer language. Machine-language programs have instructions that are similar to the following:

```
01010101  01110001
10011000  11110000
00101010  10010101
```

Machine-language programs are the fastest programs when being executed. However, there are disadvantages when writing these programs. The disadvantages of writing a program in machine language are:

- It is time consuming to write.
- It is easy to make a mistake because only 0s and 1s are used. The programmer must therefore ensure that the correct series is used.
- Programs written for one type of computer will not work on another type of computer.

Second generation

Second-generation language is called assembly language. **Assembly-language programs** use short codes to represent instructions (e.g. ADD, STO, SUB, LDA). A simple assembly-language program is shown below.

```
mov ax, 5
add ax, 10
mov ax, [bx]
xor ax, 67
jmp[bx]
sub[bx], 8
```

Assembly-language programs are easier to write than machine-language programs. However, both machine-language and assembly-language programs are machine dependent, i.e. the way the program is written depends on the operation of the computer. Therefore, the programmer has to think about how the machine is going to function when writing the program.

Third generation

The third-generation languages are known as **high-level languages**. High-level languages are not machine dependent; hence the programmer does not have to think about the machine but can concentrate on solving the problem.

Programs written in a high-level language use English-like statements and are therefore easier to write. Examples of high-level languages are Cobol, Fortran, Pascal, Basic and C. Each language was developed for a particular objective (see Table 1.1).

Fourth generation

In the first three generations of programming languages, the programmer is required to explicitly state how to do each task. In fourth-generation languages (4GLs), however, the programmer can state what tasks need to be done but doesn't have to worry about how to do them.

Some common examples of 4GLs are:

- Visual FoxPro
- database query languages such as SQL
- data analysis languages such as S and SPSS

Table 1.1 Examples of high-level languages

Name	Purpose	Sample code

Cobol	To solve business problems such as inventory control, accounts and any problems involving processing large volumes of data	`OPEN INPUT DATA - IN`
		`OUTPUT ANSWER - OUT`
		`READ DATA - IN`
		`ADD NUMBER - 1 - IN, NUMBER - 2 - IN`
		`GIVING SUM-OUT`

Fortran	To solve problems that involve complex mathematics	`      INTEGER NUM1, NUM2, SUM`
		`      READ (5,10) NUM1, NUM2`
		`10    FORMAT (14, 14)`
		`      SUM = NUM1 + NUM2`

Pascal	To assist in the teaching of programming concepts, but it can also be used for solving business problems	`Program Add-It (Input, Output);`
		`Var Num1, Num2, Sum: Integer;`
		`Begin`
		`      ReadLn(Num1, Num2);`
		`      Sum := Num1 + Num2;`
		`End.`

Basic	To solve mathematical problems. Basic is used today for solving business problems	`10 INPUT A`
		`20 INPUT B`
		`30 SUM = A + B`
		`40 PRINT SUM`

C	To write operating system programs and business software	`# INCLUDE <STDIO.H>`
		`MAIN ()`
		`{`
		`    INT APPLES, PEARS;`
		`    APPLES = 5;`
		`    PEARS = 6;`
		`    SUM = APPLES + PEARS;`
		`}`

Fifth generation

With fifth-generation languages (5GLs) you don't even have to state what tasks are to be performed; you just need to say what problem you want to solve. This is done by specifying a series of constraints.

Fifth-generation languages are common within the field of artificial intelligence. Notable examples are Prolog and Lisp.

Translating programs to machine language

Today's programmers normally use third-generation and higher languages. Unfortunately, the computer speaks another language – machine language. Just as you would for languages such as Spanish and Chinese, you need some way of translating.

The instructions written in a particular programming language are called **source code**. The two main approaches to translating source code to machine-readable code are interpreting and compiling.

Interpreting

With interpreting, the program is executed while it is being translated. A line of code is translated and executed, then the next one, and so on. The process is not unlike the one used at the Miss Universe competition when someone doesn't speak English. Not surprisingly, the program that does the translating is known as an **interpreter**.

Advantages

The main advantage of interpreting is that you can run the program right away; you don't have to wait to see the effects of changes you've made. In contrast, compilation is a fairly lengthy process – especially for large programs.

Disadvantages

There are a number of disadvantages to interpreting:

1 The program has to be interpreted each time it is run.
2 Interpreted programs cannot be run without the interpreter so whenever you distribute the program, you have to include the interpreter as well.
3 Interpreted programs run more slowly since the code is being translated while it is running.

Compiling

Compiling is a two-phase process. First, a special program known as a **compiler** converts the entire source code of file into machine-executable

instructions (see Figure 1.1). The machine-executable instructions that are produced as a result of compiling are called **object code** (also known as **binaries**).

Figure 1.1 *The compilation phase*

After the individual files of a program are compiled, another program called a **linker** combines their object code into an executable (.exe) file as shown in Figure 1.2. The user is then free to run the program as many times as he or she wants. All he or she has to do is double-click on the executable file.

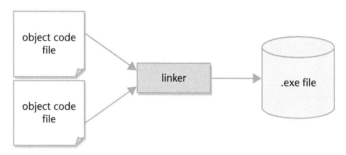

Figure 1.2 *The linking phase*

Advantages

Compiling has a several advantages over interpreting. It is no wonder that languages like C, C++ and Pascal take this approach.

1 Compiled programs run more quickly than interpreted ones.
2 You only have to compile a finished program once. After that it can be run many times.
3 Compiled programs are standalone so they are easier to distribute.

Disadvantages

The main disadvantage of compilation is that the <u>entire</u> program has to be compiled before it can be run.

> ### Note
>
> If your source code contains syntax errors it will not compile. However, a program that compiles may have logic errors or runtime errors.

Exercise 1

1 Low-level language programs are more difficult to write than high-level language programs. State two reasons for this.
2 What is a computer program?
3 Give three examples of high-level languages and the kind of processing for which they were designed.
4 Name two characteristics of three of the following:
   a fourth-generation language
   b machine language
   c assembly language
   d high-level language
5 Three specimens of programming languages are listed below. Name each language.

   a ```
      LDA 202
      ADD 300
      SUB 290
      ```
   b  ```
      01000100 11000001
      01110011 00110000
      10000100 00011101
      ```
   c ```
      10 FOR J = 1 TO 10
      20 PRINT J
      30 NEXT
      ```

6  What is the difference between fourth-generation and fifth-generation programming languages?
7  What are the advantages and disadvantages of compiling compared with interpreting?
8  What is the difference between source code and object code?
9  Why is compiling (or interpreting) necessary?
      ```

2. Introduction to Pascal

A brief history of Pascal

First published in 1970, Pascal is a high-level programming language named after the famous French mathematician Blaise Pascal. It was designed to teach students structured programming concepts and to this day is the first 'real' programming language that many students are exposed to.

The layout of a typical Pascal program

Here's what a typical Pascal program looks like.

```
(1) Program first(input, output);

(2) Const
        pi = 3.14;

(3) Var
        radius: integer;
        circumference: real;
        area: real;

    Begin
        {Find the circumference and radius}
        WriteLn('Enter radius');
        ReadLn(radius);

(4)     circ:= 2 * radius * pi;
        area:= pi * radius * radius;
        WriteLn('The circumference is ',
        circ);
        WriteLn('The area is ', area);
    End.
```

1 Program header

A Pascal program typically starts with a **program header** even though the compiler won't complain if you leave it out. It normally takes one of two forms:

- `Program meaningfulname;`
- `Program meaningfulname (input, output);`

You'll see the second form more often, but either one will do. The name that you use in your program header cannot be used anywhere else in the program.

2 Constant declaration section

You won't need constants in every program but when you do, you must place them in the **constant declaration section**. This section starts with the word **Const** (short for 'constant'). You can put as many constants as you want in this section, but nothing else.

3 Variable declaration section

The word **Var** indicates the start of the **variable declaration section** – the place where you must declare any variables that you intend to use in the program. You can't use this section to do anything else besides declare variables.

> **Note**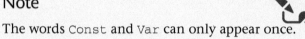
>
> The words `Const` and `Var` can only appear once.

4 The main program block

Finally there is the **main program block**, which is enclosed between the words **Begin** and **End.** (with the full stop). This is the 'meat' of the program. It contains statements which tell the computer what to do. When the computer encounters the full stop, it knows that the program is finished.

> **Note**
>
> Even though a Pascal program may contain the word END several times, only one of them will have a full stop.

Variables

Like most programming languages, Pascal requires you to declare a variable before you use it. Declaring a variable lets the computer know ahead of time what type of data it is allowed to hold. That way, the computer can make sure a user does not enter invalid data, for example typing text when the program is expecting a number.

The table shows the main data types in Pascal.

Type	Data it can hold
integer	positive and negative numbers which do NOT have a decimal point, e.g. −100, 0, 43
real	positive and negative numbers that may have a decimal point, e.g. −7.2, 0.1987, 99.0
char	a single character (letter, digit or symbol), e.g. a, Z, 9, 0, $, &, ?
string	a group of up to 255 characters
boolean	either true or false (and nothing else)

Pascal is different from most programming languages when it comes to <u>how</u> you declare a variable. There is a section <u>specifically</u> dedicated to declaring variables. A variable must be declared in this section using the following format:

```
name: type;
```

Here is an example of how you could declare some variables:

```
Var
      gender: char;
      num1, num2: integer;
      result: real;
```

Note

If two or more variables have the same type, you can declare them on the same line in order to save space.

Variable names

Pascal is fairly flexible when it comes to variable names, but as with other languages there are some rules you must follow.

1 The name must <u>not</u> contain a space.
2 A variable name must only contain letters, digits and underscores _.
3 A variable name <u>must</u> begin with a letter.
4 You cannot use a reserved word as a variable name.

Note

A **reserved word** is a word that has a special meaning to Pascal (e.g. **Program**). Some other reserved words are: **If**, **While**, **Begin** and **End**. In Turbo Pascal reserved words are shown in white.

Unlike C-like languages variables in Pascal are <u>not</u> case sensitive. This means that all of the following refer to the same variable: firstName, firstname, FIRSTNAME, FiRsTnAmE. Pascal doesn't care whether you use lowercase letters or uppercase ones.

Constants

Recall that a constant is a value that cannot and will not change throughout the execution of a program.

Pascal is unique in that is has a dedicated constant declaration section. Here's what it looks like.

```
Const
      pi = 3.142;
      VAT = 0.15;
      days_in_week = 7;
```

Notice that there are some differences from the way you declare a variable.

1 You can (and must) specify a value.
2 You don't have to specify a type. The computer can look at the value and figure out the type.
3 You use '=' instead of ':'.

Comments

If you want to put comments in a Pascal program, you place them in curly brackets { }.

```
      {circumference is pi x diameter}
      {diameter is twice the radius}
      Read(radius);                        comments
      circumference:= 2 * radius * pi;
      {calculate the circumference}
```

The computer completely ignores comments so you can put anything you want in them – even if they aren't necessarily true. For example:

```
      {I am sooooooo good looking}
```

Comments may also span several lines. For example:

```
      {This program asks the user to
enter a radius of a circle and then uses
that radius to calculate the diameter and
circumference of the circle.}
```

Note

In languages like C, C++ and Java curly brackets have a <u>completely</u> different meaning than in Pascal. They are not comments – rather, they indicate blocks of code in much the same way as Begin...End does in Pascal.

Exercise 2

1 Write suitable program headers for a program that calculates grades, using the two forms for the header shown in the chapter.

2 Which of the following variable names are allowed in Pascal? For those that are invalid, give the reason why.
   a Age
   b Item_Price
   c 1stnumber
   d Last Name
   e HeightOfPerson
   f Program

3 Which of these is the right way to declare the constant e?
   a e = 2.718
   b e: = 2.718;
   c e = 2.718;
   d e: 2.718;
   e e: real;

4 Write a variable declaration section that declares variables to store the following. Give them suitable names and appropriate types.
   a a person's address
   b a letter grade
   c the number of cars in a car park
   d a student's average grade
   e whether or not a person is married
   f job title
   g the number of tickets sold for a concert

5 What is the purpose of the full stop at the end of a Pascal program?

6 How do you write comments in a Pascal program?

3. Displaying messages on the screen

In Pascal, if you want to display messages on the screen you use the **Write** or **WriteLn** command. These correspond to the `Print` statement used in pseudocode. The two commands have a similar syntax but slightly different functionality. Most of the time you'll use `WriteLn` since it is a little more convenient.

Displaying a message

If you want the computer to display a message you must put it in single quotes. For example:

```
WriteLn('Good morning');
```

Note

Unlike most other programming languages, Pascal uses <u>single</u> quotation marks.

The computer will display the message that is <u>inside</u> the quotation marks word-for-word (but without the quotes). It doesn't care what the message is or if it makes sense. So even if the command is:

```
WriteLn('I am so smart');
```

the computer can't display:

```
Yeah, right!
```

Displaying the values of variables

Suppose you have a variable called `avg`. If you want the computer to display the value that stored in the variable, you'd use the following command:

```
WriteLn(avg);
```

Note

If you put the name of a variable in quotation marks the computer will print the <u>name</u> of the variable instead of its <u>value</u>.

If you want to display a message in addition to the value of the variable, you can do it like so:

```
WriteLn('The average is: ', avg);
WriteLn('Your total is ', sum, ' and
your average is ', avg);
WriteLn(sum, ' is your total.');
```

Suppose `sum` was 150 and `avg` was 75. Then for the above examples, the computer would display:

```
The average is: 75
Your total is 150 and your average is 75
150 is your total.
```

The difference between **Write** and **WriteLn**

The **WriteLn** command (which stands for 'write line'), displays a message on the screen and then moves down to the next line.

For example, if the following code were executed:

```
WriteLn('1');
WriteLn('2');
WriteLn('3');
```

The computer would display:

```
1
2
3
```

The **Write** command, on the other hand, does <u>not</u> move to the next line. So if you typed:

```
Write('1');
Write('2');
Write('3');
```

The computer would display:

```
123
```

Tip

If you want to print a blank line, type `WriteLn;` Notice that you don't need any brackets in this case.

Formatting real numbers

The first time you try displaying a real number you'll be in a bit of a surprise. Simple numbers like 10.2 will be displayed as 1.0200000000E+01. It's actually the same number, but in scientific notation. But how do you display real numbers in a form that <u>ordinary</u> people can understand?

Suppose you have a real variable called `Result`. Here's one way you can make it look presentable.

```
WriteLn(result:8:2);
```

That tells the computer to:

- Display `result` with 2 decimal places.
- Add additional spaces as necessary so that the result takes up <u>exactly</u> 8 characters.

The second one takes a bit of explaining so let's use an example. Suppose the result turned out to be 25.142. Since we told the computer to only display 2 decimal places, it will round the number to 25.14. That is 5 characters (including the decimal point). So the computer will put 3 additional spaces in <u>front</u> in order to make up the full 8.

Exercise 3

1 What is the difference between `Write` and `WriteLn`?

2 What is the correct way to display the message HELLO WORLD in Pascal?

  a `Print "HELLO WORLD"`
  b `WriteLn("HELLO WORLD");`
  c `WriteLn(HELLO WORLD);`
  d `WriteLn('HELLO WORLD');`

3 Suppose you wanted to display the <u>value</u> of the variable average. Why wouldn't you do it like this?

```
WriteLn('Average');
```

4 What is wrong with the highlighted line of code in following program?

```
Program exercise3a(input, output);
Var
    num: integer;
Begin
    WriteLn(number);
End.
```

5 What does the following program output?

```
Program exercise3b(input, output);
Const
    bob = 98.1234;
Begin
    Write('What does this program');
    {WriteLn('Look at this line
    carefully');}
    WriteLn('display?');
    WriteLn('Maybe this number ',
    bob: 3:3);
End.
```

4. Reading from the keyboard

In order to allow the user to type in information using the keyboard, you can use either the **Read** or the **ReadLn** Pascal commands. Just like the WriteLn command described in the previous chapter, the ReadLn command moves the cursor to a new line afterwards.

The Read and ReadLn commands use a similar syntax but ReadLn is more common so we'll use that in most of the examples.

Reading a single variable

Let's start by reading a single variable. Suppose you wanted to read a variable called fullname. Then you would type:

```
ReadLn(fullname);
```

When you run the program and the computer gets to this line, it will wait patiently for the user to type in some information. When the user presses the Enter key, the computer takes the information and stores it in the variable called fullname.

Note
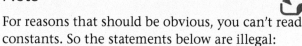

Any variables that you read <u>must</u> have been declared in the Var section.

Reading multiple variables

If you want to read multiple variables at the same time, you just separate them with commas. For example:

```
ReadLn(num1, num2, num3);
```

Now when you are <u>typing in the values</u>, you have to separate them by spaces, like so:

```
10 20 30
```

Note

Since spaces are used to separate the values, strings with spaces in them can cause problems when you are trying to read multiple variables.

Other uses for **ReadLn**

Sometimes you want the program to pause until the user presses the Enter key. One way of doing so is to use the ReadLn command without any brackets, as

shown below. In this case, you don't need to specify a variable since you aren't going to be storing anything.

```
ReadLn;
```

Note

For reasons that should be obvious, you can't read constants. So the statements below are illegal:

```
ReadLn(1);
ReadLn('Enter your name')
```

Invalid input

The ReadLn and Read commands have a major weakness – if the user enters a different type of information from what the program is expecting, your program crashes.

You can test it for yourself. Compile and run the following program.

```
Program Test(input,output);
Var
        num:integer;
Begin
        ReadLn(num);
End.
```

Instead of entering a number as the program is expecting, try entering a letter or a word. Your program will crash and give an error message. The exact error message will depend on your compiler but it may be something like 'Invalid Numeric Format'.

Note

This is an example of a **runtime error**.

The most common ways you can cause a runtime error when entering data are:

- entering text when the program is expecting a number
- entering a real number when the program is expecting an integer
- entering a number that is bigger than the type can accommodate

Unfortunately there isn't much you can do about these types of errors at this level.

Exercise 4

1 Explain what the command `ReadLn(myvar);` does.

2 Why wouldn't you read use the command `ReadLn("average");` to read the average? How should it be written instead?

3 Which of these is the correct way to read three variables?

   a `ReadLn num1, num2, num2;`
   b `Readln(num1, num2, num3);`
   c `ReadLn(num1 num2 num3);`
   d `ReadLn(num1:num2:num3);`

4 Explain why the following code would give a runtime error if the user entered 9.5.

```
Program Crashme;
Var
    num:integer;
Begin
    ReadLn(num);
End.
```

5. Assignment statements

Assignment statements allow you change the value of a variable. Assignment statements in Pascal take the following form:

`Variable:=` expression that you want to assign to the variable;

Tip

You can easily find the assignment statements in a Pascal program by looking for the := .

Here are a few examples (followed by comments).

```
Age:= 25;
Cost:= 9.99;
Sex:= 'M';        {Assigning a character
                  constant}
Name:= 'Bob';     {Assigning a string
                  constant}
Result:= 10*2;    {Storing the result of a
                  calculation}
A:= B;            {Assigning a value from
                  another variable}
count:= count+1;  {Increasing the value of
                  a variable}
```

Assignment rules

Here are some rules you must follow when writing assignment statements.

1 You can't assign something to a constant.
2 Any variables on the right-hand side should have already been assigned initial values.
3 The expression on the right of the := must be compatible with the type of variable you have on the left.

The first two points are pretty straightforward but the third is a bit more challenging. Here is a table that explains what we mean.

If the variable on the left is a	The expression on the right must work out to be...
integer	an integer
real	a real number or an integer
char	a single character or a string – if it is a string, the first character of the string is assigned to the variable
string	a string
Boolean	true or false value

Assigning values to Boolean variables

On the surface, Boolean variables don't seem very interesting since they only have two values – **true** and **false**. So a typical assignment statement might look like:

`found:= false;`

But actually, <u>any</u> expression that evaluates to true or false can be assigned to a Boolean variable. That means you can have strange looking assignment statements like the one below.

`IsGreater:= (A > B);`

This is what the computer does:

1 It tests whether A is larger than B. Depending on the values of A and B, it may be true or false.
2 Then it stores the result of the test in the variable **IsGreater**.

Calculations

You've already seen that you can assign the result of a calculation to a variable. This section will tell you how to do certain types of calculations in Pascal.

Integer division

Division in Pascal is a funny thing. <u>Every</u> time you divide using /, the result is a real number even if both numbers are integers. In fact, the following code won't even compile.

> Here is the culprit – storing a real number in an integer.

```
Program Trydivide;
Var
     num1: integer;
     num2: integer;
     result: integer;
Begin
     num1:= 10;
     num2:= 5;
     result:= num1 / num2;
     WriteLn(result);
End.
```

To get around this, Pascal has a **Div** function that allows you to perform integer division. You use it like this:

```
result:= num1 Div num2;
```

`result`, `num1` and `num2` must <u>all</u> be integers. Here are a few examples.

```
result1:= 12 Div 3; {result1 = 4}
result2:= 9 Div 4;
```

`result2` is 2 since 4 can only go into 9 twice.

Remainders

When you were doing division in primary school, you might say something like '7 divided by 2 is 3 remainder 1'. If you want to determine the remainder after one number is divided by another (i.e. the modulus) you can use Pascal's **Mod** operator.

In the line below, `r` will be assigned a value of 3 since that is the remainder you get when you try to divide 13 by 5.

```
r:= 13 Mod 5;
```

Now you may be wondering, 'What possible use would I have for the modulus function?'. Well, it turns out that it is a handy way of telling if one number is divisible by another.

Tip

To see if `num1` is divisible by `num2`, you check whether `num1 Mod num2 = 0`.

A common example is checking whether a number is even. Assuming that `isEven` is a Boolean variable, here's how you would do this:

```
isEven:= (num Mod 2 = 0);
```

`isEven` is true if and only if `num` is divisible by 2.

Exercise 5

1 Suppose `quotient` is an integer variable. Why would the following line cause an error?
```
quotient:= 10 / 5;
```
2 Write the value that would be stored in the `result` variable for each of the following calculations:

   a `result:= 25 Div 12;`
   b `result:= 25 Mod 12;`

3 Using a Boolean variable `byThree`, write a statement that checks to see if a number is divisible by 3.
4 Convert the algorithms created in Part 2 (Problem solving) Exercise 7 to Pascal programs.

6. Conditional branching

IF statements in Pascal operate following the same principle as they do in pseudocode. However, there are a few minor syntactical differences that you need to pay attention to.

If-Then

An If-Then statement in Pascal takes the following format:

```
If condition(s) Then
    single or compound statement to be executed only
    if the condition is true;
```

The condition must be written in the form: <u>something sign something else</u> as you can see in the examples below.

Condition	How you write it in Pascal
age is greater than 65.	age > 65
rating is 4 or more	rating >= 4
rating is at least 4.	
count is less than 50.	count < 50
height is less than or equal to 1.8.	height <= 1.8
grade is (equal to) A.	grade = 'A'
day is not (equal to) Sunday	day <> 'Sunday'

The following code snippet will call a person old if his or her age is more than 65.

```
If age > 65 Then
    WriteLn('Wow! You're really old!');
```

What happens when there's more than one statement to be executed if the condition is true? You need to place them in a Begin...End block so that Pascal treats them as one giant **compound statement**. This 'trick' is something you'll see time and time again in Pascal.

Here's an example that gives a 10% discount if a customer spends $100 or more.

```
If total >= 100 Then
Begin
    discount = 10/100 * total;
    total = total - discount;
    WriteLn('Customer received a
    discount of ', discount);
End;
```

Since you have three statements to be executed if the condition is true, you <u>must</u> put them in a Begin...End block. <u>Notice that there is a semicolon after the END</u>.

Tip

Although you aren't <u>required</u> to place a single statement in a Begin...End block, you are recommended to do so. It makes your code easier to read and helps you avoid tricky errors later down the road.

Conditions involving Boolean variables

Suppose you had a Boolean variable called inStock and wanted to display a message if it is true. Here is one way you could do so:

```
If inStock = True Then
Begin
    WriteLn('We have it in stock');
End;
```

There's absolutely nothing wrong with doing it this way. But since inStock is a Boolean variable, you could just as easily write:

```
If inStock Then
Begin
    WriteLn('We have it in stock');
End;
```

Remember that the message will get displayed if the condition in the If statement is true. Here, inStock <u>is</u> the condition. Therefore if inStock is true, the message will be shown.

The **And** operator

You can combine multiple conditions using the And operator. For example:

$$\underbrace{(height >= 1.8)}_{X} \quad \textbf{And} \quad \underbrace{(weight < 165)}_{Y}$$

In the above example, there are two sub-conditions (which we have called X and Y). <u>Both</u> of these sub-conditions must be true for the overall condition to be true. This is illustrated in the truth table below.

X	and	Y	Result
false		false	false
false		true	false
true		false	false
true		true	true

For example, the code below would only print 'Congratulations!' if <u>both</u> the Maths and English marks are greater than 90.

```
If (Maths > 90) And (English > 90) Then
Begin
    WriteLn('Congratulations!');
End;
```

The following IF statement checks whether a person is a teenager.

```
If (age >= 13) And (age <= 19)
```

The Or operator

The Or operator also allows you to combine multiple conditions – but the <u>overall condition will be true if</u> <u>**any** of the conditions is true</u>.

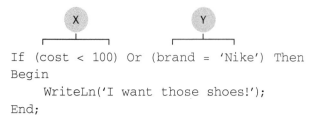

```
If (cost < 100) Or (brand = 'Nike') Then
Begin
    WriteLn('I want those shoes!');
End;
```

The If statement in the example above has two sub-conditions which (again) we will call X and Y. The truth table is given below.

X	or Y	Result
false	false	false
false	true	true
true	false	true
true	true	true

Suppose the shoes cost more than $100.00 but they are Nike shoes. It doesn't matter that the first sub-condition is false. Since the second one is true, the message is displayed.

The NOT operator

Think of the Not operator as 'the opposite'. It makes a true condition false and vice versa. Suppose you have a Boolean variable called isMarried. Then you can say:

```
If Not isMarried Then
```

Of course, this is the same thing as:

```
If isMarried = False Then
```

Which one you use is a matter of preference.

If-Then-Else

If-Then-Else statements in Pascal look almost the way you'd expect them to:

```
If condition(s) Then
    single or compound statement to be executed only
    if the condition is true
Else
    another single or compound statement to be
    executed only if the condition is false;
```

Code to print whether a person passed or failed an exam would be written like this:

```
If mark >= 50 Then
    WriteLn('You passed')   ← No semicolon
Else
    WriteLn('You failed');
End;
```

Or like this:

```
If mark >= 50 Then
Begin
    WriteLn('You passed');
End ←                        No semicolon
Else
Begin
    WriteLn('You failed');
End;
```

If-Then-Else-If

You can make an `If-Then-Else-If` construct by having multiple `If-Then-Else` statements, as in the following example.

```
If mark >= 80 Then
Begin
    WriteLn('Grade A');
End ◄──────────────── No semicolon
Else If mark >= 65 Then
Begin
    WriteLn('Grade B');
End ◄──────────────── No semicolon
Else If mark >= 50 Then
Begin
    WriteLn('Grade C');
End ◄──────────────── No semicolon
Else
Begin
    WriteLn('Fail');
End;
```

Note

The only `End` that has a semicolon is the last one in the `If-Then-Else-If` construct. That is because it indicates the end of the construct.

Exercise 6

1 What is wrong with the following `IF` construct? How would you rectify it?
```
If numHours > 40 then
    overtimeHours = numHours - 40;
    overtimePay = overtimeHours * rate
    * 1.5;
    WriteLn('Your overtime pay is: ',
    overtimePay);
```

2 Correct this `If-Then-Else` construct.
```
If numHours >= 40 then
    WriteLn('You deserve a break!');
Else
    WriteLn('Slacker!!!')
```

3 What's wrong with the condition $8 < x < 10$? Change it so that it is correct.

4 Suppose $x = 10$ and $y = 20$. Which of the following conditions would be true?
   a `x <= 10`
   b `x <> 10`
   c `y <> 14`
   d `x > y`
   e `(x <= 10) AND (x > y)`
   f `(x = 10) AND (x < y)`
   g `(x < 10) OR (x > y)`
   h `(x <=10) OR (x > y)`

5 Draw truth tables for `X OR Y` and `X And Y`.

6 Convert the algorithms obtained in Part 2 (Problem Solving) Exercise 8 to Pascal programs.

7. Loops

Recall that loops allow you to repeat instructions as long as some condition is true. Let's look at how you implement loops in Pascal.

The `For` loop

The structure of a Pascal `For` loop is:

```
For variable := startValue to endValue do
        single or compound statement to be repeated;
```

Here is an example:

```
{Prints the message 'Hello World' 100 times}
For i := 1 to 100 do
Begin
        WriteLn('Hello World');
End;
```

Since there is only one line to be repeated, you could also write it like this:

```
For i := 1 to 100 do
        WriteLn('Hello World');
```

Pascal also has an alternative version that you can use if the loop variable is <u>decreasing</u>.

```
For variable := startValue downto endValue do
        single or compound statement to be repeated;
```

The following example shows how you could count backwards.

```
For i := 5 downto 1 do
Begin
        writeLn(i);
End;
WriteLn('We have lift-off!');
```

What that would print is:

```
5
4
3
2
1
We have lift-off!
```

The `While` loop

The structure of a Pascal `While` loop is:

```
While condition(s) do
        single or compound statement to be repeated;
```

The following snippet keeps reading a number and printing its square until the user enters 999.

```
Read(num);
While num <> 999 do
Begin
        Square := num * num;
        WriteLn(Square);
        Read(num);
End;
```

Note

If you forget to put a read statement inside the `While` loop, your program could be stuck in an **endless loop**. If this happens, press Ctrl + Break to force the program to stop.

The `Repeat-Until` loop

The `Repeat-Until` loop is another type of loop that Pascal provides. It is like a `While` loop but with the condition at the bottom. This means that the <u>statements in a `Repeat-Until` loop, unlike those in a `While` loop, are guaranteed to run at least once.</u>
A `Repeat-Until` loop looks like this:

```
Repeat
        Statement;
        Statement;
        ...
        Statement;
Until Condition;
```

Note

Unlike other Pascal control structures, you do <u>not</u> have to use `Begin`...`End` blocks if you have multiple statements in a `Repeat-Until` loop. The following example will keep prompting the user until he or she enters a number that is greater than 0.

```
Repeat
        Write('Enter number greater than 0');
        ReadLn(num);
Until num > 0;
```

Tip

You can use code like this to ensure that the user enters valid data.

Exercise 7a

1. What is the difference between a `Repeat-Until` loop and a `While` loop?

2. Fix the syntax errors in this `For` loop.

   ```
   For US = 1..10
       BDS:= US * 1.98;
       WriteLn(BDS);
   ```

3. Fix this `While` loop so that it won't loop endlessly.

   ```
   Read age;
   While age > 0 do
   Begin
       If age < 13 then
               WriteLn('Child');
   End;
   ```

4. Fix the syntax error in this `Repeat` loop

   ```
   Repeat
       A:= A + 1;
       B:= A * 2;
       C:= A + B;
       D:= C - 10;
       WriteLn(A,B,C);
   Until A > 20 do
   ```

5. Write a program that reads two numbers and divides the first number by the second. Use a loop that keeps asking the user to re-enter the second number until the user enters a non-zero value.

Exercise 7b

Convert the algorithms obtained in Part 2 (Problem Solving) Exercise 9 to Pascal programs.

Exercise 7c

Convert the algorithms obtained in Part 2 (Problem Solving) Exercise 10 to Pascal programs.

Exercise 7d

Convert the algorithms obtained in Part 2 (Problem Solving) Exercise 11 to Pascal programs.

Exercise 7e

Convert the algorithms obtained in Part 2 (Problem Solving) Exercise 12 to Pascal programs.

8. Arrays

Declaring arrays

Take a look at the following array declaration:
```
Var
        numList: array[1..10] of integer;
```
Let's break it down:

- `array [1..10]` tells the computer that the array will have 10 elements. The first element will have an index of 1; the last will have an index of 10.
- `of integer` tells the computer to make it an array of <u>integers.</u>

Working with arrays

Just like with pseudocode, in order to work with a particular element in an array, place its index in square brackets. For example:

- `numList[6];`
- `numList[index];`

Note

Always make sure that the index is in bounds. So in our example, we couldn't have `numList[0]` or `numList[11]`. <u>If</u> we did it would cause an error.

Linear search

For a practical example of working with arrays, let's take a look at linear searching. This is the most basic searching algorithm – you start at the beginning of the list (or array in our case) and examine each element until you find what you are looking for.

Normally functionality such as linear searching would be enclosed in a separate function so that it can easily be reused. However, since functions are beyond the scope of this course, we'll put it in the main program instead.

The program is listed below.

```
Program linear_search;

Const
  NumItems = 10; {the number of items}

Var
  list: array[1..NumItems] of integer;
  SearchItem: integer; {the num to find}
  found: boolean; {whether it was found}
  index: integer;

Begin
  {Get some numbers from the user}
  WriteLn('Enter ', NumItems, ' items');
  For index:= 1 to NumItems do
    ReadLn(list[index]);

  {Ask which number to search for}
  Write('What number do you want to find?');
  ReadLn(SearchItem);

  {Search for the item}
  Found:= false;
  index:= 1; {start at the beginning}
  While (index <= NumItems) and (not found) do
  Begin
    If list[index] = SearchItem then
      found:= true
    Else
      index:= index + 1;
  End;

  {Display the results}
  If found then
    WriteLn ('Item found at position ',index)
  Else
    WriteLn ('Item is not in list');
End.
```

Exercise 8

1 Which of the following lines correctly declares an array named `stack` that can hold 10 integers.

   a `stack[10];`

   b `stack: integer[10];`

   c `stack: array[1 to 10];`

   d `stack: array[1 to 10] of integer;`

   e `stack: array[1..10] of integer;`

2 Suppose the first element in an array called `myArray` had an index of 1. How would you reference it?

   a `myArray[1]`

   b `myArray(1)`

   c `myArray<0>`

   d `myArray{1}`

3 Convert the problem statements from Part 2 (Problem Solving) Exercise 14 to Pascal programs.

4 This is a Bonus Question that only truly gifted programmers will get. Rewrite the linear search program given in this chapter <u>without</u> using a Found variable.

   <u>Hint</u>: Index is only greater than `numItems` if the item was not found.

9. Documentation

It is essential to document programs properly – both for the user and for any programmer who has to maintain it (including yourself). The most obvious reason to document a program is to help the user learn how to use your program properly. But documentation is also of tremendous benefit to programmers. It helps programmers to:

- understand (or remember) what each section of code does
- see any assumptions that were made when writing the program
- be made aware of any peculiarities the program may have

There are two main types of documentation: internal and external.

Internal documentation

Internal documentation is documentation that is inside the source code of the program. Below are various methods that programmers use to provide internal documentation.

Comments

The reason why comments exist in the first place is to facilitate internal documentation. If you have a tricky section of code you can sprinkle comments throughout it, explaining each step along the way. Programmers also use comments to explain what a particular variable stores.

Although comments are useful, you don't have to comment <u>everything</u>. Instead, you usually only comment things that someone reasonably familiar with the programming language would <u>not</u> know.

The following is an example of excessive commenting (which isn't very useful):

```
Var
     num: integer; {Declares num as an
integer value}
Begin {start the main program body}
     num:= 1; {set num to 1}
End. {end of the program}
```

Self-explanatory variable names

A simple trick that can save you a lot of commenting is to use self-explanatory variable names. That way, when the programmer sees the variable, he or she automatically knows what it does. For example

numIntegers is clearly the number of integers. To make it easier to recognise the words in the variable name, either:

- capitalise the first letter of each word except the first, as was done with numIntegers

or

- put underscores between the words, for example num_integers

Indentation

You may have noticed that there is a lot of indentation in the Pascal source code for the previous chapters. For example:

```
Var
     num1, num2: integer;
Begin
     If num1 > num2  Then
          WriteLn('Num 1 is larger')
     Else
          WriteLn('Num 1 is not larger');
End.
```

This is something programmers do to make it easier to read the code. Isn't the code above much easier to understand than the code below?

```
Var
num1, num2: Integer;
Begin
If num1 > num2  Then
WriteLn('Num 1 is larger')
Else
WriteLn('Num 1 is not larger');
End.
```

The indentation helps you to identify quickly which code is inside a particular construct and which isn't. It is convention to indent:

- code between a Begin ... End block
- declarations in the Var and Const sections
- the code in the If and Else parts of If statements
- the code inside loops

Effective use of white spaces

White spaces are things like blank lines and spaces. These can be used to visually divide your code into sections, making it easier for programmers to identify which pieces of code are related to a particular task.

External documentation

External documentation is documentation that is outside the program's source code. The two main types of documentation are user manuals and technical manuals.

User manuals

User manuals tell the user how to use the program. They may include:

- the hardware and software requirements of the program
- instructions on how to install and start the program
- explanations on what certain menu and toolbar items do
- instructions on how to use certain features
- troubleshooting guides

Technical manuals

These documents are meant for programmers and explain how the program was written so that future modifications can be made. A technical manual may include:

- the algorithm
- a program listing
- test cases and expected results
- information about data file structures
- known problems and workarounds

Exercise 9

1 What is the difference between internal and external documentation?
2 List four techniques used for internal documentation.
3 What are the two main examples of external documentation?
4 List four things you would expect to find in:
   a user manuals
   b technical manuals

Part 4

Microsoft Word

1. Introduction to Microsoft Word

Microsoft Word is a type of general purpose application software known as a **word processor**. This means that it allows you to create and edit documents such as letters, reports, and so on. It can usually be found under the Microsoft Office group of programs on the Start Menu.

At the time of writing, the most common versions are Word 2003 and 2007. Unfortunately there are quite a few differences between the two versions. Whenever the two differ, instructions for both versions will be given.

The Word 2003 interface

Tip

If Figure 1.1 doesn't look like your version of Microsoft Word, skip ahead to the Word 2007 Interface section.

Like other Microsoft Office 2003 programs, and indeed most Windows programs in general, the Word 2003 interface uses menus and toolbars. Let us look at the key interface features one by one.

Control Menu icon

The Control Menu icon, located at the left side of the Title bar, appears as a stylised letter 'W'. While you won't use it often, it provides a pull-down menu that allows you to Maximize, Minimize, Restore, Resize, Move or Close the Word window.

Title bar

The Title bar is the first bar from the top of the screen. In addition to displaying the Control Menu icon, it displays three buttons in the right-hand corner.

From the left, these are:

- the Minimize button, which reduces Word to an icon on the taskbar
- the Maximize button, which resizes Word so that it takes up the whole screen. When Word is maximized, the Restore button 🗗 is displayed instead, which restores Word to its previous size
- the Close button, which closes Word

Menu bar

This is where the menus that allow you to perform various tasks in Microsoft Word are displayed. Each

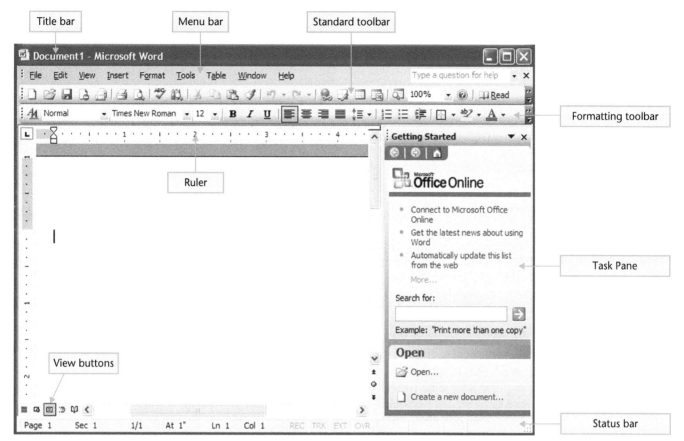

Figure 1.1 *The Word 2003 interface*

menu has a letter underlined, which you can use to access the menu more quickly. For example, since the 'F' in File is underlined, you can quickly access the file menu by pressing the Alt key (to activate the Menu bar) and then pressing F.

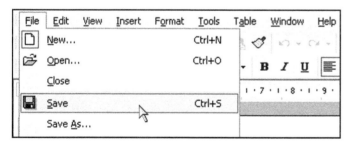

Figure 1.2 *Menu bar with File menu activated*

- File – allows you to perform various file-related tasks, for example open, save, exit and print (see Figure 1.2)
- Edit – allows you to perform basic editing tasks, for example copying and pasting; allows you to undo commands
- View – allows you to change the appearance of the Microsoft Word window, for example by showing or hiding toolbars

- Insert – inserts things such as pictures, page breaks or the current date into the current Word document
- Format – formats the appearance of the document, for example fonts, paragraphs, numbering, and borders
- Tools – provides access to tools such as Spelling and Grammar checks and the Mail Merge Wizard
- Table – allows you to access all the table-related options, for example inserting and deleting rows or columns
- Window – provides an alternate way of switching between open Word windows
- Help – provides help; allows you to see the current Microsoft Word version

Note

Another Close ('X') button also appears on this bar. Use this button when you only want to close the current Word document.

Toolbars

Toolbars provide easy access to common commands, so you don't have to remember which menu contains which command. Each toolbar button usually contains an icon (a small picture) to let you know what command it represents.

By default, Word displays two toolbars: the Standard toolbar and the Formatting toolbar.

The **Standard toolbar** has buttons for basic tasks such as creating, opening and saving documents, copying and pasting, undo and redo. The **Formatting toolbar** allows you to format the appearance of the document.

Displaying/Hiding toolbars

Microsoft Word 2003 provides several other toolbars to use for various tasks. However, in order to maximize screen space, very few of them are displayed at any given time. You may show/hide a particular toolbar at any time by doing the following:

- Click View, Toolbars.
- Click the menu item for the desired toolbar. If the toolbar was not currently being shown, it will now be displayed and a check mark will be placed next to its menu item. Otherwise it will now be hidden.

So in the example in Figure 1.3, the Formatting toolbar is currently visible. But when the Formatting option is clicked, the Formatting toolbar will be hidden.

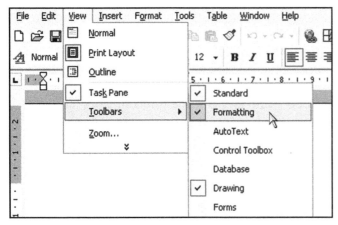

Figure 1.3 *Displaying/hiding toolbars*

Task Pane

By default, the Task Pane appears on the right of the Word 2003 window. (In Word 2007, it will only appear in certain circumstances.) Microsoft Word has a variety of task panes, each of which guides you through a particular task.

To switch to another task pane:

- Display the Task Pane menu by clicking the down arrow in the top right-hand corner of the Task Pane.
- Click the name of the desired task pane.

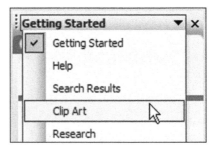

Figure 1.4 *Changing the task pane*

Note

If you don't see the Task Pane, you can display it by clicking View, Task Pane.

The Word 2007 interface

As you can see in Figure 1.5, the Word 2007 interface doesn't look like that of a standard Windows program. It doesn't have any menus or toolbars per se. Instead, it combines the two into something called The Ribbon.

The Ribbon

Your ribbon may not look <u>exactly</u> like this because items get resized according to how much space your screen has.

The Ribbon is divided into a number of tabs. These include:

- Home – which contains the most common options
- Insert – where you go anytime you want to Insert something.
- Page Layout – which allows you to change page settings such as the margins, paper size and orientation

There are also some tabs that Word will only display when you need them (e.g. the Picture tab). You will probably find the Ribbon to be pretty smart. As you work, Word 2007 tries to guess what options you need, and displays the appropriate tab to suit. So for example, when you insert a picture, the Ribbon automatically switches to the Picture tab.

The buttons on the tabs are grouped into logical sections. In Figure 1.6 you can see three sections: Clipboard, Font and Paragraph.

At the bottom-right of some sections, you'll see this button ⌐. Clicking it will give you more options to choose from. For example, if you click the one in the Font section, it will open the Font Options window.

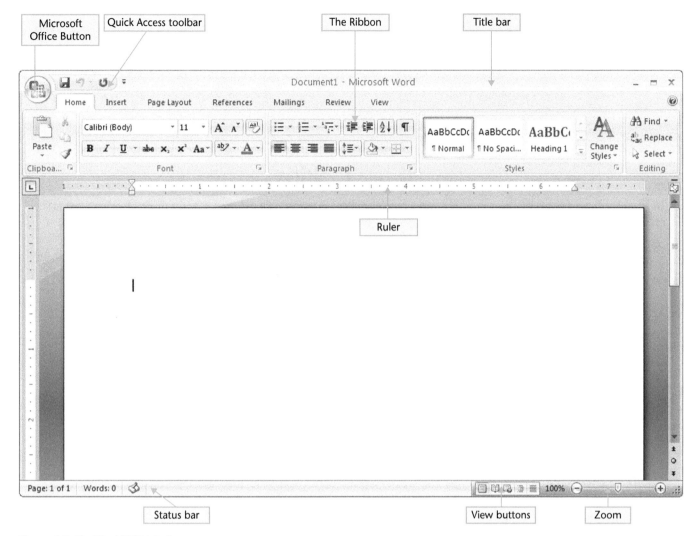

Figure 1.5 *The Word 2007 Interface*

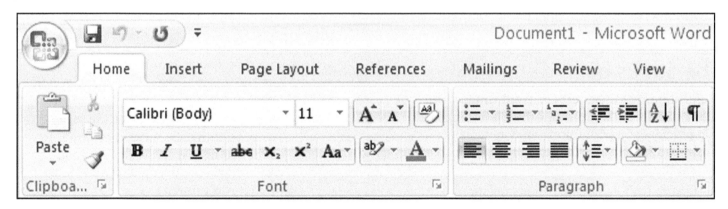

Figure 1.6 *The Word 2007 Ribbon*

The Microsoft Office button

To the top left of the Ribbon is the Microsoft Office button. Clicking this button will display the Microsoft Office menu. This menu has the items you'd find in a typical File menu, for example New, Open, Save, Print, and Close.

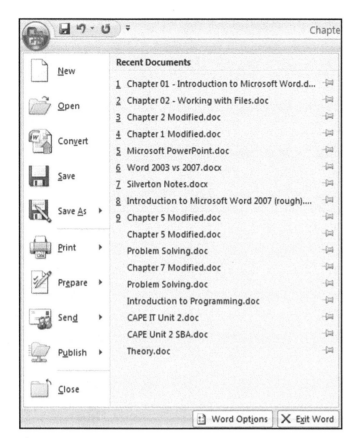

Figure 1.7 *The Microsoft Office menu*

The Quick Access toolbar

This toolbar contains buttons that allow you to quickly:

- save the document
- undo the last thing you did
- redo the last thing you undid

The Status bar

At the bottom of the Microsoft Word window – it doesn't matter which version – there is a Status bar that provides you with information about your document. Here's some of the information you can find on the Status bar:

- the number of pages in your document
- what page you are currently on
- whether or not there are any spelling errors – if there are any errors, this indicator will show an 'X'
- the line and column position (<u>Word 2003 only</u>)
- an indicator (OVR) that tells you if Overtype mode is on (<u>Word 2003 only</u>)
- the word count (<u>Word 2007 only</u>)

Note

By default, the Word 2007 Status bar displays a lot less information than the Word 2003 one.

Tooltips

Both versions of Word have so many buttons on the screen that you can forget what some of them do. If you want to see what a button does, just leave the mouse pointer over it for a few seconds. After a while, a little box pops up telling you what the item does (Figure 1.8). This is called a **tooltip**.

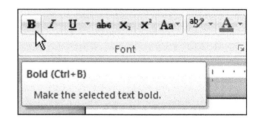

Figure 1.8 *An example of a tooltip*

Note

In Word 2003, tooltips are yellow.

Switching views

Regardless of your version of Word, at the bottom of the window are tiny buttons that allow you to switch between different views.

 Print Layout – This is the default view. The good thing about it is that while you're typing you can get a very good idea of how your document would look when it was printed.

 Draft/Normal Layout – This view allows you to type on a clean screen without worrying about headers, footers or page numbers getting in the way.

Reading Layout – This is the best view to use if you are reading a lengthy document.

Web Layout – Whenever you are working with a webpage, Word will switch to this layout. It shows you what your document would look like in a web browser.

 Outline – This view comes in handy when you don't know what to write but want to create an outline to help organise your thoughts. It makes it very easy to structure your document using different types of headings.

Exiting Microsoft Word

To exit Microsoft Word:

- Click the File menu or the Microsoft Office button.
- Click Exit.

Note

If there are any unsaved changes, a dialogue box will prompt you to save them.

2. Working with files

Creating a new document

Whenever you start Microsoft Word, it automatically creates a new blank document for you to work with. The first document is called 'Document1', the second 'Document2', and so on. If you want to create a new document <u>manually</u> you'd follow the steps below.

Word 2003

To create a new blank document in Microsoft Word 2003:

- Click File, New.
- In the New Document task pane which appears, click on Blank Document.

Figure 2.1 *The New Document Task Pane*

Alternatively, you can click the New icon in the Standard toolbar.

Word 2007

- Click the Microsoft Office button.
- Click New.
- Make sure the Blank document option is selected in the window that appears.
- Click the Create button in the bottom right-hand corner.

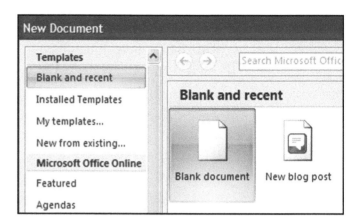

Figure 2.2 *Creating a New Blank Document in Word 2007*

Opening an existing document

To open an existing Word document:

- Click on the File menu or the Microsoft Office button.
- Click Open.
- Choose the file from the Open window.

The main part of the Open window lists the folders and documents in the current location (which is displayed in the Look in box). There are several ways you change this location:

1 by clicking on one of the common locations to the left of the Window
2 by using the Look In combo box
3 by double-clicking on the name of a folder

Once you have found the file you want to open, you can double-click it to open it, or select it and click the Open button.

Note

The Open button will be disabled until you select an item.

Saving a document

In order to save a document:

- Click File or the Microsoft Office button.
- Click Save.

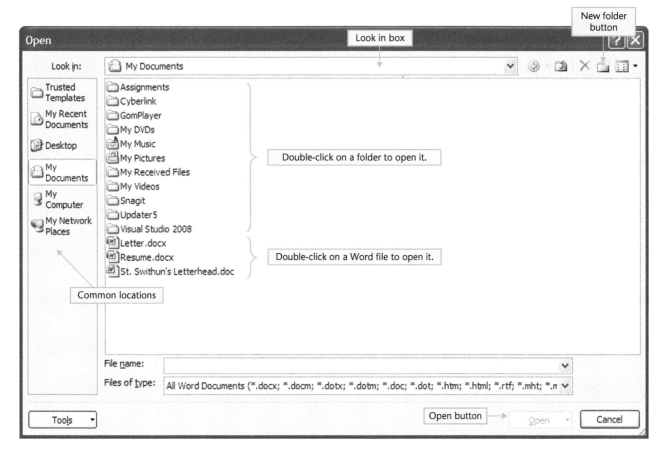

Figure 2.3 *The Open window*

• If this is your first time saving the document, the Save As window will appear. You will then have to type the name of the file and choose the location where it is to be saved.

In Word 2003, you can also click the Save button in the Standard toolbar.

Saving documents in Word 2007

Microsoft Word 2007 has introduced a new (.docx) format. Unfortunately, previous versions of Word can't read this format without a converter. So when you are saving your Word documents, you should ensure that the file type is set to the Word 97-2003 (*.doc) format, as shown in Figure 2.4.

Saving under a new name/type

If you want to save a file under a new name:

• Click on the File menu (or the Microsoft Office button).
• Click Save As.
• Go to the folder where you want to store the file.
• Type the new name of the file.
• Click Save when you're done.

Note

In Word 2007, there is also an option to Save As Word 97-2003 format.

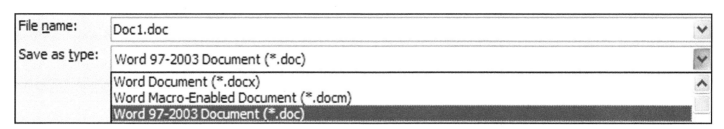

Figure 2.4 *Changing the file type*

Closing a document

In order to close the current Microsoft Word document:

- Click on the File menu (the Microsoft Office button in Word 2007).
- Click Close.

Note

If there are any unsaved changes, a dialogue box will prompt you to save them.

Moving around the document

The user can move around the document in the ways shown in Figure 2.5.

- Click the up/down arrow in the vertical scroll bar.
- Click the left/right arrow in the horizontal scroll bar.
- Drag the scroll box (on the vertical scroll bar) in the desired direction to jump to another page in your document. (Note: Use the page number label that appears to guide you.)
- Drag the scroll box (on the horizontal scroll bar) in the desired direction to move the document left or right on the screen.

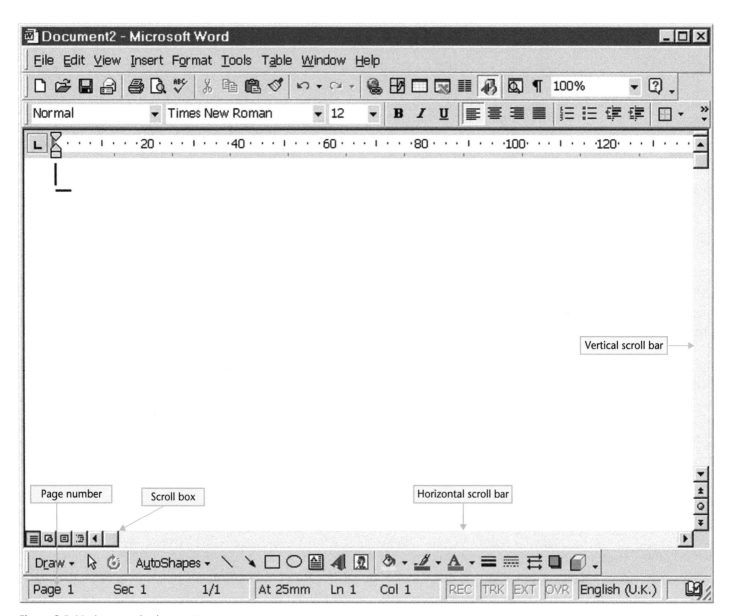

Figure 2.5 *Moving around a document*

- Double-click the page number on the Status bar.
    - Type the page number required.
    - Click Go To or press Enter.
    - Click the Close button.
- Pressing the Ctrl + Home keys together moves the cursor to the beginning of the document while pressing Ctrl + End moves the cursor to the end of the document.
- Press the PgDn key (or Page Down on some keyboards) to jump down the document one screen-length at a time.
- Press the PgUp key (or Page Up on some keyboards) to jump up the document one screen-length at a time.
- The End key moves the cursor to the end of a line, whereas the Home key moves the cursor to the beginning of a line.
- Hold down the Ctrl key and press the up or down arrow keys to jump up or down a paragraph.
- Press the down arrow key to move down one line in your document.
- Press the up arrow key to move up one line in your document.

Exercise 2

Retrieve the Media file from your class folder.

Use the keyboard for the following:

1 Move the cursor to the end of the document.
2 Move the cursor to the beginning of the last line in the document.
3 Move up one line in the document.
4 Place the cursor at the beginning of the document.

Use the mouse for the following:

5 Drag the scroll box to view the end of the document.
6 Use the up arrow in the vertical scroll bar to view the beginning of the document.
7 Double-click on the page number on the Status bar to display the Go To option.
8 Close the Go To option.
9 Close the file without saving.

3. Typing text

The cursor

Near the top of the Microsoft Word work area you'll see a short vertical black line blinking on and off. This is called the **cursor** and it indicates your current position in the document. When you type something on your keyboard, it will go where the cursor is positioned.

You can move the cursor using the arrow keys on your keyboard or by clicking the mouse where you want the cursor to go.

Note

You can't move the cursor beyond the end of the document unless you press the Enter key.

In Figure 3.1, the cursor is between the 't' and 'o' in the word 'to' in the bottom line.

Getting text on a new line

When you are typing text, you don't normally have to do anything to get it to wrap around to a new line. If you type more than can fit on a line, Microsoft Word will automatically flow the text onto a new line. This feature is called **word wrapping**. In Figure 3.1 the word 'Microsoft' couldn't fit on the first line so it went down on the next line.

However, if you want to force the cursor down on a new line – for example to type a new paragraph – , you can press the Enter key. In Figure 3.1, if you press the Enter key, it will force the part that says 'o press the Enter key' onto a new line.

Typing rules

Here are a few rules to follow when you are typing:

- Leave one space after a comma.
- It doesn't matter whether you leave one space or two after a full stop as long as you are consistent.
- In Word 2003 press Enter twice before typing a new paragraph. In Word 2007, press it once.

Erasing text

The two keys that you use to erase text are:

- the Backspace key, which erases the text to the left of the cursor. In Figure 3.1, if you pressed the Backspace key it would erase the 't'.
- the Delete key, which erases text to the right of the cursor. If you pressed Delete in Figure 3.1, it would erase the 'o'.

Note

You can also erase new lines that were created as a result of pressing the Enter key.

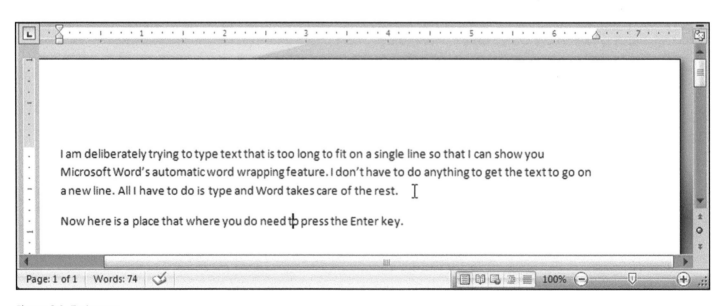

Figure 3.1 *Typing text*

Typing capital letters

There are two ways to type capital letters:

- using the CAPS LOCK key – This key works like a switch. Press it once to turn it on and press it again to turn it off. Once it is on, any letters than you type will appear in ALL CAPS.
- using the Shift key – If CAPS LOCK is off, holding down the Shift key while you type will give you uppercase letters. If CAPS LOCK is on, holding down Shift will give lowercase letters.

Typing symbols

On the upper part of certain keys such as the number keys, you'll see symbols, for example $, !, %, &, (, ?, < and '. If a key is marked with two characters and you type normally, you'll get the lower character. To get the upper character, hold down the Shift key and press the key. Try typing the following:

Customer: 'How much do the shoes cost?'
Vendor: 'They're $195 a pair.'
Customer: 'That much? That's practically $200 a pair!'

The Num Lock key

To the right of the keyboard, you'll see the numeric key pad. To use the numbers on the keypad, Num Lock must be turned on.

Typing modes

There are two operation modes in Microsoft Word. These modes may be used to assist the user in the typing and/or editing of text. These modes are the Insert mode and the Overwrite/Overtype mode.

The Insert mode

The Insert mode is the default mode of Word. This means that when you type, your newly typed text will be inserted, pushing existing text to the right.

The Overwrite/Overtype mode

The Overwrite/Overtype mode is an alternative to the Insert mode and is activated and de-activated by double-clicking the OVR button that is on the status bar. When this is done, any text that is typed wipes out the existing text. So, remember to de-activate it after you have completed your task.

AutoComplete

The AutoComplete feature assists the user in the typing process via the automatic completion of text, recognised by the first few characters typed. Once recognition is achieved, a box appears on the screen with the complete word/phrase. To accept the entry, the user simply stops typing and presses the Enter key.

To ignore the entry, the user must continue typing. Examples of AutoComplete text are months of the year, days of the week, and the current date.

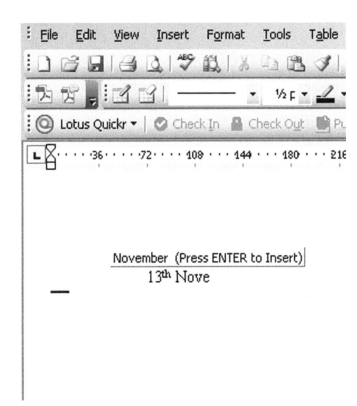

Figure 3.2 *AutoComplete*

Undoing mistakes

When you make a mistake, you can undo it by clicking the Undo button.

- To undo the last thing you did, click on the Undo button itself.
- To undo several things at once, click on the down arrow next to the Undo button and select how many actions you want to undo.

In the example shown in Figure 3.3, if we click the mouse, we will undo the last two actions.

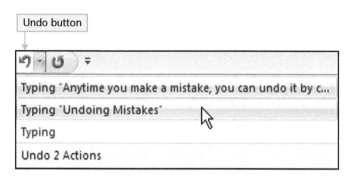

Figure 3.3 *Undoing actions*

Spelling errors

When you start typing, some of your text will appear underlined with a red squiggly line. That means that the underlined word is either spelt incorrectly or Microsoft Word isn't familiar with that word. You'll learn more about Word's spelling and grammar features in Chapter 6.

Exercise 3

Type the following document and save it to a file called `Insure` in your class folder. (<u>Note</u>: This document contains two errors; please type the document exactly as it appears.) Also save an identical copy of the file using the filename `Assure`.

INSURANCE DOCUMENTS AND TERMINOLOGY

PROPOSAL
A to the insurers to provide cover.

POLICY
A document setting out the terms to the insurance contract which provides evidence of the contract.

CERTIFICATE
An additional document used in Motor, Marine and Employer Liability incorporating elements of the contract and without which the insurance is not legal.

CLAIMS FORM
A form setting out the grounds for a claim, so that the company can decide whether it comes under the terms of the policy.

SCHEDULE
Within a given class of business (e.g. Life, Fire, Accident, Motor) each company issues standard policies, identical to each other, and divided into defined sections. The schedule contains all the information that is peculiar to that individual risk.

COVER NOTE
It normally takes some time between a proposal and the exact definition of the policy by the underwriters; during this time, legally there is no cover. This is supplied by the issue of a memorandum from the company which gives temporary legal cover.

SUM ASSURED
In some forms of insurance, e.g. Life, there can be no indemnity as such, as the financial loss of life cannot be estimated. Therefore a sum assured is covered related not to damage sustained but directly to premium. This is the sum assured.

4. Selecting text

Selecting text tells the software that the changes are to be made to this text only. This can be done in two ways:

- using the mouse
- using the keyboard

Selecting text with the mouse

Selecting a word

- Double-click on the word.

Selecting a paragraph

- Position the mouse pointer anywhere within the paragraph
- Triple-click.

Or

- Position the mouse pointer in the left margin next to the paragraph (the pointer appears as an arrow).
- Double-click.

Selecting a line

- Position the mouse pointer in the left margin next to the line (the pointer appears as an arrow).
- Click once.

Note

To deselect text, click in a blank part of the work area.

Selecting a phrase/section

- Move the mouse pointer to one end of the text you want to select (the pointer appears in this form: **I**).
- Hold down the left mouse button and drag the pointer to the other end of the text.
- Release the mouse button.

Note

If you release the mouse before all the required text is selected, you should click in a blank section of the document and try again.

Selecting text with the keyboard

The table lists the functions used to select different parts of a document with keyboard commands.

To select	Use function
entire document	press Ctrl + A
entire paragraph	press Shift + Ctrl + the up/down arrow
one line	press Shift + the up/down arrow
one word	press Shift + Ctrl + the left or right arrow
one page	press Shift + Page Up/Page Down key

Note

To deselect text, press any of the cursor control (arrow) keys.

Changing text

- Select the text.
- Type the new text.

Note

It is safer to do this when the Overtype mode is off because if the Overtype mode is on and the text being typed is more than the original text, the excess text will overwrite original text that was not even selected.

Deleting text

- Select the text.
- Press the delete key.

Exercise 4

Retrieve the `Insure` document from your class folder. Carry out the following instructions on the text in this file.

1 Using the Insert mode, add the word 'request' between 'A' and 'to' in the first sentence.
2 Using the Overwrite mode, change the word 'to' to 'of' in the second sentence of the document.

Perform the following steps using the mouse:

3 Double-click on the heading CERTIFICATE.
4 Select the paragraph under the heading SUM ASSURED.
5 Select the last sentence in the document.

Perform the following steps using the keyboard:

6 Select the entire document.
7 Select the first sentence in the document.
8 Select the heading POLICY.
9 Update the `Insure` document.

5. Editing and formatting text

In this chapter you will learn how to edit and format text.

When you edit text, you change its <u>structure</u>. For example, you can copy text from one location to another or move it altogether.

When you format text, you change its <u>appearance</u>. For example, you may underline it or change its color.

Formatting text

You can format text via the Formatting toolbar in Word 2003 (Figure 5.1) or the Home tab in Word 2007 (Figure 5.1).

Note

When you want to format <u>existing</u> text, the first step is usually to select it.

Bold, italics and underline

You can use the three buttons in Figure 5.3 to respectively:

- make the text **bold**
- put it in *italics*
- or <u>underline it</u>

Each one of these buttons works like a switch – click it once to turn it on, click it again to turn it off. When a button is on, it is highlighted in orange.

Aligning data

The alignment buttons (shown in Figure 5.4) control the alignment of the text, i.e. whether it is to the left, centred, or laid out in another way. By default, text is aligned to the left.

Figure 5.4 *The alignment buttons*

Unlike the Bold, Italics and Underline buttons, only one of these may be on at a time.

Tip

The lines in the alignment buttons represent lines of text. So you can tell what a button does by just looking at it. For example, since the lines in the first button are lined up to the left, this is the Align Left button.

Figure 5.1 *The Word 2003 Formatting toolbar*

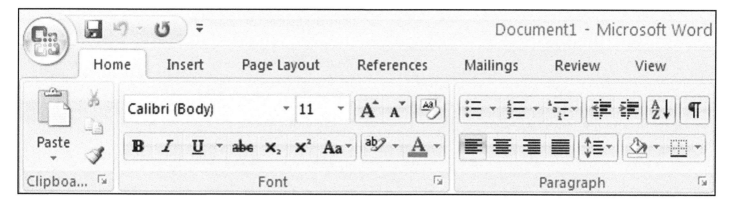

Figure 5.2 *The Home tab of the Ribbon (Word 2007)*

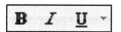

Figure 5.3 *The Bold, Italics and Underline buttons*

Changing the font and font size

Fonts are just styles of type. Microsoft Word comes with several fonts installed, for example:

- Times New Roman (size 12) is the default font in Word 2003.
- Calibri (size 11) is the default in Word 2007.
- **Arial Black is great for headings.**
- Comic Sans MS is a nice casual font.

Microsoft Word provides combo boxes that look similar to the ones below which allow you to change the font and the font size. (In Word 2003 they would say 'Times New Roman' and '12' respectively.)

A **combo box** looks like text box with a down arrow on the right. You can type in the text box portion or click the arrow in order to get a list to choose from.

Click here to see the list of fonts.

Figure 5.5 *The Font and Font Size combo boxes*

To change the font:

- Click the down arrow at the right of the Font combo box.
- Choose the font you want from the list.

To change the font size either:

- Choose the size you want from the Font Size combo box.

Or

- Type the size directly into the text box portion.

Note

The bigger the number, the bigger the text will be.

Line spacing

To change the amount of space that appears between the lines in a paragraph:

- Select the text.
- Click the line spacing button.
- Select the line spacing you want.

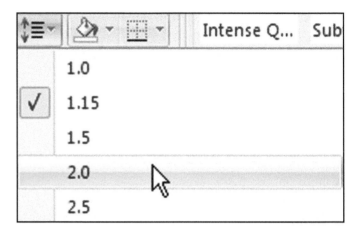

Figure 5.6 *Adjusting the line spacing*

Note

The default line spacing in Word 2003 is 1 whereas the default in Word 2007 is 1.15.

Changing the case of text

Suppose you have some existing text that you want to place in uppercase. Rather than erase the text and type it over, you can take advantage of a Word feature that allows you to change the case of text.

Word 2003

To change the case of text in Microsoft Word 2003 or earlier:

- Select the text.
- Click Format, Change Case...
- Select the case you want, then click OK.

Word 2007

In Word 2007 the steps are a little bit different.

- Select the text.
- Click the Change Case button.
- Select the case you want.

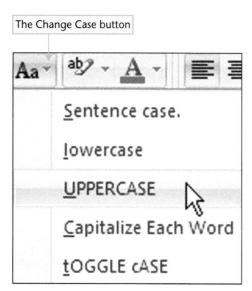

The Change Case button

Figure 5.7 *Changing Case in Word 2007*

The table explains what each of the Change Case options does.

Option	What it does
Sentence case	Puts the first letter in uppercase and the rest in lowercase
lowercase	Makes the selected text lowercase
UPPERCASE	MAKES THE SELECTED TEXT UPPERCASE
tOGGLE cASE	cHANGES aLL tHE lOWERCASE lETTERS tO uPPERCASE aND vICE vERSA
Title Case (2003) Capitalize Each Word (2007)	Capitalizes The First Letter In Each Word

Indenting paragraphs

There are two types of indentation that you need to be familiar with: first line indentation and full indentation. The difference between the two is shown below:

With first line indentation the first line of the paragraph is indented but the rest is not. You would mostly see this in letters or maybe some essays.

With full indentation, the entire paragraph is indented, not just the first line. This style isn't very common. You might do it if you want to quote large blocks of text. Whatever the reason, it definitely makes the paragraph stand out from the rest of text.

First line indentation

In order to indent the first line of a paragraph:

- Position the cursor at the beginning of the paragraph.
- Press the Tab key.

Note

You can remove the first line indentation by positioning the cursor at the beginning of the paragraph and pressing the Backspace key.

Full indentation

The indentation buttons (shown below) allow you to control the indentation of an entire paragraph. The left button <u>decreases</u> the indentation whereas the right one <u>increases</u> it. Just put the cursor inside the paragraph and click the appropriate button.

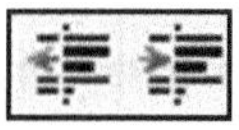

Figure 5.8 *The indentation buttons*

Moving and copying text

Moving text

If you want to move text from one position of a document to another, you don't have to delete the old text and re-type it at the new position.

To move text:

- Select the text being moved.
- Right-click on it and click Cut.
- Right-click on the new position.
- Click the Paste icon.

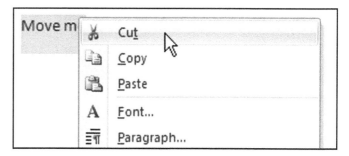

Figure 5.9 *Cutting text*

Copying text

Copying text places a duplicate of the text at another position in the document. This can significantly reduce the amount of typing you have to do.

To copy text:

- Select the text being copied.
- Right-click on it and click Copy.
- Right-click on the new position.
- Click Paste.

Keyboard shortcuts

Alternatively you can use the following keyboard shortcuts.

Command	Shortcut
Cut	Ctrl + X
Copy	Ctrl + C
Paste	Ctrl + V

Drag and drop

Text may also be moved and copied by the **drag and drop** method.

To move text

- Select the text.
- Position the mouse pointer (arrow form) on the selection.
- Hold down the left mouse button.
- Drag to the required position.
- Release the mouse button.

To copy text

Follow as instructed above, but before releasing the mouse button, hold down the Ctrl key.

Setting margins

A printed document always has space between the edges of the paper and the typed document. Those spaces are referred to as **margins**. The default margins for both versions of Word are shown below:

Word 2003

- Top and Bottom – 1".
- Left and Right – 1.25".

Word 2007

- All margins are 1".

Setting the margins for an entire page

To set the margins for an entire page you use the Page Setup window. To access this window you click:

- File, Page Setup in Word 2003.
- Page Layout, Margins, Custom Margins… in Word 2007.

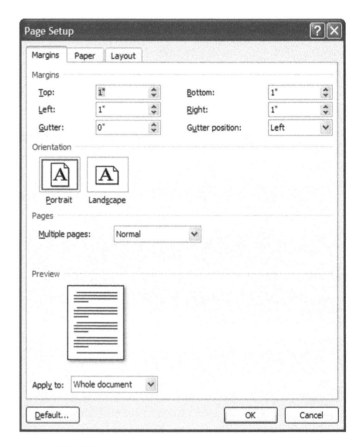

Figure 5.10 *Setting page margins*

Exercise 5

Retrieve the file called Media from your class folder and make the following changes:

1. Set the left and right margins at 1.5" for the entire document.
2. Copy the second paragraph under the heading TUNE IN RADIO to be between the second last and last paragraphs of your document.
3. Move the last paragraph of your document to be the second paragraph in the document.
4. Place all people's names in *Italics* and **Bold**.
5. Use line spacing of 2 for the entire document.
6. Save to a file called Media1.
7. Delete the heading TUNE IN TELEVISION and make your document one under the heading TUNE IN RADIO.
8. Indent the first line of each paragraph.
9. Use line spacing of 1 for the second paragraph in the document.
10. Fully indent the third paragraph of the document.
11. Save to a file called Media2.

6. Basic word processing tools

Checking spelling and grammar

Microsoft Word comes with built-in spelling and grammar checking to help you produce error-free documents. It operates in the background, highlighting spelling and grammar errors with wavy lines as you type.

- Spelling errors are underlined in red (Figure 6.1).
- Grammar errors are underlined in green (Figure 6.2).

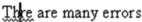
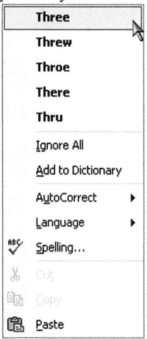

Figure 6.1 *Highlighted spelling error*

Figure 6.2 *Highlighted grammar error*

Note

The spelling and grammar checks are not perfect. For example, if you type a name that Word does not 'know' it will get underlined as a spelling error. Also, it might miss certain grammar errors. For example, even Word 2003 did not recognise the error in the following sentence: 'The boy is over their.'

To correct an individual error that has been highlighted:

1 Right-click on the wavy line.
2 Choose the appropriate correction option from the list that is displayed.

At the top of the correction options are suggested replacements that can be made. These are displayed in order of (what Word <u>thinks</u> is) most relevant. When you click on one of the suggested replacements, Word replaces the underlined text accordingly.

Note

If you accidentally type a word twice, Microsoft Word underlines the second word in red. In such a case, when you right-click on the offending word, choose the first option (Delete Repeated Word).

In addition to the suggested replacements, you are given the following correction options:

- Ignore All – ignores the error
- Add to Dictionary – adds that particular spelling to MS Word's internal dictionary so that if you type it again (even in another document), Word won't highlight it as a spelling error. Use this for names that Word doesn't recognise

Note

MS Word automatically corrects common typos. To see it in action, try typing 'teh', then press the space bar.

Performing a check of the entire document

Rather than relying on making corrections as you type, you can perform a spelling and grammar check of the entire document by pressing the F7 key. This will cause MS Word to start searching for errors starting from the point where the cursor is positioned. It stops whenever it encounters an error, displaying the Spelling and Grammar window. The window looks slightly different depending on whether the error is a spelling error or a grammar error (Figures 6.3 and 6.4). Despite the differences, there are a number of similarities:

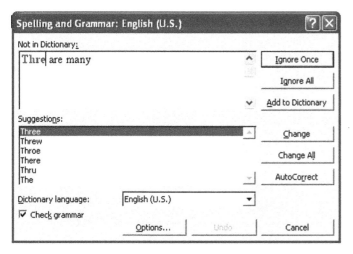

Figure 6.3 *Correcting a spelling error*

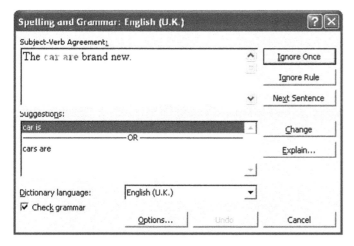

Figure 6.4 *Correcting a grammar error*

- At the top of the window there is a message such as Not in Dictionary or Subject-Verb Agreement, indicating what the error is.
- The offending text is displayed below the error message.
- A list of suggestions is displayed. To apply one of the suggestions, click the suggestion and click the Change button.

- To manually make a correction (e.g. if it is not listed among the suggestions), replace the text in the box under the error message and then click the Change button.

The Explain button is only displayed when a grammar error is encountered. If you click it, Word gives an explanation of the type of grammar error.

Note

It is important to note that the explanation is based on the type of error that Word <u>thinks</u> has occurred.

After you take some sort of action in response to the error, for example by clicking Change or one of the ignore buttons, Word continues searching for errors. When it is finished, it displays the message 'The spelling and grammar check is complete'.

Finding and replacing text

Most word processing programs include an option for finding and replacing text, to save you from having to search manually through lengthy documents. Microsoft Word is no exception.

Finding text

To find one or more occurrences of a word/phrase:

1 Click Edit (or the Home tab), then Find, or press Ctrl + F.
2 Type the word/phrase.
3 Click the Find Next button (this can be repeated to find other occurrences of the word/phrase). Word will start searching from the position of the cursor.

Search options

Word provides several options that allow you to refine the way it performs the search. These Search options are explained below.

Note

Normally the search options are hidden, but you can click the More button to display them. (Press the Less button if you want to hide them again.)

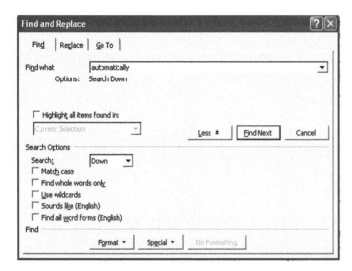

Figure 6.5 *Finding text (with the Search options displayed)*

Match case

The Match case option is usually disabled, meaning that Word does <u>not</u> distinguish between uppercase and lowercase characters. So searching for 'Bell' would find 'Bell', 'bell', 'BELL' or even 'beLL'. If it were <u>enabled</u>, Word would only find 'Bell'.

Find whole words only

If this option is disabled, Microsoft Word will find the text in the Find what box, even if it is part of another word. For example, a search for the word 'ever' would find 'what<u>ever</u>'. But when enabled, it forces Word to ignore instances of the search text that are part of other words. So if you repeat the search for the word 'ever', with the Find whole words only option enabled, it would no longer find 'whatever', 'every' or any word besides 'ever'.

Use wildcards

If this option is disabled, Word treats all characters the same. But when this option is selected, certain characters like '*' and '?' have special meanings, as shown in the table.

Meaning	Example
? any single character	c?t finds 'cat' and 'cut'
* any string of characters	s*t finds 'sat', 'short', 'st'

Sounds like

Tells Microsoft Word to find words that sound the same as the text in the Find what box. For example, a search for the word 'hair' will find 'hair', 'here', 'hear' and 'hare'. If this option is selected, Word dims the Match case and Find whole words only checkboxes since these features cannot be combined with Sounds like.

Find all word forms

This feature tells Microsoft Word to not only find the particular word, but find other tenses of that word as well. For example, if you search for the word 'sing' with this option enabled, Word will find 'sing', 'sang' and 'sung'.

Replacing text

To use the replace function:

1 Click Edit (or the Home tab), then Replace, or press Ctrl + H.
2 Type the text you want to search for in the Find what box.
3 Type the text you want to replace it with in the Replace with box.
4 Use the Replace or Replace All button, as appropriate:

- Clicking the Find Next button causes Word to find the next occurrence of the text in the Find what box and select it.
- Click the Replace button to replace the currently selected instance of the search text with the replacement text. After replacing the text, Word finds the next occurrence of the search text.
- Click Replace All to replace all instances of the Find what text with the replacement text.

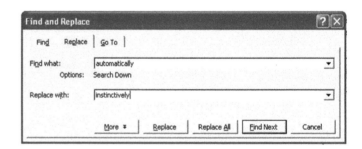

Figure 6.6 *Replacing text*

As you can see from Figures 6.5 and 6.6, the Find function and the Replace function are both tabs in the Find and Replace window. So you can quickly switch between them by clicking the appropriate tab.

Numbering pages

Numbering pages in Microsoft Word is <u>not</u> something you'd ever want to want to do manually. Fortunately, you don't have to since Word can easily do it for you automatically.

Word 2003

To number pages in Word 2003:

1 Click Insert, Page Numbers.
2 Choose the position of the page numbers (either 'Top of page' or 'Bottom of page').
3 Choose the alignment of the ('Left', 'Right', 'Center', etc.)
4 (Optional) If you don't want to show the page number on the first page, uncheck the 'Show number of first page' box.
5 Click the 'OK' button.

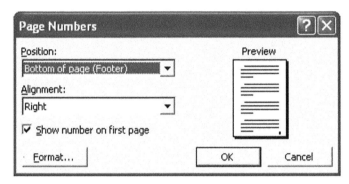

Figure 6.7 *Inserting page numbers in Word 2003*

Word 2007

Inserting page numbering in Word 2007 is completely different.

1 Switch to the Insert tab of the Ribbon.
2 Click the Page Number button.
3 Select whether you want the numbers to go to the 'Top of Page' or 'Bottom of Page'.
4 From the resulting submenu, choose the page numbering style you want to use. For example, if you just want to insert the page numbers in the centre, you'd choose the 'Plain Number 2' style.

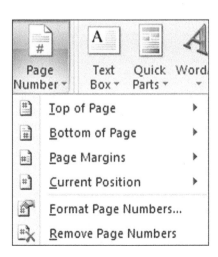

Figure 6.8 *Inserting page numbers in Word 2007*

Tip

As you can see from Figure 6.8, there are also options to remove the page numbers and to format them.

Page number formats

Instead of numbering pages 1, 2, 3, 4,... you might want to number them as I, II, III, IV, or even as a, b, c, d. To do so:

1 Open the Page Number Format window. You can do so as follows:

- In Word 2003, click the Format... button from the Page Numbers dialogue box.
- In Word 2007, click the Page Number button then click Format Page Numbers...

2 Choose the appropriate number format.
3 Click the OK button.

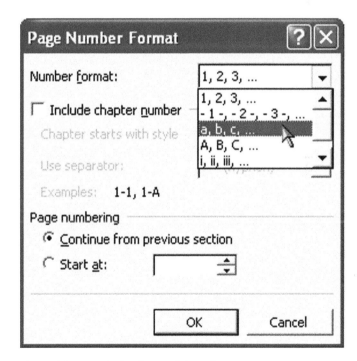

Figure 6.9 *Page Number Format dialogue box*

Exercise 6

Retrieve the `Insure` document from your class folder and perform the following:

1 Centre, underline and bold all headings.
2 Set top and bottom margins to 2.5" and left and right to 1.5".
3 Use double-line spacing for the paragraph with the heading SCHEDULE.
4 Use line spacing of 1.5 for the paragraph with the heading SUM ASSURED.
5 Use italics for the example in brackets: (e.g. Life, Fire, Accidents, Motor).
6 Indent the paragraph with the heading CERTIFICATE.
7 Copy the main heading to the bottom of the document.
8 Move the paragraph with the heading CERTIFICATE to a new position before COVER NOTE.
9 Change the case of all subheadings to title case.
10 Indent the first line of the paragraphs headed COVER NOTE and CLAIMS FORM.
11 Number each page in the top right-hand corner.
12 Save the file as `Insurance`.
13 Replace all occurrences of the word 'sum' with 'amount'.
14 Save the file as `Insurance1`.

7. Inserting files, footnotes and breaks

Combining files

Combining may be necessary when files relating to one particular topic have been stored separately. If you want all the information in one file, you have to combine the files.

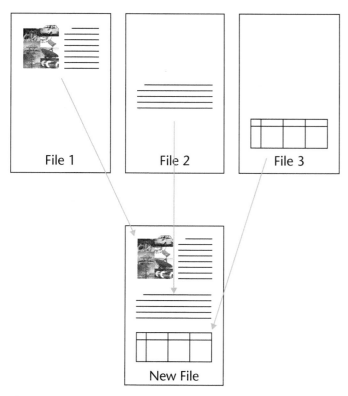

Figure 7.1 *Combining files into a new file*

To combine multiple files:

- Open the first file.
- Position the cursor at the bottom of the document (or wherever you want the next file to go).
- Insert the next file.
- Repeat the previous two steps until all the files have been inserted.
- Use the Save As option to save the combined file.

Inserting files

As you will have seen, the key step in combining files is inserting the text from a file. To do so you:

- Click Insert, File... (Word 2003).

Or

- Click the Insert Tab, Object, Text from File... (Word 2007).

In either case, the Open File dialogue box will appear for you to select the file.

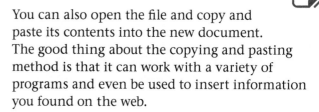

Note

You can also open the file and copy and paste its contents into the new document. The good thing about the copying and pasting method is that it can work with a variety of programs and even be used to insert information you found on the web.

Footnotes and endnotes

When you are reading certain types of books, such as the Bible or Shakespeare plays, you'll often see a little number next to a word. Then at the bottom of the page you will find a short note explaining what the particular word/phrase means. This is known as a footnote.

Note

A footnote appears at the end of the page whereas an endnote appears at the end of the document or current section.

Inserting a footnote or an endnote

To insert a footnote/endnote:

- Position the cursor to the right of the text being explained.
- Open the Footnote and Endnote window (Figure 7.2).
- Choose the type of note (Footnote/Endnote), as well as the location where the note is to be displayed.
- Click the Insert button.
- In the area provided, type the note.
- When you have finished typing, click anywhere in the document.

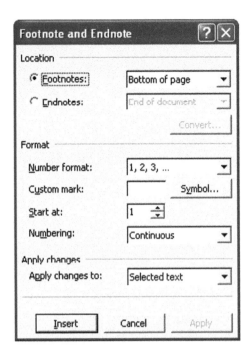

Figure 7.2 *Footnote and Endnote window.*

Opening the Footnote and Endnote window
Word 2003

To open the Footnote and Endnote window in Word 2003, click Insert, Reference, Footnote...

Word 2007

To open the Footnote and Endnote window in Word 2007:

- Switch to the References tab of the Ribbon.
- Click the More Options button at the bottom of the Footnotes section (see Figure 7.3).

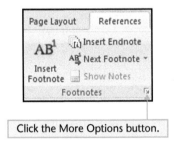

Click the More Options button.

Figure 7.3 *Opening the Footnotes and Endnotes window in Word 2007*

Deleting a footnote or an endnote

To delete a footnote or endnote, you must delete its footnote/endnote number from within the document.

Breaks

You can use breaks to divide a document into sections or force text on to a new page or column. To insert a break in your document:

- In Word 2003, click Insert, Break... then select the type of break.
- In Word 2007, switch to the Page Layout tab, click Breaks then select the type of break.

Page breaks

A page break identifies where one page ends and another begins. There are two types of page breaks:

- Automatic or Soft break
- Manual or Hard break

Word inserts an Automatic page break when the page is full of text. However, you can also create your own Manual page break at any point on a page.

In Normal/Draft view an Automatic page break appears as a dotted horizontal line from the left margin to the right and a Manual page break appears as a dotted horizontal line from the left margin to the right with the words 'Page Break' in the centre of the line.

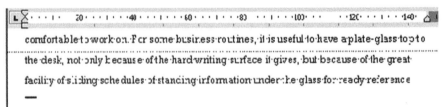

Figure 7.4 *Automatic page break*

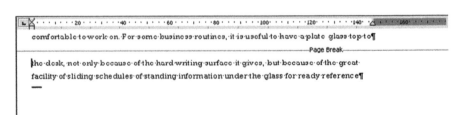

Figure 7.5 *Manual page break*

In Print Layout view you cannot distinguish a Manual page break from an Automatic break, as shown in Figure 7.6. Therefore, when you want to know if an Automatic or Manual break has been inserted, you will need to select the Normal/Draft view.

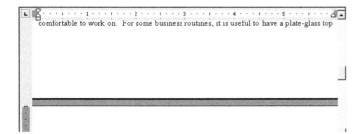

Figure 7.6 *A page break in the Print Layout view*

Section breaks

A section break is a mark that indicates the end of one section and the beginning of a next. This feature allows you to have more than one page format in the same document. Some instances where section breaks are used in a document are different orientation (see Figure 7.8), different paper sizes, different margins, different headers/footers or one page with multiple sections (see Figure 7.7).

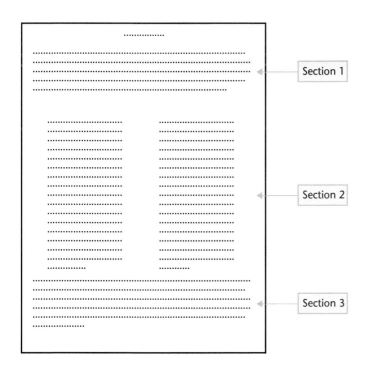

Figure 7.7 *Three sections on one page*

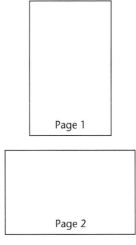

Figure 7.8 *In this document, page 1 is in portrait orientation and page 2 is in landscape. Each section is on a new page.*

Types of section break

Next page

This option inserts a section break and starts the new section on the next page.

Figure 7.9 *Next page section break*

Continuous

This option inserts a Section break and starts the new section on the same page. Multiple formats can be combined on one page.

Figure 7.10 *Continuous section break*

Odd page

This option forces a section break and starts the new section on the next odd-numbered page.

Figure 7.11 *Odd page section break*

Even page

This option forces a section break and starts the new section on the next even-numbered page.

Figure 7.12 *Even page section break*

Column breaks

If your document is divided into multiple columns, inserting a column break forces the text below the cursor into the next column.

Deleting breaks

Although you don't have to be in the Normal/Draft view when you are deleting breaks, it certainly helps since you can easily see where the breaks are.

To delete any type of break:

- (Optional) Switch to the Normal/Draft view.
- Click on or just in front the break you want to delete.
- Press the Delete key.

Exercise 7

1 Retrieve the file Quality_Manual. This document contains three pages. Check the Status bar.
2 Switch to the Normal view.
3 Use the down arrow scroll button on the vertical scroll bar to view what is on pages 2 and 3. Please note that page 2 is separated from page 1 by an Automatic page break and page 3 is separated from page 2 by a Manual page break.
4 Press the Ctrl and Home keys to move back to the beginning of the document.
5 Place the cursor at the beginning of the sentence 'Generally 10 ...' to place this sentence on page 2.
6 Insert a page break.
7 Click on the page break above the heading 'Fittings' and press Delete. Page 3 was just deleted from the document. You should now have two pages in the document and the information on page 3 now joins the information on page 2.
8 Press the Ctrl and Home keys to move to the beginning of the document.
9 Place the cursor between the first paragraph and the heading 'Purpose'.
10 Insert a Continuous section break.
11 Place the cursor between the heading 'Retention of Records' and the paragraph above.
12 Insert a Continuous section break.
13 Select the information between the section breaks.
14 Click the Columns button shown in Figure 7.13 and select two columns. You can find this button:

- in the Standard toolbar (Word 2003)
- in the Page Layout tab of the Ribbon (Word 2007)

(Columns will be explained in Chapter 9.)

Figure 7.13

15 Save the adjustments to a file called Quality Manual1.

8. Headers and footers

Headers and footers refer to text used to identify pages of your document. They may appear at the top (header) or bottom (footer) of every page of a document. Common headers and footers are page numbers, document titles, notices to turn over the page and dates. MS Word offers a number of options for positioning headers and footers. You may:

- control the alignment of the header/footer (right/left/centre)
- place headers/footers on all pages except the first (e.g. where the first page is a cover page)
- have a different header/footer on the first page
- have a different header/footer on the last page
- have different headers/footers on each section of the document
- place headers/footers on odd/even pages

The Header and Footer view

The Header and Footer view is a special view that allows you work with headers and footers. There are a number of ways that you can switch to this view:

- Double-click an existing header.
- Click View, Header and Footer (Word 2003).
- Click the Insert tab, Header, Edit Header (Word 2007).

Note

Page numbers are also headers and footers.

The Header and Footer toolbar (Word 2003)

In Word 2003, when you view a header or footer, the Header and Footer toolbar will be automatically displayed.

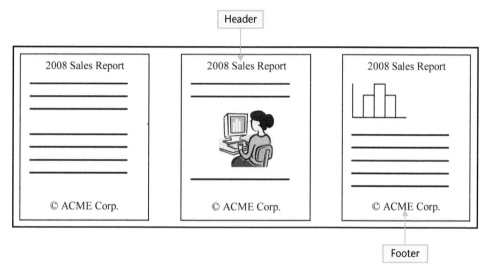

Figure 8.1 *Headers and footers*

Figure 8.2 *The Header and Footer toolbar*

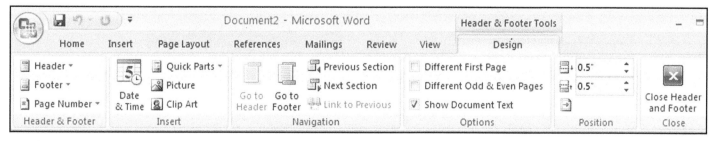

Figure 8.3 *The Header Design tab of the Ribbon*

The Header Design tab (Word 2007)

When you view a header in Word 2007, the Ribbon will automatically switch to the Header Design tab.

Viewing the footer

By default, when you switch to the Header and Footer view, you'll actually be viewing the header. In order to view to the footer:

- Scroll down to the bottom of the page (simple, but it works).
- Click the Go to Footer button. In Word 2003 it says 'Switch between Header and Footer'.

Closing the Header and Footer view

To close the Header and Footer view either:

- Double-click anywhere outside the header or footer box.
- Or click the Close button in the Header and Footer toolbar or the Header Design tab.

Inserting a header or footer

In order to insert a header or footer:

- Switch to the Header and Footer view.
- Type the header or footer in the designated area.
- Close the Header and Footer view.

Note

The header or footer will appear on all pages unless you specify otherwise.

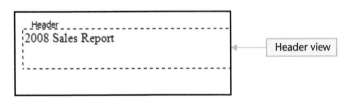

Figure 8.4a *Inserting a header in Word 2003*

Figure 8.4b *Inserting a header in Word 2007*

Formatting the header or footer

A header or footer is just ordinary text. This means that you can do all the usual formatting, for example making it bold, changing its alignment or changing the font.

Advanced options

Having a different first page

Sometimes you don't want a header or footer on the first page. For example, you don't normally have them on a cover page. In other cases you may want to use a <u>different</u> header or footer on the first page. In both of these cases you'd select the Different First Page option.

To have a header/footer appear on every page except the first:

- Insert the header or footer as normal.
- Turn <u>on</u> the Different First Page option as described below.

Word 2003

To have a different first page in Word 2003:

- Click the Page Setup button on the Header and Footer toolbar. (See Figure 8.5a.)
- Switch to the Layout tab.
- Select the Different first page option. (See Figure 8.5b.)

Word 2007

To have a different first page in Word 2007, put a check mark in the 'Different First Page' box which is located in the Options section of the Header Design tab.

Note

The header and footer boxes will now say 'First Page Header' and 'First Page Footer', respectively.

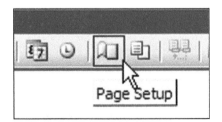

Figure 8.5a *The Page Setup button*

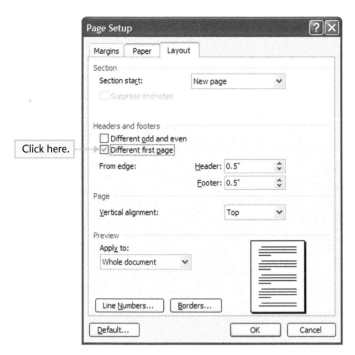

Figure 8.5b *Different First Page option (Word 2003)*

Click here.

Figure 8.6 *Different First Page (Word 2007)*

Having a different header on part of the document

Sometimes you may want to have a different header (or footer) on part of your document. In order to do so you must:

- Put that part of the document in a separate section (if it isn't already) using section breaks.
- Click in that section and switch to the Header and Footer view.
- Turn off the 'Link to Previous' option in the toolbar or the Header Design tab.

Note

The headers and footers operate independently so you can have a different header but have the same footer as the rest of the document.

Exercise 8a

Retrieve the file BusLett from your class folder, and carry out the following instructions.

1 Change the text to double-line spacing and justify throughout.
2 Number the pages of the document in the bottom right-hand corner of each page.
3 Use the header LETTER WRITING, positioning it in the top left-hand corner of each page and another header PRINCIPLES OF BUSINESS, positioning it in the top right-hand corner.
4 Centre the footer FINAL DOCUMENT on all pages of the document.
5 Make any grammatical corrections using the spell-check feature to assist you and save the document as BusLett1.
6 Then using the same document, change the document to single-line spacing, indenting one inch (1") from the left margin.
7 Place all headings in uppercase. Bold and centre each one.
8 Delete the underlines from the paragraph headings.
9 Save the edited document as BusLett2.
10 Use left and right margins of 2" and top and bottom of 1.5" for the entire document.
11 Insert the following section between the sections headed 'Body of Letter' and 'Complimentary Close'.

CLOSING PARAGRAPH
The closing paragraph is a single sentence which establishes the atmosphere of courtesy whatever the content of the letter.

12 Insert today's date at the top of the document.
13 Move the sections so that they appear in the following order:

1 Reference
2 Date
3 Name of Addressee
4 Salutation
5 Subject Heading
6 Opening Paragraph
7 Body of Letter
8 Closing Paragraph
9 Complimentary Close
10 Enclosures and Copies

14 Create as an endnote the following, which refers to the main heading: Extracted from *The H_2O of Letter Writing* by Alexis Keaton.

15 Save as `BusLett3`.

Exercise 8b

1 Combine the files `Valentine`, `Hearts`, `Perfume` and `Food` as one file.

2 Spell-check the document and save using the name `Love1`.

3 Swap the paragraphs under the heading STRAIGHT FROM THE HEART.

4 Centre, bold and underline the heading LOVE! LOVE!! LOVE!!! and place the letters at a size of 16.

5 Bold and underline all shoulder headings and change the appearance to Title Case.

6 Use double-line spacing in the entire document.

7 Save the file using the name `Love2`.

8 Insert page breaks before the sections headed STRAIGHT FROM THE HEART, ROMANCE IN A BOTTLE and THE FOOD-SEX CONNECTION so that each section appears on a different page.

9 Search for '14th century' and '18th century' in the document and place in italics. Also place the 'th' so that it appears 14th and 18th.

10 Use top and bottom margins of 1.5" and left and right margins 2".

11 Indent the first line of each paragraph.

12 Change all occurrences of the word 'seduce' to 'entice'.

13 Save the file using the name `Love3`.

14 Underline the phrases 'flirtatious romantic' and 'passionate romantic'.

15 Remove the underline from the word 'chocolate'.

16 Copy the main heading LOVE! LOVE!! LOVE!!! to the bottom of the document.

17 Use the header 'Love Fest '97' to the right of the document. The header should be bold and in italics.

18 Use the footer 'New Edition' which should be in the centre of the page. The footer should be in the font size of 16.

19 Add the following footnote in the document to explain the word 'chocolate': *'Edible substance made from cacao seeds'*. Taken from the Oxford Dictionary.

20 Save the file using the name `Love4`.

Exercise 8c

You are provided with the files `Laser`, `Thermal` and `Inkjet`. Do the following:

1 Combine the files into one file called `Printers`. `Thermal` should be first, `Inkjet` second and `Laser` last.

2 Make a copy of `Printers` and call it `Printout`.

Make the changes below to the file called `Printers`:

3 Place the entire document in 1.5 line spacing.

4 Change the margins as follows: Top – 1.5", Bottom – 1.5", Right – 0.5", Left – 2".

5 Move the second paragraph under the heading 'Laser printers' so that it now becomes the first paragraph under that heading.

6 Centre, bold and underline <u>all</u> headings and place them in uppercase.

7 Indent the first line of each paragraph.

8 Insert a page break at the section headed 'Laser printers'.

9 Replace <u>all</u> occurrences of 'paper' with 'sheets'.

10 Number <u>all</u> pages at the top left of each page.

11 Use a footnote which corresponds with the first occurrence of cps. The note should read: 'This is an acronym for characters per second.' This note should appear in italics.

12 Save the file using the name `Printing`.

Make the changes below to the file called `Printout`:

13 The paragraph beginning with 'Until recently …' should have left and right indentation of 1.0" and double-line spacing.

14 Use the header SILENT PRINTERS. The header should be right-aligned, bold, italicised and on every page.

15 Use the footer THE HALLMARK OF QUALITY at the centre of every page except the last, where THE END should appear.

16 Insert the heading 'A⁺ Printer Technology' at the top of the document. Centre and use a font size of 16.

17 Spell-check the document and save as `FinalPrint`.

Exercise 8d

You are provided with the following files: USA, Travel, EatngOut and EatngIn. You are required to:

1 Combine the above files into one file called Vacation. USA should be first, Travel next, then EatngOut and finally EatngIn.

2 Make the following changes to the Vacation file:

a Allow 1.5" top margin and 2" left and right margins.

b Insert at the top of the document the following text as it appears below. Take special note of the bold text.

MEMORANDUM
TO: Michael Arthur
FROM: Charles Haynes
DATE: (insert today's date)
RE: Travel and Eating in the USA

c Run the spell-check on the <u>entire</u> document and correct any errors which you find.

d Change the line spacing within the body of the document to 2 and repaginate appropriately.

e Add the header 'Memo (Cont'd)' to the extreme right of every page except page 1.

f Add the footer 'Memo 1' which should be centred and on every page.

g Underline, bold and use a consistent uppercase with the following headings: USA, Getting around, Eating Out and Eating in.

h Place <u>all</u> sections on a separate page.

i Replace <u>all</u> occurrences of 'USA' with United States of America.

j Move the sub-headings under 'Getting Around' so that they appear in alphabetical order.

k Number the pages at the top centre of every page.

l Place a note at the bottom of the page to explain the meaning of the abbreviation RV, which stands for 'Recreational Vehicles'.

m Save the corrected memorandum as Holiday.

Exercise 8e

1 Combine the files Family1, Family2, Family3 and Family4 into one file called Insight.

2 Correct any spelling errors in the document and save using the filename Vision1.

3 Put the section headed 'The Family's Solution' on a separate page.

4 Bold and enlarge the two headings in the document.

5 Centre the last line of the document and place in uppercase.

6 Locate the phrase 'Such a paradox' and place it in italics.

7 At the top of the document, add a centred heading 'Preserving the Family'. Underline it and use a font larger than the other heading.

8 Save the file as Vision2.

9 In the last section 'The Family's Solution' join the fifth paragraph to the third paragraph.

10 With the paragraph beginning 'Dr James Dobson ...' use left and right margins of 1.5" each.

11 Place the paragraph beginning 'Of course there are ...' in double-line spacing.

12 Change all occurrences of the word 'kids' to 'children'.

13 Change the top and bottom margins to 0.6" each.

14 Number each page in the bottom right-hand corner.

15 Create a header which should appear in the top centre of each page and which should read:

For Family Week '98

16 Place a note at the end of the document to correspond with the occurrence of the name Dr James Dobson, which appears in the second paragraph. The note should read: *A world-famous Christian psychologist.*

17 Resave Vision2.

9. Bullets, numbering and columns

Bullets and numbering

Microsoft Word makes it easy to create numbered lists like this:

1. First item
2. Second item
3. Third item

Or bulleted items like this:

- bananas
- apples
- oranges

In fact, it has buttons dedicated to these tasks (Figure 9.1).

Figure 9.1 *Bullets and Numbering buttons*

In addition, if you start manually typing a numbered list, sometimes Word will recognise what you are doing and convert it to an automatically numbered list.

Tip

Try typing '1. This is a test' (without the quotes) and then press the Enter key.

Here's how you could reproduce the numbered list given in the first example:

- First you would click the Numbering button to turn it on. The number '1.' should appear.
- Then you'd type 'First item' and press Enter to go to the next item, which would be automatically numbered as '2.'
- After typing the third item, you'd press Enter twice, which would automatically turn off the numbering.

Note

You don't have to type the numbers. Microsoft Word does that for you!

Using another style of bullets or numbers

Suppose, instead of numbering your items 1., 2., 3.,… you want to number them a, b, c. Or maybe you want to have square bullets instead of the normal round ones. This is done in a different way in Word 2003 and Word 2007.

Word 2003

In Word 2003, to change the bullets or numbering style:

- Click Format, Bullets and Numbering.
- Click the appropriate tab.
- Choose the style you want.
- Click the OK button.

Figure 9.2 *Bullets and Numbering window (Word 2003)*

Word 2007

To choose a different style of numbering or bullets in Word 2007, just click the arrow next to the list button and choose from the set that appears.

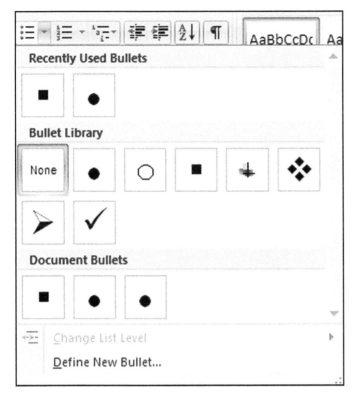

Figure 9.3 *Choosing another type of bullet (Word 2007)*

Creating columns

You may want to lay your text out in columns. The easiest way to put existing text into columns is:

- Select the text.
- Click the Columns button in the Standard toolbar (in Word 2003) or the Page Layout tab (in Word 2007).
- Select the number of columns you want.

Figure 9.4 *Columns button*

Columns window

If you need to do something more advanced, for example put a line between the columns or have unequal columns, you need to use the Columns window.

To access this window:

- In Word 2003, click Format, Columns…
- In Word 2007, click Page Layout, Columns, More Columns…

Tip

Be sure to change the Apply to combo box so that the correct part of the document gets put into columns.

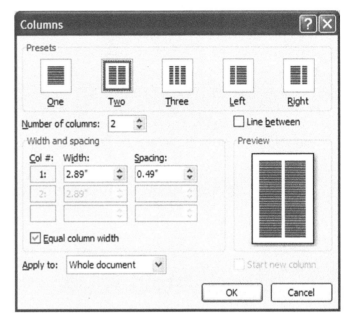

Figure 9.5 *Columns window*

Exercise 9a

Open the `Water_Bodies` file from the appropriate exercise folder and make the following changes:

1. Use Word's numbering feature to number the five seas and the seven oceans.
2. Type the following text at the bottom of the document. Be sure to use the same numbering and bullet styles as shown here.

Lakes

A lake is a large body of water, surrounded by land. But some lakes are 'greater' than others. In Eastern North America, along the Canada–United States border, you can find the five Great Lakes. They are:

   i. Lake Superior
   ii. Lake Michigan
   iii. Lake Huron
   iv. Lake Erie
   v. Lake Ontario

Rivers

Wikipedia defines a river as 'a natural watercourse, usually freshwater, flowing toward an ocean, a lake, a sea or another river'. When people hear the word 'river', they normally think of either:

- **The Nile** – At over 6500 kilometres long, the Nile is the longest river in the world. Although it is primarily associated with Egypt, the Nile passes through several other African countries including Ethiopia, Uganda and Kenya.
- **The Amazon** – While the Nile is the *longest* river in the world, the Amazon is the *largest*. In fact, more water flows through this South American river than the next eight largest rivers <u>combined</u>. It is also the world's second longest river.

---

3. Change the numbering of the oceans to letters with brackets after them. For example:
   a) The Pacific Ocean
   b) The Atlantic Ocean
   c) ....
4. Use bullets instead of numbers for the seven seas.
5. Change all the headings except for the Introduction to the Century Gothic font, bolded and underlined.
6. Place the entire document apart from the Introduction into two newspaper columns.

7. Ensure that the entire Lakes section (including the heading) is in the second column. Use a column break if necessary.
8. Save the document as `Water_Bodies2`.

Exercise 9b

1. Combine the following files in order as listed – `Technician`, `Groomer`, `Surgeon` and `Nurse`, placing each file on a separate page. Save the combined files as `Animals`.
2. The entire document is to have line spacing of 1.5.
3. Justify all paragraphs of the document.
4. Spell-check the document and save as `Animal_Care1`.
5. Use top margins and bottom margins of 1.5" and left and right of 1" each.
6. Indent the first line of all paragraphs.
7. Save as `Animal_Care2`.
8. Change all occurrences of 'Required Attributes' to 'Personal Qualities'.
9. Insert a note, with reference to the term 'parasites' at the bottom of the appropriate page.
   The note, which should appear in italics, should read as follows:

   'An animal that lives upon or in another.' (Taken from the New Webster's Dictionary, 1992 Edition.)

10. <u>Each</u> main heading should appear in uppercase and bold print while <u>all</u> subheadings should be underlined.
11. Create a header on all pages of the document. Each header should consist of the title 'Small Animal Care' and the position discussed on that page. The headers should appear on the right side of the page. A font size of 14 should be used. Below is an example of the header for page 1.

    Small Animal Care
    Animal Technician

12. Add a main heading at the top of the document titled INFORMATION SHEET, emboldened and of size 16.

13 On a new page, which should be divided into two columns (portrait) and insert the file called `Seminar`, which must fit only on the first column of the page.

14 Add the programme below on the second column of the page, appropriately spaced and save the amended file as `Animal_Care3`.

SMALL ANIMAL CARE SEMINAR PROGRAMME

Saturday 15th May 2001

9:00 a.m.	**COFFEE**
9:30 a.m.	Introduction and Welcome
9:45 a.m.	Working in a Veterinary Surgery *Roles*
11:00 a.m.	**COFFEE**
11:45 a.m.	Working in a Veterinary Surgery *Qualifications and training*
12:30 p.m.	**BUFFET LUNCH**
1:30 p.m.	Working in a Hospital *Duties and training*
3:00 p.m.	**TEA**
3:15 p.m.	Working as a Dog Groomer *Duties, location and training*
4:15 p.m.	*CLOSE*

Exercise 9c

Divide your document screen into two columns and key in the text shown below.

MEMORANDUM

Date: (Today's Date)

Ref: JH/(your initials)

To: All Departments

From: Personnel Manager

BAD TIME KEEPING

Reports have recently been brought to my attention of instances of bad time keeping by some members of staff, i.e. reporting late to their work stations in the morning and taking unofficial extended lunch hours. May I remind all staff of the following points:

Working Hours

The contract of employment states the working hours:

(a) 9:00 a.m.–12.00 p.m. / 1.00 p.m.–5.00 p.m.

(b) Two 15-minute coffee breaks allocated morning and afternoon to be taken at the convenience of each department.

Signing-in Book

(a) All staff must sign in and out.

(b) If necessary, the reason for lateness must be recorded in the book.

Disciplinary Procedure

Staff should note that in the event of persistent bad time keeping, without improvements, the disciplinary procedure outlined below may come into operation.

(a) Verbal warning.

(b) First written warning signed by Department Manager.

(c) Final written warning signed by Functional Manager.

(d) Dismissal.

Notification of Absence

(a) All staff should notify their immediate superiors if they are aware of impending absence, e.g. doctor/dental appointment.

(b) In the event of sickness, notify the Assistant Personnel Manager (ext 273) not later than 0830 hrs.

Punctuality is the obligation of every member of staff. Persistent lateness by individuals puts additional pressure on others and this may have a detrimental effect on morale and good working relationships.

Your co-operation is requested in this matter.

JOHN HUTCHINSON

10. Tables

The table feature may be used to enhance the display of information, define and explain text, help to organise columns of numbers, produce data-entry forms and add spreadsheets to documents. A table consists of columns and rows that form a grid of cells. The table can be edited to change the appearance of an entire column, an entire row or a single cell.

Creating a table

To create a table:

- In Word 2003, click Table, Insert, Table...
- In Word 2007, click Insert, Table, Insert Table...

This will bring up the Insert Table dialogue box.

Figure 10.1 *The Insert Table dialogue box*

Changing the number of columns and rows

To change the number of columns and rows in a table, you can either:

- Click the arrows in order to increase or decrease the value.
- Type the number directly into the box.

AutoFit behaviour

The following table explains the different AutoFit options.

Option	What it does
Fixed Column Width (default)	Makes all columns a specific size. You can use the arrows to choose the width you want or type it in directly.
AutoFit to contents	Automatically adjusts the width of columns in the table based on the amount of text you type.
AutoFit to window	Automatically resizes the table within the window of a web browser.

AutoFormat button

This button is only available in Word 2003. When you click the AutoFormat button, it brings up a window with a list of table styles for you to choose from.

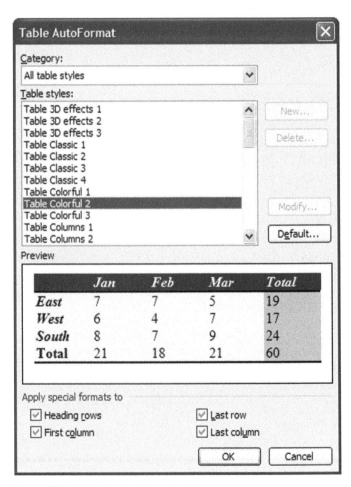

Figure 10.2 *The Table AutoFormat window*

Changing the appearance of a table

Word 2003

To change the way a table looks in Word 2003:

- Click inside the table.
- Then click Table, Table AutoFormat... to bring up the AutoFormat window.

Word 2007

Word 2007 has an entire tab of the Ribbon dedicated to changing the appearance of a table. See Figure 10.3. The Table Design tab only appears when you click on a table.

Drawing tables

If you want to create a complex looking table, or add some lines to an existing table, you can draw the table yourself.

To start drawing a table:

- In Word 2003, click Table, Draw Table.
- In Word 2007, click Insert, Table, Draw Table.

Then you drag the mouse to form the lines of the table.

Note

To stop drawing a table, press the Esc key.

Changing the table layout

When you change the layout of a table, you change its structure. For instance, you can add rows, delete columns or merge cells.

Table menu (Word 2003)

In Word 2003, most of the table layout options are located in the Table menu (Figure 10.4).

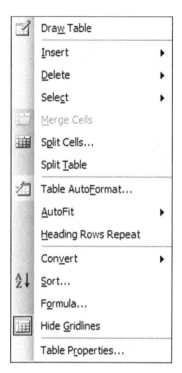

Figure 10.4 *The Table Menu (Word 2003)*

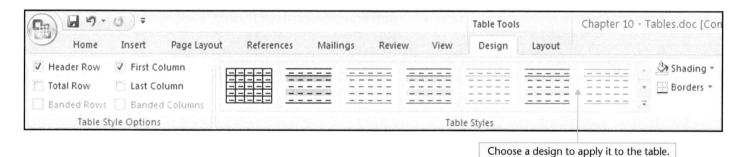

Figure 10.3 *The Table Design tab*

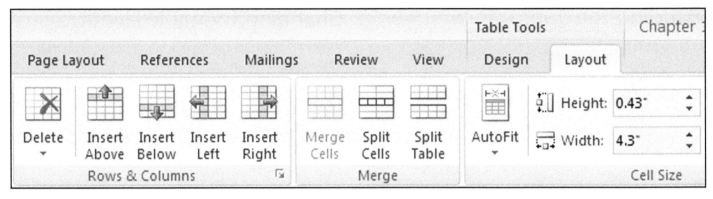

Figure 10.5 *The Table Layout tab (Word 2007)*

Table Layout tab (Word 2007)

Word 2007 doesn't have a Table menu, but it does have a Table Layout tab (Figure 10.5).

Inserting rows and columns

To insert a row or column:

- Click in a cell next to where you want to insert the row or column.
- Choose the appropriation insertion option from the Table menu or the Table Layout tab.

Deleting rows and columns

To delete a row or column:

- Click in the row or column to be deleted.
- Choose the appropriation deletion option from the Table Menu or the Table Layout Tab.

Deleting tables

To delete an entire table:

- Click inside the table.
- Choose the Delete Table option from the Table menu or the Table Layout tab.

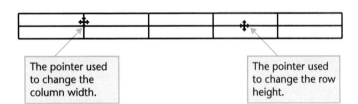

Figure 10.6 *Changing column width or row height*

Resizing rows and columns

- Place the mouse pointer on the column or row boundary you want to change. (Note: The appearance of the mouse pointer will change; see Figure 10.6.)
- Drag the boundary until the column or row is the required width or height.

Merging cells

When you merge cells you join two or more cells to form a single, larger cell. To merge cells in a table:

- Select the cells you want to merge.
- Right-click on the selected cells and click Merge Cells (Figure 10.7).

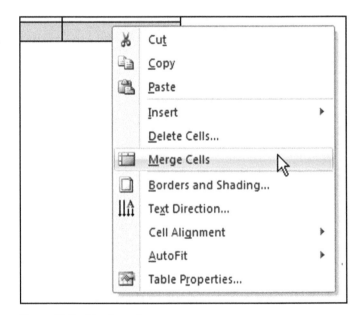

Figure 10.7a *Merging cells*

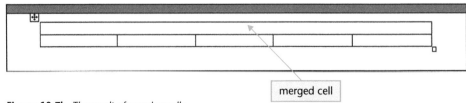

Figure 10.7b *The result of merging cells*

Splitting cells

In order to split a cell into two or more smaller cells:

- Right-click in the cell you want to split.
- Click Split Cells... The Split Cells window will appear (Figure 10.8a).
- Type the number of rows and columns you want the cell to be split into.
- Click OK.

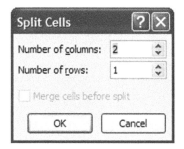

Figure 10.8a *The Split Cells window*

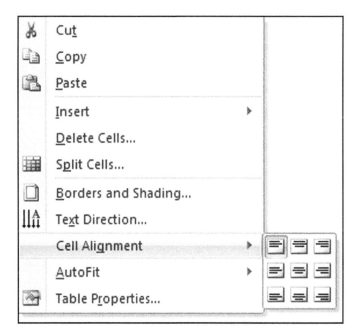

Figure 10.9 *Changing the cell alignment*

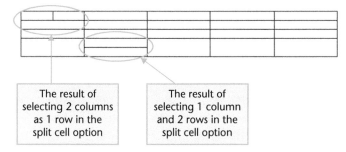

The result of selecting 2 columns as 1 row in the split cell option

The result of selecting 1 column and 2 rows in the split cell option

Figure 10.8b *The results of splitting cells*

Changing cell alignment

To change the alignment of cell(s):

- Select the cell(s).
- Right-click on the selected cell(s).
- Choose the desired cell alignment (Figure 10.9).

Changing the alignment of the table itself

In order to align the table itself, as opposed to its <u>contents</u>:

- Position the mouse pointer in the top-left corner of the table.
- Click the four-headed arrow that appears.
- Click an alignment button (the same ones you normally use to align text).

Exercise 10

1 a Using the Insert table icon, create a table that has 3 columns and 7 rows.

b Click in the first cell of the table and insert a row above.

c Click in the last cell of the first row and insert a column to the left.

2 a Type the following in the table as it appears below.

AUTHOR	BOOK	PRICE	
AUTHOR	**BOOK**	**PRICE**	
Alfred Skinner	The House of Horror	$34.00	
Keith Lager	All the Parents	$67.89	
Jake Curor	We Were	$45.28	
Riffle Peters	Children	$23.40	
Vitra Clarke	Top of the Pops	$25.15	
Jason Moore	Flowers for Him	$14.87	

b Place the column headings in bold.

c Click in the first cell of the table and insert a row above.

d Click anywhere in the last column and delete that column.

e Centre the table horizontally.

f Merge the cells in the first row and type the following in all uppercase, bold and aligned in the centre.
BOOK SUPPLIERS

g Merge the cells in the second row, type the following in title case, bold and aligned in the centre.

Best Sellers

h Click in the cell where 'The House of Horror' appears and split that cell into 1 column, 2 rows and type 'Murder on Death Street'.

i Click in the cell where the price $34.00 appears. Split that cell into 1 column, 2 rows and type $30.00.

j Centre the price information in the table.

k Click in the cell where the author Alfred Skinner appears and centre the name vertically in the cell.

l Change the format of the table to List6.

m Save the file as Best_Sellers.

3 Place the following data in a table as it appears below. Please include all the necessary formatting and alignment. All data must be centred vertically and horizontally within the cells.

MCDONALD'S ELECTRONIC COMPANY
ELECTRONIC OFFICE EQUIPMENT

Machines	Actual Figures			Estimated Figures		
	1998	1999	2000	1998	1999	2000
Calculations	43	48	53	47	50	60
Electronic typewriters	24	25	26	21	26	20
Automatic typewriters	3	4	4	5	5	6
Electronic cash registers	6	7	8	3	8	9
Electronic accounting systems	31	34	37	30	35	30
Dictation equipment	4	5	5	5	5	6
Plain paper copiers	9	12	14	10	16	11
Direct electrostatic copiers	10	46	70	12	50	80
Small copiers	25	30	50	26	35	14

11. Tabs

Tabs are primarily used to indent the first line of a paragraph or to line up columns of text or numbers. By default, the tab key takes the cursor 0.5" from the left margin and between columns. The space may be widened by pressing the Tab key more than once (twice to get 1" etc.). However, this method does not make alignment very accurate and sometimes the space bar has to be used to give a line an additional space to match the others. An alternative is to change the tab settings to suit the information that will be used.

Setting and clearing tabs

Setting tabs with the Ruler
An easy way to set tab stops is to use the Ruler (Figure 11.1). On the far left of the Ruler bar is the Tab Alignment button, which allows you to select of the type of tab required.

- Click on the Tab button to the left of the horizontal Ruler bar to choose the required tab stop.
- On the Ruler bar, set the tab stops by clicking at the point where you want a stop to appear (this is based on the length of the information).

To clear a tab stop from the Ruler bar

- Place the mouse pointer over the tab stop you want to clear.
- Drag the tab stop down from the horizontal Ruler bar.

To move a tab stop on the Ruler bar

- Drag the tab stop to the right or the left on the horizontal Ruler bar.

Type of tab	Description
Left	Text is left-aligned after the tab
Right	Text is right-aligned before the tab
Centre	Text is centred around the tab
Decimal	The decimal points of numbers are positioned in line with the tab

Tab dialogue box

If you double-click on a tab stop in the ruler, you will open the Tab dialogue box (Figure 11.2).

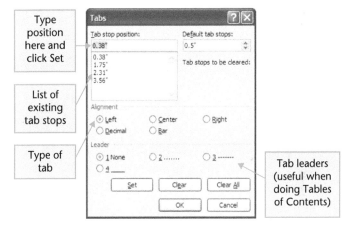

Figure 11.2 *The tab dialogue box*

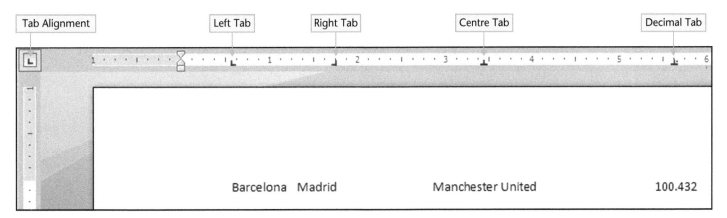

Figure 11.1 *The Ruler bar*

To add tabs using this window:

- Type the required position in the Tab Stop Position box.
- Choose the type of tab.
- Click the Set button.

To clear all the tabs, click the Clear All button. If you only want to erase a particular tab:

- Select the entry for that tab.
- Click Clear.

Tabs using tables

You can simulate tabs using tables (which are often easier to work with). Just be be sure to hide the borders.

Exercise 11a

1 Key in the following information using left tab stops at 2.5" and 5". Save the completed document as School.

TEACHER	SCHOOL	PARISH
Husband	Garrison School	St Michael
Elcock	Queens College	St James
Waterman	St James Secondary	St James
King	The Lodge Secondary	St John
Price	Foundation School	Christ Church
Henry	Ellerslie School	St Michael
Augustine	Alexandra	St Peter
Smith	Coleridge & Parry	St Peter
Roberts	Combermere	St Michael
Browne	Harrison College	St Michael
Calder	St Michael's School	St Michael
Haynes	St Lucy Secondary	St Lucy

2 Key in the following information using a decimal tab stop at 2.5" and a left tab stop at 4". Save the completed document as Crop.

January	$345.77	Satisfactory
February	$657.50	Very Good
March	$221.00	Fair
April	$78.90	Poor
May	$432.00	Very Satisfactory
June	$121.00	Moderate
July	$45.00	Poor
August	$600.00	Good
September	$333.90	Very Fair

Exercise 11b

1 Open your class folder for Chapter 11. Retrieve and combine the following word files in the order: Intro, Checklist and Bahamas.

2 Add the following text at the end of the paragraph headed 'Packing Luggage'.

Never agree to take someone else's bag for them. Never leave your luggage unattended.

3 From the section on the Bahamas, delete the text 'This is an area ... accidents can be limited.'

4 Add the following data in a table on a new page at the end of the document and double-space it.

FISHING

FISH	DATE	AREA
Tuna	June	Deep Waters
	July	
	August	
Bonefish	Year round	Shallows
Amberjack	November–May	Reefs and Wrecks
Barracuda	Year round	Reefs and Shallows
Grouper	Year round	Reefs

5 Start new paragraphs at the beginning of the sentences.
   a Great Exuma...
   b The shores of...

6 Spell-check the document and save as Travel1.

7 Change the headings 'Activities in the Bahamas' and 'Happy Holidays' to UPPERCASE.

8 Place the following headings in bold:

ACTIVITIES IN THE BAHAMAS
CHECKLIST FOR TRAVELLERS
HAPPY HOLIDAYS

9 Underline the headings INSURANCE, PASSPORT, MONEY, TICKETS, PACKING LUGGAGE and CURRENCY.

10 The text 'A super holiday for all!' which appears at the beginning of the section headed ACTIVITIES IN THE BAHAMAS should be emboldened and centred and should appear at the end of the document.

11 Change all occurrences of seasports to watersports.

12 Bold and italicise all occurrences of Globetrotters Ltd.

13 Change the current margins to 2.5" top, 1.5" bottom and 2" left and right.

14 Justify the entire document at both margins.

15 The following header should appear centred on the first page only. The company name should be in a larger font than the address and telephone number.

Globetrotters Ltd.
Suite 911, 1st Floor
Mid-Air Building
Journey's End
Christ Church
(246) 428-7576

16 On all other pages the header should be as follows:

Globetrotters
The Ideal Vacation Packagers for You
Call us Today!!

17 A footer, font size of 10, should appear on all pages centred, bold and italics.

Other branches are located at ...
Speightstown, Holetown and The City

18 Insert the following endnote which describes Mystery Cove:

A 400-foot tunnel extending into the island

19 Change all occurrences of Ltd. to Limited and save the completed document to the name `Travel2`.

12. Enhancing a document's appearance

Inserting pictures

Adding images can quickly enhance the appearance of your document. You can insert a picture either from a file, or from the library of images and other media (called Clip Art) that comes with Microsoft Word. You do not have to know where the Clip Art files are actually located on your disk – Word takes care of this for you.

Inserting a picture from a file

If you have an image (e.g. a .jpg or .bmp or .gif or .tiff file) and want to insert it into a Microsoft Word document:

1 Position the cursor where the picture is to be inserted.
2 Click Insert, Picture, From File (Word 2003) or Insert, Picture (Word 2007).
3 Go to the folder where the picture is located.

4 Select the correct file.
5 Click the Insert button.

This causes a <u>copy</u> of the image to be inserted into the document. This means that if you change, delete or move the original file, the image you see in the document is not affected.

Inserting Clip Art

Microsoft Word provides you with a wide variety of images that you can use in your documents, called Clip Art. You insert Clip Art via the Clip Art task pane (Figure 12.1).

To open the Clip Art task pane:

• In Word 2003, click Insert, Picture, Clip Art.
• In Word 2007, click Insert, Clip Art.

Repositioning an image

To reposition an image, just drag it to another location.

Type what you are looking for then click 'Go'.

Search results are displayed here.
If you are connected to the Internet, results from the Microsoft Office website will also be included. Click on an image you like to insert it or click on the arrow next to it for more options.

Images with a tiny globe in the bottom-left corner are coming from the Internet so they may take longer to load.

Figure 12.1 *The Clip Art task pane*

Resizing an image

1 Click the image. (<u>Note</u>: The sizing handles appear at the corners and along the edges of the graphic.)

Figure 12.2 *Resizing an image using the sizing handles*

2 Drag any of the sizing handles to resize the image:

- The left and right handles change the width.
- The top and bottom handles change the height.
- The corner handles change the height and width together while maintaining the original proportions of the image.

Formatting images

In order to format an image you must first click on it. Then you use the facilities that your version of Word provides in order to format the image.

Word 2003

To format images in Microsoft Word 2003 you can use the Picture toolbar.

Figure 12.3 *The Picture toolbar (Word 2003)*

Word 2007

Microsoft Word 2007 doesn't have a Picture toolbar. Instead you use the Picture Format tab (Figure 12.4).

Text wrapping

Normally you are limited in where you can put an image. When you adjust the text wrapping, you allow text to flow around the image, giving you a lot more freedom to move around the image.

To change the text wrapping, click the Text Wrapping button and choose an option. Here are some key wrapping styles:

- <u>In Line With Text</u> – This is the default (not much positioning flexibility).
- <u>Tight</u> – Text flows around the image, giving you a lot of flexibility with where you can put it.
- <u>Behind Text</u> – Text flows over the image. Use this option for watermarks.

Watermarks

To use an image as a watermark:

- Change its text wrapping to Behind Text.
- Recolour it using the Washout option from the Color button.

Borders and shading

There are many situations where you might want to change the borders or shading of certain parts of your Word document. For example, you may want to make text stand out, or put a border around a cover page, or even change the background colour of table headings. All of these things (plus much more) can be done via the Borders and Shading window.

To change the borders or shading:

- Right-click on the object, then click Borders and Shading...
- Click the appropriate tab.
- Make the necessary changes.
- Click the OK button to close the Borders and Shading window.

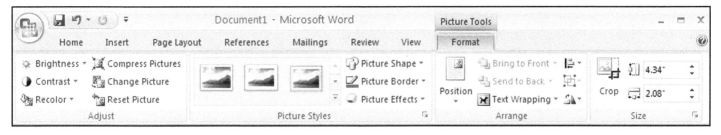

Figure 12.4 *The Picture Format tab (Word 2007)*

Changing borders

Microsoft Word allows you to add borders to text, tables (and table cells), graphical objects and pictures via the Borders tab (Figure 12.5) of the Borders and Shading window.

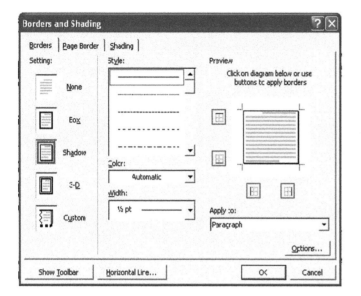

Figure 12.5 *Changing the borders*

Even though the Border tab looks complicated, it isn't that difficult to use once you understand its various sections. Below are some explanations for these sections.

Setting

The Setting choices affect the type of border being applied. To remove borders, choose the None setting. In Figure 12.5, the Shadow setting is selected.

Style, Colour, Width

These sections change the style (dashed, dotted, double-lined, etc.), width and colour of the border. As long as the border setting is not Custom, changes to any of these options are automatically reflected in the preview. Custom borders work differently. When you change the style, width or colour of a Custom border, it has no visible effect. Instead, these changes are applied to any borders you add in the Preview section <u>from that point onwards</u>.

Apply to

This section is where you can change the region to which the border is applied. Some of these regions are:

Text	Puts the border around the selected text
Paragraph	Puts the border around the current paragraph
Cell	Puts the border around the current cell of a table
Table	Puts the border around the entire table

Preview

The Preview section shows a preview of how the selected Border options would affect the region in the Apply to combo box. It also allows you to selectively show/hide individual borders, for example top, bottom, left, right. Just click the appropriate button in the Preview area.

Figure 12.6 *This Preview button shows/hides the top border.*

The position of the button determines which border it affects. On the button itself there is a dotted grid, with the border that will be affected shown by a solid line. When you start showing/hiding individual borders, the border setting automatically changes to Custom.

Changing page borders

The Page Borders tab allows you to create a page border that is applied to one page or multiple pages. It has all of the areas from the Borders tab, as well as an additional area, labelled Art. If you find the usual straight-line borders too boring, you can use the Art combo box to choose a graphical border, as shown in Figure 12.7.

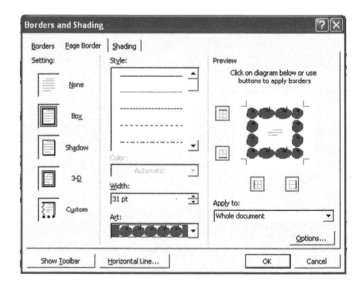

Figure 12.7 *Page Border tab (with a custom border)*

Shading

You can add shading to text, tables (and table cells), graphical objects and pictures via the Shading tab (shown in Figure 12.8) of the Borders and Shading window. The term 'shading' refers to changing the background colour of the selected region. For example:

This is some shaded text whereas this is not.

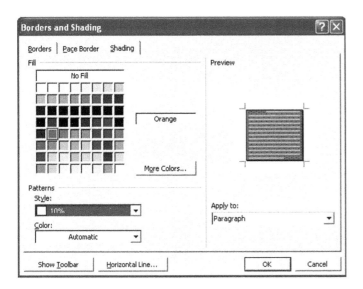

Figure 12.8 *Shading tab*

There are two layers of shading. You'll normally only use the first one – changing the fill (background) colour. But you can also have a pattern on top of the background colour. The Pattern section allows you to change the colour and style of this pattern.

Drop Caps

Another feature you may wish to use is a Drop Cap. An example is shown in Figure 12.9.

This schedule establish
Hydraulic House Ass
established and maint
contractual requirements

Figure 12.9 *Drop Cap*

Inserting a Drop Cap

To insert a Drop Cap:

- Place the cursor in the paragraph you want to begin with a drop cap.
- Click Format, Drop Cap (Word 2003) or Insert Drop Cap (Word 2007).
- Choose the Dropped or In Margin option.

Removing a Drop Cap

To remove a Drop Cap:

- Place the cursor in the paragraph you want to begin with a drop cap.
- Click Format, Drop Cap (Word 2003) or Insert Drop Cap (Word 2007).
- Choose the None option.

Exercise 12

Reproduce the documents that follow on the next two pages. Save them as Graphics1 and Graphics2, respectively. You will find two of the images in the Exercise 12 folder. The remaining images can be found via the Clip Organizer.

OFFICE FURNITURE

Volume 3, Number 3   A Publication of Mac's Office Supplies   Summer 2001

Ideally the size and design of office furniture, particularly of desks, should be suitable for the work to be performed on it. Unfortunately this is not always possible, and desks have to be bought which can be fitted into the available office space. If a clerk is working for most of the time on small 5 x 3 inch index cards, a very small desk would be sufficient, but if another clerk needs to spread out ledgers and working paper, a 6-feet-square desk might be necessary and should be provided – regardless of prestige consideration. There is, however, an advantage in having all desks of a standard size. It adds to the appearance of the office, allows interchange of units, and better terms are usually obtained when buying. Within a chair of standard height,

the height of a desk should not be more than 28 inches. Some clerks with long limbs will doubtless state that desks are never high enough for them to sit at comfortably, and although the height of desk should be adjustable, it is usual to have chairs of adjustable height to fit the desk. It is preferable on grounds of hygiene and portability that desks should be light in construction, and they should be so made that the floor beneath can easily be cleaned. Some storage space is desirable, and the two drawers usually provided are adequate for normal purposes, but too much storage space should be avoided, as the inside of such extra drawer space is apt to get cluttered up with office bric-à-brac and personal belongings.

As far as material surface of a desk, bare wood is

apt to get scratched and look rather dilapidated very quickly. Linoleum and rexine tops can be obtained which are warm and comfortable to work on. For some business routines, it is useful to have a plate-glass top to the desk, not only because of the hard writing surface it gives, but because of the great facility of sliding schedules of standing information under the glass for ready reference.

When buying desks, cost should not be forgotten by the office manager, and the standard two-drawer desk meets the average requirements at a reasonable cost. Simple wooden tables without drawers, and topped with linoleum, are a most useful adjunct for filing or for sorting correspondence, or occasional use in private or general offices.

Productivity Software

Productivity software is the term given to application programs that make people more effective and efficient in their daily activities. Three popular application programs are word processing, spreadsheet and database

Word processing programs are used for creating, editing and formatting documents such as reports, memos and letters. Some features of word processing programs include spelling and grammar checker; headers and footers, character formatting, page formatting, inserting clipart and finding and replacing text. Microsoft Word and Corel WordPerfect are examples of word processing programs

Spreadsheet software is used to organize data in rows and columns in a worksheet. Data is stored in cells, the intersection of rows and columns. Text, numbers, formulas and functions can be entered into cells. One important feature of a spreadsheet program is automatic recalculation. A formula or a function in a cell will automatically recalculate when cells relating to the formula or function change. Most spreadsheet programs include the feature to create charts such as pie charts, line charts and column and bar charts. Microsoft Excel and Lotus 1-2-3 are examples of spreadsheet program

Database software is used to store, maintain, organize, retrieve and present data in an organized manner. A database can contain one or more tables. Microsoft Access and Corel Paradox are examples of database programs

Type of Productivity Software	Examples
Word Processing	Microsoft Word, WordPerfect
Spreadsheet	Microsoft Excel, Lotus 1-2-3
Database	Microsoft Access, Corel Paradox

13. Using text boxes

If you've ever tried to position text precisely in Microsoft Word using the techniques you've learnt so far, you'll appreciate how difficult it is to get the text positioned exactly where you want it. Fortunately, you can use text boxes to do just that.

Creating a text box

There are two main ways you can create a text box.

Method 1

This is the easiest method and can be used if you have already typed the text you want to put in the text box.

- Select the text that is to be in the text box.
- Click Insert, Text Box. If you are using Word 2007, then click Draw Text Box.

Method 2

- Click Insert, Text Box. If you are using Word 2007, then click Draw Text Box.
- If the Drawing Canvas appears (Figure 13.1), press the Delete key once to get rid of it.
- Position the mouse where you want the upper left-hand corner of the text box to be.
- Hold down left-hand mouse button and drag the mouse until the text box is the desired size.
- Type the text.

Note

Starting with Microsoft Word XP, a new 'feature' known as the Drawing Canvas was introduced. When you are creating certain items such as text boxes or shapes, it may automatically appear. Since it tends to get in the way when working with simple documents, it is recommended that you press the Delete key when it appears.

Figure 13.1 *The Drawing Canvas*

Changing the text in a text box

If you ever want to change the text in a text box, all you have to do is click inside the text box. Then you can make the changes the same way you would change any other text in Microsoft Word.

Tip

You can even use the alignment buttons to change the alignment of the text in the text box.

Changing the format of a text box

You can change the format of a text box (e.g. line colour or fill colour) by doing the following:

- Double-click the text box.

Or

- On the text box, then click Format Text Box.
- Select the tab that allows you to make the necessary changes.
- Click OK.

Figure 13.2 *Format Text Box dialogue box*

Note

The Colors and Lines tab provides a lot of the functionality found in the Borders and Shading Window.

Changing the orientation of text in a text box

- Select the text box.
- Go to the Text Box toolbar (Word 2003) or the Textbox Format tab of the ribbon (Word 2007).
- Click Text Direction.
- Click the orientation needed.

Moving a text box

Once you're satisfied with the layout of your text you can drag the text box to a new position. If you just want to move it a little bit, you can 'nudge' it in a given direction:

- Click the boundary of the text box.
- Use the arrow keys to move the text box in the desired direction. (Hold the Ctrl key while pressing the arrows to nudge it in 1-pixel increments.)

Exercise 13

1 Retrieve the file called `Letters` from the folder for Exercise 13.
2 Justify the entire document.
3 Place the first three paragraphs in the font size of 12.
4 Perform the following tasks:

You are required to bold the following:	Location
Letters	main heading
BUSINESS, PERSONAL and CIVIL SERVICE	third paragraph
Styles of display	second heading
The Block, the Semi-blocked and the Indented	third heading
Parts of the letter	fourth heading

5 Place the heading 'Letters' in the font size of 18.
6 Place the word 'ambassadors' and the sentence beginning with 'This is the style chosen ...' in italics.
7 Enter 12 spaces between the heading 'Styles of display' and the paragraph above.
8 In the space created, draw a text box of 1.2" height and 5" width (make sure the box is centred horizontally).
9 Type the following in the text box:

The Business Letter

Business letters, depending on their length, can be typed on three sizes of paper: A4 for ordinary-length letters, A5 for small-length letters, and two-thirds A4 for medium-length.

Note: The heading should be centred, bold and have the font size of 16. Leave the rest in the font size of 10.

10 Place the sections above and beneath the text box in columns. The two columns should be applied to the remainder of the document.
11 Insert the file called `MPOBL` (from the Exercise 13 folder) at the bottom of the document (this file should not be included in the column format above).
12 Save the altered file as `Typing`.

14. Advanced word processing features

Labelling an envelope

To print labels on envelopes, you have to open the Envelopes and Labels window (Figure 14.1). To do this:

- In Word 2003, click Tools, Letters and Mailings, Envelopes and Labels.
- In Word 2007, click the Mailings Tab then click the Envelopes button.

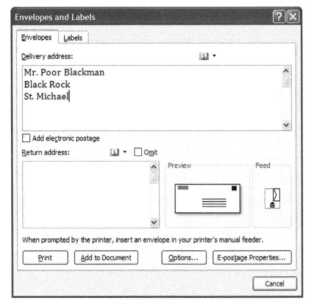

Figure 14.1 *The Envelopes and Labels window*

1 Click in the Delivery address box and type in the appropriate address.

2 (Optional) Click in the Return address and type in the appropriate address.

3 (Optional) Change the envelope size and fonts:
   - Click the Options button.
   - Choose the Envelope Options tab and make the appropriate changes.
   - Click the OK button.

4 Click the Print button.

Mail Merge

Why Mail Merge?

Suppose you wanted to mail out 100 invitations to a wedding. The invitations would be almost identical – each would have information such as:

- the name of the couple being married
- the date, time and location of the wedding

In fact, the only difference between the invitations would be the name of the person(s) being invited. The invitations are not quite identical because they are personalised for the recipients. To solve this problem, you do what is known as a Mail Merge. You start off with two documents:

1 a data file (sometimes called a recipient list) containing the personalised data such as the name and address of each recipient

2 a main document that acts as a template from which the personalised letters are generated

Suppose your recipient list contains the following information:

FirstName	LastName
Jane	Doe
George	Bush
Owen	Arthur

It contains two **fields**: FirstName and LastName. When typing your main document, you use the fields as placeholders to indicate where the personalised information should be inserted. For example, your main document might say:

Dear <<FirstName>> <<LastName>>

When you perform the Mail Merge, you will get a document containing three letters – one for each recipient. None of them will actually contain the words <<FirstName>> or <<LastName>>. Instead, the first letter will say 'Dear Jane Doe', the second will say 'Dear George Bush', and so on.

Microsoft Word has a built-in Mail Merge facility. However, the way you use this facility varies slightly according to the scenario. These are described below as Scenarios A, B and C.

Scenario A

- Main document does <u>not</u> already exist.
- Recipient list does <u>not</u> already exist.

1 **Start the Mail Merge Wizard.**
   Open a new document.

   - In Word 2003, click Tools, Letters and Mailings, Mail Merge Wizard.
   - In Word 2007, click Mailings, Start Mail Merge, Step By Step Mail Merge Wizard.

2 Ensure Letters is selected as the document type. This should be selected by default (Figure 14.2). Click Next to continue to the next step of the Wizard.

Figure 14.2 *Mail Merge Wizard (Word 2003)*

3 Make the current document the starting document. The Current Document option should be selected by default (Figure 14.3). Click Next to go to the next step.

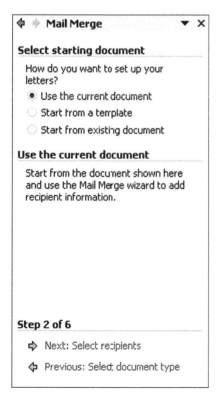

Figure 14.3 *Select the starting document*

4 Type a new recipient list.
- Select the Type a new list option (Figure 14.4).
- Click Create.
- (Optional) To add, delete, rename or reorder the field names, click the Customize button (Figure 14.5a).

Figure 14.4 *Create new recipient list*

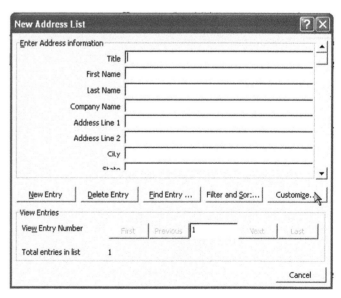

Figure 14.5a *Customizing the Address List (optional)*

- Fill in the recipient information for each entry (Figure 14.5b).
- Click the Close button when you have finished entering all the entries.
- Select the folder where you want to save the list.
- Type a file name and click the Save button.
- Ensure that check marks are next to all the recipients you want included in the merged document (Figure 14.6).

- Click the OK button.
- Click Next to continue to the next step of the Wizard.

5 Type your main document.

Type the main document the same way you would type any other Word document, except that when you have to insert a merge field, do the following:

- Open the Insert Merge Field window (Figure 14.7). Either click More Items... or click the ▣ button.
- Ensure the Database Fields option is selected.
- Double-click each field you wish to insert (or use the Insert button).
- Click the Close button.

When the main document is finished, click Next to continue to the next step of the Wizard.

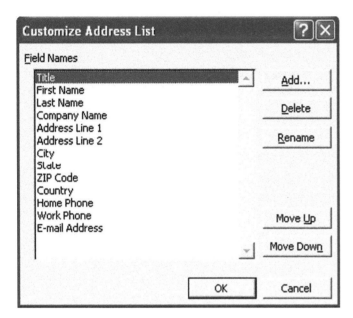

Figure 14.5b

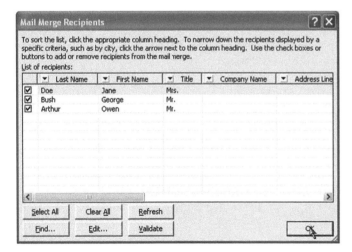

Figure 14.6 *Selecting the recipients*

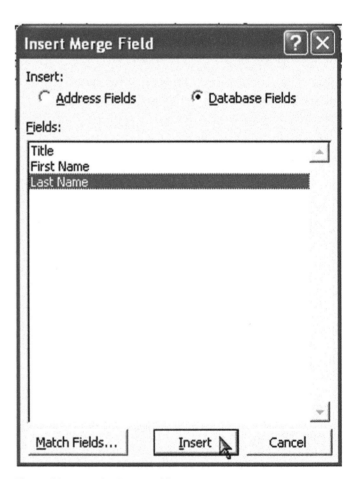

Figure 14.7 *Inserting Merge Fields*

6 Preview your letters.
- Use the navigation buttons 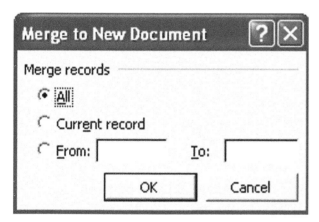 to cycle through the recipients' letters.
- (Optional) You can make any necessary changes directly in the preview letters.
- Save the main document by clicking File, Save.
- Click Next to continue to the next step of the Wizard.

7 Complete the merge.
- Click Edit individual letters... This will cause the Merge to New Document window to appear (Figure 14.8).
- Click the OK button.
- Save the merged document.

Figure 14.8 *Merge to New Document window*

Scenario B

- Main document does <u>not</u> already exist.
- Recipient list already exists.

1 Start the Mail Merge Wizard
Open a new document.
- In Word 2003, click Tools, Letters and Mailings, Mail Merge Wizard.
- In Word 2007, click Mailings, Start Mail Merge, Step By Step Mail Merge Wizard.

2 Ensure Letters is selected as the document type.
This should be selected by default. Click Next to continue to the next step of the Wizard.

3 Make the current document the starting document.
The Current Document option should be selected by default. Click Next to continue to the next step of the Wizard.

4 Open an existing list.
- Ensure the Use an existing list option is selected (Figure 14.9).
- Click Browse ...

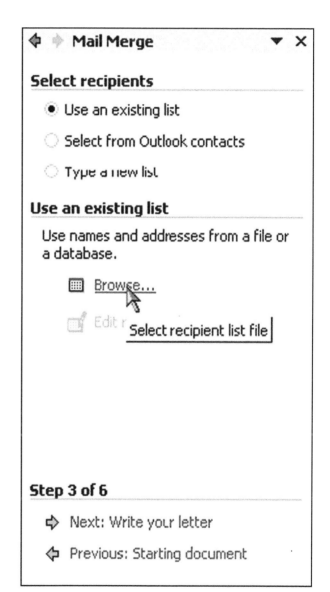

Figure 14.9 *Selecting the recipient list file*

- Select the file containing the list and click the Open button.
- (Optional) To edit an existing entry, click the record, then click the Edit button. Any changes made will be automatically saved after you press the Close button.
- (Optional) To add an additional entry, click the last record, click the Edit button, then click the New Entry button. When you click the Close button, the new entries will be automatically saved.
- Ensure that check marks are next to all the recipients you want included in the merged document.
- Click the OK button.
- Click Next to continue to the next step of the Wizard.

5   Type your Main document.

Type the Main document the same way you would type any other Word document, except that when you have to insert a Merge Field, do the following:
- Open the Insert Merge Field window. Either click More Items… or click the ▭ button.

- Ensure the 'Database fields' option is selected.
- Double-click each field you wish to insert.
- Click the Close button.

When the Main document is finished, click Next to continue to the next step of the Wizard.

6   Preview your letters.
- Use the ⏮ ◀ 1 ▶ ⏭ navigation buttons to cycle through the recipients' letters.
- (Optional) You can make any necessary changes directly in the preview letters.
- Save the Main document by clicking File, Save.
- Click Next to continue to the next step of the Wizard.

7   Complete the merge.

- Click Edit individual letters… This will cause the Merge to New Document window to appear.
- Click the OK button.
- Save the merged document.

Scenario C

- Main document already exists.
- Recipient list already exists.
- You want to make changes to them.

1   Open the existing Main document.

2   Start the Mail Merge Wizard.
- In Word 2003, click Tools, Letters and Mailings, Mail Merge Wizard.
- In Word 2007, click Mailings, Start Mail Merge, Step By Step Mail Merge Wizard.

3   (Optional) Edit the Recipient List.
- Click Edit recipient list.
- Click the Edit button.
- Use the Next and/or Previous buttons to navigate to the right entry.
- Make any desired changes or click the New Entry button to add a new entry.
- Click the Close button.
- The changes you made will be automatically saved.
- Ensure that check marks are next to all the recipients you want included in the merged document.
- Click the OK button.
- Click Next to continue to the next step of the Wizard.

4   (Optional) Edit the Main document.

If you want to move or delete merge fields from the Main document, you must first highlight them completely (including the << and the >>).

To insert merge fields:
- Open the Insert Merge Field window. Either click More Items… or click the ▭ button.

- Ensure the Database Fields option is selected.
- Double-click each field you wish to insert.
- Click the Close button.

When the Main document is finished, click Next to continue to the next step of the Wizard.

5   Preview your letters.
- Use the ⏮ ◀ 1 ▶ ⏭ navigation buttons to cycle through the recipients' letters.

- (Optional) You can make any necessary changes directly in the preview letters.
- Save the Main document by clicking File, Save.
- Click Next to continue to the next step of the Wizard.

6 Complete the merge.
- Click Edit individual letters...
- Click the OK button.
- Save the merged document.

Automatically save backup copies

This feature is for those of us who have ever accidentally saved over a file. Microsoft Word can automatically create a backup copy whenever you click Save. Here's how it works:

Suppose you have a file called `Bob`. You make changes to it and then click Save. If the Automatic Backup feature is turned on, Word would save the old version of `Bob` to a file called `Backup of Bob`, <u>before</u> replacing the existing `Bob` file. So if you accidentally save over `Bob`, you would simply open the `Backup of Bob` file.

Here's how you turn on this feature:

Word 2003

- Click Tools, Options...
- Switch to the Save tab (Figure 14.10).
- Ensure that the 'Always Create Backup Copy' option is selected, then click OK.

Word 2007

- Click the Microsoft Office button.
- Click Word Options.
- Click Advanced.
- Scroll down to the Save section (Figure 14.11).
- Place a tick in the box that says 'Always Create a Backup Copy'.
- Click OK.

Password protection

Microsoft Word allows you to password protect your documents. You can require that a user have to enter a password:

1 To open your file.
2 To modify your document. If the person can't provide the password, he/she will still have the option of opening the document in Read Only mode.

Note

If you want to password protect a file you have to do it while you are saving it.

To password protect a file:

- Open the Save As dialogue box.
- Click on the Tools button.
- If you are using Word 2003, click 'Security Options'. If you are using Word 2007 click 'General Options'. A window similar to the one in Figure 14.12 will appear.
- Type in the passwords in the appropriate boxes.
- Click OK. Word will ask you to retype your password as confirmation.

Tracking changes

If you turn on the Track Changes option, Microsoft Word will keep track of the changes that people make to your document <u>from that moment onwards</u>. Each person is given a different colour so you can quickly identify who changed what.

Here's a quick key:

- Things that have been added are underlined.
- Things that have been deleted will be struck through.
- A vertical black line is displayed on the left of each line that contains a change.
- Formatting changes are listed to the right of the document.

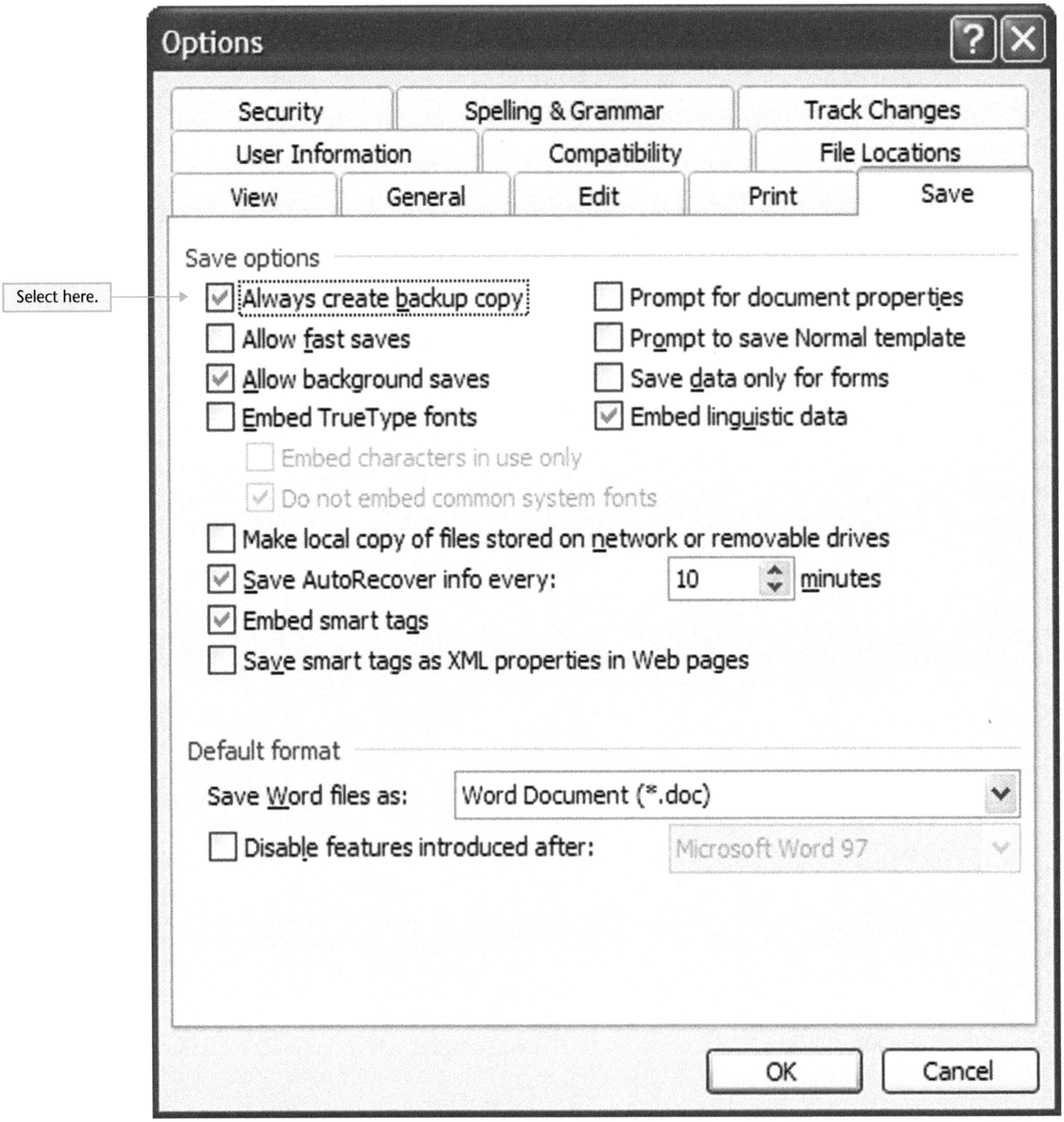

Options [?][X]

Security	Spelling & Grammar	Track Changes
User Information	Compatibility	File Locations
View	General	Edit	Print	**Save**

Save options

Select here. →

[✓] Always create backup copy   [ ] Prompt for document properties
[ ] Allow fast saves   [ ] Prompt to save Normal template
[✓] Allow background saves   [ ] Save data only for forms
[ ] Embed TrueType fonts   [✓] Embed linguistic data

     [ ] Embed characters in use only
     [✓] Do not embed common system fonts

[ ] Make local copy of files stored on network or removable drives
[✓] Save AutoRecover info every: 10 [▲▼] minutes
[✓] Embed smart tags
[ ] Save smart tags as XML properties in Web pages

Default format

Save Word files as: Word Document (*.doc) [▼]

[ ] Disable features introduced after: Microsoft Word 97 [▼]

[OK] [Cancel]

Figure 14.10 *Automatic Backup (Word 2003)*

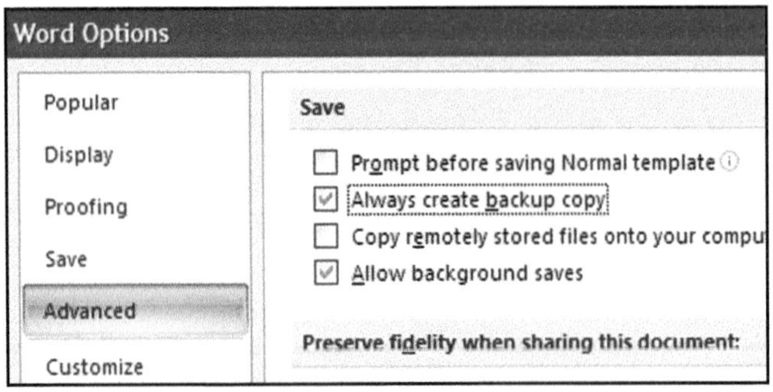

Word Options

| Popular |
| Display |
| Proofing |
| Save |
| Advanced |
| Customize |

Save

[ ] Prompt before saving Normal template ⓘ
[✓] Always create backup copy
[ ] Copy remotely stored files onto your compu
[✓] Allow background saves

Preserve fidelity when sharing this document:

Figure 14.11 *Automatic Backup (Word 2007)*

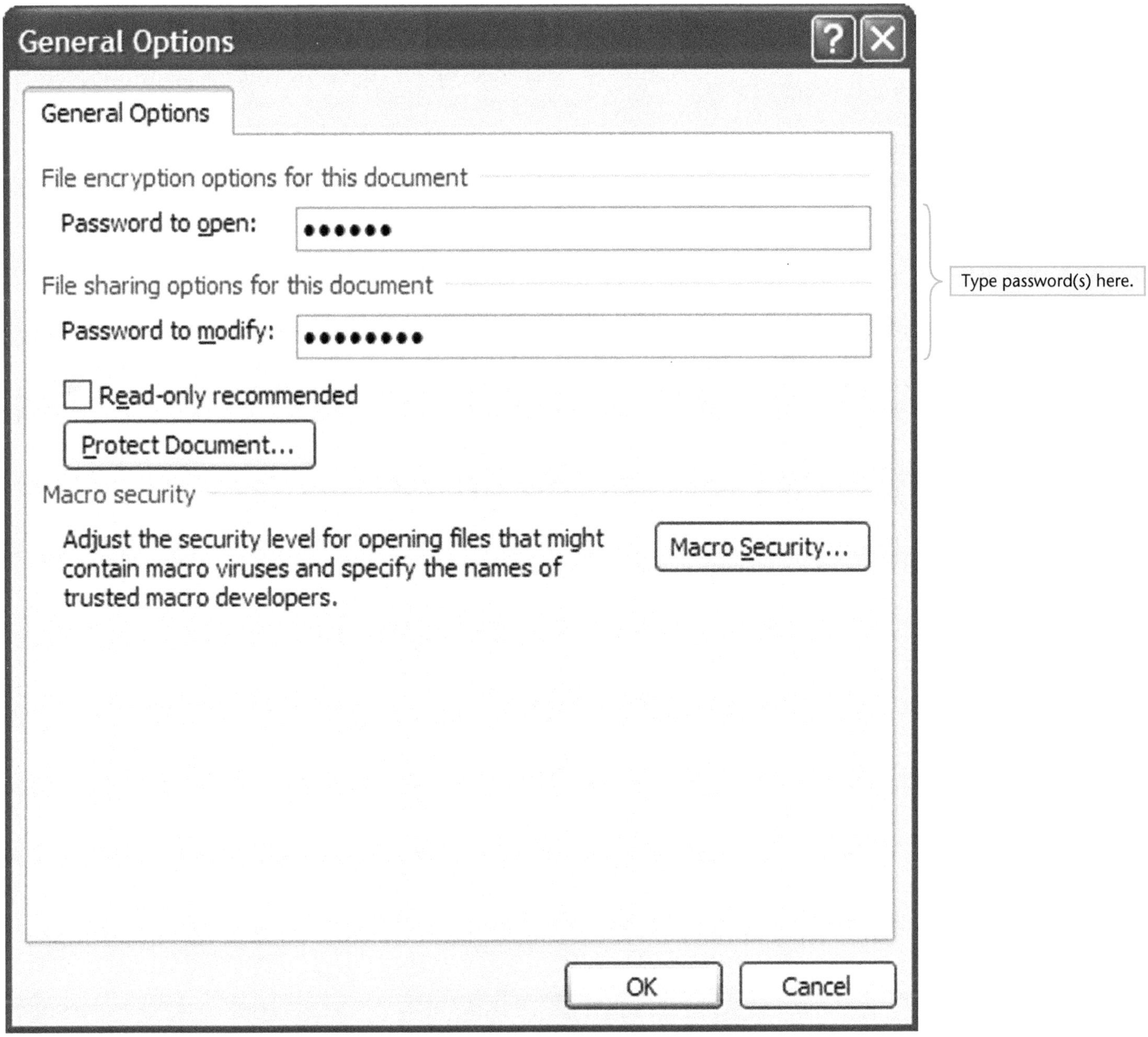

General Options

General Options

File encryption options for this document

Password to open: ••••••

File sharing options for this document

Password to modify: ••••••••

☐ Read-only recommended

[Protect Document...]

Macro security

Adjust the security level for opening files that might contain macro viruses and specify the names of trusted macro developers.

[Macro Security...]

Type password(s) here.

[OK]   [Cancel]

Figure 14.12 *Password protection*

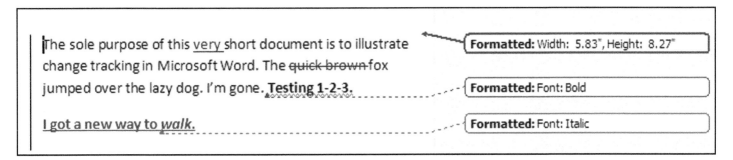

The sole purpose of this <u>very</u> short document is to illustrate change tracking in Microsoft Word. The ~~quick brown~~ fox jumped over the lazy dog. I'm gone. **Testing 1-2-3.**

<u>I got a new way to *walk*.</u>

Formatted: Width: 5.83", Height: 8.27"

Formatted: Font: Bold

Formatted: Font: Italic

Figure 14.13 *Tracking changes*

Note

Whenever you are viewing a document that is tracking changes, the changes you made will always be in red.

So in the example shown in Figure 14.13:

- Three users (red, blue and purple) made changes to our document.
- All the lines contain changes.
- You changed the word 'walk' to italics.
- Another user inserted the word 'very' and deleted the words 'quick brown'.

Turning on change tracking

To turn on change tracking:

- In Word 2003, click Tools, Track Changes.
- In Word 2007, click Review, Track Changes, then click Track Changes.

Note

To turn off change tracking, simply repeat these steps.

Reviewing toolbar (Word 2003)

In Word 2003, when you turn on the Track Changes option, the Reviewing toolbar will appear (Figure 14.14).

Review tab (Word 2007)

In Figure 14.15 you can see the part of the Review tab that deals with tracking changes.

Showing/hiding markup

When you track changes in a document, by default Word shows you the final version along with the markup showing what changes have been made. That is why you still see deleted words.

Word gives you four views to choose between. Their names are self-explanatory:

- Final Showing Markup
- Final
- Original Showing Markup
- Original

If you want to hide the markup, choose either the 'Final' or 'Original' option from the combo box.

Accepting/rejecting changes

You can use the Accept and Reject buttons to accept or reject the changes one at a time or all at once.

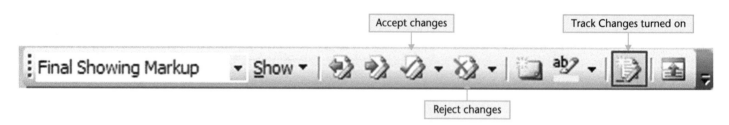

Figure 14.14 *Reviewing toolbar*

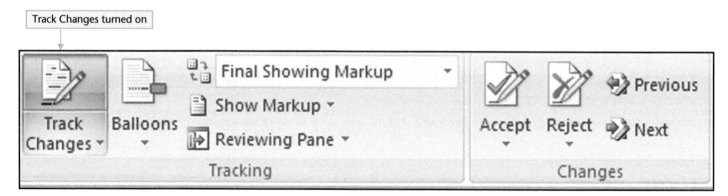

Figure 14.15 *Review tab (tracking changes)*

Exercise 14a

You have been asked to send a letter to three different recipients. Neither the main document nor the recipient list already exists (Scenario A). Using Microsoft Word's Mail Merge facility:

1 Create a new blank document.
2 Type a new recipient list to store the following information for each recipient: first name, last name, district and parish. You will have to click the Customize button and make the following changes to the list of fields:
   • Add fields for District and Parish.
   • Delete any unnecessary fields, e.g. Title, Company Name.
3 Type in the following information, clicking the New Entry button after each record.

FirstName	LastName	District	Parish
Mary	Sobers	Hope Road	St Lucy
Pamela	Best	Orange Hill	St James
Trudi	Gittens	Deacons	St Michael

4 Save this recipient list (also known as the data source) in the appropriate folder. Name it `WMembers`.

5 Type the following letter, inserting appropriate fields in the specified location. (To insert a field, click the Insert Merge fields button ☐).

<<FirstName>> <<LastName>>
<<District>>
<<Parish>>

Dear Madam

Please be advised that the Women of the 21st Century meeting has been postponed until the 6th of April, 2007.

Sorry for any inconvenience caused.

Yours sincerely

....
Kate Windsor
Meeting Director

6 Preview the letters, checking for things like having a space between the first name and last name.
7 Save the main document that you have typed as `Meeting`.
8 Complete the mail merge, saving the merged document as `MeetingLet`.

Exercise 14b

Use the Mail Merge feature to send the following letter (Notice) to the four customers below (Clients):

Teller Green
1st Avenue Blue Rd
Hillaby, St Andrew
$25.52

Evadne Lewis
2nd Avenue Halls Road
Well Gap, St Michael
$87.00

Beulah Burke
St Christopher Road
Spooners Hill, St James
$56.90

Lorna Garnes
Mud Gap
Water Road, Christ Church
$45.85

Notice

<<Insert current date>>
<<Full Name>>
<<Address1>>
<<Address2>>

Dear Mr/Mrs <<LastName>>:

This is our second letter to you concerning your overdue balance of <<Amount>>.

We know that sometimes in the rush of things customers forget the date on which their bills are due. Maybe you missed the date of payment.

Your balance of <<Amount>> is due on the 10th of each month. It is now the 23rd and we have not heard from you.

We would appreciate if you would come into our Broad Street Office and settle your account before the next due date of your balance.

Yours sincerely

Edwin Yearwood

Save the merged letters as `Overdue`.

Exercise 14c

1 Create a Data file using the information below.
2 Save to a file called `Names`.

Mary Lamping Tweedside Road St Michael Barbados 427-7900	James Cobbler Deepen Road Christ Church Barbados 425-7777	Edwin Fuller Kirks Road St Michael Barbados 433-8900
Hallam Greenidge Eden Lodge St Michael Barbados 427-0909	Althea Street Holders Land St James Barbados 432-7876	Heather Small Pie Corner St Lucy Barbados 428-4837

3 Create a Form file.
4 Fill in the merge codes for the address and the phone number of each client.
5 Save to a file called `Telephone`.
6 Merge both documents. Save to a file called `Clients`.

The general format of the document is as follows:

Insert current date

<<Full Name>>
<<Address>>

Dear Sir/Madam:

Your new telephone number <<tel. no.>> is now installed. We are sorry for any inconvenience caused by the lack of telephone service. There was a cable problem in the general area and our men worked day and night to correct that problem.

If there is any further problem with your line please let us know immediately.

Thank you.

Keith Allers
Barbados Telephone Company

Exercise 14d

You are a new teacher at a school and wish to introduce yourself to the parents of a particular class. In your class folder is a data file called `Parents` containing three completed records. You are required to:

1 Retrieve this data file.
2 Add an additional field called <<ChildsFirstname>> to enter the relevant information. Add the following records. Save the file as `Parents1`.

Parent:	Mrs Stephanie Bleeds	Mr and Mrs Glen Cyrus	Mr Levere Jordan
Address:	Blades Hill	Spring Garden	Road View
Parish:	St John	St Michael	St Peter
Child:	Steffan Bleeds	Shanice Cyrus	Janelle Jordan

The general format of your letter is given below. Type and date the letter.

<<Parents' Name>>
<<Address>>
<<Parish>>

Dear <<Mr/Ms Parent Surname>>

Let me introduce myself. I'm Jean Thomas, a first-form teacher at Combermere school, and I have the pleasure to have your child <Child's full name> in my class this year.

Every year, I like to get together with the parents of each of my first-formers early in the school year to talk about their child's progress. This also gives you a chance to ask any questions you may have about how <child's first name> is doing.

I've tentatively scheduled a meeting on October 20th at 5:00 p.m., at the school. If this is not convenient for you, please feel free to call me or drop me a note. I can schedule conferences any day after school.

I'm looking forward to meeting you!
Sincerely

Jean Thomas

3 Merge the documents saving the final document as `Meeting` and the general letter as `Teacher`.

Exercise 14e

Prepare this letter to be sent in the mail to the three customers listed below. Use the Mail Merge feature. Name the Primary document `Orders`, the Secondary document `Reply` and the merged document `Stock`.

Ref MG/(your initials)

Today's date

<<Name>>
<<Address>>

Dear <Name>

Thank you for your order of <Order date>.

I regret that we are currently out of stock of <Item>. However this will be dispatched to you within <Number> weeks.

We are pleased to enclose a copy of our current brochure which contains many special offers. May I draw your attention to pages 45 and 46 where details of free gifts according to the value of your order are itemised.

We look forward to your continued custom.

Yours sincerely

GREENSDALE GARDEN CENTRE
Martin Greensdale

Enc

RECORD ONE	RECORD TWO	RECORD THREE
Mr T Gardner	Mr T Shah	Ms C Cheltenham
14 Elm Tree Close	27 The Poplars	29 Athol Crescent
BRIGHOUSE	HUDDERSFIELD	PEMBERTON
HD4 3LM	HD4 3NR	WA17 4XM
Order Date:	Order Date:	Order Date:
16 Sept	18 Sept	21 Sept
Item: Cymbidium	Item: Slugget	Item: Gromoxone
No Weeks: 4	No Weeks: 3	No Weeks: 5

Exercise 14f

From the letter and accompanying data below, use the Mail Merge feature to create appropriate letters. Save the data file as `Majors`, the form file as `Show` and the merged document as `Annual`. The letter should have left and right margins of 1.5″ and top margin of 2″.

COMMITTEE OF ANNUAL SHOWTIME

>
> <<Fullname>>
> <<District>>
> <<Parish>>
>
> Dear <<Firstname>>

The annual student <<type of show>> will be held this year in the <<name of the gallery>>. The gallery is on the <<location>> of the building. All the work you are planning **must** be dropped off at this location before <<date>>. The gallery will be open from 10:00 to 12:00 and 3:00 to 5:00 during the day and from 7:00 to 10:00 in the evening. You must register all your work with the gallery director when you drop it off.

>
> Sincerely
> Dr Dawn Barber

The letters should go to:

1. Kristen Barclay of Black Rock, St Michael. Her display is for the Science show which will be held in the John Newton Gallery situated on the second floor. The closing date for the arrival of displays is 12th March, 2006.
2. Randall Clarke of Mangrove, St Philip. Her display is for the Music show which will be held in the John Fletcher Gallery situated on the first floor. The closing date for the arrival of displays is 9th March, 2006.
3. Julie Velmer of Pie Corner, St Lucy. Her display is for the Art show which will be held in the Elsie Vaughan Gallery situated on the second floor. The closing date for the arrival of displays is 10th March, 2006.

Exercise 14g

A number of persons from various companies sent requests for the use of facilities at the Monksfield Hotel. You are required to:

1. Retrieve the data file called **Event**, which already contains two (2) records.
2. Delete the <<Title>> field and rename the <<Address3>> field to <<Country>>.

3 Add the records from the table below:

Name	Mr Bumble Bee	Ms Butter Fly	Mrs Centi Pede	Mr Grass Snake
Position	H R Assistant	Office Manager	Director	Manager
Company	Honey's Ltd.	Flowers Galore	Bite Hard College	Hissing Gear Inc.
Address	Hive Street	Garden Grove	#100 Feet Rd	Glide Ave
	Christ Church	St Johns	Stingington	Long Town
	BARBADOS	ANTIGUA	ST LUCIA	TRINIDAD
Event	Staff Retreat	Workshop	Reunion	Conference
Time	Two-day	One-week	Three-day	Two-day
Persons	Ten (10) persons	Fifteen (15) persons	Fifty (50) persons	Twenty (20) persons
Room	The Buzz Lounge	The Pollen Hall	The Swollen Suite	The Forest Room

4 Save the changes as `EventData`.

5 Type the following letter and save it to a file `EventLet`.

(Current Date)
Our Ref. JJ/you

<<Name>>
<<Position>>
<<Company>>
<<Address>>

Dear <<Name>>

Thank you for your recent inquiry concerning <<Event>> facilities at our hotel.

You stated in your letter that the <<Event>> is expected to be over a <<Time>> period. I have therefore arranged for biscuits and coffee for <<No. Persons> to be available in the reception area of your floor each day of your <<Event>.

Seating and tables will be set up in <<Room> which is most suitable for the activities you listed as taking place during your <<Event>>.

If you have any further requests or queries concerning your arrangements and accommodation, please do not hesitate to telephone me or my personal assistant.

Yours sincerely

Mos Quito

6 Merge both files together and save the merged letters using the filename **Eventful**.

Exercise 14h

1 Use the Mail Merge feature to create appropriate letters.

   a Retrieve the secondary document `Member` from your class folder.
   b Delete the <<Parish>> field
   c Rename the <<Land>> field to <<Country>>.
   d Add the records from the table below.

FULLNAME:	Henry Tanui	Miss K Robinson	Alice Banda
ADDRESS:	Medley Close	17 Stoney Bridge	Uhuru Road
	PO Box 462	Victoria 2714	Blantyre
	Nairobi	Australia	Malawi
FIRSTNAME:	Henry	Katie	Alice
MAGAZINE:	Philately	Philately	African Stamps
COUNTRY:	Kenya	Australia	Malawi

   e Save the changes to a file called `Members`.
   f Create a primary document or form file to store the following. Save the file as `ISC`.

   <<Full Name>>
   <<Address>>

   Dear <<First Name>>:

Thank you for your subscription to ISC. The free magazine of your choice is enclosed. We hope you enjoy reading <<name of magazine>> and will consider taking out an annual subscription on this or any of our numerous publications.

May we take this opportunity to welcome you to the world of stamps. Names and addresses of all members will be circulated shortly so that you may write and exchange information from all parts of the world. Alternatively, we at ISC have access to stamps of all prices and types.

As a special offer to new members, we are offering a rare Indian stamp at a very low price. Stamps may be ordered directly from our ISC office.

Next month, we are going to issue a free catalogue to new members. Your catalogue will focus mainly on <<name of country>> and will contain many interesting features. We hope you have countless hours of enjoyment from your hobby.

Yours sincerely

Lisa Lovell

Executive Manager

   g Mail Merge `Members` and **ISC**. Save the result as `Freemag`.

Exercise 14i

The following letter is to be sent to six people. The records for three of these people have been provided. Create the form data file and save it as a file called `Travellers`. Add three records of your choice based on the data below and create the letter which should be saved as `Reservations`. Save the six completed letters as `Confirmation`.

Reservations have been made for:

Mr Anthony Moses of 18 Oak Ridge, Long Bay, St Philip to travel and tour with Sunshine Tours on his visit to the Bahamas. He will receive his ticket 10 days before departure.

Mr & Mrs Dennis Carutheres of Apartment 8, Medbourne Development, St Michael to travel and tour with Island Hoppers on their visit to St Lucia. They will be receiving their tickets 21 days before departure.
Ms Angela John of Lot#84, Orange Hill, St James to travel and tour with Island Hoppers on her visit to Martinique. She will receive her ticket 14 days before departure.

The letter should read as follows:

(Today's Date)
<<Name>>
<<Address>>

Dear Customer

Thank you for confirming your forthcoming travel arrangements with Globetrotters. Enclosed is your confirmation detailing your reservation with <<Travel/Tour Company>>. Please check all details and contact us immediately if you have any queries. Once final payment has been received your tickets will be mailed to you at the address shown on your booking form approximately <<days>> before departure.
Thank you for booking with us and we wish you a pleasant trip. We hope you will re-book next year.

Yours sincerely

Maria Kassim

Director

Enc

Exercise 14j

Using Mail Merge facilities, prepare the following letter (Bookings) to be sent to the persons listed in the table below (Attendees). The letter should have 2.5" top margin to make provision for printing on letter-head. Highlight the topic, presenter's name and number of seats.

<<Date of Letter>>

Our Ref: MLP/VK/me

<<Name>>
<<Address>>

Dear <<Name>>

Thank you for your application to attend the <<Topic>> seminar.

I am sure you will find that a great deal of relevant information is forthcoming and you will have a chance to speak to experts on the subject – both in training and in employment. Your presenter will be <<Presenter's Name>>.

We have booked <<No. Seats>> as you requested and a buffet will be provided at lunchtime.

Please find enclosed an Information Sheet giving a summary of topics.

Yours sincerely

Val Knight

Enc

Date of Letter	May 2nd 2006	May 3rd 2006
Name	Latifa Fing	Mandisa Abraham
Address	Shakespeare Drive	Sunflower Drive
	St George	St Philip
Seminar	Pets and the Weather	Indoor and Outdoor Pets
Presenter	Peter Weatherhead	Ingrid Outram
No. Seats	10	6

Date of Letter	May 9th 2001	May 10th 2001
Name	Safia Lynch	Kyla Pulmar
Address	3rdAvenue Grazettes	Nr Hothersal Turning
	St Michael	St George
Seminar	Behavioural Patterns of Pets	Small Animal Care
Presenter	Beverly Small	Mike Wills
No. Seats	8	9

Save the merged letters as All_Seminars.

15. Printing

Print Preview

Eventually you are going to want to print your document. But before you click Print, you should look at a **Print Preview** to see <u>exactly</u> what the document will look like when it is printed.

Some of the things that the Print Preview will show you that you might not be able to see clearly in the Print Layout view are:

- whether or not a table has any borders
- whether any parts of your document are being 'cut off'

To view the Print Preview:

- Click File or the Microsoft Office button.
- Click Print Preview (in Word 2003) or Print, Print Preview (in Word 2007).

Note

To exit the Print Preview, click the Close preview button.

Using the Print dialogue box

Once you have finished previewing your document, you can choose to print it. The Print dialogue box (shown below) provides you with several options of how to do so. To open this dialogue box:

- Click File (or the Microsoft Office button).
- Click Print.

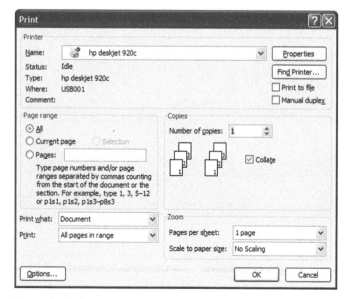

Figure 15.1 *The Print dialogue box*

To print the entire document, just click the OK button. You don't have to change any of the options since Microsoft Word is set up to print <u>all</u> the pages in the document by default.

If you need advanced functionality, such as printing a number of copies or printing selected pages, you'll have to change the appropriate options. The Print dialogue's most useful options are explained below.

Printing the current page

If you just want to print the page where the cursor is currently located, choose the 'Current page' option in the Page range section.

Printing some of the pages

If you want Microsoft Word to print <u>some</u> of the pages in the document:

- Click on the Pages option in the Page range section.
- Type the numbers of the pages you want printed.

Note

You separate individual page numbers by commas and use dashes to indicated page ranges. So if you wanted to print pages 1 and 3 as well as pages 7 to 10, you would type: <u>1, 3, 7–10</u>.

Printing multiple copies

You can control how many copies will be printed via the Number of Copies box (to the right of the window). You can either click on the arrow buttons or type the number directly.

Changing the printer

Microsoft Word normally prints using the default printer that your computer is set up to work with. If you want to change the printer, choose the one you want from the combo list at the top of the Print dialogue box (Figure 15.2).

Note

If you choose the wrong printer, your document may not print at all or may appear as gibberish.

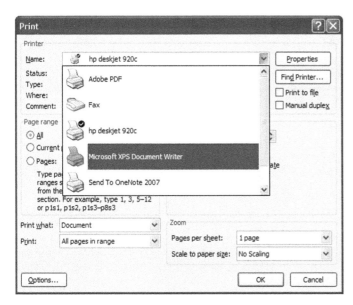

Figure 15.2 *Changing the printer*

Useful shortcut keys

Task/Function	Keyboard command
normal	Ctrl – space bar
italic	Ctrl – I
bold	Ctrl – B
underline	Ctrl – U
double underline	Ctrl – Shift – D
small caps	Ctrl – Shift – K
all caps	Ctrl – Shift – A
subscript	Ctrl – =
superscript	Ctrl – Shift – =
select font	Ctrl – Shift – F
select font size	Ctrl – Shift – P
increase font size	Ctrl – Shift – >
decrease font size	Ctrl – Shift – <
to force a page break	Ctrl + Enter
to cut	Ctrl + X
to copy	Ctrl + C
to paste	Ctrl + V
to save	Ctrl + S
to centre text	Ctrl + E
to position text to the left of the document	Ctrl + L
to position text to the right of the document	Ctrl + R
to spell-check	F7

Part 5

Microsoft PowerPoint

1. Introduction to Microsoft PowerPoint

Microsoft PowerPoint, which is part of Microsoft Office, is the most commonly used **presentation** software in the world. Presentation software allows you to create slideshows that can be used:

- as teaching tools during lectures and training sessions
- to present reports (in business meetings, in class, etc.)
- to illustrate points made during speeches
- to enhance sales pitches.

Presentation software should <u>supplement</u> what the speaker is saying. What do we mean by that?

- You shouldn't read from the slides.
- Your slides shouldn't be packed with text – they should only show the <u>main</u> points you are talking about.
- The slide show should have some pictures or charts to illustrate what you are talking about.

Microsoft PowerPoint can usually be found under the Microsoft Office group of the Start menu.

The PowerPoint 2003 interface

If you have PowerPoint 2003, your interface will look similar to the one in Figure 1.1. Let's look at the main features of this interface.

The Task Pane

By default, the Task Pane is on the right of the PowerPoint 2003 window. (In PowerPoint 2007, it will only appear in certain circumstances.) There are a variety of task panes to choose from including:

- Slide Layout
- Slide Design
- Clip Art.

Each task pane aims to simplify the process of carrying out its particular task. In PowerPoint 2003 (only) you can use the Task Pane menu to switch between the different task panes.

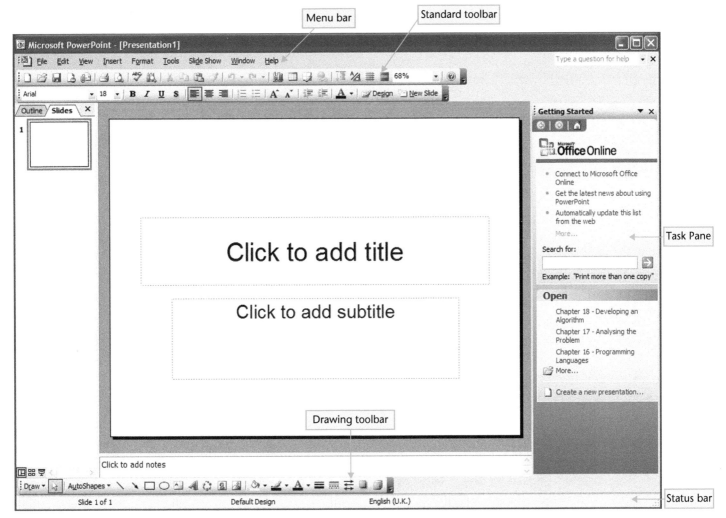

Task Pane

Drawing toolbar

Status bar

Figure 1.1 *The PowerPoint 2003 interface*

The PowerPoint 2007 interface

Like most other programs in the Office 2007 package, the PowerPoint 2007 interface does not have any menus or toolbars (Figure 1.3). Also, the Task Pane is turned off by default. Instead, the main component of the interface is the Ribbon (Figure 1.4).

The Ribbon

The PowerPoint 2007 Ribbon is divided into a number of tabs (Home, Insert, Design, etc.). You can switch to a tab manually by clicking on it. However, in many cases, PowerPoint detects which tab you currently need and automatically switches to it.

Each tab of the Ribbon is divided into a number of groups to make it easier for you to find the various options. For example, the Home tab is divided into groups such as Clipboard, Slides and Font.

The Microsoft Office button

To the top left of the Ribbon is the Microsoft Office button. Clicking this button will display a menu

Click to open the Task Pane menu

Figure 1.2 *The Task Pane*

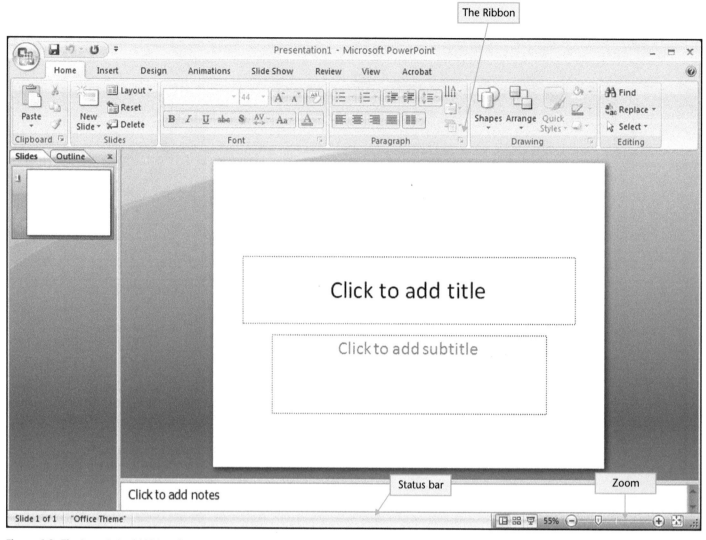

Figure 1.3 *The PowerPoint 2007 interface*

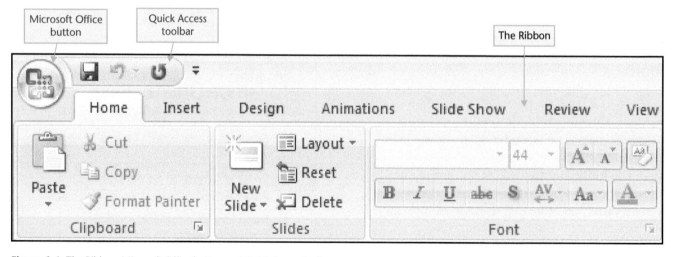

Figure 1.4 *The Ribbon, Microsoft Office button and Quick Access toolbar*

that has the items you'd find in a typical File menu, for example: New, Open, Save, Print, Close and Exit.

The Quick Access toolbar

This toolbar contains buttons that allow you to quickly:

- save the slideshow
- undo the last thing you did
- redo the last thing you undid

Similarities between the 2003 and 2007 versions

While there are some significant differences between the PowerPoint 2003 and 2007 interfaces, there are a number of things they have in common.

1 In the middle of the window you'll see the current slide you're working on.

Figure 1.5 *The current slide*

2 To the left of the window there is a list of the slides in your slideshow. By default, the Slides tab is selected (but you can switch to the Outline tab by clicking on it). The Slides tab shows thumbnails of the slides in your presentation.

- To switch to a particular slide, just click on its thumbnail.
- To select multiple slides use the Shift or Ctrl keys.

Figure 1.6 *The Slides tab*

3 Near the bottom is the window is a place where you can type notes for the current slide.

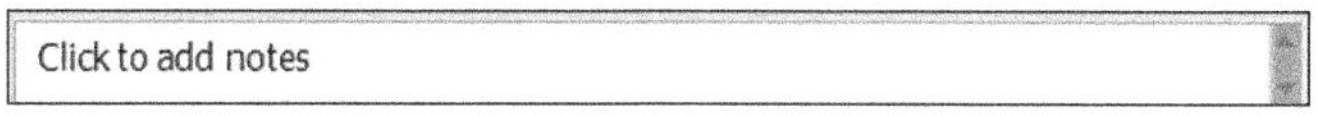

> Click to add notes

Figure 1.7 *The Notes box*

Similarities to Microsoft Word

If you are comfortable with formatting text in Microsoft Word, you should feel completely at home doing so in PowerPoint. Making text bold, changing the font and alignment all work just as you'd expect them to.

Differences from Microsoft Word

PowerPoint uses slides instead of pages. Working with presentations therefore requires a different mindset from working with Word documents. The most important thing to remember is this:

> You can't type directly on slides – you have to use text boxes.

Opening an existing presentation

To open an existing slideshow:

- Click File (or the Microsoft Office button).
- Click Open.
- Go to the folder that contains the file.
- Double-click on the file's icon.

In PowerPoint 2003 and before, files normally have the extension `.ppt` or `.pps`. PowerPoint 2007 adds several new file types including `.pptx` and `.ppsx`, but it can also open files created in previous versions.

Note

PowerPoint 2003 can't open the PowerPoint 2007 files (`.pptx`, `.ppsx`, etc.) unless you install a special converter.

Opening a recent presentation

All Microsoft Office programs keep track of the documents that you have recently worked with and

PowerPoint is no exception. You can see a list of recent documents:

- at the bottom of the File menu (PowerPoint 2003)
- to the right of the Microsoft Office menu (PowerPoint 2007).

Viewing a slideshow

To view a slideshow click View, Slideshow, or press the F5 key. Some slideshows are designed to automatically advance to the next slide. Others require you to manually go from one slide to the next.

There are several ways you can go to the **next** slide:

- Click the left mouse button.
- Press the Enter key.
- Press the right or down arrow.

You can go to the **previous** slide by pressing the left or up arrow on your keyboard.

Navigation controls

If you move the mouse during a slideshow, a semitransparent overlay will appear at the bottom left-hand corner of the screen.

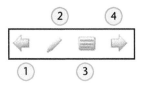

Figure 1.8 *The navigation controls*

These controls have the following functions (corresponding to the numbered buttons in Figure 1.8):

1 Go to the previous slide.
2 Click here to change the current annotation settings. You can make the mouse pointer behave like a pen or highlighter, change the colour and more.

3 Clicking here displays a menu from which you can jump to particular slide, pause the slideshow, and get help on what keys do what during the slideshow. <u>Note that you can get this same menu by right-clicking on the slide.</u>
4 Go to the next slide.

Keyboard shortcuts

Here are some additional keyboard shortcuts you may find useful.

In order to …	Press …
end the slideshow	Esc
go to a particular slide	the number for that slide, followed by Enter
erase annotations from the screen	E

Exercise 1

1 List four uses of presentation software.
2 Open the Island file from your class exercise folder.
3 Use the scroll bar on the right to scroll through the different slides.
4 Use the Slides tab to return to the first slide.
5 Switch to the Outline tab to see what it looks like then switch back to the Slides tab.
6 View the slide show. Navigate through it by using the mouse, keyboard and navigation controls.
7 Close the presentation.

2. PowerPoint basics

Creating a new blank presentation

Whenever you first open PowerPoint, it automatically creates a blank presentation for you to work with (usually called Presentation1). However, if you need to do so manually, it is very simple.

PowerPoint 2003

- Click File, New...
- Click the Blank presentation option from the top of the Task Pane.

Or you could just click the New icon from the Standard toolbar.

PowerPoint 2007

- Click the Microsoft Office button.
- Click New.
- Choose the Blank presentation option from the New presentation window.
- Click the Create button.

A new blank presentation contains only one slide – the Title Slide. On it there are two placeholder text boxes – one for the title and one for the subtitle.

Figure 2.1 *Title Slide*

When you click in one of the text boxes, the placeholder text disappears, allowing you to insert some text of your own.

Adding a new slide

Although the way you insert a new slide differs a bit between the two versions of PowerPoint, in both cases

you have the option of using the default slide layout or choosing another one. We'll talk more about slide layouts in a little while.

Note

New slides are inserted <u>after</u> the current slide.

PowerPoint 2003

To insert a new slide in PowerPoint 2003:

- Click Insert, New Slide.
- (Optional) If you wish, change the slide layout by choosing one from the Slide Layout task pane.

PowerPoint 2007

In PowerPoint 2007, if you want to insert a new slide:

- Switch to the Home tab.
- Click the New Slide button. If you click on the button itself PowerPoint will insert a new slide with the default layout (Title and Content). If you click on the arrow, you'll get a menu like the one shown below that you can use to choose an alternative layout.

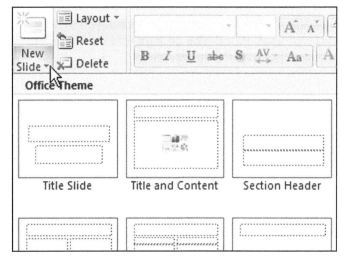

Figure 2.2 *Inserting a new slide in PowerPoint 2007*

Deleting a slide

To delete a slide, right-click on its thumbnail in the Slides tab and click Delete (Figure 2.3).

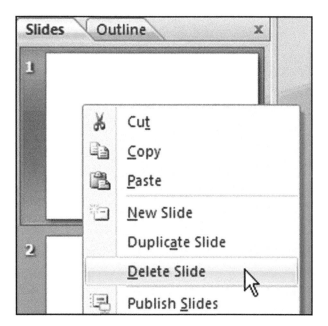

Figure 2.3 *Deleting a slide*

Reordering slides

To change the order of your slides, just drag the slide thumbnails to the desired positions. You can do this via the Slides tab, but if you have several slides it may be easier to reorder them via the Slide Sorter.

To switch to the Slide Sorter view, click View, Slide Sorter.

Figure 2.4 shows the third slide being repositioned so that it will now be the second. You should notice the following:

- The mouse pointer has a little rectangle at the bottom. Whenever you see this icon, you are in the process of dragging an item to a new location.
- The vertical line indicates where the slide will go.

Tip

If you want to get back to the view you are accustomed to, click View, Normal.

Saving a presentation

In order to save your PowerPoint presentation:

- Click File (or the Microsoft Office) button.
- Click Save.
- Type the name of the file and choose the location where it will be saved.
- (Optional) If you are using PowerPoint 2007 and you want people using previous versions to be able to view your presentation, change the file type to PowerPoint 97-2003 Presentation (*.ppt).
- Click the Save button.

Exercise 2a

1 Open the Island file from the folder for Exercise 2a.
2 Interchange the second and third slides.
3 Delete the fourth slide.
4 Save the presentation as Island1.

Exercise 2b

1 Create a new blank presentation.
2 In the appropriate placeholder, insert the title 'All about me'. Put your name as the subtitle.
3 Add the following slides and fill in the appropriate information:
   - My family
   - My hobbies
   - My favourite things
4 Insert a slide after the title slide called 'Words that best describe me'.
5 Save the presentation as Myself.

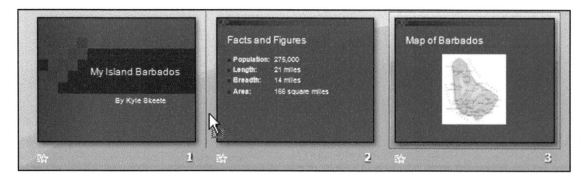

Figure 2.4 *Reordering a slide via the Slide Sorter view*

3. Slide layouts

PowerPoint provides multiple layouts that you can use in your slides. These layouts have placeholders where you can insert text or various media.

Changing the layout

You can change the layout of a slide at any time. When you change a slide's layout, you don't erase the material you already have on the slide. Instead, the material is repositioned to fit the new layout.

To change the layout of a slide:

- Right-click on the slide's thumbnail in the Slide tab.
- Click (Slide) Layout.
- Choose the layout you want. In PowerPoint 2003, you have to do this from the Task Pane.

Choosing the right layout

You can divide the slide layouts into two broad categories: text layouts and content layouts. Text layouts are straightforward – you just click in the text box and replace the placeholder text with some text of your own.

Content layouts require a bit more work. But the good thing about them is that they allow you to insert different types of media – tables, pictures, clip art, charts and video clips.

Below is an explanation of when to use a particular layout.

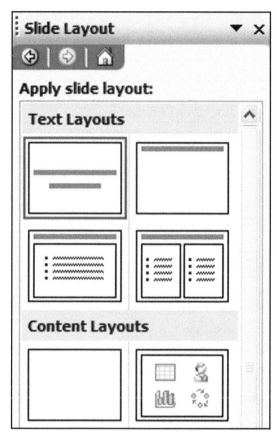

Figure 3.1 *Changing layout in PowerPoint 2003*

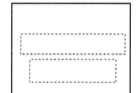

Title Slide

Use this layout on the first slide of your presentation. Give the title of the presentation and a subtitle or the name of the presenter.

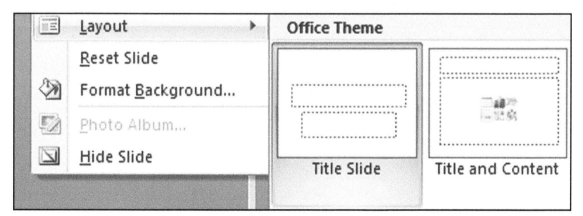

Figure 3.2 *Changing slide layout in PowerPoint 2007*

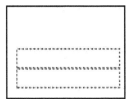

Section Header (PowerPoint 2007 only)
You should use a section header slide to let the audience know whenever a new section is beginning.

Title and Content / Title and Text
This is the default layout for any new slides that you add.

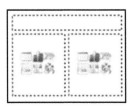

Title and 2 Content / Two Column Text
A two-column layout is a good way to show or compare two items.

Blank Slide
With this layout, you'll have to add each item manually, but you have full control over where each item goes on the slide.

Title Only
You'd use this layout if you want to manually position information on the slide but still want to have a title that is consistent with the rest of the slides.

Using content layouts

Each content layout has a cluster of icons that you can click to insert different types of media. PowerPoint 2003 has slightly different icons from 2007, but very similar functionality. The icons and what they do are shown in Figures 3.3 and 3.4 and the table.

Figure 3.3 *Content icons in PowerPoint 2003*

Figure 3.4 *Content icons in PowerPoint 2007*

Icon number	What it inserts
1	table
2	chart
3	clip art
4	picture from a file on your computer
5	smart chart / diagram
6	media clip, e.g. video, sound

We'll only cover inserting pictures and Clip Art. If you want to insert a table or chart it is often easier to copy it from another Microsoft Office program as opposed to creating one in PowerPoint.

Inserting Clip Art
When you click on the Clip Art content button in a slide, it will open the Clip Art task pane. You can also show the Clip Art task pane by clicking:

- Insert, Picture, Clip Art… (in PowerPoint 2003)
- Insert, Clip Art (in PowerPoint 2007).

Figure 3.5 illustrates how you use the Clip Art task pane.

Inserting a picture
In order to display the dialogue box that allows you to insert a picture from a file on your computer, either:

- Click the picture content button on the slide.

Or
- Click Insert, Picture (from file).

Once you've inserted a picture, you can drag it to another location or use the picture handles to resize it (Figure 3.6).

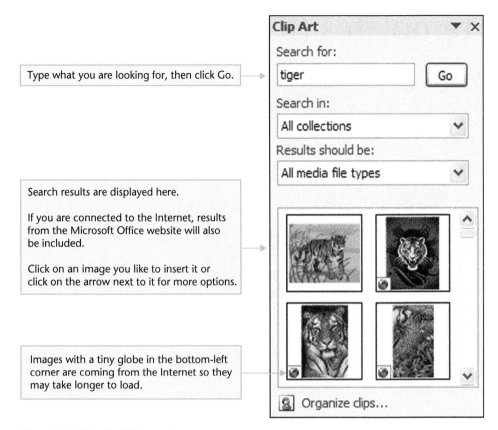

Type what you are looking for, then click Go.

Search results are displayed here.

If you are connected to the Internet, results from the Microsoft Office website will also be included.

Click on an image you like to insert it or click on the arrow next to it for more options.

Images with a tiny globe in the bottom-left corner are coming from the Internet so they may take longer to load.

Figure 3.5 *Using the Clip Art task pane*

Figure 3.6 *Using the picture handles to resize a picture*

Exercise 3

1 Create a new blank presentation.
2 In the title slide, add the title 'Computer hardware'. Put 'Basic stuff you should know' as the subtitle.
3 Add a new slide. Put its title as 'Types of hardware'. Mention the following types:
   • Central Processing Unit (CPU)
   • Input Devices
   • Output Devices
   • Storage Devices.

4 Add a Section Header for 'Input Devices'. If you are using PowerPoint 2003 use a Title Slide instead.
5 Add slides for the following input devices. Use layouts that have a Title and Content and insert a clip art image of each of the following devices:
   • keyboard
   • mouse
   • joystick.
6 Add a Section Header (or Title Slide) for 'Output Devices'.
7 Add a two-column layout called 'Monitors'. Add the following content:

Cathode Ray Tube	**Liquid Crystal Display**
CRT for short	Better known as LCD
Looks like an old TV	Thin and compact
Big and heavy	

8 Add a Title and Content slide for 'Printers' and add the following points:
   • **Dot-matrix** – Uses a ribbon
   • **Inkjet** – Uses ink
   • **Laser** – Uses a laser and toner
   • **Thermal** – Uses heat.
9 Save the presentation as `Hardware`.

4. Using design templates (themes)

The presentations that we've created so far have looked a bit dull. Fortunately, PowerPoint comes with a set of design templates that can be used to make a presentation look more interesting. Each one has been carefully designed so that the background and the text go well together.

Note

In PowerPoint 2007 design templates are called themes. Here we use the terms 'design template' and 'theme' interchangeably.

Creating a new presentation from a design template

When creating a new presentation, if you want to use a design template you have to take some additional steps.

PowerPoint 2003

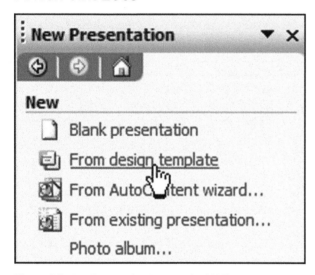

Figure 4.1 *New Presentation (PowerPoint 2003)*

In order to create a new presentation from a design template:

- Click File, New...
- Click From design template on the task pane.
- Select the template you want.

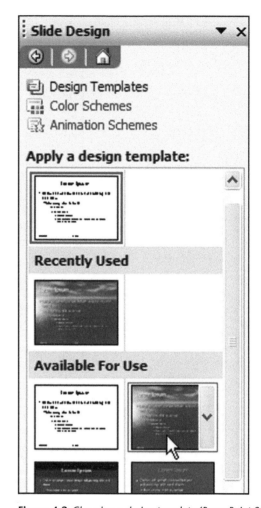

Figure 4.2 *Choosing a design template (PowerPoint 2003)*

PowerPoint 2007

To create a new presentation from an installed theme:

- Click the Microsoft Office button.
- Click New.
- Click Installed Themes.
- Select the theme you want to use.
- Click the Create button at the bottom of the window.

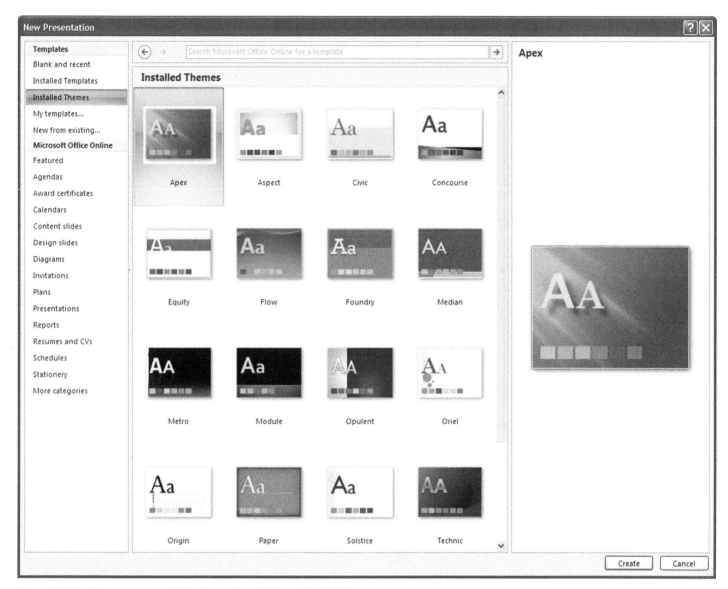

Figure 4.3 *Creating a new presentation from a theme in PowerPoint 2007*

Changing the design template (theme)

If you don't like your presentation's design template (or if it doesn't have one), you can always change it later.

PowerPoint 2003

In PowerPoint 2003, there is a task pane dedicated to changing the design template (the same one you use when creating a new presentation from a design template). You can access it by clicking Format, Slide Design…

When you position the mouse over a design, you'll see an arrow appear at the side. If you click on it, you'll see the list of options in Figure 4.4. Choose the option that suits your particular situation.

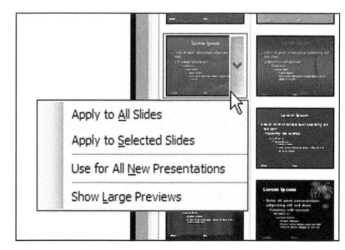

Figure 4.4 *Changing the design template in PowerPoint 2003*

PowerPoint 2007

To change the theme utilised by your presentation, you use the Design tab of the Ribbon.

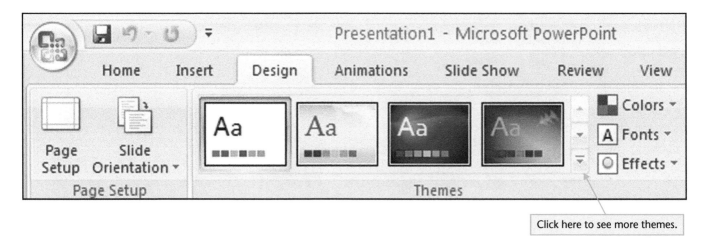

Figure 4.5 *Changing the theme in PowerPoint 2007*

To apply the theme to the entire presentation, just click on the theme.

To apply the theme to selected slides:

- Select the thumbnails of the slides in the Slides tab (to select multiple slides use the Shift or Ctrl key).
- Right-click on the theme you want from the Ribbon.
- Click Apply to Selected Slides.

Changing the colour scheme

Sometimes you may like a particular design but would prefer it in another colour. Fortunately, PowerPoint makes it easy to change a presentation's colour scheme.

PowerPoint 2003

PowerPoint 2003 loves task panes so, not surprisingly, it has one for colour schemes as well. There are a couple of ways to access it.

1 If a Slide Designs task pane is currently open, click on the Color Schemes link at the top.
2 Alternatively, you can switch to the Slide Design – Color Schemes task pane via the Task Pane menu.

Then click the arrow by the colour scheme you like and choose whether you want to apply it to all slides.

Figure 4.6 *The same slide using three different colour schemes*

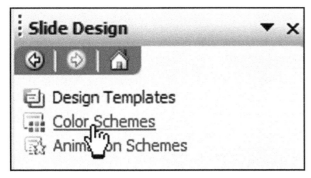

Figure 4.7 *Accessing colour schemes from the Slide Design tab*

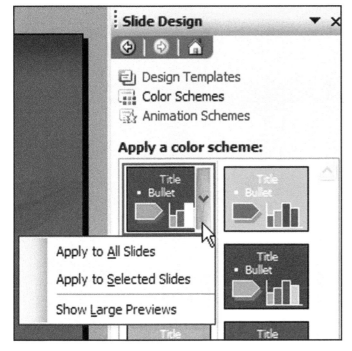

Figure 4.8 *Changing the colour scheme in PowerPoint 2003*

PowerPoint 2007

As expected, PowerPoint 2007 takes a ribbon-based approach. To change the colour scheme in PowerPoint 2007:

- Switch to the Design tab.
- Click on the Colors button.
- Click on the colour scheme you want.

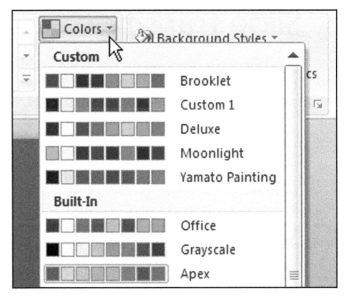

Figure 4.9 *Changing the colour scheme in PowerPoint 2007*

If you only want to apply the scheme to selected slides, right-click on the colour scheme and choose Apply to Selected Slides.

Note

The current scheme has an orange box around it. So in Figure 4.9, Apex is the current colour scheme.

Exercise 4

1. Open the `Hardware` file that you created in Exercise 3.
2. Apply a design template/theme to the presentation.
3. Change the colour scheme to one of your choosing.
4. Apply a new design template/theme to the first slide only. Change its colour scheme.
5. Save the file as `Hardware1`.
6. Create a new presentation from a design template/theme. Add a few slides with different layouts. Change the colour scheme and save it as `Templates`.

5. Slide transitions

Slide transitions allow you to control how PowerPoint moves from one slide to the next. You can make PowerPoint advance to the next slide after a specified number of seconds, use transition animations, or use any of a range of other options.

Applying slide transitions

Although PowerPoint 2003 and 2007 provide the same functionality when it comes to slide transitions, they use different interfaces. From what we have seen before, this should not be too surprising.

PowerPoint 2003
PowerPoint 2003 has a task pane dedicated to slide transitions which can be accessed by clicking Slide Show, Slide Transition... You can also use the Task Pane menu.

PowerPoint 2007
In PowerPoint 2007, the Slide Transition options (shown in Figure 5.2) are part of the Ribbon's Animations tab.

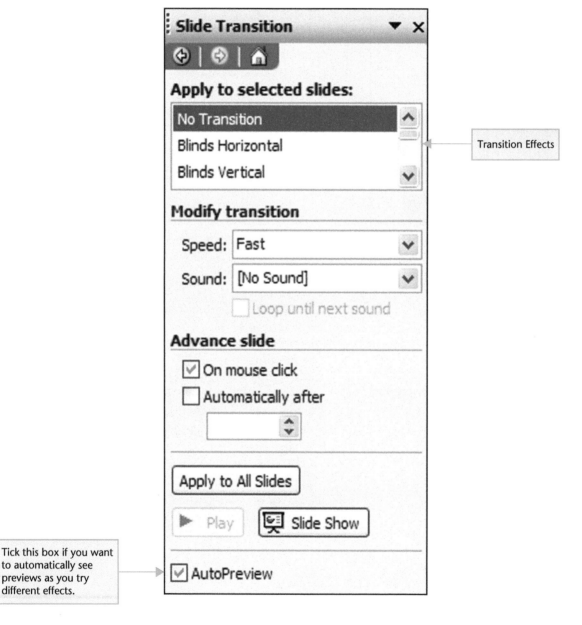

Figure 5.1 *Slide Transition task pane in PowerPoint 2003*

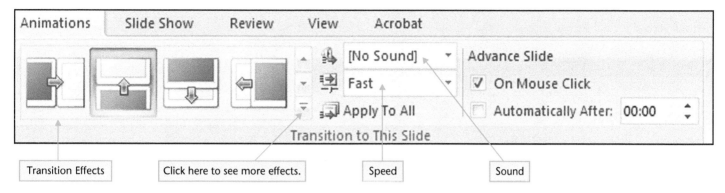

Figure 5.2 *Slide transition options in PowerPoint 2007*

Transition options

Here's what the various options are for:

1 <u>Transition Effects</u> – These control how your slide appears on the screen. For example you can have a dissolve effect or make the new slide fade in from black.
2 <u>Speed</u> – This allows you to control whether the animation occurs at a Fast, Medium or Slow speed.
3 <u>Sound</u> – Makes PowerPoint play a sound as the slide appears on the screen. You can choose from the list or use a file stored somewhere else on your computer.
4 <u>Advance Slide</u> – This allows you to control what causes this slide to advance to the next one. By default PowerPoint requires you to click the mouse or press a button to go to the next slide. But you can also make it advance automatically after a certain amount of time. Using the settings shown in Figure 5.3, the slide will advance when you click the mouse or after 5 seconds (whichever comes first).

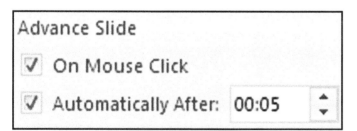

Figure 5.3 *Advance Slide dialogue box*

5 <u>Apply to All</u> – Click this button if you want to apply these settings to all the slides in the show.

Tip

You can tell which slides have transition effects by checking their thumbnails. The ones with effects have a tiny image that looks like the one below next to their thumbnails.

Rehearsing timings

This is a very useful feature, especially if your presentation is accompanying a speech or has to be a certain length.

Here's how it works. You rehearse your presentation while looking at each slide. As you do this there are two timers going – one that lets you know how long you've spent on the current slide and another that tells you the total time that has elapsed.

When you are ready to go to the next slide, you click the Next button. When you're finished, PowerPoint asks you if you want to keep the new slide timings. If you click Yes, PowerPoint will update your slide transitions so that the slides automatically advance according to the rehearsed timings.

You access this feature the same way in both PowerPoint 2003 and 2007:

• Click Slide Show.
• Click Rehearse Timings.

The first slide of the presentation will be displayed full-screen, with the Rehearsal window on top.

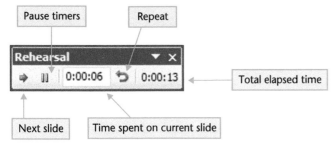

Figure 5.4 *The Rehearsal window*

Some parts of the window aren't self-explanatory:

- <u>Pause Timer</u> – Click it once to pause both timers. Click it again to continue timing.
- <u>Repeat</u> – This allows you to start the current slide again and resets the timers to suit. The first timer gets reset to 0:00:00 whereas the total elapsed time gets rolled back to whatever it was when you first got to this slide.

Note

The rehearsed timings can also affect your custom animations. You will find out more about custom animations in the next chapter.

Exercise 5

1 Open the file `Hardware1` from your exercise folder.
2 Add a dissolve effect to <u>all</u> the slides and have each slide automatically advance after 5 seconds.
3 Apply a fade effect to the title slide as well as to the slides with the section headers (Input Devices, Output Devices). These slides should automatically advance after 2 seconds.
4 Save the file as `Hardware2`.
5 Use the Rehearse Timings feature to set timings for the slides. Pretend that you are talking to the class about these various devices.
6 Save the file as `Hardware3`.

6. Custom animations

Custom animations are similar to transition effects except that they work on the individual elements on a slide rather than on the slide itself. Both PowerPoint 2003 and 2007 use the same interface to add custom animations – the Custom Animation task pane.

Displaying the Custom Animation task pane

If the Custom Animation task pane is not currently being displayed, you can see it by clicking:

- Slide Show, Custom Animation… (if you are using PowerPoint 2003)
- Animations, Custom Animation (if you are using PowerPoint 2007)

Understanding the Custom Animation task pane

The Custom Animation task pane is one of the more complicated parts of PowerPoint since it has so many different features. It helps if you think of the task pane as being divided into four sections, as shown in Figure 6.1.

Adding a custom animation

To add a custom animation:

- Select the element you want to animate, for example a picture or paragraph.
- Click Add Effect.

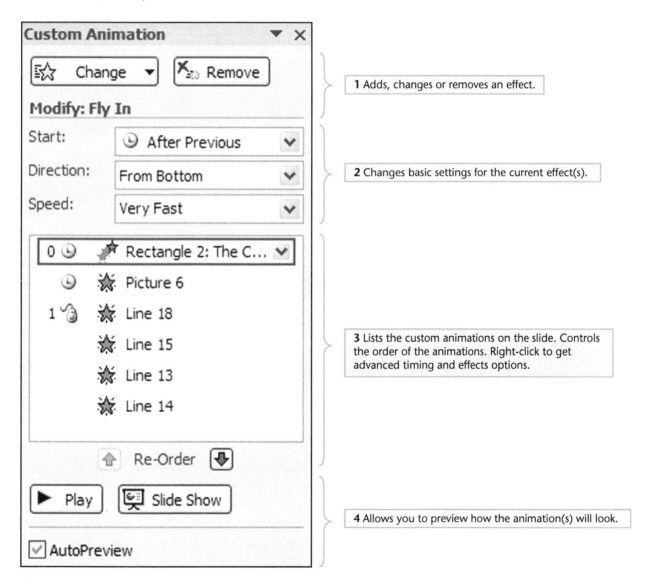

Figure 6.1 *The Custom Animation task pane (with effects already added)*

- Choose an effect from one of the four categories. The effect that you choose is then added to the list of custom animations for the slide.
- Change the settings for the effect to suit your needs.

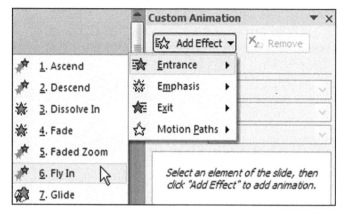

Figure 6.2 *Adding an entrance effect*

Categories of effects

The effects are grouped into four categories:

1 <u>Entrance</u> – Effects where the object is hidden at first but then animates into view.
2 <u>Emphasis</u> – Emphasises objects that are currently on the screen by changing their size and/or colour, making them flicker for example.
3 <u>Exit</u> – These effects make objects on the screen disappear.
4 <u>Motion Paths</u> – Cause an object that is already on the screen to move to another position along a straight line, curve or custom path.

Of these four types, you only really need to know how to use the Entrance effects. The rest are more difficult to use effectively.

Removing an animation or switching to another one

After you've added a custom animation, you can always switch to another one or remove it altogether.

- Select the custom animation from the list of custom animations that are currently being applied.
- Click the Change or Remove button.

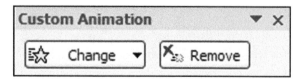

Figure 6.3 *Change and Remove animation buttons*

Changing basic animation settings

After you've added a custom animation, you may want to tweak basic settings such as the speed and when the animation starts.

To change the basic settings:

- Make sure the animation that you want to modify is currently selected in the list.
- Use the Start, Direction or Speed combo boxes to make the changes you want.

The Start settings are quite complicated and need a little bit more explaining.

Option	When the animation will start
On Click	when the user clicks the mouse or presses Enter
With Previous	at (roughly) the same time as the previous animation
After Previous	after the previous animation has completed

Changing advanced settings

You have to dig a bit deeper to access advanced features like delaying effects or adding sounds.

Delaying custom animations

In order to delay a custom animation:

- Right-click on the animation you want to delay, then click Timing...

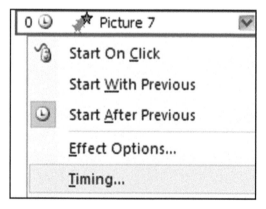

Figure 6.4 *Changing the timing*

- Type the number of seconds you want the effect delayed (or use the arrows to increase/decrease the delay in intervals of 0.5 seconds).

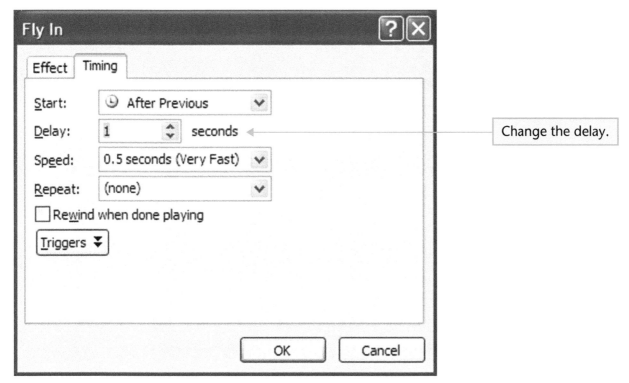

Figure 6.5 *Timing settings*

Adding sound effects

To add a sound effect to a custom animation:

- Right-click on the animation you want to add the sound to, then click Effect Options...

- Choose a sound from the Sound combo box. If you don't want to use one of the built-in sounds, scroll down to the bottom of the box and click Other Sound.... Then you can choose a sound file from anywhere on your computer.

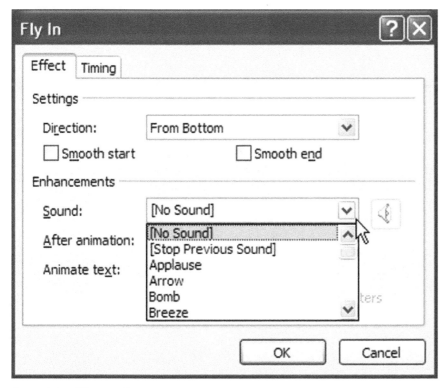

Figure 6.6 *Adding sound*

Exercise 6

1 Open the `Hardware2` file from your exercise folder.
2 Add some custom animations. Each one should start after a delay of 0.5 seconds.
3 Add some sound effects.
4 View your handiwork.
5 Save the file as `Hardware4`.

7. The Slide Master

In PowerPoint there is a special slide called the **Slide Master**. Anything you put on this slide will appear on all the other slides. For instance, if you need a company logo to automatically appear on every slide, you'd put it on the Slide Master. This is how PowerPoint does things like footers, slide numbers and even design templates – it just modifies the Slide Master accordingly.

Viewing the Slide Master

In order to view the Slide Master:

- In PowerPoint 2003, click View, Master, Slide Master.
- In PowerPoint 2007, click View, Slide Master.

You can see what a slide master looks like below. If you don't have a design template it is normally blank. Otherwise, is formatted with the background, bullet style and colours of your template.

Figure 7.1 *Blank Slide Master*

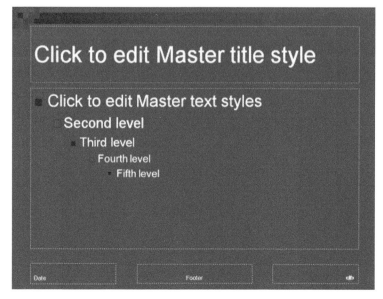

Figure 7.2 *The Slide Master for the Island presentation*

Editing the Slide Master

The first thing you will notice about the Slide Master is the placeholders. For example, at the top of Figure 7.1, you can see a box that says 'Click to edit Master title style'. This isn't normal text, or else you would see it on all your slides. It is actually the placeholder for the title. Any changes you make to its appearance (e.g. underlining it) will get reflected on all your slide titles.

Editing the Slide Master is very much the same as editing any other slide. You can change the font and colour, change the background and so on.

Closing the Master View

To close the Master View and get back to the view you were in before, click Close Master View on the Slide Master View toolbar.

Footers

There are two ways you can add footers to your slides:

1 Add them to the Slide Master.
2 Use the Header and Footer window.

Adding a footer via the Slide Master

To add a footer via the Slide Master:

- Open the Slide Master.
- Click in the footer placeholder at the bottom.
- Type the text you want as the footer.

Using the Header and Footer window

If you prefer, you can use the Header and Footer window (Figure 7.3). To open it:

- In PowerPoint 2003, click View, Header and Footer...
- In PowerPoint 2007, click Insert, Header & Footer...

Once you've opened the window:

- Tick the footer box.
- Type the footer.
- Click Apply to All.

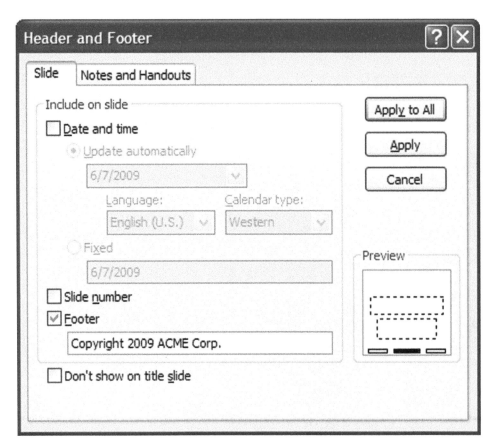

Figure 7.3 *Header and Footer window*

Inserting slide numbers

In order to insert numbers on your slides:

- Click Insert, Slide Numbers.
- When the Header and Footer box appears, tick the Slide Number box.
- Click the Apply to All button.

A slide number is a special kind of footer, so it will get added to the master slide.

Exercise 7

1 Open the Hardware2 file from your exercise folder.
2 Open the Slide Master.
3 Underline the title.
4 Close the Master View. When you view your slides you should see that all of their titles are underlined.
5 Add the name of your school as a footer.
6 Insert slide numbers.
7 Save the file as Hardware5.

8. Printing

After you have prepared your presentation and rehearsed the timing, your presentation is ready for viewing. Normally the presentation is shown to the audience via a laptop that is connected to a projector. So what could you possibly need to print?

You may want to print handouts of your presentation to give to members of your audience. But more importantly, you'll probably want to print out your slide notes so you can refer to them while you are doing the presentation.

Slide notes

We mentioned in Chapter 1 that you can type notes in the notes box at the bottom of the Slide View (Figure 8.1). You can also use the Notes Page. Just click View, Notes Page.

> Click to add notes

Figure 8.1 *Notes Box*

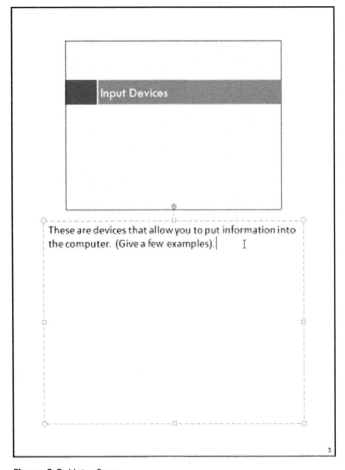

Figure 8.2 *Notes Page*

Print Preview

Before you print something, you should use the Print Preview option to see what it will look like. To access Print Preview:

- In PowerPoint 2003, click File, Print Preview.
- In PowerPoint 2007, click the Microsoft Office button, point at Print then click Print Preview.

At the top of the Print Preview is either the Print Preview toolbar (if you are using PowerPoint 2003) or the Print Preview tab (PowerPoint 2007).

The following table explains what each of the various options does.

Button	What it does
Next/ Previous	go to the next or previous slide
Print	opens the Print dialogue
Options	allows you to set options such as whether you are going to print in greyscale or colour
Print What	allows you to choose whether to print slides, handouts or notes pages
Zoom	allows you to zoom in or out of the preview
Close	closes the Print Preview

Print What

Before you print, choose what you want to print via the Print What combo box. In addition to being able to print slides and notes pages, you can choose among several handout options that allow you to fit multiple slides on a page.

Print dialogue

Once you are satisfied with the preview, click the Print button. The Print dialogue (Figure 8.5) will be displayed. Adjust the options to suit your needs then click the OK button to print.

Note

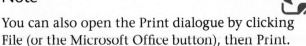

You can also open the Print dialogue by clicking File (or the Microsoft Office button), then Print.

Figure 8.3 *Print Preview toolbar (PowerPoint 2003)*

Figure 8.4 *Print Preview tab (PowerPoint 2007)*

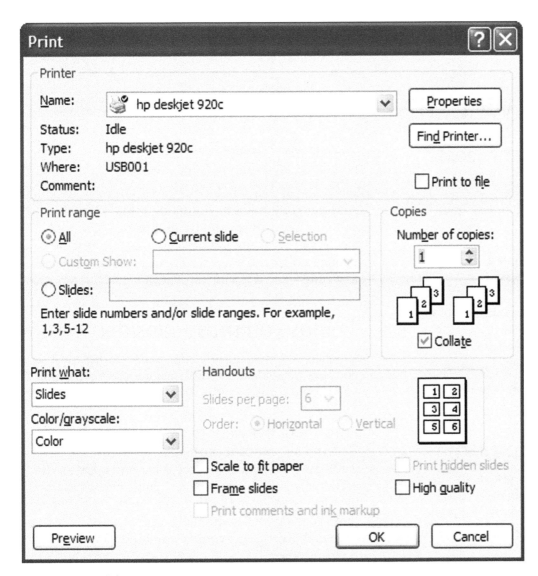

Figure 8.5 *Print dialogue*

Part 6

Microsoft FrontPage

1. Planning a website

The website creation process

In the next few chapters, you will learn how to create a **website**. The process of creating a website normally goes like this:

1 Plan the website.
2 Create the website on your computer.
3 Test the website (first on your own, then with a test audience).
4 Choose the domain name of the site (e.g. www. mysite.com).
5 Choose a company to host the website.
6 Upload the website so that people can access it.

We will cover all these steps in more detail, but this chapter is all about planning.

Why it is important to plan

Planning your website is absolutely crucial. In Microsoft Word, if you want to reorganise your document you can simply cut and paste. But if you decide to restructure a website, you have to:

• reorganise its files and folders

• change the layout of each page
• change your links to reflect the new structure

And this is the absolute minimum. This is why it can take many weeks and thousands of dollars for a company to change its website. It is a lot easier to change a plan and a few sketches than it is to change a website – and it is a lot cheaper too.

Things you must consider

So when you are planning your website, what must you take into consideration? Here are the main points you should think about.

Purpose of the website
First and foremost you must ask yourself, 'What is the purpose of this website? What do I hope to accomplish?' This purpose must guide every design decision or you could easily end up with a site that looks gorgeous but is ultimately useless.

The table lists some common website types and their purposes.

Type of website	Normal purpose
personal	to tell people about yourself or something you are interested in
information	to provide visitors with a wealth of information about a particular topic
business	to promote a company and the services it provides
e-commerce	to sell products and services
news	to provide visitors with the latest news

Figure 1.1 shows Amazon.com's e-commerce site. Since the purpose of the site is to sell products, the products are prominently displayed.

Intended audience

Next you must ask some questions about the typical visitor to your website:

- Demographics – male or female? How old? From where?
- Is the visitor computer savvy?
- Is the visitor an existing client of your business?
- What is the visitor hoping to achieve?

Structure of the website

Once you are clear on why you are doing the website and who it is for, the next step is to come up with a rough sketch of the website structure. When are you doing the sketch you have to ask yourself questions like:

- How many pages will there be? What will be on each page?
- How will the pages be connected?

Figure 1.2 shows a possible structure of a personal website.

Layout of the web pages

Having decided on your website layout, the next step is to choose the general layout of the individual pages. Things to consider are:

- where the logo will go

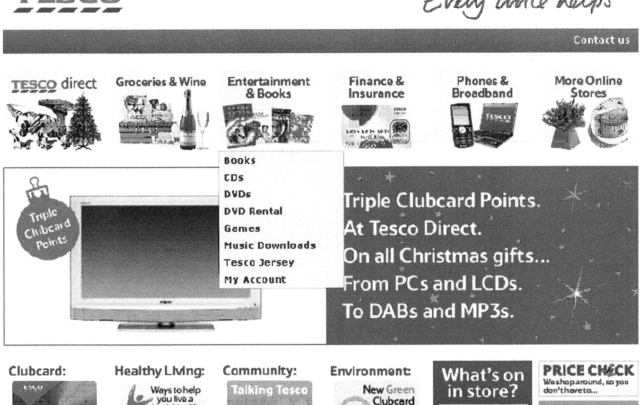

Figure 1.1 *An example of an e-commerce site.*

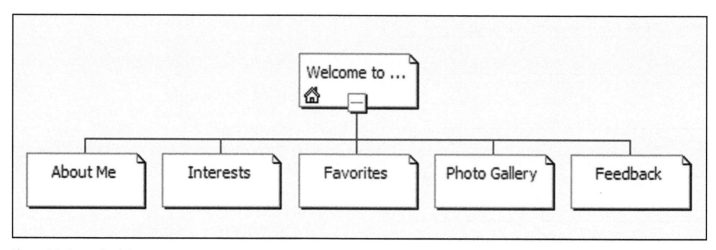

Figure 1.2 *Personal website structure*

- whether the navigation links will be on the left, right or top
- how many columns the page be divided into
- if the pages will have a footer section and if so, what will go in it (normally contact information goes in the footer)

Whatever you choose, you must be <u>consistent</u>. Nothing says 'amateur' like a website that looks as if it has been coloured at random.

The website in Figure 1.4 is aimed at children. Notice the bright colours and the large type.

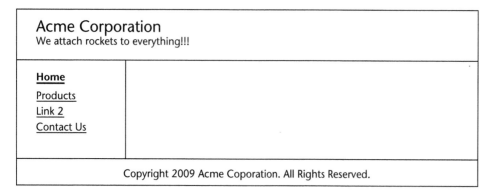

Figure 1.3 *A general page layout for a company*

Colour schemes

If you are designing a website for a company you may need to incorporate the company's colour scheme. Even if you are designing a personal website, you'll need to pay special consideration to the colours you use. These colours often reflect the purpose of the site and the target audience. For example, websites for women normally contain a lot of pink whereas travel sites may use a lot of blues.

Other considerations

Some other things you'll want to consider are:

- the budget you have to work with
- when the website needs to be finished
- how to manage the transition from the old website to the new one

Once you've considered all these things, you are ready to proceed.

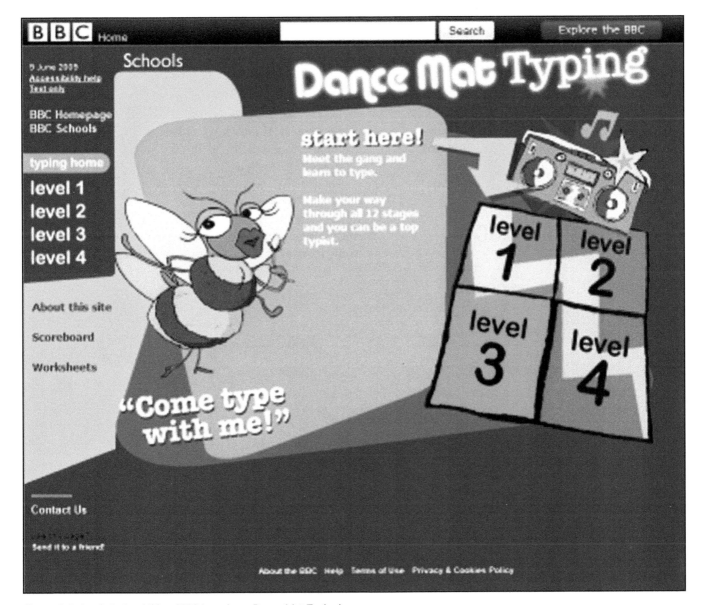

Figure 1.4 *A website for children* (BBC Learning – Dance Mat Typing)

Exercise 1

1 Describe the process of creating a website.
2 List five things you must consider when you are planning your website.
3 Plan a website for a project based on one of the following:
   a your own personal website
   b a simple website for a fictitious company
   c an informative website about your school, country or a topic you have covered in Information Technology

2. Introduction to Microsoft FrontPage

What is Microsoft FrontPage?

Microsoft FrontPage is a popular website design tool. It allows you to design your website as well as edit its individual pages. Microsoft is no longer updating FrontPage, so FrontPage 2003 is the final version.

Microsoft FrontPage can usually be found in the Microsoft Office group of the Start Menu.

The initial FrontPage 2003 interface

The first time you start FrontPage, you will be presented with the interface shown in Figure 2.1.

Note

After you start creating websites, FrontPage will automatically open the last site you worked on when it starts up.

This is the interface you use for creating an individual standalone web page. If you are working with a website, the interface is more complicated.

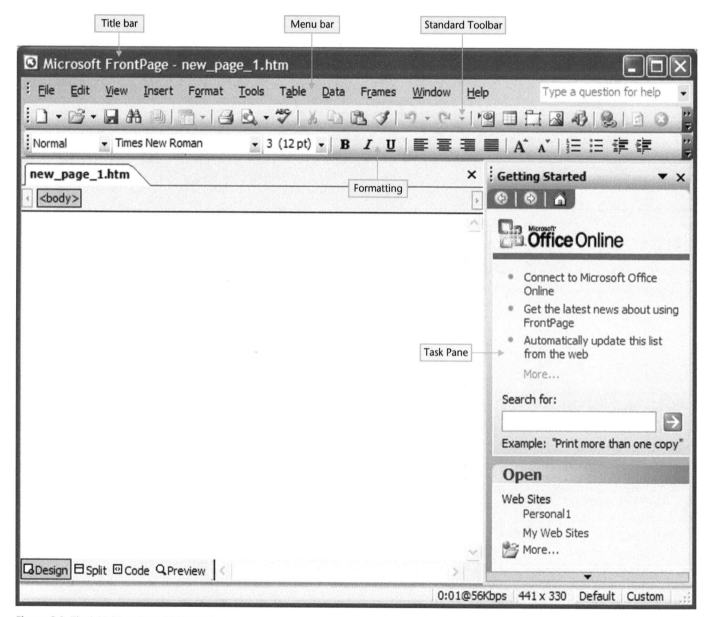

Figure 2.1 *The initial FrontPage 2003 interface*

Creating a new website

A website is simply an organised collection of web pages, folders, images and other types of files. When you create a new website you normally start from a template and then make changes to suit your needs. Websites that you create in FrontPage will also include some hidden files and folders that FrontPage uses to keep track of certain information. If you see _vti_ cnf and _vti_pvt folders while browsing your files, that's what they are for.

Choose a template

The first step is to choose a template from which the website will be created.

- Click the File menu, then click New... .
- On the New task pane that appears at the right of the window, click the More Web site templates... option.
- Select one of the templates from the Web Site Templates window.

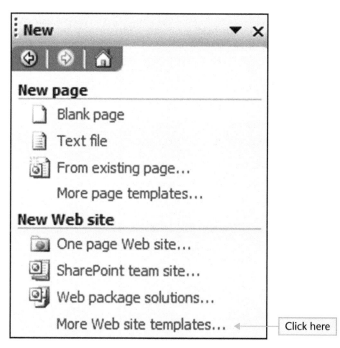

Figure 2.2 *The New task pane*

Unless you choose the Empty Web Site template, FrontPage will automatically add content to your new website. Of course, the content depends on which template you choose.

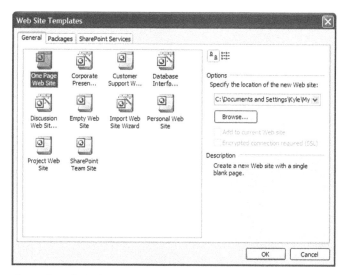

Figure 2.3 *The Web Site Templates window*

Choose a location for the website

The next step is to choose a location on your computer where the website will be stored. Remember that you work with a website on your computer before publishing it on the Internet.

Note

If you want FrontPage to choose a location for you, just click the OK button at the bottom of the Web Site Templates window.

- Click the Browse... button.
- Choose an existing location for your website or create a new one. Click Open when you're done.
- Click the OK button at the bottom of the Web Site Templates window.

Creating a new website folder

If you need to create a website folder, you can do so via the Open window. Here's how you would create a folder inside the My Web Sites folder.

- Go to My Documents, then My Web Sites.
- Click the New folder button.
- Type a name for the folder and click OK.

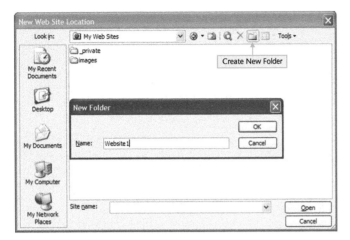

Figure 2.4 *Creating a folder*

FrontPage will then generate the files for the website and open it so that you can work with it.

FrontPage's website interface

The first thing you will notice is that the interface (see Figure 2.5) looks more complicated than before.

This is the interface that FrontPage shows you when you are working with a website. Its main features are described below.

Folder List
To the left of the window is the Folder List. This is a list of the folders and the files in your website.

Tabs
To the right of the Folder List is a set of tabs – one for each object that is currently open. When you first create a website, only one tab will be open – the Web Site tab.

View buttons
At the bottom of each tab is a set of buttons that allow you to switch between that tab's different views. The different views will be explained shortly.

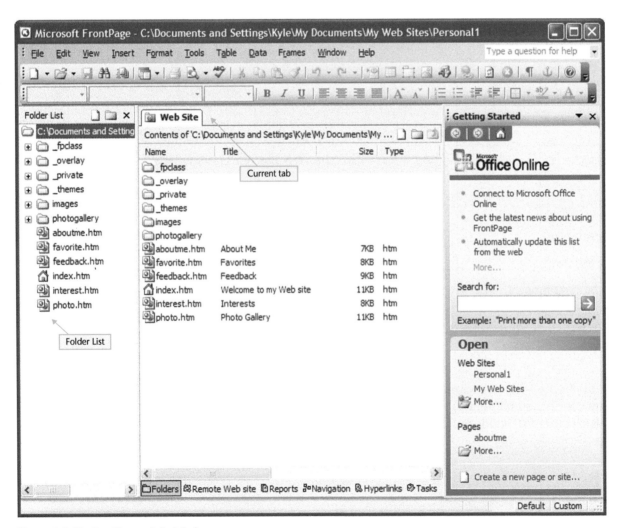

Figure 2.5 *The FrontPage website interface*

Using the Folder List

Figure 2.6 shows the Folder List with explanations of some of the features.

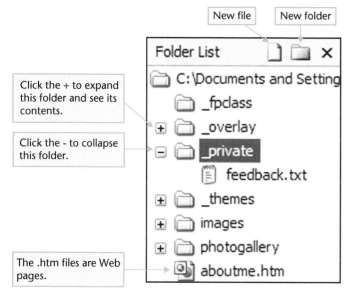

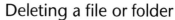

Figure 2.6 *The Folder List*

Opening a web page
To open a web page, double-click on it. It will appear as a new tab on the right-hand side of the window. You can close the tab by clicking on the 'X' on the far side of the window.

Creating a new file/folder
To create a new file of folder:

- Select the folder inside which you want the new file or folder to be created.
- Click the New File or New Folder button.
- Type the name of the new object.
- Press Enter.

Renaming a file or folder
To rename a file or folder:

- Right-click on it and click Rename.
- Type the new name.
- Press Enter.

Note

When you are rename a web page be sure to leave the .htm extension.

Deleting a file or folder
To delete a file or folder:

- Right-click on it and click Delete.
- Click Yes to confirm the deletion.

Views

Tabs in Microsoft FrontPage have several different views. The views may be divided into two categories: website views and page views.

Website views
You will only see these views on the Web Site tab because they apply to the website as a whole. If you look at the bottom of the Web Site tab you'll see six tabs. The table below explains what each one does.

Web Site View	What it does
Folders	the default view. It shows you the files and folders that make up the web page
Remote Web Site	allows you to publish your website and manage the files on the web server
Reports	provides reports on your website
Navigation	shows the structure of the website
Hyperlinks	shows the hyperlinks to and from a web page
Tasks	allows you to keep track of what tasks you need to perform

Page views
You only see these views at the bottom of a web page tab. They present you with different views of your web page, which are very helpful while editing.

Design View
This view allows you to design a web page the same way that you would work with a Word document (Figure 2.7).

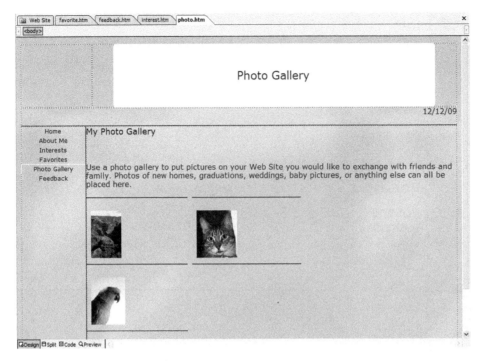

Figure 2.7 *Design View*

Split View

This view shows you the HTML code and the resulting web page at the same time (Figure 2.8).

Code View

If you prefer writing HTML by hand you can use this view. However, other than in the next chapter, we won't be using this view very much.

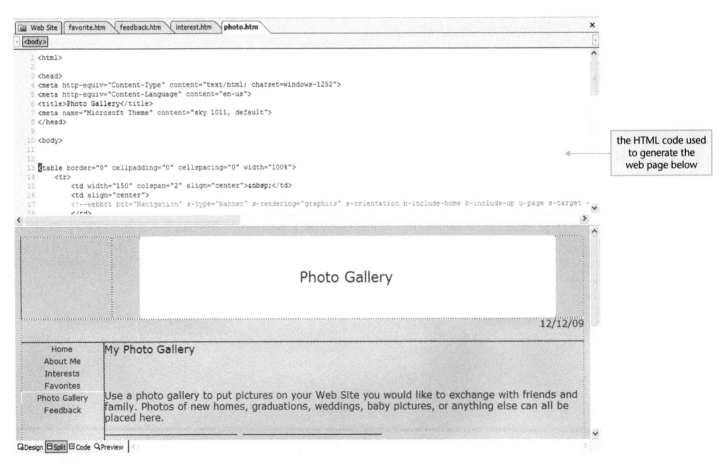

Figure 2.8 *Split View*

Figure 2.9 *Code View*

Preview View

This view allows you to get a preview of how the page would look in a web browser. It looks very similar to the Design View but has two important differences:

- you can't design the web page in this view
- unlike the Design View, you get to see how the web page would behave in a browser

Closing a website

To close a website, click File, Close Site.

Opening a website

To open an existing website, either:

- Click File, Open Site... Go to the folder that contains the website. Then click Open.

Or

- Click File, Recent Sites and choose the website from the list.

Exercise 2a

1. Create a new website based on the Personal Web Site template. Put it in a new folder called `Test` inside the My Web Sites folder.
2. Expand the Images folder to see the images created by the template.
3. Switch between the six views of the Web Site tab.
4. Open the Index, Favorite and About Me web pages.
5. Close the Favorite tab.
6. Go to the Index tab.
7. Switch between the four different views (Design, Split, Code, Preview).
8. Add a new web page called Blank.
9. Open it and switch to the Code view.
10. Close all the open web pages.
11. Close the website.

Exercise 2b

Create an empty website. You will eventually turn this website into the one you planned for your project in Chapter 1, so name it appropriately.

3. Introduction to HTML

In this chapter, you'll get a quick crash course in **Hypertext Markup Language** (better known as HTML).

How HTML works

Think of HTML as a special sort of programming language that gives instructions to the web browser. A web browser such as Internet Explorer or Firefox then interprets the instructions and generates the web page you see when you surf the 'net.

In the example shown in Figure 3.1, the web browser interprets the HTML and realises that it is supposed the show the message 'Hello World' and display the image globe.jpg next to it. Notice that HTML is just plain text so you could write it in Notepad if you wanted to.

The fact that HTML is interpreted means that different browsers may display the same web page in different ways. This is (part of the reason) why some web pages don't work properly in certain browsers.

How HTML is structured

HTML is made up of tags – which are instructions to the web browser. HTML tags are enclosed in angled brackets < >. If you look at our example HTML, you'll see several tags such as:

- `<html>`
- `<head>`
- `</title>`

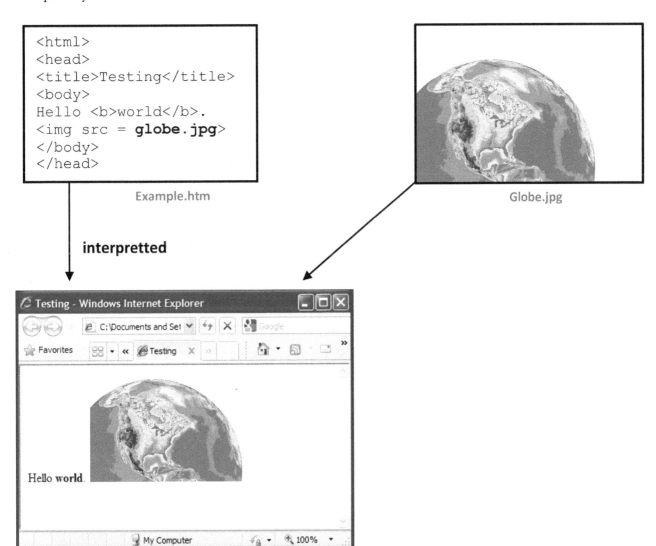

```
<html>
<head>
<title>Testing</title>
<body>
Hello <b>world</b>.
<img src = globe.jpg>
</body>
</head>
```

Example.htm

interpretted

Globe.jpg

Figure 3.1 *How HTML works*

The last tag is what is called a **closing tag**. Each tag normally has a closing tag, for example `<title>` and `</title>`. That's because tags normally work in pairs. In the line `<title>Testing</title>`, the first title tag tells the browser, 'This is the start of the title' and the closing tag tells it 'This is the end of the title'.

Note

There are a few cases where it doesn't make sense to have a closing tag. In those cases, one tag is used and written like this `<p/>`.

Let's look at another example
```
Hello <b>world</b>
```

The first `<b>` tag tells the browser to turn on the bold effect and the `</b>` tells it to turn the bold off. The result is to make the word 'world' bold.

Nested tags

In HTML, you can have tags inside tags. For example the title tags are inside the `<head>` tags which are inside the `<html>` tags. Nested tags must not overlap.

The following is an example of correct nesting.
```
<head><title>Blah blah</title></head>
```
This is an example of incorrect nesting because the head tag was closed before the title tag; the two pairs of tags overlap.
```
<head><title>Blah blah</head></title>
```

How web pages are structured

The typical web page structure is as follows:

- The entire web page is enclosed in `<html> ... </html>` tags.
- It is divided into two parts: the head and the body.

Let's look at an example:

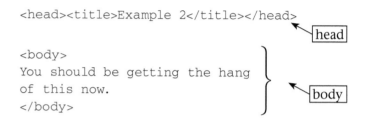
```
<html>

<head><title>Example 2</title></head>

<body>
You should be getting the hang
of this now.
</body>

</html>
```
This is rendered as shown in Figure 3.2.

The body

The body section controls what you see <u>inside</u> the web page. This is where the majority of the html code goes.

The head

The head deals with things that won't get displayed inside the web page, such as the title.

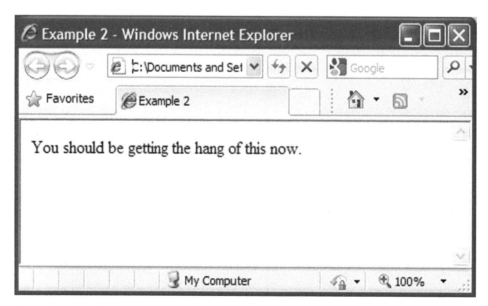

Figure 3.2 *Example 2*

Common HTML tags

The following table lists the most common HTML tags.

Tag	What it does	Example
html	encloses the entire web page	
head	encloses the head of the web page	
body	encloses the body of the web page	
b	makes text bold	`<b>This is to be bold</b>`
i	puts text in italics	
u	underlines text	
p	starts a new paragraph	`<p/>`
br	starts a new line	` This will go on a new line`
hr	insert a horizontal rule	`<hr/>`
h1	the largest heading	
h2 to h6	smaller headings (the higher the number the smaller the heading)	`<h2>This is a smaller heading</h2>`
a	defines a hyperlink	`<a href=index.html>Back to home</a>`
img	includes an image	`<img src = globe.jpg>`

Arguments

The examples for the `img` tag (and the `a` tag above it) don't look like those for the other tags. In between the angled brackets there is some additional text `src = globe.jpg`. This coding is known as an **argument**. Arguments control the way that tags work.

Typing HTML inside FrontPage

Having learned a bit about HTML, now let's learn how to work with it in FrontPage. You will need to create a blank web page to work with. To do this:

- Click File, New...
- Select Blank New Page from the task pane.

- Switch to the Code View (if necessary) by clicking the Code button at the bottom of the web page's tab.

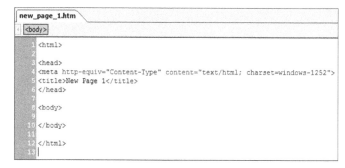

Figure 3.3 *New web page code*

Even though we created a blank web page, there is some code in it. It looks fairly <u>similar</u> to our examples. The main difference is the long line with `<meta...>`. We can ignore that. You'll find that FrontPage often inserts things like this that aren't <u>required</u> but are still useful.

Type the following line in the body (i.e. between two body tags):

```
Not <u>much</u> to see here
```

IntelliSense

When you start to type a tag, you'll notice a list of tags pop up for you to choose from. This is a type of code assistance called IntelliSense.
You use it as follows:

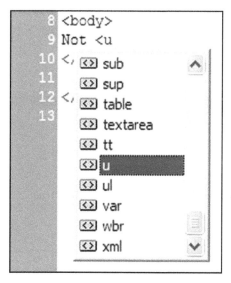

Figure 3.4 *IntelliSense*

- As you type, IntelliSense will make suggestions and help you remember what to type.
- To accept a suggestion, press the tab key. IntelliSense will complete the word for you.
- When you finish, type a tab, IntelliSense will automatically put in the closing tag.

Previewing the web page

Now let's get back to our web page. Here's how our example web page would look in the web browser.

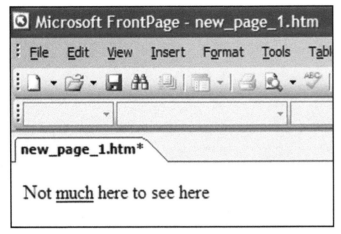

Figure 3.5 *Previewing the web page*

Note

To preview what your example will look like in the web browser, click on the Preview View button.

Notice that although we typed things with angled brackets, such as <u>, there are none in the preview. That is because the browser treated them as instructions, in this case to underline the text.

Split View

Finally, let's see how to work with code in the split view. If you select the word 'here' in the Design part of the split view (the bottom part), it will also be selected in Code part (Figure 3.6).

Similarly, if you click the Bold icon in the formatting toolbar, FrontPage automatically surround the 'here' with <b> tags.

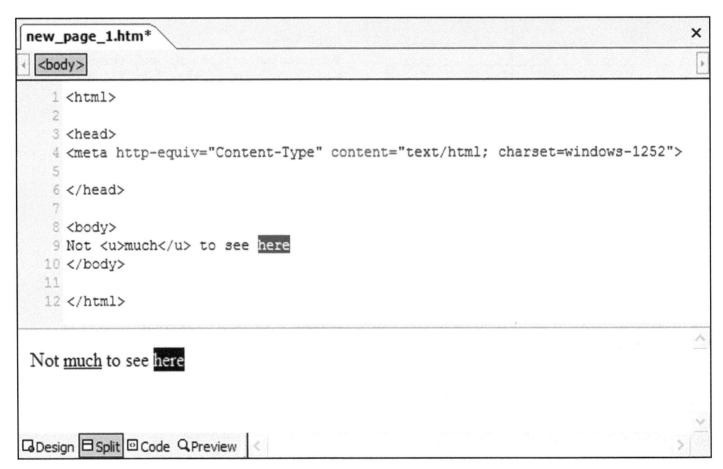

Figure 3.6 *Split View*

However, if you remove the `<u>` tags from the Code part, the Design part won't automatically get updated. The two parts will be out of sync.

Note

If you make a change in the Code section of the Split view, press F5 to update the Design part.

Exercise 3a

1 Identify the opening and closing tags from the following list:

   a `</head>`
   b `<body>`
   c `<i>`
   d `</b>`
   e `</h1>`

2 When coding a web page, is the title placed inside the head or the body?
3 What goes inside the body of a web page?
4 Explain how the following line of HTML will get displayed in a web browser:

```
The <b>quick</b> brown fox jumped over
the <b>lazy <i>dog</i></b>.
```

Exercise 3b

1 Create a new blank web page.
2 Using the examples in this chapter as a guide, type the HTML for a web page that has the title 'Learning HTML' and displays the text 'HTML is so cool!' in bold.

4. Designing a web page

In this chapter you will learn how to design a <u>simple</u> web page using the Design View. This is not too difficult. You edit the web page in almost the same way as you would edit a normal Word document.

Adding a blank web page to the website

The first step in designing a web page is to create a new Empty website. Then add a new web page to it:

- Click the New file button in the Folder list.

If this is the first web page, it will get added as the Home Page `index.htm`. A **home page** is the first page you see when you visit a website. Otherwise it will get added as something like `new_page1.htm`. In that case you would rename it.

Tip

To make another page the Home Page, right-click on it in the Folder List and click Set as Home Page.

Opening the page

To open the web page so that you can add content to it:

- Double-click on the icon for the web page in the Folder List. It will open in a new tab.
- Switch to the Design view by clicking on the Design button at the bottom of the tab.

Basic editing

As we mentioned above, web pages are edited in almost the same way as a Word document. Instead of repeating things you are already familiar with, we'll cover the special things you need to consider and remind you of things you may have forgotten.

Fonts

Although FrontPage allows you to choose any font, there is no guarantee that your viewers will have it on their computers. That would force their web browsers to substitute alternative fonts and your web page won't look as you intended.

The following is a list of some safe fonts which virtually everyone will have on their computer. Feel free to use any of these:

Arial	Arial Black	Comic Sans MS
Georgia	Impact	Lucida
Times New Roman	Trebuchet	Verdana
Webdings	Wingdings	MS Sans Serif
Courier New	Tahoma	Symbol
MS Serif		

Font sizes

As you can see in Figure 4.1, FrontPage only provides you with a few sizes.

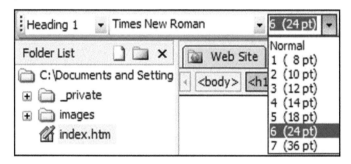

Figure 4.1 *The limited font sizes in FrontPage*

Colours

If your web page uses a theme, the theme colours will be at the bottom of the list. These are colours that will go well with your theme. If you need more colours to choose from, click the More Colors... button.

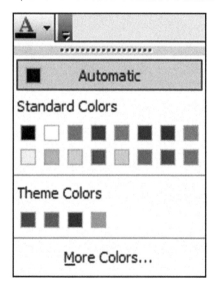

Figure 4.2 *Changing the text colour*

Inserting separator lines

To insert a horizontal line to (visually) separate two parts of your document:

- Click Insert, Horizontal Line

Themes

An easy way to make a web page look more interesting is to use a theme. Themes in FrontPage work in a similar manner to design templates in PowerPoint.

To apply a theme:

- Click Format, Theme...
- Click on a theme from the list.

Figure 4.3 *Themes*

Layout tables

One thing you'll quickly realise is that it is very difficult to position items precisely on a web page. One technique that was popular in the 1990s was to place the items in a table as shown in Figure 4.4. There are more modern techniques involving CSS (Cascading Style Sheets), but they are more difficult to master.

Web Page header goes here	
Home Page Link 1 Link 2 Link 3	Main text goes here.
Footer goes here	

Figure 4.4 *Using a table to lay out a web page*

To add a layout table to your webpage:

- Click Table, Layout Table and Cells...
- Choose the layout you want from the task pane that appears.

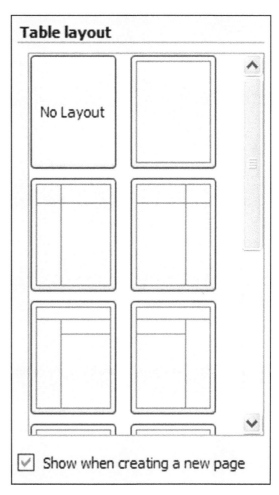

Figure 4.5 *Using Table layout to structure a web page*

Once you've added the table to the web page, you just put the relevant information in the different sections.

Note

When you add a layout table, the borders are hidden. So someone viewing your page wouldn't know that you used a table.

Giving the page a title

In order to give a page a title:

- Click File, Properties.
- Type the title in the Page Properties dialogue box (Figure 4.6).
- Then click OK.

Of course, if you are feeling adventurous, you could switch to the Code view and type the title in manually.

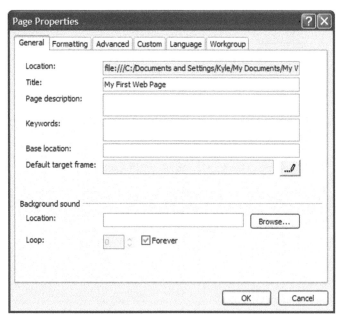

Figure 4.6 *Adding a title*

5. Working with pictures

Inserting a picture

Inserting a picture is the same as in Microsoft Word and PowerPoint.

From a file

To insert a picture from a file on your computer:

- Click Insert, Picture, From File.
- Locate the file on your computer and click OK.

From Clip Art

To insert a picture from Clip Art:

- Click Insert, Picture, From Clip Art.
- Type what you are searching for and click Go.
- Click on the one you want.

The picture will be inserted where the cursor was positioned.

Importing the picture to the website

Whenever you add an external object to your website such as a picture, you need to import it into your website folder. Then, when you upload your website, the file will be uploaded as well. To import the picture:

- Save the web page that contains the picture. If the file needs importing, you will see it in the Save Embedded Files window.
- (Optional) Change the folder to the Images folder.
  - Click the Change Folder button.
  - Click on the Images folder, then click OK.
- Click OK to import the file.

Figure 5.1 *Saving embedded pictures*

Repositioning images

To reposition an image:

- Click on it.
- Click one of the alignment buttons from the formatting toolbar.

Using this method, you are very limited in terms of where you can put an image on a web page.

Note

You can get around this by putting your picture in the cell of a table.

Wrapping text

To allow text to wrap around a picture:

- Right-click on the picture.
- Click Picture Properties. The Picture Properties window will appear.
- Choose one of the wrapping styles.
- Click OK.

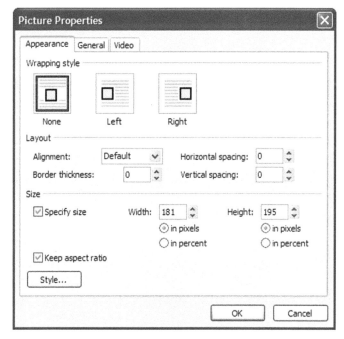

Figure 5.2a *Picture Properties window*

Merry Christmas

We wish you a merry Christmas,

We wish you a merry Christmas,

We wish you a merry Christmas

And a happppyyyy new yearrrrrrrr.

Figure 5.2b *This text needs wrapping.*

Merry Christmas

We wish you a merry Christmas,

We wish you a merry Christmas,

We wish you a merry Christmas

And a happppyyyy new yearrrrrrrr.

Figure 5.2c *This text has been wrapped.*

Creating thumbnails

Thumbnails are miniaturised images of larger originals. You see them all the time when you are surfing the web. For example, when you are shopping online, you can click on a thumbnail of a product and then see a larger image.

To use FrontPage's useful Auto Thumbnail feature:

- Right-click on the original image.
- Click Auto Thumbnail.

FrontPage will then:

- Create a thumbnail image.
- Put the thumbnail image where the original one was located on the page.
- Replace the original image with the thumbnail.
- Create a link so that when you click on the thumbnail, you are taken to the original image.

Note

You will need to import the thumbnail to your folder, the same way you would a regular file.

Exercise 5

Make your website look more interesting by inserting some pictures. Be sure to try some of the different wrapping options.

6. Hyperlinks

Anyone who has used the Internet will be familiar with hyperlinks (even if not by name). A hyperlink is a link on your webpage to another file or location.

Pep's Gladiator Video

Many Barcelona fans will be aware that Pep Guardiola played a specially-commissioned inspirational film to his troops ahead of their Champions League final win over Man Utd. Now, Goal.com readers can see for themselves what brought several Blaugrana starts to tears...

Figure 6.1 *A hyperlink on a web page*

Inserting a hyperlink

There are two ways to insert hyperlinks:

1 Creating them from scratch.
2 Adding them to existing text or images.

Creating a hyperlink from scratch

To create a hyperlink from scratch:

- Position the cursor where you want to insert the link.
- Click Insert, Hyperlink. The Insert Hyperlink window will appear.
- Type the text you want the user to see.
- Select the file or location that you want to link to.
- Click OK.

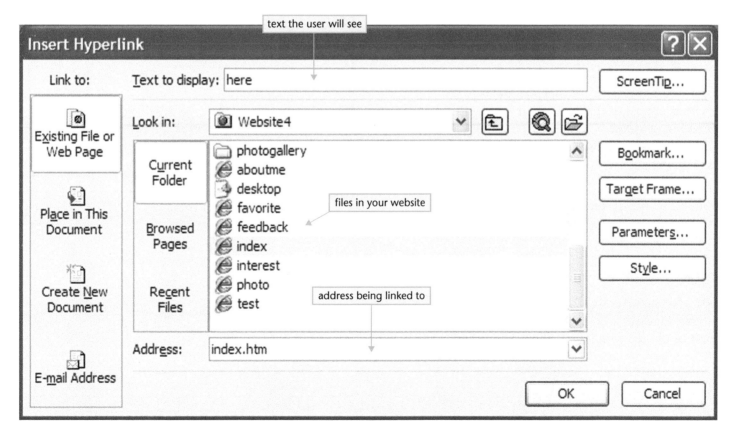

Figure 6.2 *Insert Hyperlink window*

Adding a hyperlink to existing text or images

- Select the existing text or image.
- Click Insert, Hyperlink.
- Select the file or location being linked to, then click OK.

Things you can link to

Link to an existing file or web page

If the file you want to link to is in your website, click on it in the Insert Hyperlink window. The relative address of the file or page will be inserted in the Address box.

A **relative address** is the location of a file with respect to your website folder. Two examples are given in the table below.

If the relative link is this	The browser opens
index.itm	the index.htm file within your website folder
Images/acme.jpg	the acme.jpg file within your website's images folder

Note

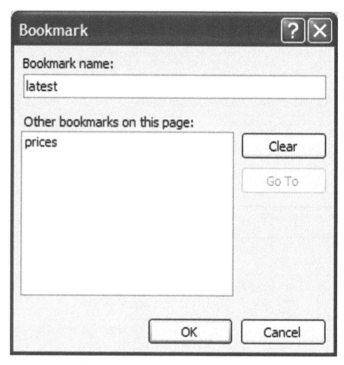

The good thing about relative addresses is that if you move your website folder or rename it, you don't have to go back and update the links.

If you want to link to another website, type its absolute address in the Address box of the Insert Hyperlink window.

An **absolute address** is the full address of a web page or file. For example:

- http://www.msn.com
- C:\Documents and Settings\Kyle\My Web Sites\Website4\images\acme.jpg

Note

Avoid using links like the one to acme.jpg above. Links to specific locations on your computer will be broken when you publish the website.

Link to a location within a web page

In order for you to link to a specific location in a web page:

- Create a bookmark to the location (if there isn't one already).
- Open the Insert Hyperlink window.
- Click the Place in This Document button.
- Select the bookmark from the list and click OK.

Bookmarking a location

To bookmark a location on your web page:

- Put the cursor at the location you want to bookmark.
- Click Insert, Bookmark.
- Type the name you want to give to the bookmark and click OK.

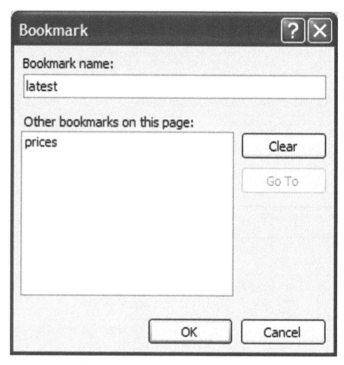

Figure 6.3 *Bookmark window*

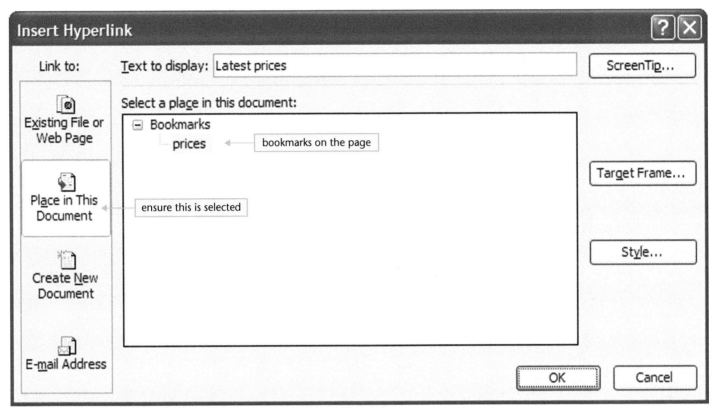

Figure 6.4 *Linking to a bookmark*

Linking to an e-mail address

You can also create links to e-mail addresses. When a user clicks on one of these links, the user's e-mail client (e.g. Microsoft Outlook) will open and automatically address a new e-mail to the specified address.

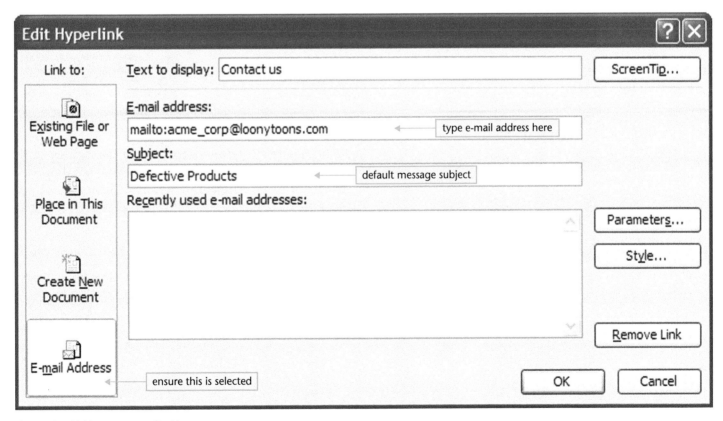

Figure 6.5 *Linking to an e-mail address*

To link to an e-mail address:

- Open the Insert Hyperlink window.
- Click on the E-mail Address button.
- Type the e-mail address.
- Type the default subject for the e-mail message.
- Click OK.

Note

When you start typing the e-mail address, FrontPage will put `mailto:` in front of it. Ignore this and continue typing.

Removing hyperlinks

To remove a hyperlink:

- Make sure you are in the Design view.
- Right-click on the hyperlink.
- Click Hyperlink Properties.
- Click the Remove Hyperlink button.

Testing hyperlinks

Once you've inserted your hyperlinks you should test them in different web browsers to make sure they work correctly.

To open a web page in a web browser:

- Click File, Preview in Browser.
- Choose one of the web browsers from the list.

Alternatively, you can press the F12 key to preview it in the default web browser.

Using website reports

FrontPage has several reports that allow you to quickly find problems with your links such as broken hyperlinks. Some of the things it can check for are:

- <u>Broken hyperlinks</u> – links to files that don't exist or are no longer at the specified location.
- <u>Unlinked files</u> – files that are in your website folder but have no links pointing to them.

To view a website report:

- Save all the files in your website (or else the reports won't be up to date).
- Click on the Web Site tab.
- Click on its Reports view.
- Choose the report you want.

Note

You can easily tell which web pages haven't been saved. An unsaved web page has an asterisk (*) to the right of its tab.

Figure 6.6 *Web Site tab selected*

☐Folders 🖳Remote Web site 📄Reports 🔁Navigation 🔗Hyperlinks 🕘Tasks

Figure 6.7 *Reports view selected*

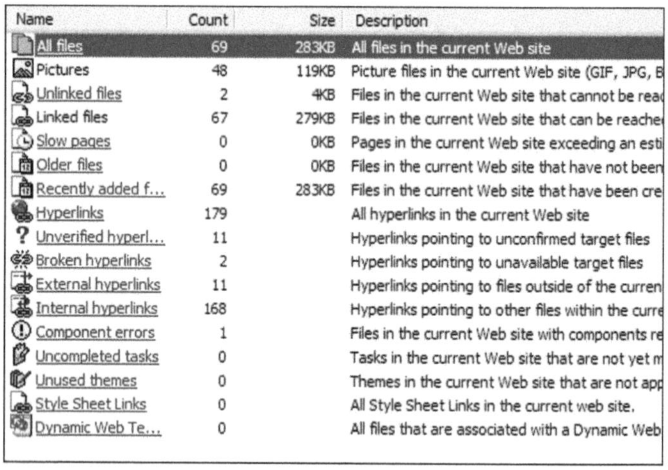

Name	Count	Size	Description
All files	69	283KB	All files in the current Web site
Pictures	48	119KB	Picture files in the current Web site (GIF, JPG, B
Unlinked files	2	4KB	Files in the current Web site that cannot be rea
Linked files	67	279KB	Files in the current Web site that can be reache
Slow pages	0	0KB	Pages in the current Web site exceeding an esti
Older files	0	0KB	Files in the current Web site that have not been
Recently added f...	69	283KB	Files in the current Web site that have been cre
Hyperlinks	179		All hyperlinks in the current Web site
Unverified hyperl...	11		Hyperlinks pointing to unconfirmed target files
Broken hyperlinks	2		Hyperlinks pointing to unavailable target files
External hyperlinks	11		Hyperlinks pointing to files outside of the curren
Internal hyperlinks	168		Hyperlinks pointing to other files within the curre
Component errors	1		Files in the current Web site with components re
Uncompleted tasks	0		Tasks in the current Web site that are not yet m
Unused themes	0		Themes in the current Web site that are not app
Style Sheet Links	0		All Style Sheet Links in the current web site.
Dynamic Web Te...	0		All files that are associated with a Dynamic Web

Figure 6.8 *Website reports*

The Reports view lists summaries of the various reports. For example, the reports in Figure 6.8 show that there are two broken hyperlinks. The names of the reports are actually hyperlinks themselves, so you could click a report to open it.

Broken hyperlinks

To view the Broken hyperlinks report, click on its link in the website's Report view. If FrontPage asks you about verifying links, click Yes.

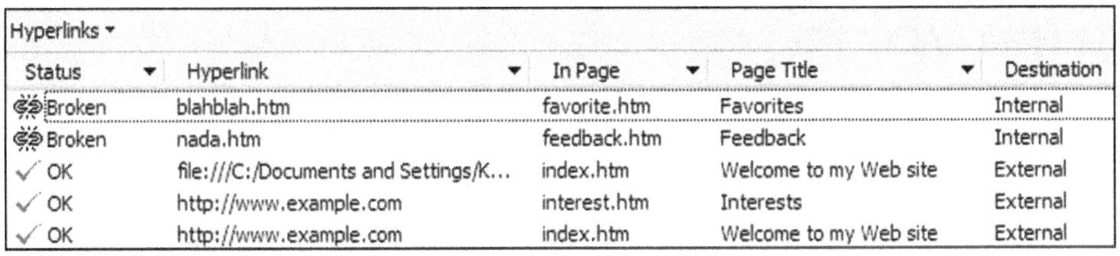

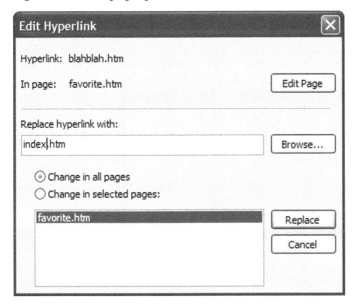

Hyperlinks ▾				
Status ▾	Hyperlink ▾	In Page ▾	Page Title ▾	Destination
⚷ Broken	blahblah.htm	favorite.htm	Favorites	Internal
⚷ Broken	nada.htm	feedback.htm	Feedback	Internal
✓ OK	file:///C:/Documents and Settings/K...	index.htm	Welcome to my Web site	External
✓ OK	http://www.example.com	interest.htm	Interests	External
✓ OK	http://www.example.com	index.htm	Welcome to my Web site	External

Figure 6.9 *Broken hyperlinks report*

Note

Internal hyperlinks are links inside your website.
External links are links to things outside your website.

The broken hyperlinks are clearly indicated as well as the pages they are on. To fix a broken link:

- Right-click on an item in the report.
- Click Edit Hyperlink or Edit Page.

If you click Edit Hyperlink, the window shown in Figure 6.10 will pop up.

Edit Hyperlink

Hyperlink: blahblah.htm

In page: favorite.htm   [Edit Page]

Replace hyperlink with:

[index|htm]   [Browse...]

◉ Change in all pages
○ Change in selected pages:

[favorite.htm]   [Replace]
                    [Cancel]

Figure 6.10 *Edit Hyperlink window*

Returning to the list of reports

In order to get back to the list of reports:

- Click on the arrow next to Hyperlinks in the top left-hand corner of the tab.
- Click Site Summary.

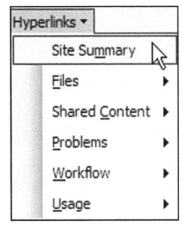

Hyperlinks ▾	
Site Summary	
Files	▶
Shared Content	▶
Problems	▶
Workflow	▶
Usage	▶

Figure 6.11 *Returning to Site Summary*

Exercise 6

1 Add hyperlinks to your website's pages. Be sure to add:

- links to other pages on your site
- links to pages outside your website
- links to sections on a web page
- an e-mail link

2 Use FrontPage's Broken Hyperlinks report to identify and fix any broken hyperlinks in your site.
3 Test your hyperlinks in your web browser to make sure they take you to the right locations.

7. Publishing your website

Before you publish your website, you should first make sure it works correctly. In particular:

- test it in different web browsers
- run reports to find problems such as broken hyperlinks
- use a test audience to see if they have any issues with your site

Finding hosting for your site

There are plenty of free hosting solutions that you can choose from. Just Google for something like 'free websites'. Be sure to get one that offers FTP access because that is what we will be using to transfer our files.

Once you have found a host for your website, you'll need certain information in order to access your FTP account:

1 the URL of your FTP account
2 a username
3 a password

You'll normally get the URL after you sign up for your account. The username and password will be the same ones you provided during the sign-up process.

Using the Remote Site view

Microsoft FrontPage has a view dedicated to transferring files between your personal computer and the remote computer that will be hosting your site. This is called the Remote Site view. In order to access this view:

- Switch to the Web Site tab.
- Click on the Remote Web site button at the bottom of the window.

When you first open this view, there won't be much to see because you'll have to enter the settings for the remote web site. To do so, click on the Remote Web Site Properties button at the top of the tab.

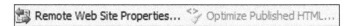

Figure 7.1 *Remote Web Site Properties button*

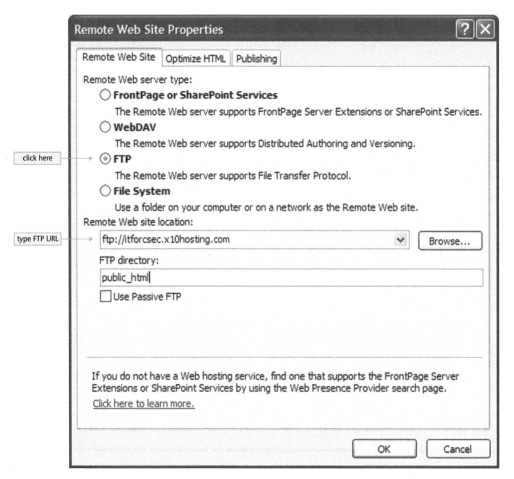

Figure 7.2 *Remote Web Site Properties window*

The Report Web Site Properties window (Figure 7.2) will be displayed. You'll then have to:

- Select the FTP option.
- Type in your FTP address.
- (Optional) Specify the directory (folder) on the remote site where your website files will go. This will depend on your host, but is usually `public_html` or `www`. Whatever directory you specify will be opened automatically when you connect to the remote site.

Once you have finished typing in the information, click OK. FrontPage will then try to connect to the remote FTP site. A dialogue box will pop up asking you to enter your name and password (see Figure 7.3). These are the same ones you entered when you were signing up for an FTP account with your host.

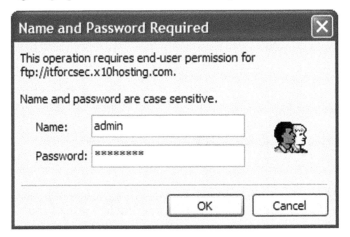

Figure 7.3 *Name and Password dialogue box*

Once you've successfully connected, you will see the files on your computer (on the left) and those on the remote host (on the right).

In Figure 7.4, all the files that are marked with a blue arrow pointing to the right are going to be transferred to the remote site. These are the ones that either don't exist on the remote site, or have changed since you last published the site.

To publish the site, click the <u>Publish Web site</u> button in the bottom right-hand corner. If your hosting provider does not have FrontPage extensions, you'll probably receive a few warnings. You can usually ignore these.

Depending on the speed of your connection, it may take a while for your files to be uploaded. Even after they have been uploaded, it may be a few minutes before you can access your website via the web.

Manually transferring files

To manually transfer a file or folder from your computer to the remote host or vice versa:

- Select the file(s).
- Click one of the transfer buttons in the middle of the window.

Exercise 7

1 Sign up for a free hosting provider. Make sure the provider offers FTP access.
2 Fill in the Remote Site Properties for your site.
3 Publish your website.
4 Test it to make sure it works correctly.

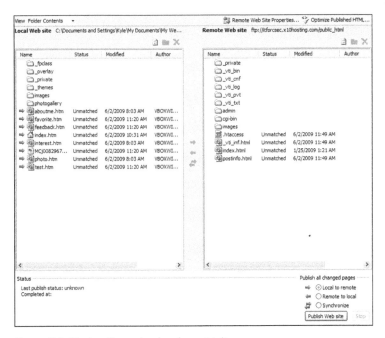

Figure 7.4 *Viewing files on local and remote sites*

Part 7

Microsoft Excel

1. Introduction to Microsoft Excel

Microsoft Excel is a type of general purpose application software known as a **spreadsheet**. Spreadsheet programs allow you to work with large amounts of numerical data, making it easy to manipulate the figures and to perform calculations on them. One really useful feature is that when you change a value, any figures that use that value are automatically recalculated.

Microsoft Excel can usually be found in the Microsoft Office group of the Start Menu. At the time of writing the two most common versions are Excel 2003 and 2007. Unfortunately there are quite a few differences between the two versions. Whenever the two differ, instructions for both versions will be given.

The Excel 2003 interface

If you are using Excel 2003 or an earlier version your interface should look very similar to the image shown in Figure 1.1. If your version looks different, skip ahead to the Excel 2007 interface section.

The Excel 2003 interface, like most Windows programs, relies heavily on menus and toolbars. Let us look at the key interface features one by one.

Control Menu icon

The Control Menu icon, located at the left side of the Title bar, appears as a stylised letter 'X'. While you won't use it often, it provides a pull-down menu that allows you to Maximize, Minimize, Restore, Resize, Move or Close the Excel window.

Menu bar

The Menu bar displays menu options which, when clicked, display drop-down menus that you can use to perform particular tasks.

The menus you'll most commonly use are shown in the table.

Menu	What you'll use it for
File	to open, save and print spreadsheets
Edit	to cut, copy and paste and to find and replace text
Insert	to insert items such as rows, columns and functions
Data	to sort items and to perform advanced filtering

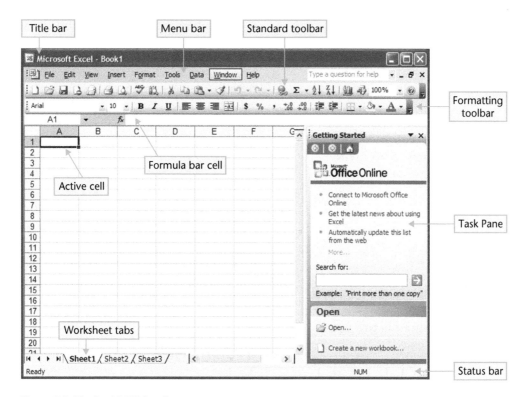

Figure 1.1 *The Excel 2003 interface*

To select a menu:

- Use the mouse to point to a menu on the Menu bar and click once.

Or

- Press Alt + the underlined letter in the menu option.

Figure 1.2 shows the drop-down menu that appears when the Insert menu is selected. Several commands have icons that may be selected from the toolbar or can be added to a customised toolbar.

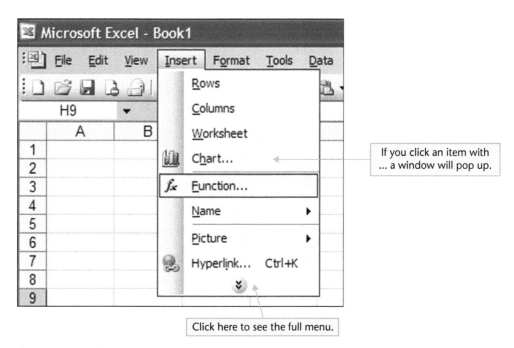

Figure 1.2 *Drop-down menu*

Toolbars

A toolbar is a group of buttons that you can use to quickly perform common tasks instead of having to go through the menus.

The main toolbars are:

- the Standard toolbar – which you'll use to do things like save, print, copy, paste and sort
- the Formatting toolbar – which you'll use to change the appearance of cells

Toolbars can be shown or hidden using the steps below.

Displaying/Hiding toolbars

- Select the View option from the menu.
- Position the mouse pointer on Toolbars (this will display the option for the different types of toolbars).
- Click the type of toolbar required (a tick will appear next to the option selected).

- Toolbars may also appear on the screen when the option with which they are associated has been chosen (as will be seen with Charts).

Task Pane

Like Microsoft Word, Microsoft Excel has a Task Pane to the right of its window. However, you won't use this very often.

The Excel 2007 interface

Like Word 2007, Excel 2007 introduces a brand new interface that is quite different from that of a standard Windows program. The following features were introduced in Office 2007 (including Excel 2007):

- the Ribbon
- the Microsoft Office button
- the Quick Access toolbar

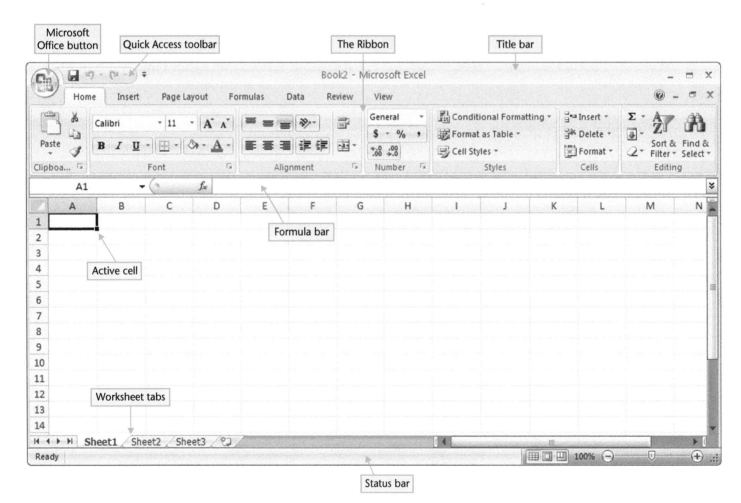

Figure 1.3 *The Excel 2007 interface*

The Ribbon

Your Ribbon may not look exactly like this because items are automatically resized according to how much space your screen has.

The Excel 2007 Ribbon is divided into a number of tabs. For example:

- Home – which contains the most common options.
- Insert – where you go whenever you want to insert something.
- Page Layout – which allows you to change page settings such as the margins and orientation.
- Data – which allows you to sort and filter data.

In addition there are tabs that will appear when you need them, for example the Chart tabs. Each tab is divided into a number of groups. Some groups have a tiny square box in the bottom right-hand corner. You can click these boxes to view additional options.

1. The Minimize button, which reduces Excel to an icon on the taskbar.
2. The Maximize button, which resizes Excel so that it takes up the whole screen. When Excel is maximized, the Restore button ⟐ is displayed instead, which restores Excel to its previous size.
3. The Close button, which closes Excel.

File names

The Title bar at the top of your screen will be reading Book1 whenever you start up the program. Book1 is the default file name that remains there until you,

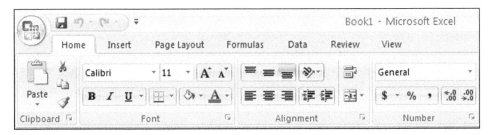

Figure 1.4 *The Ribbon*

The Microsoft Office button

To the top left of the Ribbon is the Microsoft Office button. Clicking this button will display the Microsoft Office menu. This menu has the items you'd find in a typical File menu, for example New, Open, Save, Print, Close and Exit.

The Quick Access toolbar

This toolbar contains buttons that allow you to quickly:

- save the Workbook
- undo the last thing you did
- redo the last thing you undid

Similarities between the two interfaces

Despite the differences, the two interfaces do have things in common.

Title bar

The Title bar is the first bar from the top of the screen. In addition to displaying the Control Menu icon in

the user, save and name the file with which you are working or until you open a file with another name. Each new file created thereafter is named in numeric sequence Book2, Book3, etc. These names may be used when saving your files.

Status bar

The Status bar is located at the bottom of the Excel window. This bar displays information about the current mode, selected command, or option. At the right of the Status bar is the AutoCalculator box. The results of automatically calculating selected cells using a variety of formulas are displayed here.

The Workbook

A workbook (Book1) displaying the active **worksheet** (Sheet1) is the document window that opens when you start Microsoft Excel (Figure 1.5). By default, workbooks contain three worksheets (Sheet1–Sheet3). You can have up to 255 sheets in a workbook to enter your data and formulae or to create charts and macros.

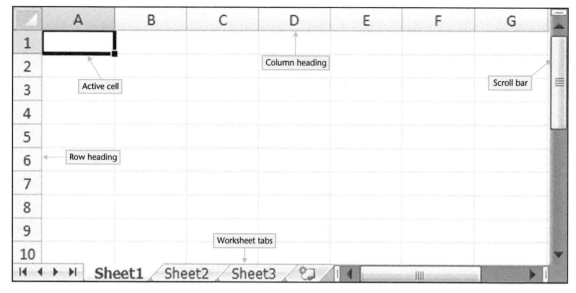

Figure 1.5 *An Excel Workbook*

Worksheets

A worksheet is like a giant table. Each row has a number – the first row is row 1, the second is row 2, etc. You can see the row numbers along the <u>left</u> side of Excel. At the <u>top</u> of Excel you'll see some letters (A, B, C, …) that are used to identify the columns. The first column is A, the second is B and so on.

The column letters and row numbers act as coordinates to identify a particular cell in Excel. The column is always given first, then the row (e.g. A1 or B14).

In order for a user to enter data or formulae in a cell, it must be active. The **active cell** (Figure 1.6) is distinguished by a heavy black border and its address is given in the Name box. When you first create a worksheet, cell A1 will be active.

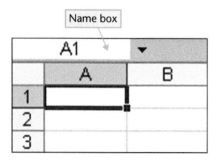

Figure 1.6 *Active cell*

Sheet tabs

A book/file usually starts with three sheets. This allows the user to save related data in one file under grouped headings. The sheets are pre-named but may be renamed to suit the user. Here is a practical example where the use of sheets may be understood. Let's say you keep budgetary data for home or office use. The income and expenditure accounts would always be the same but the figures would most likely change. The entire budgetary data may be saved in a book/file called BUDGET09. Then the data for each quarter of that year may be stored in sheets named 1ST QUARTER, 2ND QUARTER, 3RD QUARTER, and so on.

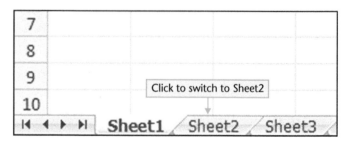

Figure 1.7 *Worksheet tabs*

Figure 1.8 *Name box and Formula bar*

Formula bar

The Formula bar is located next to the Name box. It allows you to type or edit data and formulae in the active cell.

Exiting Excel

In order to exit Excel either:

- Click File (or the Microsoft Office button) and click Exit.
- Or click the 'X' in the top right-hand corner.

2. Working with files

Creating a New Workbook

Whenever you start Microsoft Excel, it automatically creates a new blank workbook for you to work with. The first workbook is called 'Book1', the second 'Book2', and so on. If you want to create a new workbook <u>manually</u> you'd follow the steps below.

Excel 2003

To create a new blank workbook in Microsoft Excel 2003:

- Click File, New.
- In the New Workbook task pane which appears, click on Blank Workbook.

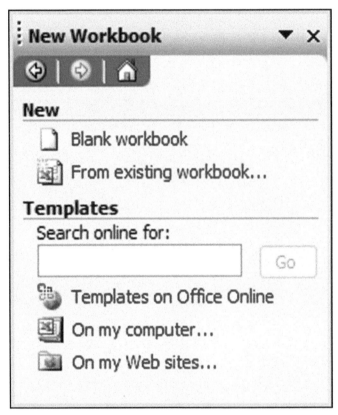

Figure 2.1 *The New Workbook task pane*

Alternatively, you can click the New icon in the Standard toolbar.

Excel 2007

- Click the Microsoft Office button.
- Click New.
- Make sure the Blank Workbook option is selected in the window that appears.
- Click the Create button in the bottom right-hand corner.

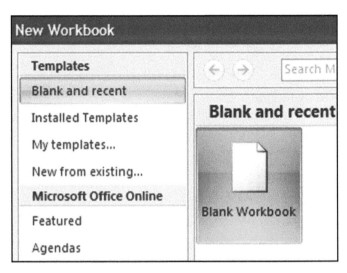

Figure 2.2 *Creating a New Blank Workbook in Excel 2007*

Opening an existing workbook

To open an existing Excel workbook:

- Click on the File menu or the Microsoft Office button.
- Click Open.
- Choose the file from the Open window (Figure 2.3).

The main part of the Open window lists the folders and workbooks in the current location (which is displayed in the Look in combo box). There are several ways in which you can change this location:

1 by clicking on one of the common locations to the left of the window
2 by using the Look in combo box
3 by double-clicking on the name of a folder.

Once you have found the file you want to open, you can double-click it to open it, or select it and click the Open button.

Note

The Open button will be disabled until you select an item.

Saving a workbook

In order to save a workbook:

- Click File or the Microsoft Office button.
- Click Save.

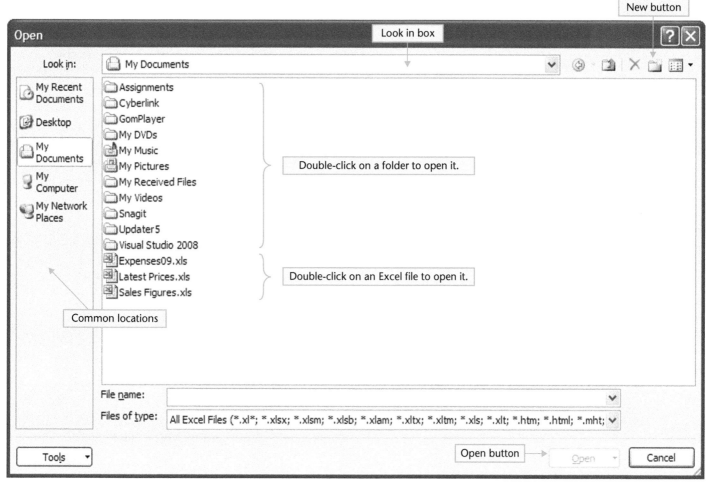

Figure 2.3 *The Open window*

- If this is your first time saving the workbook, the Save As window will appear. You will then have to type the name of the file and choose the location where it is to be saved.
- You can also click the Save button ▤

Saving workbooks in Excel 2007

Microsoft Excel 2007 has introduced a new (.xlsx) format. Unfortunately, previous versions of Excel can't read this format without a converter. So when you

are saving your Excel workbooks, you should change the file type to the Excel 97–2003 (*.xls) format as shown in Figure 2.4.

Saving under a new name/type

If you want to save a file under a new name:

- Click on the File menu (or the Microsoft Office button).
- Click Save As.

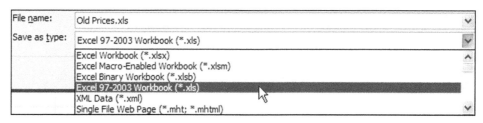

Figure 2.4 *Changing the file type*

- Go to the folder where you want to store the file.
- Type the new name of the file.
- Click Save when you're done.

Note

In Excel 2007, there is also an option to Save As Excel 97–2003 format.

Moving around the sheet

To move from cell to cell, you may use the **arrow keys** or simply <u>click in the cell</u> required. If the spreadsheet data spreads to cells that cannot be seen on the screen, you may use your scroll bars to shift the screen before clicking, or click on the arrow in the name box, key in the cell name and press the Enter key. From any point of the spreadsheet, you may return to the beginning cell A1 by pressing Ctrl and Home.

Other methods of moving around

- Press Ctrl + G to open the Go To dialogue box.
- Type the cell name (letter and number).
- Click OK or press Enter.

- Ctrl + End moves the cell pointer to the end of a workbook.
- Press the PgDn key (or Page Down on some keyboards) to jump down the worksheet one screen-length at a time.
- Press the PgUp key (or Page Up on some keyboards) to jump up the worksheet one screen-length at a time.
- Press the End key and then press the up, down, left and right arrow keys to jump to the top/bottom or beginning/end of data in the current row or column.

Closing a workbook

In order to close the current Microsoft Excel workbook:

- Click on the File menu (the Microsoft Office button in Excel 2007).
- Click Close.

Note

If there are any unsaved changes, a dialogue box will prompt you to save them.

Figure 2.5 *Go To dialogue box*

Exercise 2

Perform the following using the keyboard:

1 Starting at the beginning of the worksheet, press the right arrow key → four times, then the down arrow key ↓ nine times. Your cell pointer should now be positioned on cell E10. (Note: The cell address appears in the Name box and the column and row headings are boldface.)

2 Press the left arrow key ← twice, then the down arrow key ↓ 16 times. Your cell pointer should now be positioned on cell C26. (Note: Some of the rows scroll off the top of the screen.)

Perform the following using the mouse:

3 Move to cell A19 by positioning the mouse pointer that appears as a cross ✛, over cell A19 and click the left mouse button.

4 Move to cell B24.

Perform the following using the Page Up and Page Down keys:

5 Press the Page Down key until you can see cell B200 in view. Press either the ↑ or the ↓ to move the cell pointer to cell B200.

Perform the following using the scroll bars:

6 Press the arrow positioned to the right on the horizontal scroll bar until the column AZ is in view.

7 Press the up arrow positioned at the top of the vertical scroll bar until row 100 is in view.

8 Using the mouse, click in cell AZ100.

9 Drag the scroll box back to the top of the vertical scroll bar then drag the scroll box back to the left of the horizontal scroll bar.

10 Using the mouse, click in cell D10.

Perform the following using the Name box:

11 Position the I-beam mouse pointer over the Name box and click. Type cell E14, then press the Enter key.

Perform the following using the Go To option:

12 Under the heading Other methods of moving around, following the steps to bring up the Go To dialogue box, type AX200 and press Enter or click the OK tab.

Perform the following using shortcut keys:

13 Press Ctrl + Home to take the cell pointer back to cell A1.

3. Excel basics

Entering data

To enter data in a cell:

- Go to that cell using any of the methods you learnt (e.g. clicking on it).
- Type the data.

To let Excel know that you have finished typing in that cell, you can do any of the following:

- Press the Enter key (which would take you down to the next row).
- Press an arrow key.
- Press the tab key.
- Click on another cell.
- Click the Enter box on the Formula Bar.

Tip

If you are entering the data row by row, press the tab key after you finish each cell. If you are entering the data column by column, press the Enter key after you finish each cell.

Automatic completion

Sometimes when you type in a cell, Excel will automatically complete the text for you.

	A
1	Item
2	Pens
3	Pens
4	

Figure 3.1 *Automatic completion*

In the example shown in Figure 3.1, you can see that when you start typing 'Pencils', Excel thinks you're typing 'Pens' again and automatically completes the word for you. To accept an automatic completion, press the Enter key. If you don't want the completion, simply ignore it and continue typing.

Modifying data

Replacing the contents of a cell

To replace the contents of a cell, click <u>once</u> on the cell then type the new data.

Making minor adjustments

You can make minor adjustments to a cell either by editing it in place or using the Formula Bar.

To edit a cell in place:

- Double-click on the cell or click on it and press the F2 key. The cursor will start flashing in the cell indicating that it is being edited.
- Make the necessary changes.

To edit a cell using the Formula Bar:

- Click on the cell.
- Click in the Formula Bar and make the necessary changes.

When you start editing a cell, an X and a tick appear to the left of the Formula Bar. To cancel the change, click the 'X' or press the Esc key. To accept the change, press the Enter key or click the tick.

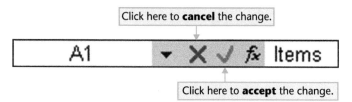

Click here to **cancel** the change.

Click here to **accept** the change.

Figure 3.2 *Editing a cell*

Undoing mistakes

Any time you make a mistake (e.g. accidentally deleting something), just click the Undo button to undo it.

Values and labels

Data in Excel can be placed into two broad categories – values and labels. **Values** are numbers that can be used in calculations. **Labels** are usually made up of letters but may contain numbers and symbols, for example '424-5662'. They are usually used to identify rows, columns or values.

	A	B	C	D
1	Items	Jan	Feb	
2	Books	30	45	
3	Pencils	21	35	
4	Rulers	20	25	
5	Erasers	50	30	
6				

Figure 3.3 *Values (in black) and labels (in red)*

In the example shown in Figure 3.3, the labels have been formatted in red to distinguish them from the values.

Note

Labels are automatically aligned to the <u>left</u>. Values are automatically aligned to the <u>right</u>.

Sometimes you'll want certain types of number to be formatted as labels, for example numbers of years. Here are some reasons why:

- So that you can have 0s in front. If you try and enter the value '001' (without the quotes), Excel will get rid of the zeros – <u>unless</u> you format it as a label.
- Because you won't be using them for calculations.
- So that Excel will recognise them as headings.

The last point is illustrated in Figure 3.4. Here the years have been formatted as labels since they are meant to be column headings. If they were left as values, Excel would be confused and this could cause problems later on when sorting or creating charts.

	A	B	C	D
1		2008	2009	2010
2	Maths	45.8	56.2	59.1
3	English	60.4	66.2	66.1
4				

Figure 3.4 *Numeric labels*

Note

Labels are automatically aligned to the <u>left</u>. Values are automatically aligned to the <u>right</u>.

To format a number as a label, put an apostrophe ' in front, for example '2008.

Working with worksheets

Switching worksheets
To switch to another worksheet, simply click on its Sheet tab at the bottom left-hand corner of the workbook.

Inserting a new worksheet
To insert a new worksheet:

- Right-click on the tab of the worksheet that you want the new sheet to appear <u>in front of</u>.
- Click Insert…

- Click OK in the dialogue box that appears.

In the example in Figure 3.5, the new sheet (Sheet 4) would be inserted in front of Sheet1.

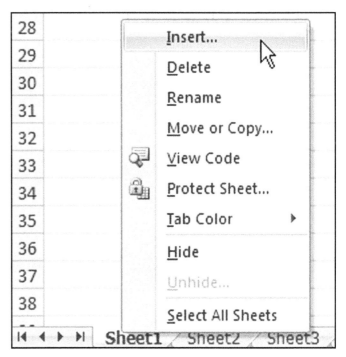

Figure 3.5 *Inserting a new worksheet*

Renaming a worksheet
To rename a worksheet:

- Right-click on the tab of the worksheet that you want to rename.
- Click Rename.
- Type the new name of the sheet.

Deleting a worksheet
To delete a worksheet:

- Right-click on its tab.
- Click Delete.

Working with rows and columns

Resizing rows and columns
To change the size of a column:

- Position the mouse pointer over the line to the <u>right</u> of the column <u>heading</u>. The cursor should turn to a double-headed arrow.
- Hold down the left mouse button and drag the mouse to the right to widen the column (or to the left if you want to make it narrower).

You can resize a row using a similar method.

Note

Whenever a cell contains ##########, it means that the column is not wide enough to display the full number. To see the full number, you just have to widen the column.

In the example shown in Figure 3.6, the Unit Cost heading looks as if it has gone into column D. But if you were to click inside cell D1, you'd realise that this isn't the case. The column just needs widening. To do this, drag the column separator to the right.

Figure 3.6 *Resizing a column*

Inserting rows and columns

To insert a row above a chosen row:

- Click in the chosen row.
- Then click Insert, Row (if you are using Excel 2003 or earlier). If you are using Excel 2007 or later, click the Insert button on the Home tab, then click Insert Sheet Rows.

Tip

If you select multiple rows before you click Insert, then you will insert multiple rows at one time. You can insert columns using a similar method.

Deleting rows and columns

In order to delete a row or a column:

- Right-click on its heading.
- Click Delete.

Exercise 3a

1 Create a new spreadsheet file containing the information below:

	A	B UNIT PRICE	C NUMBER
1	ITEM		
2	SUITE	1400	10
3	CORNER TABLE	100	5
4	4 PC. DINING SET	900	4
5	LAMP STAND	215	12
6	BOOK SHELF	500	6
7	DOUBLE BED	959	8
8	BEDSIDE CABINET	320	6
9	CHEST OF DRAWERS	875	7
10	COMPUTER DESK	995	15
11	LIVING ROOM SUITE	1500	8

2 Save the file as `Furnt`.

Exercise 3b

1 Create a new spreadsheet file containing the information below:

	A	B	C
1	ITEM	QTY	PRICE
2			
3	APPLES	10	1.5
4	BANANAS	12	0.5
5	ORANGES	20	1
6	PEARS	50	1.2
7	MANGOES	24	1.25
8	GRAPES	12	1.75

2 Save the file as `Task1`.

Exercise 3c

1 Create a new spreadsheet file containing the information below:

	A	B	C	D	E
1	ITEM	ORDER NO.1	ORDER NO.2	ORDER NO.3	PRICE
2	PENCILS	30	45	25	0.5
3	ERASERS	21	35	30	1
3	BOOKS	20	25	19	0.9
4	SHARPENERS	50	30	40	0.45
5	PENS	24	20	21	1.2
6	RULERS	12	22	19	4.75
7	MARKERS	40	27	36	4.75
8	CRAYONS	26	36	41	3.55

2 Save the file as Stationery.

Exercise 3d

1 Create a spreadsheet, which will display loan history information on books borrowed over a 4-year period from the READ-A-BOOK PUBLIC LIBRARY. Use the apostrophe (') before each year.

	A	B	C	D	E
1	BOOK ID	2003	2004	2005	2006
2	QA276	100	98	80	50
3	QA972	10	50	32	56
4	CL419.33	30	35	33	40
5	AC52.1.91	25	32	49	89
6	PP 235	47	55	35	78
7	BL908	125	100	103	110
8	FD111	24	34	44	54

2 Save the file as Books.

4. Selecting ranges

Ranges of data

A **range** is simply a group of cells in Excel. When you are referring to ranges, you use the colon notation. The colon (:) means 'to'. So to represent the range A1 to A5 you could type A1:A5.

Selecting ranges

Whenever you want to do something with a range of cells, for example format it or delete it, the first step is always to select it. The easiest way to do this is with the mouse.

Selecting a single cell

To select a single cell, just click on it or use one of the other methods to go to that cell. When you select a cell, you make it the active cell.

Selecting multiple cells

Selecting multiple cells is a little more difficult.

- Move the mouse to the top left part of the region you want to select.
- Make sure the cursor is a fat white cross.
- Drag the mouse to the bottom right part of the region you want to select.

The selected region will appear in blue except for the active cell which will remain white.

Tip

This also works if you start at the bottom right and go towards the top left.

To select cells from two or more non-adjacent regions:

- Select the first region.
- Hold down the Ctrl key and select the next region.
- Repeat the previous step until all the regions are selected.

Let's look at the example in Figure 4.1 again. Suppose you only wanted to select the cells in the Items and Feb columns. If you did a normal selection you would include the Jan column as well. So to select the two columns you would:

- First select the Items column.
- Then, while holding down the Ctrl key, select the Feb column.

	A	B	C	D
1	Items	Jan	Feb	
2	Books		30	45
3	Pencils		21	35
4	Rulers		20	25
5	Erasers		50	30
6				

Figure 4.2 *Selecting non-adjacent regions*

Selecting entire rows and columns

To select an entire row or column simply click on its heading.

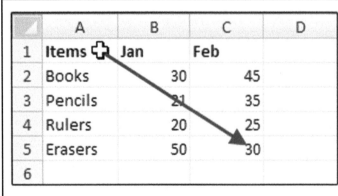

Before / After

Figure 4.1 *Selecting adjacent cells*

⬓	A	B	C ⬇	D
1	Items	Jan	Feb	
2	Books	30	45	
3	Pencils	21	35	
4	Rulers	20	25	
5	Erasers	50	30	
6				

Figure 4.3 *Selecting an entire column*

Selecting the entire spreadsheet

To select the entire spreadsheet, click the Select All button (where the column and row headings meet).

✛	A	B	C	D
1	Items	Jan	Feb	
2	Books	30	45	
3	Pencils	21	35	
4	Rulers	20	25	
5	Erasers	50	30	
6				

Figure 4.4 *Selecting the entire spreadsheet*

Exercise 4

1 Retrieve the Stationery file you created in Exercise 3 from your exercise folder.
2 Select all the information in the file.
3 Select the ORDER NO.1 and the ORDER NO.3 columns.
4 Select Column C and Row 5.
5 Close the Stationery file without saving.

5. Formulae and formatting

Formulae

Rules for calculating
Always start with the equal sign (=). Use cell names rather than the values in the cell (clicking in the required cell allows for more accuracy).

Examples of formulae

= B4 * C4   to multiply the value in B4 and C4
= D3 / D10   to divide the value in D3 by the value in D10
= C20 - D20   to subtract the value in D20 from the value in C20
= F15 + E15   to add the values in F15 and E15 together

Copying formulae
The copying formulae function speeds up the calculating process by allowing the user to repeat a calculation for a range of cells:

- Enter the formula for the first cell in the range.
- Click on that cell to make it active.
- Position the cursor in the bottom right-hand corner of the cell until the mouse pointer changes to a hairline cross (see Figure 5.1).
- Hold down the left mouse button and drag down/across to copy the calculation.

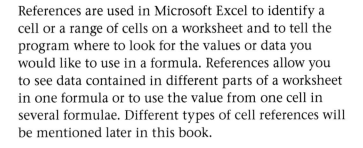

Note
As the formula is copied down, the rows in the formula change relative to the position of the mouse. As the formula is copied across, the columns in the formula change

References are used in Microsoft Excel to identify a cell or a range of cells on a worksheet and to tell the program where to look for the values or data you would like to use in a formula. References allow you to see data contained in different parts of a worksheet in one formula or to use the value from one cell in several formulae. Different types of cell references will be mentioned later in this book.

Functions in Excel
Adding numbers is probably the most frequently used calculation on a spreadsheet and at some time or another, spreadsheet users will have to add large amounts of data, for example adding figures from C1 through to C30. When entering this calculation, you will probably become very frustrated because the formula would look like this =C1+C2+C3+C4+C5+C6+C7+C8 all the way to C30. To assist the user, a shortcut for adding numbers is available. There are also shortcuts for finding the average, maximum (highest) and minimum (lowest) for a group of data. This shortcut is called a **function**. There are over 200 functions that can be performed in Excel; the six basic ones used in this book are SUM, MIN, MAX, AVERAGE, COUNT and IF. All functions follow the same fundamental set of rules, but not all work alike.

The fundamental parts of functions
The fundamental parts of functions are:

- the equal sign (=), which indicates the beginning of a formula
- the function name, for example = SUM
- the function's arguments. An **argument** is the information required to calculate the function. It may be a list of numbers contained within

	A	B	C	D
1	Items	Jan	Feb	Total
2	Books	30	45	75
3	Pencils	21	35	
4	Rulers	20	25	
5	Erasers	50	30	
6				

Before

	A	B	C	D	E
1	Items	Jan	Feb	Total	
2	Books	30	45	75	
3	Pencils	21	35	56	
4	Rulers	20	25	45	
5	Erasers	50	30	80	
6					

After

Figure 5.1 *Copying formulae*

brackets (or parentheses). A function can have a maximum of 30 arguments and a minimum of 1.

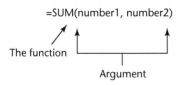

=SUM(number1, number2)

The function

Argument

- brackets in the appropriate places

If you are adding a range of cells, for example D5 through to D15, only one argument is needed. The function will appear as =SUM(D5:D15). However, if you wanted to add two ranges together, for example D5 through to D15 and E5 to E15, a second argument would have to be used. The function will appear as =SUM(D5:D15,E5:E15).

A comma separates each argument. The SUM function can be inserted manually or by using the AutoSum icon.

Inserting a SUM function manually

- Click in the cell where you want the answer to appear.
- Type =SUM (you can also type sum or SUM) and the open brackets symbol '('.
- Select the data in the range of cells for which the function is required =SUM(B6:B10.
- Close brackets, for example =SUM(B6:B10). This is optional. Some people do it to feel a sense of completeness but if you do not manually close brackets, when you press Enter, the software will automatically insert the close bracket.
- Press the Enter key.

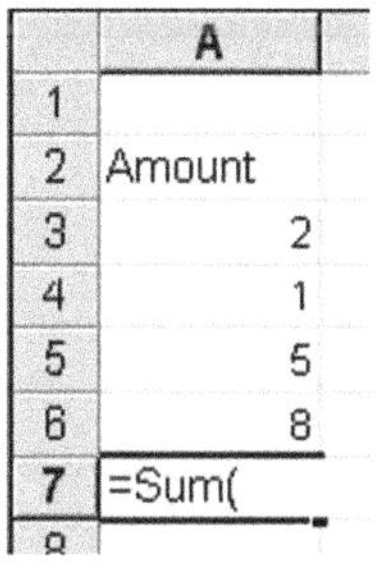

	A
1	
2	Amount
3	2
4	1
5	5
6	8
7	=Sum(

Figure 5.2 *Manual SUM function*

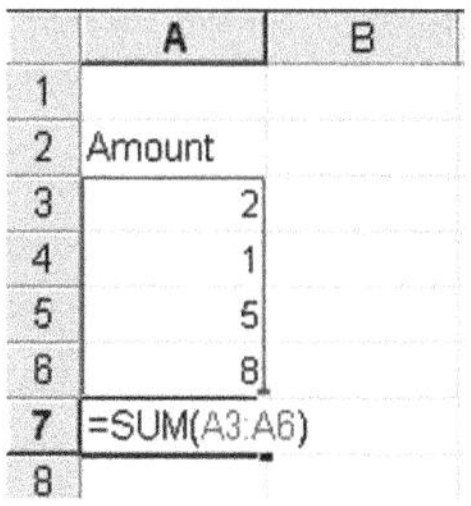

	A	B
1		
2	Amount	
3	2	
4	1	
5	5	
6	8	
7	=SUM(A3:A6)	
8		

Figure 5.3 *AutoSum function*

Using AutoSum

- Click in the cell where you want the answer to appear.
- Click the AutoSum button Σ. (You can find it in the Standard toolbar of Excel 2003 or the Home tab of Excel 2007.)

To change the suggested AutoSum formula

The AutoSum formula may sum a different range of values from those you want to add. You will then need to change the range. There are two ways a range of cells can be changed in a formula. These are:

1 Edit the defaulted range by typing directly in the formula.
2 Use the mouse to select an alternative range. Press the Enter key when you have finished selecting the correct range of cells.

Adding non-consecutive ranges

If non-consecutive ranges are to be added, each range of cells has to be separated by a comma. Figure 5.4 provides an illustration of adding three ranges in columns B, C, and D. Note how a comma separates each range.

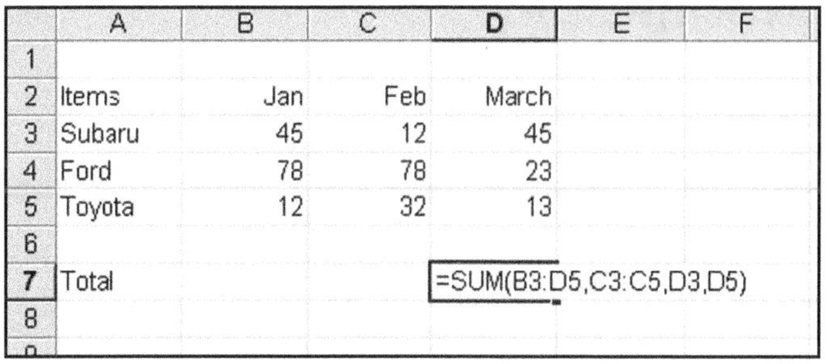

	A	B	C	D	E	F
1						
2	Items	Jan	Feb	March		
3	Subaru	45	12	45		
4	Ford	78	78	23		
5	Toyota	12	32	13		
6						
7	Total			=SUM(B3:D5,C3:C5,D3,D5)		
8						

Figure 5.4 *Non-consecutive ranges*

Other functions

So far all the examples have used the SUM function. But you can just as easily use these techniques with other functions. For example, if you click the arrow next to the AutoSum button, you can choose other functions like MAX and MIN. Or you can type them in manually, for example =AVERAGE(A2:A10).

The table below gives a list of the functions and their uses:

Function	Purpose
=SUM(range of cells)	to calculate totals for a list of numbers
=AVERAGE(range of cells)	to calculate the average number of a list of numbers
=MIN(range of cells)	to display the lowest number in a list
=MAX(range of cells)	to display the highest number in a list
=COUNT(range of cells)	to count the number of entries in a list (must be done using values)
=IF(condition,true,false)	makes an entry or performs a calculation when a stated condition is met and performs an alternative action if the condition is not satisfied
=TODAY()	this function inserts the current date from your system onto the spreadsheet
=NOW()	provides the current date and time

Error messages

Below is a list of error values that may appear in a cell when Excel cannot calculate the formula value.

#DIV/O!
Indicates that the formula is trying to divide by zero.
In formula: Divisor is a zero. Divisor is referencing a blank cell or a cell that contains a zero value.

#N/A
Indicates that no value is available.
In formula: An invalid argument may have been used with a LOOKUP function. A reference in any array formula does not match the range in which results are displayed. A required argument has been omitted from a function.

#NAME?
Indicates that Excel does not recognise the name used in formula.
In formula: A named reference has been deleted or has not been defined. A function or named reference

has been misspelled. Text has been entered without required quotation marks. A colon has been omitted in a range reference.

#NULL!
Indicates that the intersection of two range references does not exist.
In formula: Two range references (separated with a space operator) have been used to represent a non-existent intersection of the two ranges.

#NUM!
Indicates a number error.
In formula: An incorrect value has been used in a function. Arguments result in a number too small or large to represent.

#REF!
Indicates references to an invalid cell.
In formula: Arguments refer to cells that have been deleted or overwritten with non-numeric data. The argument is replaced with #REF!.

#VALUE!
Indicates the invalid use of an operator or argument.
In formula: An invalid value, or a referenced value, has been used with a formula or function (i.e. =SUM("John")).

Circular
This message indicates that the formula is referencing itself.
In formula: A cell reference used in the formula is the same as the cell containing the formula result.

#####
The number value calculated or entered is too large for the cell width.

Formatting cells

When you format cells, you either change their appearance or the way their data is presented. For example you could put a border around a cell or you could format its data to display a $ and 2 decimal places.

Using the formatting buttons
The following table explains what the various formatting buttons do. In Excel 2003, you would find most of these buttons in the Formatting toolbar. In Excel 2007, you would find them in the Ribbon's Home tab.

If you want to...	Use these buttons
change the font or font size	Calibri ▾ 11 ▾
bold, italicise or underline text	**B** *I* U ▾
horizontally align cells	(align left) (align centre) (align right)
vertically align cells	(align top) (align middle) (align bottom)
merge and centre cells	(merge and centre)
change the cell background colour and text colour	◇ ▾ A ▾
change the number of decimal places	←.0 .00 / .00 →.0
change the border	(border) ▾
format as currency, percentage or with a comma	$ ▾ % ,

Using the Format Cells window

If there isn't a formatting button that does what you want to do, you may have to use the Format Cells window instead.

To format cells using the Format Cells window:

- Select the cells.
- Right-click on the selection, then click Format Cells...
- Make the formatting changes, then click the OK button.

The Number tab

The Number tab of the Format Cells window allows you to change the way that data is presented within the cells. To the left of the Number tab is a list of categories that you can choose from. When you choose a category, options related to that category will be displayed on the right side of the window.

Figure 5.5 *The Format Cells window (Number tab)*

The following table explains <u>some</u> of the categories.

Category	What it does
General	removes the formatting from the data
Text	formats the data as a label
Date	formats the data as a date; you can choose from several predefined formats
Custom	allows you to specify the format, for example 'yy/mm/dd'

Wrapping text

If you want to wrap the text in a cell, change its alignment or orientation, use the <u>Alignment</u> tab of the Format Cells window.

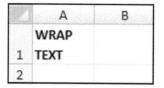

Figure 5.7 *Wrapped text*

Centring data across columns

This function may be used for centring main headings and subheadings:

Position the cursor in the row where the data is to appear.

- Select the cells in that row covering only the range of columns over which the data is to be centred.
- Click the Merge and Centre icon.
- Type the data.

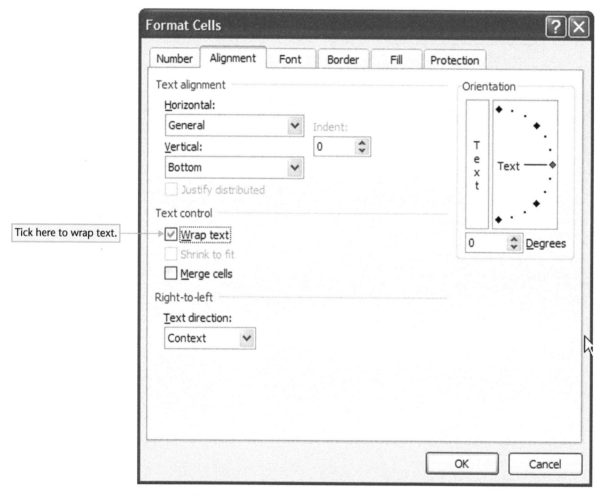

Figure 5.6 *The Format Cells window (Alignment tab)*

Wrapping text allows long headings to take up multiple rows. To wrap text in a cell:

- Right-click on the cell and select Format Cells.
- Switch to the Alignment tab.
- Place a tick next to the Wrap text option.

	A	B	C	D	E	F
1	KATHY'S GROCERY					
2						
3						
4	GROCERY	WEEK1	WEEK2	WEEK3	WEEK4	UNIT PRICE
5	SARDINE	55	66	45	50	0.99
6	TUNA	40	25	30	35	1.99
7	KETCHUP	20	15	17	25	3.99
8	BISCUIT	99	79	89	100	0.64
9	HORLICKS	10	15	12	16	4.19
10	MACARONI	35	34	30	32	1.30
11	BUTTER	15	10	11	16	2.35
12	CORN FLAKES	21	25	19	20	4.55
13	HOT DOGS	13	12	14	15	3.65
14	SALT	12	11	10	10	0.45
15	SUGAR	35	24	46	49	2.66
16	RICE	22	23	21	25	5.99

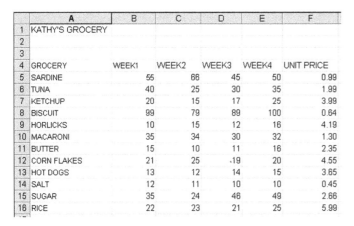

Figure 5.8 *Centring data*

	A	B	C	D	E	F
1	KATHY'S GROCERY					
2						
3						
4	GROCERY	WEEK1	WEEK2	WEEK3	WEEK4	UNIT PRICE
5	SARDINE	55	66	45	50	0.99
6	TUNA	40	25	30	35	1.99
7	KETCHUP	20	15	17	25	3.99

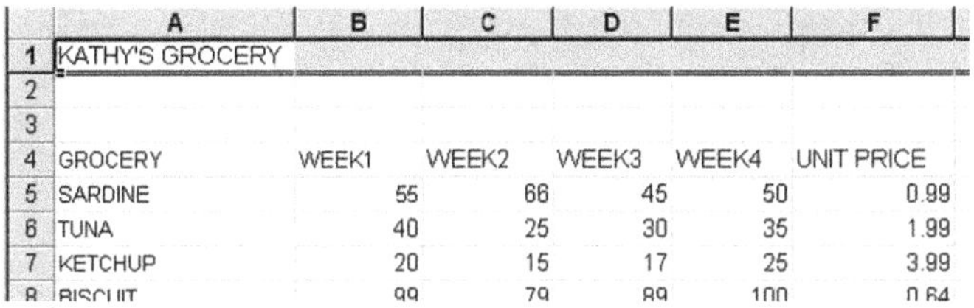

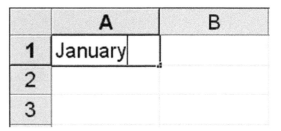

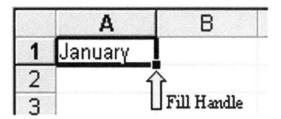

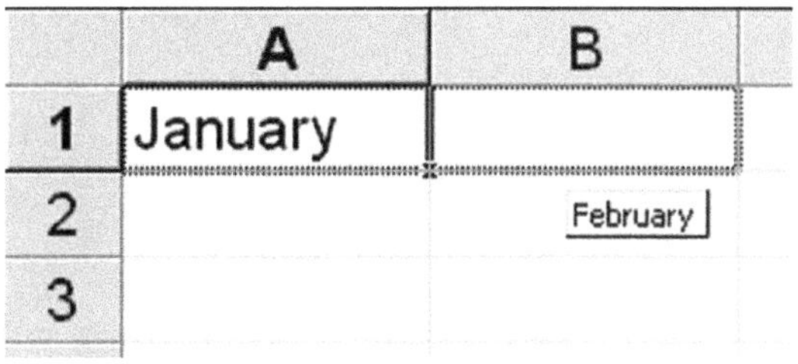

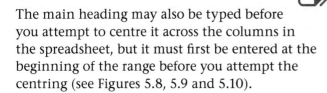

Figure 5.9 *Centring data – the heading is selected.*

	A	B	C	D	E	F
1			KATHY'S GROCERY			
2						
3						
4	GROCERY	WEEK1	WEEK2	WEEK3	WEEK4	UNIT PRICE
5	SARDINE	55	66	45	50	0.99
6	TUNA	40	25	30	35	1.99
7	KETCHUP	20	15	17	25	3.99

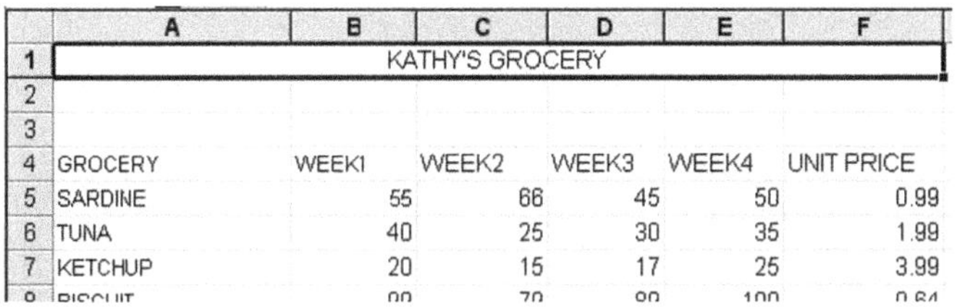

Figure 5.10 *Centring data – the heading is now centred.*

Note

The main heading may also be typed before you attempt to centre it across the columns in the spreadsheet, but it must first be entered at the beginning of the range before you attempt the centring (see Figures 5.8, 5.9 and 5.10).

Using AutoFill

The AutoFill function quickly fills in data which follows a sequence (e.g. days of the week/months of the year/ID numbers for stock/clients/years, etc.).

- Type the first piece of data, for example January.
- Select the cell with January.

Figure 5.11

- Position the mouse pointer at the bottom right of the cell until it changes to a hairline cross sign.

Figure 5.12

- Hold down the left mouse button and drag in the required direction.

Figure 5.13

- Release the mouse button when complete.

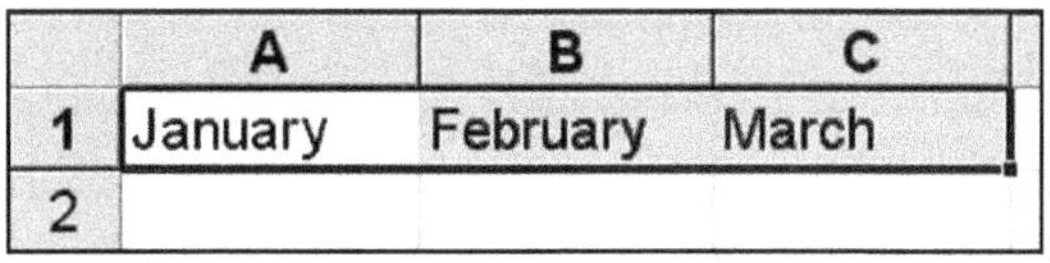

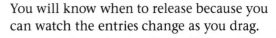

Figure 5.14

Note

You will know when to release because you can watch the entries change as you drag.

Exercise 5a

Your task is to create an Income Statement following the steps below:

TASK: Use the Merge and Centre feature to create a main heading.

STEPS:
  i   Click in cell A2. Type 'INCOME STATEMENT'.
  ii Highlight cells A2 to H2.
  iii Click on the Merge and Centre icon.

TASK: Fill in the months of the year using the Autofill feature

STEPS:
  i   Move to cell B4, type Jan and press Enter.
  ii Return to the same cell in which you entered the text, i.e. click in cell B4.
  iii Place the mouse pointer in the lower right-hand corner of that cell until you see a hairline cross.
  iv Drag the mouse pointer to the right until June appears. Release the left mouse button.

TASK: Widen Column A using AutoFit Selection.

STEPS:
  i   Place the cell pointer on cell A14 (because that cell has the longest data in column A).
  ii Select Format, Column and AutoFit Selection.

TASK: Add up Sales from January to June using the SUM function.

STEPS:
  i   Place the cell pointer on cell H5.
  ii Press the Alt key and the equal sign. This brings up the SUM function.
  iii Since the program has selected the correct range of cell (i.e. B5:G5), press the Enter key.

TASK: Add up the Expenses for the month of January by typing the SUM formula manually.

STEPS:
  i   Click in cell B14 (this is the cell where the total is to appear).
  ii Type the formula =SUM(B8:B12), then press the Enter key.

Type the data from Table 5.1 in the respective cells.

Table 5.1 Data for Exercise 5a

	A	B	C	D	E	F	G	H
1								
2				INCOME	STATEMENT			
3								
4		Jan	Feb	Mar	Apr	May	Jun	Total
5	Sales	1500	1250	1800	1300	980	1650	
6								
7	Expenses							
8	Rent	100	100	100	100	100	100	
9	Utilities	50	50	50	50	50	50	
10	Salaries	400	400	420	400	400	400	
11	Suppliers	300	390	500	500			
12	Consultants			90		200		
13								
14	Total Expenses							
15								
16	Profit or Loss							

TASK:	Copy the formula for the other months.		**ii**	Type =B5–B14 (this subtracts the Total Expenses from the Sales).
STEPS:	**i** Click on cell B14 (where the formula was keyed).		**iii**	Press the Enter key.

TASK: Copy the formula for the other months.
STEPS:
  i Click on cell B14 (where the formula was keyed).
  ii Move the mouse pointer to the fill handle in the bottom right-hand corner of cell B14.
  iii Drag the formula until you reach the column containing the last month.

TASK: Add up each expense over the six months.
STEPS:
  i Position the cell pointer in cell H8.
  ii Type: =SUM(
  iii Click in cell B8 and drag to cell G8. Note that a moving border will appear around the six cells. This formula should appear after the open bracket, i.e. =SUM(B8:G8).
  iv Press the Enter key.

TASK: Copy the formulae for the other expenses.
STEPS:
  i Position the cell pointer in cell H8.
  ii Move the mouse pointer to the fill handle in the bottom right-hand corner in cell H8.
  iii Drag the formula until you reach the cell of the row of the last expense.

TASK: Calculate the Profit and Loss.
STEPS:
  i Position the mouse pointer in cell B16.
  ii Type =B5–B14 (this subtracts the Total Expenses from the Sales).
  iii Press the Enter key.

TASK: Copy the Profit and Loss calculation for the other months.
STEPS:
  i Position the cell pointer in cell B16.
  ii Highlight from cell B16 to G16.
  iii Select Edit from the Menu Bar.
  iv Select the Fill option.
  v Click Right.

TASK: Format the figures in the spreadsheet to dollar sign and two decimal places.
STEPS:
  i Highlight cells B5 through to H16.
  ii Click the dollar sign icon on the Formatting toolbar.

TASK: Align the column headings in the spreadsheet to the right of the cell.
STEPS:
  i Highlight the cells January to June.
  ii Click on the Right Alignment icon.

TASK: Bold multiple cells.
STEPS:
  i Highlight the following heading by clicking in cell A2. Keeping your finger on the Ctrl key, select the following cells to place in bold: Jan to Jun, Total, Sales, Expenses, Total Expenses and Profit or Loss.
  ii Click on the bold icon.

TASK: Save the file as `Income_Statement`.

Exercise 5b

Type the data from Table 5.2 into an Excel worksheet, starting from cell A5. Note that the students' ID numbers are labels, so place the apostrophe (') before the first number. Since these numbers are consecutive, after typing the first number, you may use the AutoFill function to quickly fill in the others (see the section Using AutoFill in the text).

Table 5.2 Data for Exercise 5b

STUDENTID	STUDENT	TEST 1	TEST 2	TEST 3	TEST 4	TEST 5
101	KIM BANFIELD	58	85	88	94	100
102	DERICK BEST	0	74	75	0	0
103	NATASHA WEEKES	62	65	99	75	65
104	KIM WOODS	71	68	100	63	92
105	KURT MICHAELS	90	100			
106	DANIEL JOHN	85	89	95	85	50
107	SUE NORVILLE	95	78	75	55	85
108	MICHELLE IFILL	40	50	55	60	66
109	TOM DASH	85	67	65	78	
110	JOHN LUKE	20	77	50	50	61

Then carry out the following tasks.

1. Add a column to the right called NO. OF TESTS TAKEN and calculate the number of tests taken per student. FORMULA: =Count(C6:G6).
2. Add a column to the right called TEST AVERAGE to calculate the average test score per student. FORMULA: =Average(C6:G6).
3. Add a column to the right called FINAL EXAM and enter the following score each student received.

STUDENT	FINAL EXAM
KIM BANFIELD	100
DERICK BEST	80
NATASHA WEEKES	86
KIM WOODS	70
KURT MICHAELS	70
DANIEL JOHN	85
SUE NORVILLE	80
MICHELLE IFILL	85
TOM DASH	70
JOHN LUKE	82

4. Add a column to the right called FINAL AVERAGE to calculate the final average each student received. FORMULA: =Average(I6,J6).
5. Format the last three columns to one decimal place.
6. Perform the following calculations starting from row 17 for all numeric columns.

Label	Calculation
No. of papers	= COUNT(C6:C15)
Class average	= AVERAGE(C6:C15)
Highest grade	= MAX(C6:C15)
Lowest grade	= MIN(C6:C15)

7. Format the results of the calculations above to one decimal place.
8. In the first row of the spreadsheet, centre the following heading across the data in the spreadsheet:
   FRENCH 202
   Format this heading to size 14 and place in bold print.
9. In the second row of the spreadsheet, centre the heading EXAM GRADES across the data in the spreadsheet. Make the heading bold.
10. Save the file as Exam.

Exercise 5c

1. Retrieve Furnt file created in Exercise 3a from your exercise folder.
2. Add a column called TOTAL PRICE and calculate the total price for each item.
3. Format the UNIT and TOTAL PRICES to show the dollar sign but no decimal places.
4. In new rows at the bottom of the spreadsheet calculate the total, average, lowest and highest figures of the TOTAL PRICE.
5. Save the file as Furnt1.

Exercise 5d

1. Retrieve Task1 created in Exercise 3b from your exercise folder.
2. Add a column to the right of the PRICE column called TOTAL PRICE.
3. Calculate the TOTAL PRICE for each item.
4. Format all monetary figures to display the dollar sign ($) and two decimal places.
5. Save the file as Task2.

6. Copying, moving and linking data

Basics of copying and moving data

Copying data

- Select the required data.
- Click the Copy icon.
- Select the specific cell position where the data is to be copied.
- Click the Paste icon.

Moving data

- Select the required data.
- Click the Cut icon.
- Select the specific cell position where the data is to be moved.
- Click the Paste icon.

Copying or moving data (from one sheet to another)

- Select the required data.
- Click the Cut or Copy icon.
- Select the target sheet.
- Select the specific cell position where the data is to be moved.
- Click the Paste icon.

Copying and moving calculated values

It is important to understand the difference between copying calculated values and moving them.

Copying calculated values

When you try copying a value that is the result of a calculation, Excel does not copy the value. Instead it copies its formula, changing it to reflect the new location.

Consider the example shown in Figure 6.1.

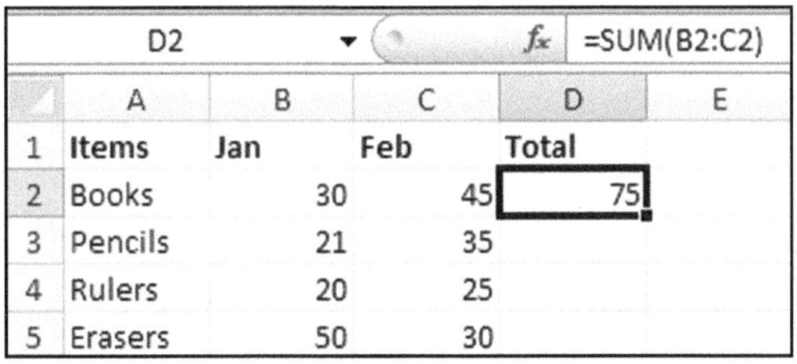

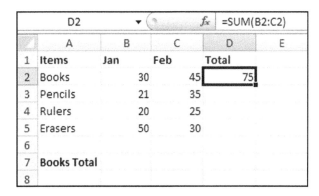

Figure 6.1a *Selecting the formula to be copied*

Suppose we copy the calculated value from cell D2 to cell D4. You might expect that cell D4 will now contain the value 75. But remember, Excel copies (and adjusts) the formula, not the calculated value.

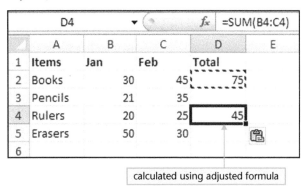

Figure 6.1b *The adjusted formula is now located in the new cell.*

Looking at Figure 6.1b, we can see that Excel puts the formula =SUM(B4:C4) in the new location. This is similar to the original formula – but the arguments have been adjusted.

How does Excel come up with the new arguments? Because the new location is two rows down from the old one, Excel increases the addresses in the formula by two rows.

Note

If you want to copy the old formula to a new location, go in the formula bar and copy it.

Moving calculated values

When you try moving a calculated value from one location to the next, what Excel does is move the formula to the new location (without trying to adjust it).

Let's look at an example (Figure 6.2).

Figure 6.2a *Selecting a cell to move its contents*

Suppose you move the total in cell D2 to cell B7.

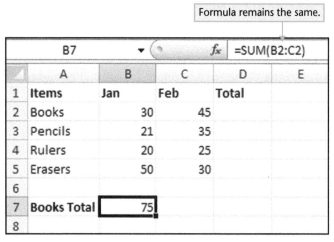

Figure 6.2b *The contents of cell D2 have been moved to B7.*

Because Excel does not adjust the formula when it moves it, the formula and hence the result remains the same.

Paste Special

The Paste Special feature is very useful. It allows you to paste data while providing you with options that the normal paste button doesn't. For instance you can use it to paste links.

To use the Paste Special feature:

- Copy some data.
- Right-click on the new location.
- Click Paste Special.
- Choose one of the options from the Paste Special window.

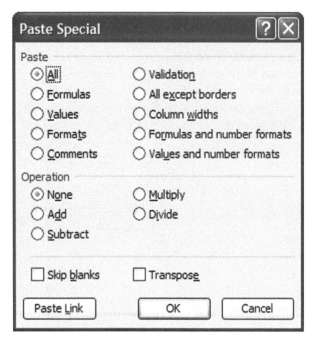

Figure 6.3 *Paste Special window*

Pasting values

When you copy a calculated value, you can use the Paste Special window to paste the value instead of an adjusted formula. Looking back at the example in Figure 6.1, you would use this feature if you wanted to copy the value '75' to cell D4.

To copy and paste a calculated value (without its formula):

- Copy some data.
- Right-click on the new location.
- Click Paste Special.
- Choose either the Values option or the Values and number formats option.
- Click OK.

Linking data

A 'link' provides an automatic update of copied data as long as the original data is changed. Links may be done when copying a) to another part of the spreadsheet, b) to another sheet within the same workbook or c) to another file.

- Select the data to be copied.
- Click the Copy icon.
- Right-click on the starting position for the copied data.
- Click Paste Special.

From the Paste Special window, click the Paste Link button Paste Link

Note

If you just want to link a single cell, you may move the cell pointer to the required position, type the equal sign followed by the name of the cell which contains the data you want repeated.

Linking worksheets

Sometimes in a workbook, you may be required to calculate cells which are in different sheets. For example, in a workbook you may want to add the value of cell A15 in the current worksheet and cell A17 in a second worksheet. These two cells can be added by using the format 'sheetname!celladdress'. The formula for this example would be =A15+Sheet2!A17. This formula indicates that the value of cell A15 in the current worksheet is added to the value of cell A17 in the worksheet named Sheet2.

- Move the cell pointer on the sheet and to the position where you want to perform the formula.
- Type the equal sign (=).
- Type or select with the mouse, the cell(s) in the current sheet, for example =A17.
- Type the calculation sign, for example +.
- Select the sheet which contains the next value and click on the cell.
- Press the Enter key.

Exercise 6a

1 Retrieve the `Furnt1` file created in Exercise 5c from your exercises folder.
2 Copy the items and number of items from the first sheet to a second sheet.
3 In the new sheet, insert a column called SUPPLIERS to the right of Item and add the following:
COURTS
DACOSTA MANNINGS
COURTS
MODERN LIVING
DACOSTA MANNINGS
CONTEMPO
STANDARD
MODERN LIVING
CARIBBEAN FURNISHING
CONTEMPO
4 Still using the new sheet, add the headings below to span the columns that contain information.

WOOD DESIGNS LIMITED
CHRISTMAS ORDERS
Use font size 14 and bold for the main heading and font size 12 and italic for the second heading.

5 Delete the records of the two suites from both sheets.
6 In the second sheet, insert a new record between BOOKSHELF and DOUBLE BED as follows:

ITEM	SUPPLIER	NUMBER
KITCHEN STOOL	MODERN FURNISHING	9

7 Make the following amendments to both sheets:
   a Change CORNER TABLE to GOSSIP CHAIR.
   b Change DOUBLE BED to SINGLE BED.
   c Change 4 PC. DINING SET to 11 PC. DINING SET.
   d Change the unit price for BEDSIDE CABINET to 290 (first sheet only).
8 Rename the first sheet as COSTS and the second sheet as ORDERS.
9 Save the file as `Furnt2`.

Exercise 6b

1. Retrieve `Task2` created in Exercise 5d from your exercise folder.
2. Copy data from Sheet1 to Sheet2.
3. Rename Sheet1 as PRICES.

Perform questions 4–11 in Sheet 2:

4. Bold, italicise and underline all column headings.
5. Calculate the average, lowest and highest QUANTITY and TOTAL PRICE.
6. Centre the heading ITEM, and right align PRICE and TOTAL PRICE.
7. Add two new rows – one between Apples and Bananas and the other between Pears and Mangoes and enter the following information:

Item	Qty	Price
Pineapples	7	$8.00
Coconuts	25	$2.00

8. Add a column between ITEM and QTY called COLOUR and key in colours of your choice.
9. Add the title 'Kay's Fruit Stall' and centre it across the columns that contain information.
10. Delete the Total Price column and the Banana record.
11. Save as `Task3`.

Exercise 6c

1. Retrieve the `Stationery` file created in Exercise 3c from your exercise folder.
2. Make a copy of the data from Sheet1 into Sheet2.

Perform questions 3–11 in Sheet 2:

3. Insert a column between ORDER NO.3 and PRICE and calculate the total number of orders for each item.
4. Add a column at the end of the spreadsheet and calculate the total price of orders for each item.
5. Format the monetary figures to display the $ and two decimal places.
6. Add two new rows – one between BOOKS and SHARPENERS and the other between MARKERS and CRAYONS. Enter two items of your own and calculate.
7. Underline all column headings. Also place them in **bold** print, and in a larger font size.
8. Place all item names in *italics*.
9. Insert a column headed ITEM # in the first column of the spreadsheet and enter item numbers for each item in the order 00901, 00902, etc.
10. Delete the record of the SHARPENERS.
11. Centre <u>all</u> column headings.
12. In Sheet1, perform the following calculations:
    a. the total number of orders for each order
    b. the average number of orders for each order
    c. the highest number of orders for each order
    d. the lowest number of orders for each order
13. Resave the file.

7. Absolute cell references

What is an absolute cell reference?

So far, all the formulae that you have done have used **relative cell references**. These are cell references that do not contain a $. For example, in the formula =MIN(A2:B2), the following are relative cell references:

- A2
- B2

An **absolute cell reference** is one that has a dollar sign in front of <u>both</u> the column and the row, for example: $A$2.

A mixed cell reference is one that has a dollar sign in front of <u>either</u> the column or the row, for example: $A2 or A$2.

So what is so important about the dollar sign? Think of it as meaning 'do not change'. Remember that normally, when you copy a formula to a new location, Excel adjusts the rows and the columns in that new location. By using the dollar signs, you can tell Excel, 'do not change this address when you copy the formula'.

Below is an explanation of the different types of cell references.

Cell reference	What it means
A2	When the formula is copied, both the row and the column can change.
$A2	Do not change the column (A). However, the row can change.
A$2	Do not change the row (2). However, the column can change.
$A$2	Do not change the row or the column, i.e. fix the cell reference so it doesn't change.

Inserting an absolute reference

To insert an absolute reference, you can:

- Manually type in the dollar signs.
- Press the F4 key. Excel will automatically put in the dollar signs around the current address in the formula.

Note

If you press the F4 key more than once, Excel will toggle through the different types of references.

Why you need absolute references

To understand why you need absolute cell references consider an example where we are using Excel to calculate percentages. Remember that in order to find a percentage you divide the number by an overall total.

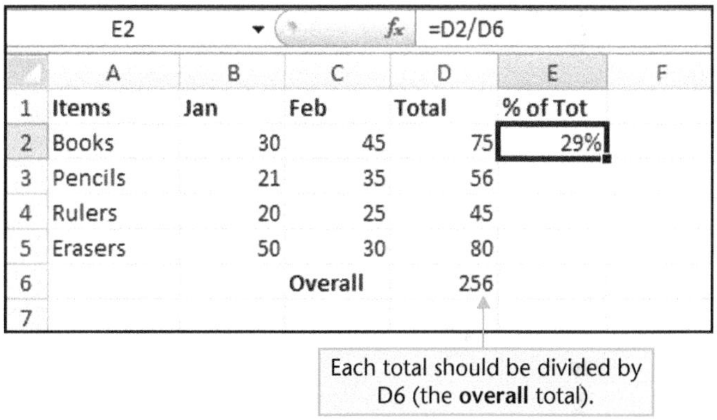

*Each total should be divided by D6 (the **overall** total).*

Figure 7.1a *Why you need absolute addressing – setting up the first division*

First we calculate and format the percentage for Books. Notice that we are dividing by D6 (the overall total). It looks correct so we copy it down to the other rows.

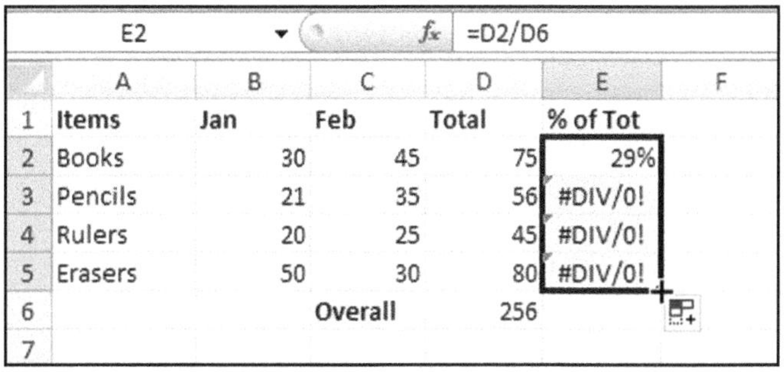

Figure 7.1b *Why you need absolute addressing – copying the formula to other cells*

Instead of getting the expected result, we get a set of errors as shown in Figure 7.1c. Why do we have those errors? Looking at the formula in cell E3 reveals the problem. The formula is =D3/**D7**. What a minute, aren't we supposed to be dividing by D6?

What happened is that when we copied down the formula, Excel increased its row numbers. This is what Excel <u>normally</u> does, but we don't want this behaviour in this case.

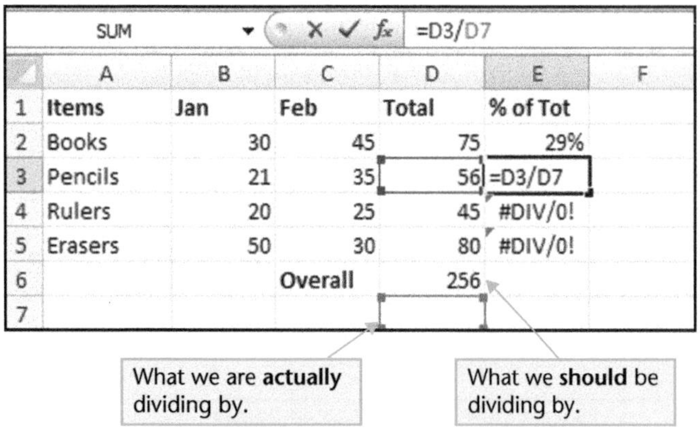

	A	B	C	D	E	F
			fx	=D3/D7		
1	Items	Jan	Feb	Total	% of Tot	
2	Books	30	45	75	29%	
3	Pencils	21	35	56	=D3/D7	
4	Rulers	20	25	45	#DIV/0!	
5	Erasers	50	30	80	#DIV/0!	
6			Overall		256	
7						

What we are **actually** dividing by.

What we **should** be dividing by.

Figure 7.1c *Why you need absolute addressing – showing how the formula has been copied by Excel*

How do we solve it? We absolute the reference to the overall total like this: =D2/$D$6. Now when we copy down the formula, the D6 part remains fixed as we can see in Figure 7.1d.

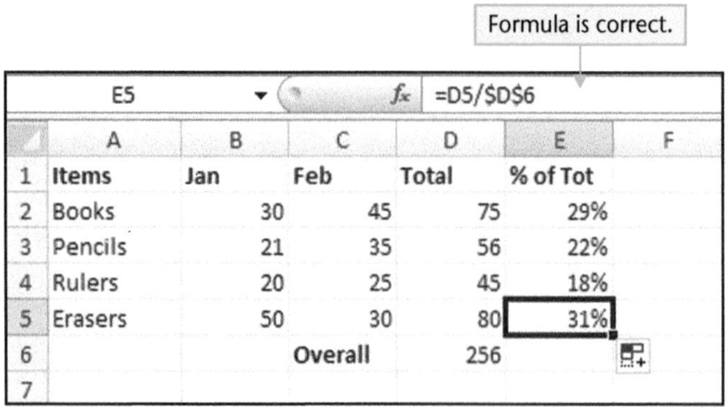

Formula is correct.

	A	B	C	D	E	F
	E5		fx	=D5/$D$6		
1	Items	Jan	Feb	Total	% of Tot	
2	Books	30	45	75	29%	
3	Pencils	21	35	56	22%	
4	Rulers	20	25	45	18%	
5	Erasers	50	30	80	31%	
6			Overall		256	
7						

Figure 7.1d *Why you need absolute addressing – the correct calculation*

Tip

If a formula seems to be correct but when you copy it you get an error message like <u>#DIV/0!</u> or <u>#VALUE!</u>, you probably need to use an absolute reference.

Exercise 7a

Create a spreadsheet of the information in Table 7.1 and perform the tasks that follow.

Table 7.1 Data for Exercise 7a

	A	B	C
1	COST OF CARPETING (per sq m)	$15.00	
2	STANDARD DISCOUNT	10%	
3			
4	CUSTOMER	ROOM LENGTH (m)	ROOM WIDTH (m)
5	LINDA BECKLES	4.0	3.0
6	WENDELL ALLEN	5.0	7.0
7	HEATHER CYRUS	3.2	4.0
8	CHARLES MAXWELL	6.2	6.8
9	VALERIE SKEETE	5.5	6.0
10	PETER GILKES	4.0	7.5
11	MICHELLE GERALD	8.5	9.2
12	KELVIN KANI	6.4	5.8
13	TAMA WELCH	9.1	3.4
14	VEDA BEST	4.2	6.7

TASK: Calculate the floor area for each customer. Format the floor area to one decimal place.

STEPS:
   i Place the cell pointer on cell D4 and type the heading FLOOR AREA.
   ii Place the cell pointer on cell D5.
   iii Type the formula: =B5*C5.
   iv Copy the formula to calculate the floor area for the other customers.

TASK: Calculate the total cost of carpeting for each customer. Format the totals to show $ and two decimal places.

STEPS:
   i Place the cell pointer on cell E4 and type the heading COST OF CARPETING.
   ii Place the cell pointer on cell E5.
   iii Type the formula: =D5*B1.
   iv Press the F4 function key.
   v Copy the formula.
   vi Select the data from cell E5:E14.
   vii Click the dollar sign icon ($).

TASK: Calculate each customer's discount. Format the answers to show $ and zero decimal places.

STEPS:
   i Place the cell pointer on cell F4 and type the heading DISCOUNT.
   ii Place the cell pointer on cell F5.
   iii Type the formula: =E5*$B$2.
   iv Copy the formula to calculate the discount for the other customers.
   v Select the data from cell F5:F14.
   vi Click the dollar sign icon ($).
   vii Click the Decrease Decimal Place icon twice to take off the decimal places.

TASK: Show the net due for each customer. Format the totals to show $ and two decimal places.

STEPS:
   i Place the cell pointer on cell G4 and type the heading NET DUE.
   ii Place the cell pointer on cell G5.
   iii Type the formula: =E5-F5.
   iv Copy the formula to calculate the net due for the other customers.
   v Select the data from cell G5:G14.
   vi Click the dollar sign icon ($).

TASK: Calculate the total revenue gained by the company.

STEPS:
   i Place the cell pointer on cell A16 and type the heading TOT. REV. GAINED.
   ii Place the cell pointer on cell G16.
   iii Click the AutoSum icon.
   iv Press the Enter key twice.

TASK: Calculate the total expenses incurred by the company.

STEPS:
   i Place the cell pointer on cell A17 and type the heading TOT. EXPENSE.
   ii Place the cell pointer on cell F17.
   iii Type the formula: =SUM(F5:F14).
   iv Press the Enter key.

TASK: Centre the following heading across the information in your spreadsheet. The heading should have the font size of 14 and should appear in bold.

CARPET GALORE JOB REPORT

Save the file as CARPET.

Exercise 7b

In this exercise you will create a worksheet that calculates prices for various magazines according to the length of subscription.

1 Type the information in Table 7.2 into a new worksheet.

Table 7.2 Data for Exercise 7b

	A	B	C	D	E
1		Hot	Madd	Teen	
2	Price	1.56	2.00	1.15	
3					
4	Months				
5	3				
6	4				
7	5				
8					

2 Click on cell B5.
3 Type the formula: =B$2*$A5
4 Copy the information to find out the prices of each magazine for the number of subscription months.
5 Save the file as MagPrices.

8. The BODMAS rule in calculations

BODMAS is a mathematical principle which means that where a user inserts <u>no brackets</u> in a formula, the calculation will be performed with preference to <u>d</u>ivision first, then <u>m</u>ultiplication, then <u>a</u>ddition, and <u>s</u>ubtraction last. The following example is based on this principle:

The calculation: $2 + 6 \times 3 - 10 / 2$
means: $2 + (6 \times 3) - (10/2)$
                              $2 + 18 - 5$
                              $20 - 5$
The answer is: 15

If we want a calculation done in a different order from that dictated by the BODMAS rule, we must enforce the order we want done by inserting our own brackets in the formula. Let's take a look at the following example:

Scenario

Given the following sales figures for the first three months of the year, with a selling price of $1.50, calculate the quarterly revenue.

Selling price	Jan	Feb	Mar
1.50	5	2	3

To calculate the quarterly revenue would require adding the three sale figures together first and then multiplying the answer by the selling price. The calculation `5 + 2 + 3 * 1.50` would return the answer 7 + 4.50 = 11.50, because, based on the BODMAS principle, the multiplication will be done first. Since that is not the requirement for this calculation, the user should insert brackets, using the formula:

> `(5 + 2 + 3) * 1.50`

This will return the answer $10 \times 1.5 = 15.00$

Note

As the user, you must determine when to insert brackets based on the requirement of the calculation.

Exercise 8a

1   Type the following information:

	A	B	C
1	6	10	2
2			
3			

2   Click in cell C3.
3   Type the formula: `= A1 + B1 * C1`

Note

Cells B1 and C1 are multiplied first $(10 \times 2 = 20)$. Then 6 is added to this total which results in the answer 26 $(20 + 6 = 26)$.

4   With the cell pointer in cell C3, press the F2 function key.

Note

Each cell is in a different colour so that you can easily identify cell references.

5   Moving the cursor using the arrow key(s), surround cell A1 and B1 in brackets:
    `= (A1 + B1) * C1`
    A different answer should appear because the bracketed calculation will be given priority; so $(6 + 10 = 16)$ is done first, and then the result is multiplied by the value in C1 $(16 \times 2 = 32)$.

Exercise 8b

1 Type the following information:

	A	B	C
1	DISCOUNT	3%	
2			
3			
4	ITEM	PRICE	
5	STOVE	$2,000.00	
6	REFRIGERATOR	$3,500.00	
7	MICROWAVE	$1,050.00	
8	LIVING ROOM SUITE	$3,600.00	
9	AD-DOER	$ 250.00	
10			

2 Create a heading to the right of the price column called PRICE AFTER DISCOUNT.

3 In cell B5, type the formula,

```
= B5 - (B5 * $B$1)
```

Note

In the calculation above, the discount is worked out first, then taken away from the original price to obtain the PRICE AFTER DISCOUNT.

4 Save the file as Discount.

9. Sorting data

In this chapter you will learn the <u>correct</u> way to sort data. Throughout the chapter we will be working with the following data.

ID	FirstName	LastName	Salary
HC	Horatio	Caine	$15,000.00
JA	John	Alleyne	$2,500.00
JB	John	Brown	$4,000.00
LC	Lisa	Cuddy	$10,000.00
MS	Michael	Scofield	$8,000.00
TA	Tonya	Alleyne	$3,000.00

The Sort buttons

The Sort buttons make it very easy to sort by one column.

Excel 2003
In Excel 2003, you can find the Sort buttons towards the right of the Standard toolbar.

Figure 9.1 *The Sort buttons (Excel 2003)*

Excel 2007
In Excel 2007, the Sort buttons are hidden under the Sort & Filter button to the right of the Ribbon's Home tab.

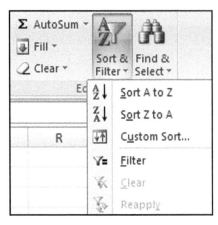

Figure 9.2 *The Sort buttons (Excel 2007)*

Sorting by one column
To sort by one column:

- Click a cell inside the column (but do not select the column).
- Click one of the Sort buttons.

Figure 9.3a shows what the data looks like when it is correctly sorted in descending order by ID. Notice that when one part of the row (in this case the ID) moves, the rest of the row moves with it. Thus, the integrity of the data is preserved.

	A	B	C	D	E
1	ID	FirstName	LastName	Salary	
2	TA	Tonya	Alleyne	$3,000.00	
3	MS	Michael	Scofield	$8,000.00	
4	LC	Lisa	Cuddy	$10,000.00	
5	JB	John	Brown	$4,000.00	
6	JA	John	Alleyne	$2,500.00	
7	HC	Horatio	Caine	$15,000.00	
8					

Figure 9.3a *Data correctly sorted by descending ID*

Figure 9.3b shows how the data might look if it were sorted incorrectly (for example, if you selected the ID column before sorting). If you look at the IDs you'll realise that the IDs have moved but the rest of the row didn't, thus corrupting your data.

	A	B	C	D	E
1	ID	FirstName	LastName	Salary	
2	TA	Horatio	Caine	$15,000.00	
3	MS	John	Alleyne	$2,500.00	
4	LC	John	Brown	$4,000.00	
5	JB	Lisa	Cuddy	$10,000.00	
6	JA	Michael	Scofield	$8,000.00	
7	HC	Tonya	Alleyne	$3,000.00	
8					

Figure 9.3b *Data <u>incorrectly</u> sorted by descending ID*

Disadvantages of using the Sort buttons
Although the sort buttons are very convenient, they have some disadvantages:

- They shouldn't be used to sort by more than one column.
- They have trouble sorting data that has a total row directly underneath.

Sort window

The Sort window gives you total control over how your data is sorted. It allows you to sort by multiple columns even if their sort orders are different.

Unfortunately the Sort windows in Excel 2003 (Figure 9.4) and 2007 (Figure 9.5) are very different. Figures 9.4 and 9.5 explain how to use these sort windows.

Note

If the Headers option is not enabled, when you go to select the columns, you will see A, B, C, for example.

2 Choose the columns to sort by.

3 Choose the sort orders.

1 Click here if the data has headers.

Figure 9.4 *The Excel 2003 Sort window*

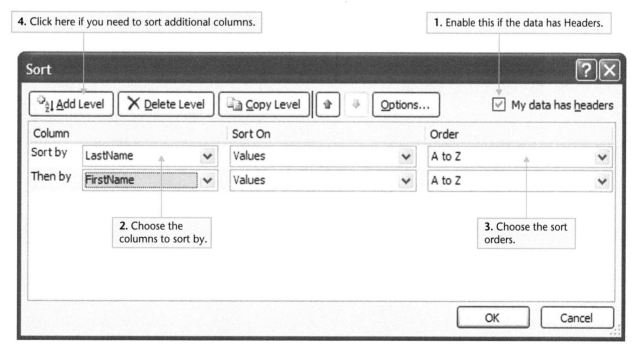

4. Click here if you need to sort additional columns.

1. Enable this if the data has Headers.

2. Choose the columns to sort by.

3. Choose the sort orders.

Figure 9.5 *The Excel 2007 Sort window*

Sorting by more than one column

The following method allows you to sort by more than one column and it works under all circumstances. To sort by more than one column:

- Remove any blank rows between the column headings and the data.
- Select the entire table of data (excluding any summary rows).
- Open the Sort window.
- Ensure the Header row option is selected
- Choose the fields you want to sort by and the sort order.
- Click OK.

If you sort by two columns, the first column is called the primary field and the second one is called the secondary field. In the following example, LastName is the primary field and FirstName is the secondary field. So in the cases where two people have the same LastName, Excel then sorts them by their first names.

Select all the columns of the table.

ID	First Name	Last Name	Salary
HC	Horatio	Caine	$15,000.00
JA	John	Alleyne	$2,500.00
JB	John	Brown	$4,000.00
LC	Lisa	Cuddy	$10,000.00
MS	Micheal	Scofield	$8,000.00
TA	Tonya	Alleyne	$3,000.00
		Total Salary	$42,500.00

Do not include summary rows like the total.

Figure 9.7 *The correct way to select data before sorting*

	A	B	C	D	E
1	ID	FirstName	LastName	Salary	
2	JA	John	Alleyne	$2,500.00	
3	TA	Tonya	Alleyne	$3,000.00	
4	JB	John	Brown	$4,000.00	
5	HC	Horatio	Caine	$15,000.00	
6	LC	Lisa	Cuddy	$10,000.00	
7	MS	Michael	Scofield	$8,000.00	
8					

Figure 9.6 *Sorting by two fields.*

The correct way to select data before sorting

Figure 9.7 illustrates the correct way to select data when you're going to sort it.

Exercise 9

1 Reproduce the spreadsheet in Figure 9.6.
2 Use the sort buttons to sort in DESCENDING order by Salary.
3 Save the file as SALARY1.
4 Use the sort window to sort in ASCENDING order by Salary.
5 Save the file as SALARY2.
6 Sort the data by FirstName then LastName.
7 Save the file as SALARY3.

10. Inserting charts

Graphs and charts are common ways of depicting data found in spreadsheets. This means of representing data may be used to show:

- fluctuations in figures – column, bar or line graph
- contribution of single items to a whole – pie chart
- percentages – pie chart

Types of chart

Pie
Pie charts are used to compare all parts to the whole. Two ranges of data are required – one range of labels and one range of values. The range of values is called a **data series**. No axes are required.

Line
Line charts are used to show data trends at equal intervals (fluctuations). The line chart consists of a category axis (X-axis) and a value axis (Y-axis). Because of its potential for comparison, more than two ranges of data may be used – one range of labels and one or more data series.

Column
A column chart is used to display data changes over a period of time or illustrates comparison among items. It consists of a category axis (X-axis) organised horizontally, and a value axis (Y-axis) organised vertically. Again, one range of labels and more than one data series may be used.

Bar
The bar chart consists of a category axis (X-axis) organised vertically and a value axis (Y-axis) organised horizontally. Like the line and column charts, this also has the potential for comparison and may use more than one data series.

Chart components

A chart is constructed using the following:

Data series
This is a group of related data plotted in a chart that originates from rows or columns on a single worksheet. Each series in a chart has a unique colour pattern. You can plot one or more data series in most charts.

Axis
This is a line that borders one side of the plot area, providing a frame of reference for measurement or comparison in a chart. For most charts, data values are plotted along the value axis, which is vertical (the Y-axis), and categories are plotted along the category axis, which is usually horizontal (the X-axis).

To decide which of these axes is which, remember that the category axis (or X-axis) is determined by the group of labels which were selected, while the Y-axis is determined by the data series selected.

Legends
These consist of a box that identifies the patterns or colours assigned to the data series or categories in a chart.

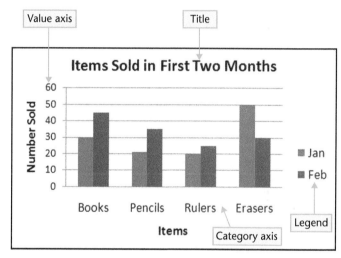

Figure 10.1 *Column chart*

In the example shown in Figure 10.1, there are two series (sets of values). The January values are in blue whereas the February ones are in red.

Selecting data

The first step of plotting a chart is always to select the data. In many cases, this is actually the trickiest part.

Note

If the areas you have to select are disconnected you will have to use the Ctrl key.

Selecting data for a pie chart

This is the easiest type of chart to construct. You simply select the values you want to plot as well as their corresponding labels.

In the example shown in Figure 10.2a, we've selected the data needed to plot the names of the items and the number sold in January. In this case the items (A2:A5) are acting as the labels.

	A	B	C	D
1	Items	Jan	Feb	
2	Books	30	45	
3	Pencils	21	35	
4	Rulers	20	25	
5	Erasers	50	30	
6				

Figure 10.2a *Selecting data for a pie chart (series in columns)*

Figure 10.2b shows how you would select the data if you wanted to plot the number of erasers sold in each month. In this case the months are acting as the labels. Since the values are values are going across, we say that the series are in rows.

Note

Note that the 50 is included in the selection, but it is outlined because it is the active cell.

	A	B	C	D
1	Items	Jan	Feb	
2	Books	30	45	
3	Pencils	21	35	
4	Rulers	20	25	
5	Erasers	50	30	
6				

Figure 10.2b *Selecting data for a pie chart (series in rows)*

Selecting data for a bar, column or line chart

The way you select the data for these types of chart depends on how many sets of <u>values</u> (i.e. series) you are going to plot.

Plotting one series

If you are plotting <u>one</u> series, you select the data the same way you would for a pie chart.

Plotting two or more series

If you are plotting <u>more than one</u> series, you'll need to include the column/row heading as well so that Excel knows how to label them in the legend.

Using the selection shown in Figure 10.3a, we are plotting two series, the figures for Jan and Feb. Therefore we <u>also</u> include the three column headings: Items, Jan and Feb. This is the selection that was used to plot Figure 10.1.

	A	B	C	D
1	Items	Jan	Feb	
2	Books	30	45	
3	Pencils	21	35	
4	Rulers	20	25	
5	Erasers	50	30	
6				

Figure 10.3a *Plotting two series in a column chart (Part A)*

In the example shown in Figure 10.3b we are plotting the number of books and erasers sold each month. We need to use the row headings for the legend so they are selected as well. The resulting chart is shown in Figure 10.3c.

	A	B	C	D
1	Items	Jan	Feb	
2	Books	30	45	
3	Pencils	21	35	
4	Rulers	20	25	
5	Erasers	50	30	
6				

Figure 10.3b *Plotting two series in a column chart (Part B)*

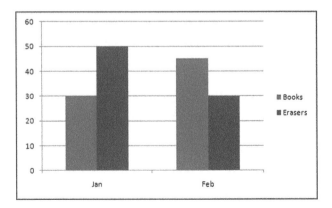

Figure 10.3c *The resulting chart*

Creating a chart

Excel 2003 and 2007 take very different approaches to creating charts. However, once you've created a chart, they both allow you to move it and resize it just like with a picture. You are also free to make changes to the chart.

Excel 2003

In order to create a chart in Excel 2003 or earlier, you:

- Select the data you want included in the chart.
- Click the Chart Wizard icon in the Standard toolbar 📖 (or click Insert, Chart...).
- Follow the steps in the Wizard.

By the time you finish the Wizard, you usually have a complete chart including a title and labelled axes.

Excel 2007

Excel 2007 takes a completely different approach. When you first create a chart, it is very basic and doesn't include a title or axes (see Figure 10.3c). You have to add these things later.

To create a chart in Excel 2007:

- Select the data you want included in the chart.
- Switch to the Insert tab of the Ribbon.
- Choose the type of chart you want.
- Customise the chart.
- Choose the location of the chart.

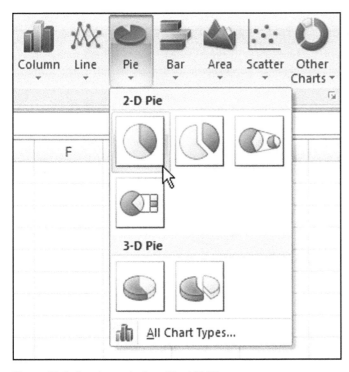

Figure 10.4 *Creating a pie chart (Excel 2007)*

The Chart Wizard (Excel 2003)

The following section explains the various steps of the Chart Wizard found in Excel 2003 and earlier. If you are using Excel 2007, skip ahead to the Modifying charts section on page 319.

Step 1 – Chart Type (Figure 10.5)

- Select the type of chart on the left, for example 'Pie'.
- Once you do that, you can select the subtype on the right (for example, what <u>type</u> of pie chart).

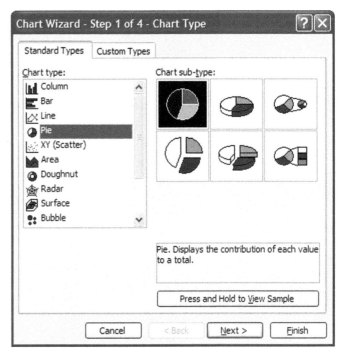

Figure 10.5 *Chart Wizard (Chart Type)*

Tip

You can get an idea of how your data will look with the selected type by clicking the big button near the bottom of the window.

Step 2 – Chart Source Data (Figure 10.6)

- If the preview looks right, then click the Next button.
- If you realise the incorrect data was selected, click the Collapse button and reselect the data.
- If the preview looks 'wrong' but the right data is selected, try changing whether the series is in rows or in columns.

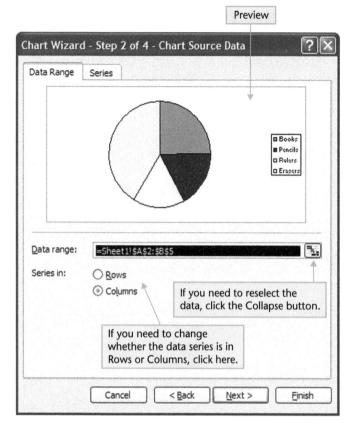

Figure 10.6 *Chart Wizard (Source Data)*

Step 3 – Chart Options (Figure 10.7a, b, c)

This is the step where most of the work is done. The following table explains what tab does what.

Tab	What it allows you to do
Titles	add a title or label the axes
Legend	determine where the legend is positioned or whether to have a legend at all
Data Labels	display percentages or values on the chart itself

Note

If you are creating a column, bar or line chart you will see additional tabs such as Axes, Grid Lines and Data Table. You won't be using those.

Titles tab

- Type in the title.
- If the chart has axes you can label them.
- The Category axis normally goes on the bottom of the chart (unless it is a bar chart).

Note

A pie chart doesn't have any axes. This is why the axis boxes are disabled in the image below.

Figure 10.7a *Chart Wizard (Titles tab)*

Legend tab

- If you want to hide the legend (for example if it just says Series 1), uncheck the Show Legend box.

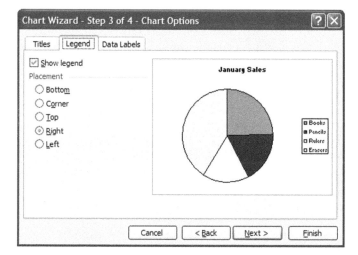

Figure 10.7b *Chart Wizard (Legend tab)*

Data Labels tab

- Tick Value if you want to show the data values on the chart.
- Tick Percentage if you want to show percentages (good for pie charts).

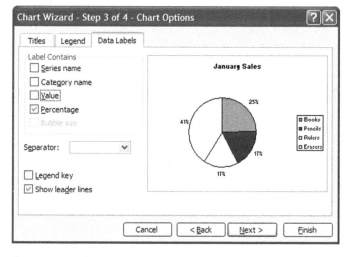

Figure 10.7c *Chart Wizard (Chart Options tab)*

Step 4 – Chart Location (Figure 10.8)

- Click <u>As new sheet</u> if you want the chart to appear on its own sheet.
- Otherwise, leave the <u>As object in</u> option selected.

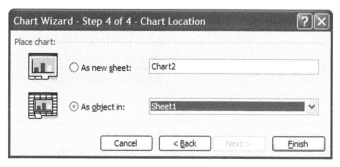

Figure 10.8 *Chart Wizard (Chart Location)*

Modifying charts

After you have created a chart, the easiest way to modify it is to right-click on its background (the white area) and choose the appropriate option. Alternatively, you can use:

- the Chart toolbar buttons (Excel 2003)
- the Chart tabs on the Ribbon (Excel 2007).

Tip

To change the Chart type, right-click on the chart and click Chart Type.

Excel 2003

In Excel 2003, the Chart toolbar appears whenever you click on the chart. To change the appearance of an object on the chart, select the object from the combo box, then click the Format button.

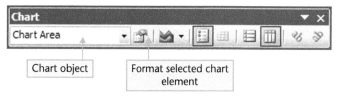

Figure 10.9 *Chart toolbar (Excel 2003)*

Excel 2007

There are three chart tabs that appear to the right of the Ribbon.

Note

If you don't see the Chart tabs, click on the chart.

Chart tab	What it allows you to change
Design	the location of the chart and how it looks in general, e.g. its colour scheme
Layout	whether the chart has a title or axes labels as well as the position of the legend
Format	the appearance of individual objects on the chart

Changing the chart location

To change whether the chart is on the current sheet (default) or its own sheet:

- Click on the Chart Design tab of the Ribbon.
- Click the Move Chart button (located at the far right).
- Choose the desired option from the dialogue box that appears.

Figure 10.10 *Move Chart button (Excel 2007)*

Changing the chart layout

Although you can manually add chart objects such as titles, it is <u>much</u> easier to choose from one of Excel's predefined chart layouts. To do so:

- Switch to the Chart Design tab of the Ribbon.
- Choose a layout.

Figure 10.11 *Changing Chart Layouts (Excel 2007)*

Then it is just a matter of editing the title, axes labels and so on.

Adding a title

To add a title to a chart:

- Switch to the Chart Layout tab of the Ribbon.
- Click the Chart Title button.
- Click the Above Chart option.
- Click on the title that appears then select the existing text.
- Type the new title.
- Click anywhere outside the chart when you are done.

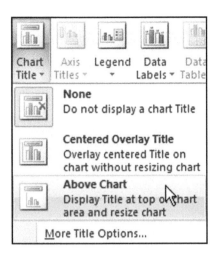

Figure 10.12 *Add Chart Title (Excel 2007).*

Adding an axis label

To add an axis label to the chart:

- Switch to the Chart Layout tab of the Ribbon.
- Click the Axis Title button.
- Choose which axis you want to label.
- Choose to display the axis label.
- Click on the axis label that appears then select the existing text.
- Type the new axis label.
- Click anywhere outside the chart when you are done.

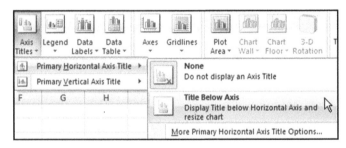

Figure 10.13 *Adding the Category Label (Excel 2007).*

Repositioning the legend

To reposition the legend or turn it off/on:

- Switch to the Chart Layout tab of the Ribbon.
- Click the Legend button.
- Choose the appropriate option.

Adding data labels

To add data labels, for example to display percentages on a pie chart:

- Switch to the Chart Layout tab of the Ribbon.
- Click the Data Labels button.
- Click More Data Label Options.
- Select the options that you want.
- Click Close.

Figure 10.14 *Adding data labels (Excel 2007).*

Copying charts

If you want to copy a chart (for example so that you can paste it into Microsoft Word):

- Click on the <u>background</u> of the chart.
- Click the Copy button.

Note

Excel 2003 does not allow you to copy a chart by right-clicking on it.

Exercise 10a

1 Retrieve the `Books` file from your exercise folder.
2 Select cell range A1:E8. The Book IDs will be placed on the horizontal or X-axis and the Years will be plotted on the vertical or Y-axis.
3 Insert a <u>column</u> chart with the following options:

- Title: BOOK LOANS 2003–2006
- X-axis: BOOK ID
- Y-axis: NO. OF LOANS
- Location: New sheet

4 Save the file as `Books1`.

Exercise 10b

1 Retrieve the `Books` file from your exercise folder.
2 Select cell range A1:B8.
3 Insert a pie chart with the following options:

- Title: BOOK LOANS FOR 2003
- Show percentages
- Location: New sheet

4 Save the file as `Books2`.

11. Advanced features

The IF function

The IF function is the most powerful of the logical functions. This function returns one value if a condition is true, another if the condition is false.

Syntax for IF function

The IF function has the following syntax:

```
= IF(condition, value_if_true, value_
  if_false)
```

The following is an example of where this function might be used.

Example

A teacher uses an IF statement to determine whether a student passed or failed based on the final average. The pass mark is 50.

Here an IF statement is used to test whether the final average is 50 or more. If the condition is true, i.e. the average is greater than or equal to 50, the student passes and the word 'Pass' is entered in the function location. If the condition is false, the word 'Fail' is entered in the function location.

The analysis of one of the IF statement used in this problem is shown below.

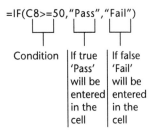

Note

Since the words 'Pass' and 'Fail' are labels, you must enclose them in quotation marks (").

IF statements may use the following conditional operators to state the condition question:

= equal to	<= less than or equal to
< less than	>= greater than or equal to
> greater than	<> not equal to

The VLOOKUP function

The VLOOKUP function is used to look up values in a table. Let's look at a simple example:

	C2	▼		fx	=VLOOKUP(B2,$E$2:$F$4,2,FALSE)	
	A	B	C	D	E	F
1	Name	Seat Class	Ticket Cost		Class	Cost
2	George Bush	First	2500		First	2500
3	Poor Blackman	Economy	1000		Business	2000
4	Lisa Cuddy	Business	2000		Economy	1000
5	Michael Scofield	Economy	1000			
6						
7						

Figure 11.1 *The VLOOKUP function (Example 1)*

In this example we have a table of ticket prices to the right of the spreadsheet. Each row of the table gives a particular ticket class and its associated cost. This table was used to fill in the Ticket Cost column (column C).

How would we fill in this column manually? We would look at the person's seat class, then look up the price that corresponds to that class. <u>This is exactly what VLOOKUP function does</u>. The function used to look up the price for George Bush is given below:

= VLOOKUP (B2, $E$2:$F$4,   2,   FALSE).

As you can see, there are four arguments, separated by commas. Let's look at what each one does.

1 <u>the lookup value</u> – this is the value that you want to look up in the table. In our example we use the reference B2 because that's where we can find George Bush's seat class.

2 <u>table array</u> – this is a reference to the table you want to search (<u>excluding the headings</u>). You normally make the range absolute so that it doesn't change when you copy the formula.

3 <u>column index</u> – this is the index of the column that contains that value you want to find. In this case we want to find the cost, which is in column 2 of the table.

4 <u>approximate match</u> – in our example we put 'false' because we do <u>not</u> want to use an approximate match. This means that we're using <u>exact matching</u>. Approximate matches will be explained next.

Approximate matches

Let's look at an example that uses approximate matches.

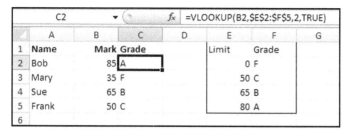

Figure 11.2 *The VLOOKUP function (Example 2)*

A common use of the VLOOKUP function is to look up what grade a student received. Here we can't use exact matching because it would require that our lookup table contains a value for <u>every</u> possible grade. So we use approximate matching instead.

The formula that looks up Bob's grade illustrates this:

```
= VLOOKUP(B2,    $E$2:$F$5,    2,    TRUE)
```

Note

For approximate matching to work correctly, you need to ensure that the <u>first column of the lookup table is sorted</u>.

Here's how approximate matching works. When Excel goes to look up Bob's grade, it doesn't find an entry for 85, so it uses the largest one that is less than 85 (in this case 80). Then it goes across to the second row of the table and notes that the grade is A.

The RANK function

Excel's RANK function ranks a value's position in a list of values. For instance, you could use it to rank a student's position in a class based on his or her average.

In the example below, we are ranking four students in a class. Since Bob has the highest average, he gets a rank of 1. Sue has the next highest average so she gets a rank of 2, and so on.

Figure 11.3 *The RANK function*

As you can see, the formula used to rank Joe is:

= RANK (B2, $B$2:$B$5,   0).

There are three arguments, separated by commas. Let's look at what each one does.

1 <u>number</u> – this is the value that you want to rank. In this case it is B2 since we are referring to Joe's mark

2 <u>ref</u> – this is a reference to the list in which the number is being ranked. In our case this is the list of averages in cells B2 to B5. Since we intend to copy this formula down, we use absolute cell references. Otherwise Sue would get ranked according to list B3:B6, Bob would get ranked according to list B4:B7, and so on

3 <u>order</u> – this is the order in which the values are being ranked. If you want:

   - the biggest value to have a rank of 1, set the order to 0 (default)
   - the smallest value to have a rank of 1, set the order to 1

The order field has a default of 0, so in our example we could have also said:

```
=RANK(B2,  $B$2:$B$5)
```

The Insert Function window

When you are inserting a function, sometimes it is difficult to remember what the various arguments do – particularly with the more complex functions covered in this chapter.

The Insert Function window (Figure 11.4) provides you with an interface that helps you insert a function. To access this window:

- Click in the cell where you want this function to go.
- In Excel 2003, click Insert, Function…
- In Excel 2007, click the Insert tab of the ribbon then click the Insert Function button.

You have the option of searching for a function, or browsing through the various categories until you see something that looks useful. Once you've selected the function you want, click the OK button. In this example, we are getting assistance with inserting the IF function (Figure 11.5).

Excel provides you with a box for each argument. You can either type the argument directly into the box, or you can click the Collapse button and then select cells from your worksheet. As you are building the function, you can see what value the formula would give.

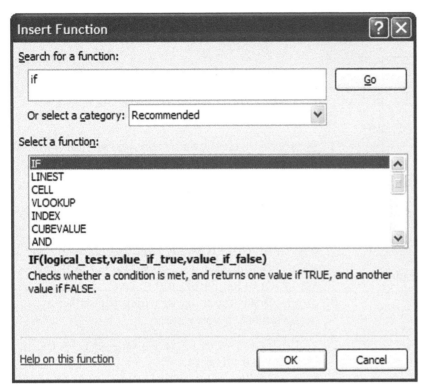

Figure 11.4 *The Insert Function window*

When you click OK, the formula will be inserted into the active cell using the arguments you provided.

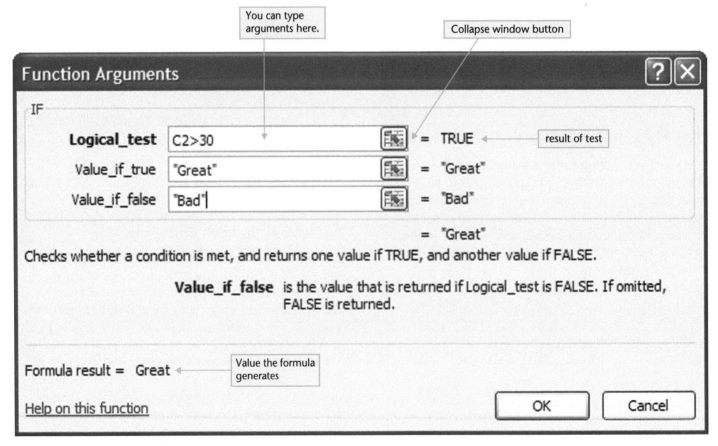

Figure 11.5 *The IF function window*

Exercise 11a

Use the `Furnt2` file from your exercise folder to perform the following exercises on entering a calculation based on values.

Note that cell addresses must be used when carrying out these exercises on the worksheet.

1 A warehouse owner is planning to give a discount on the total price of items customers purchase. The discount is as follows:

   If the total price of the customer's purchase is greater than $5000.00, then that customer is given a 5% discount on the total price; otherwise, a 2% discount is given. Calculate the discount value for each customer.

   <u>Syntax</u>: = IF(Total Price>5000,Total Price*5%,Total Price*2%)

2 A warehouse owner is planning to give a discount on the total price of items customers purchase. The discount is as follows:

   If the total price of the customer's purchase is greater than $5000.00, then that customer is given a 5% discount on the total price; otherwise, a 2% discount is given. Calculate the discounted price for each customer.

   <u>Syntax</u>: = IF(Total Price>5000,Total Price-(Total Price*5%),Total Price-(Total Price*2%))

Exercise 11b

1 Retrieve the `Ages` file from your exercise folder.
2 Use the VLOOKUP function to fill in the Category column (Adult, Teenager, etc.), but use exact matching. Why are there errors? What type of matching should you use instead?
3 Change the VLOOKUP formulae to use approximate matching. Why don't they work correctly?
4 Sort the Lookup table by the Min Age column. Notice that the values in the Category column will change.
5 Save the file as `Ages1`.

Exercise 11c

1 Retrieve the `Movies` file from your exercise folder.
2 Insert columns to the right of <u>each</u> of the following columns: Cost, Gross, Rating and Profit. Give each new column the heading 'Rank'.
3 Use each ranking column to rank the column immediately to its left.

   • The Cost and Gross columns are to be ranked so that the largest value has a rank of 1.
   • The Rating and Profit columns are to be ranked so that the smallest value is ranked first.

12. Criteria ranges (Advanced Filter)

The Advanced Filter feature allows you to extract from a table of data those records that meet certain criteria. If you are familiar with databases, the Advanced Filter works in a similar manner to a query.

Look at the example in Figure 12.1. We want Excel to extract the records that have more than 650 000 visitors in 2007. Let's look at the steps we must follow in order to do so.

Performing an Advanced Filter

Step 1 – Set up the criteria

The criteria will tell Excel how to extract the records. To set up the criteria:

- Copy and paste the heading(s) at the bottom of the spreadsheet.
- Put the condition(s) under the heading(s) (see Figure 12.1).

Note

If you misspell the headings, the Advanced filter won't work. This is why you copy and paste them instead of typing them.

Step 2 – Select the table of data

- Make sure you include the column headings.
- Do not include any summary rows.

Step 3 – Open the Advanced Filter window

- In Excel 2003 and before, click Data, Filter, Advanced Filter.
- In Excel 2007, click the Data Tab, then click the Advanced button in the Filter group.
- Select the option Copy to another location.

	A	B	C	D	E	F
1	**Caribbean Cruise Visitors**					
2	For 2006 & 2007					
3						
4	Destination	2006	2007	Increase	% Increase	
5	St. Lucia	359,573	610,345	250,772	69.7%	
6	Antigua & Barbuda	471,623	672,788	201,165	42.7%	
7	Grenada	218,684	270,932	52,248	23.9%	data we want to filter
8	Barbados	539,092	616,354	77,262	14.3%	
9	Puerto Rico	1,388,019	1,437,239	49,220	3.5%	
10	US Virgin Islands	1,901,275	1,917,878	16,603	0.9%	
11	Total	4,878,266	5,525,536	647,270		
12						
13	2007	criteria				
14	>650000					
15						

Figure 12.1 *Selecting the data*

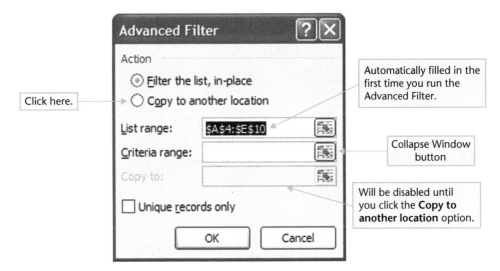

Figure 12.2 *The Advanced Filter window*

Step 4 – Fill in the options

You are given a number of items to fill in. Below is a table explaining what each one is for.

Option	What to do
List range	Ensure that the table of data is selected.
Criteria range	Select the criteria you set up earlier (including the headings).
Copy to	Click the cell where you want the top of the extracted data to go.

Using the Collapse window buttons

To the right of each option is a Collapse window button:

- Click it to collapse the Advanced Filter window. This makes it easier to select data on the sheet.
- Select the desired range.
- Click the button again (now showing a Restore window icon) to restore the window.

Figure 12.3 *Collapsed window*

Step 5 – Click OK

When you are finished, click the OK button. The results are shown in Figure 12.5.

Figure 12.4 *Completed window*

Multiple criteria

AND

If you have two or more criteria that must be true, put them on the <u>same</u> line.

Suppose you wanted the countries that had more than 600000 visitors in 2007 <u>and</u> a greater than 30% increase. Then you would use the following criteria:

2007	% increase
>600000	>30%

The following criteria select countries that had between 600000 and 1000000 arrivals in 2007.

A	B	C	D	E	F
Caribbean Cruise Visitors					
For 2006 & 2007					
Destination	2006	2007	Increase	% Increase	
St. Lucia	359,573	610,345	250,772	69.7%	
Antigua & Barbuda	471,623	672,788	201,165	42.7%	
Grenada	218,684	270,932	52,248	23.9%	
Barbados	539,092	616,354	77,262	14.3%	
Puerto Rico	1,388,019	1,437,239	49,220	3.5%	
US Virgin Islands	1,901,275	1,917,878	16,603	0.9%	
Total	4,878,266	5,525,536	647,270		
2007					
>650000					
Destination	2006	2007	Increase	% Increase	
Antigua & Barbuda	471,623	672,788	201,165	42.7%	
Puerto Rico	1,388,019	1,437,239	49,220	3.5%	
US Virgin Islands	1,901,275	1,917,878	16,603	0.9%	

extracted data

Figure 12.5 *Results of extracting the destinations with > 650000 visitors in 2007*

2007	2007
>=600000	<=1000000

OR

If you have multiple criteria and any of them may be true, put them on the <u>different</u> lines.

The following example selects the countries that had more than 600000 visitors in 2007 <u>or</u> a greater than 30% increase.

2007	% increase
>600000	
	>30%

The following example selects the countries that had more than 1000000 visitors or less than 300000 arrivals in 2007.

2007
>1000000
<300000

Exercise 12

Retrieve the `Cruise` file from your exercise folder and try the following filters:

1 List all the countries that had fewer than 100000 arrivals in 2006.
2 List all the countries that had an increase of more than 50% or less than 1%.
3 List all the countries that had more than 1 million arrivals in both 2006 and 2007.

Retrieve the `Climate` file from your exercise folder and try the following filters:

4 List all the months that had a temperature of at least 30 degrees Celsius.
5 List all the months that had 9 hours of sunshine a day and a temperature of at least 30 degrees Celsius.
6 List all the months that had a temperature of 28 or 31 degrees Celsius.
7 List all the months that had less than 50 mm of rainfall or more than 175 mm.

13. Printing

Print Area

The Print Area is the part of the spreadsheet that would be printed if you clicked Print. Normally Excel will simply print all the data on the sheet but, by setting the print area, you can control which part gets printed.

Setting the Print Area
To set the Print Area:

- Select the range that you want printed.
- Click File (or the Page Layout tab), Print Area, Set Print Area.

Clearing the Print Area
If you clear the Print Area, Excel will go back to printing the entire spreadsheet. To do this:

- Click File (or the Page Layout tab), Print Area, Clear Print Area.

Print Preview
You can use Print Preview to see how the selected print area will look when it is printed and how many pages it will be printed on.

To open the Print Preview window:

- In Excel 2003, click File, Print Preview.
- In Excel 2007, click the Microsoft Office button, select Print, and click Print Preview.

Depending on whether you have Excel 2003 or 2007, the Print Preview window will have either a toolbar (Figure 13.1) or something that resembles it (Figure 13.2) at the top.

The table lists what the various options do.

Option	Purpose
NEXT	displays the next print page
PREVIOUS	displays the previous print page
ZOOM	allows you to 'zoom in' to get a closer view of the document or to 'zoom out' to see more of the page at a reduced size – this feature does not affect the printing size
PRINT	brings up the Print dialogue box which allows you to set the required print options
SETUP	displays the Setup dialogue box which allows you to adjust the document to your specification, including page orientation, scaling, paper size, margins, page centring, headers and footers and sheet settings such as showing gridlines
MARGINS	displays or hides the margin indicators, which allows you to change the page margin, header and footer margins, and column widths
PAGE BREAK PREVIEW	allows you to adjust the page breaks and print area
CLOSE	exits Print Preview
HELP	displays information about the Print Preview window

Figure 13.1 *The Print Preview toolbar (Excel 2003)*

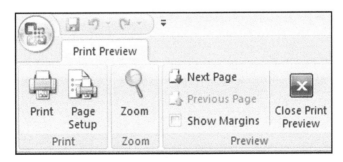

Figure 13.2 *The Print Preview tab (Excel 2007)*

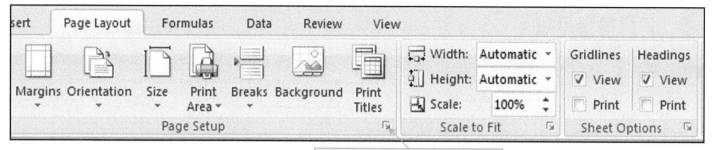

Figure 13.3 *The Page Layout tab (Excel 2007)*

Click to open the Page Setup window.

Page Setup window

The Page Setup window (Figure 13.4) has several page layout options that are very helpful when printing. To open the Page Setup window:

- In Excel 2003, click File, Page Setup.
- In Excel 2007, click Page Layout, then click the more options button in the Page Setup group.

Note

In Excel 2007, many of the options in the Page Setup window can be found in the Page Layout tab (Figure 13.3).

The following table explains what each tab in the window does.

Tab	Why you would use it
Page	to change the orientation; to fit a spreadsheet onto one page
Margins	to change the margins; to centre the spreadsheet on the page
Header/Footer	to add a header or a footer
Sheet	to show gridlines or repeat rows

Fitting the data on one page

If you want to force your spreadsheet to fit on one page:

- Open the Page Setup Window.
- Go to the Page tab (Figure 13.4).
- Select the Fit to option.
- Click OK.

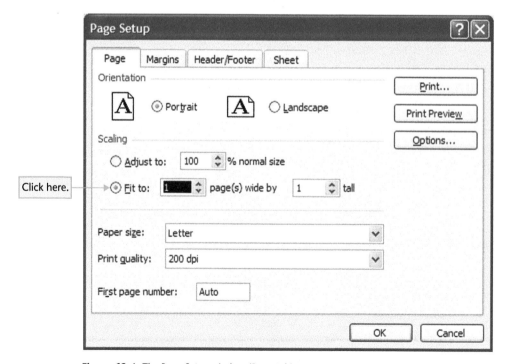

Figure 13.4 *The Page Setup window (Page tab)*

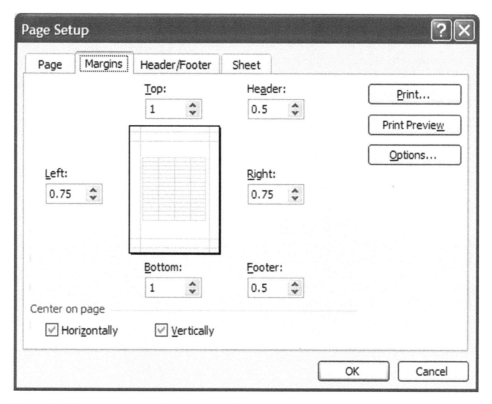

Figure 13.5 *The Page Setup window (Margins tab)*

Centring the spreadsheet on the page

If you want to centre the spreadsheet on the page:

- Open the Page Setup Window.
- Go to the Margins tab (Figure 13.5).
- Place ticks in the two Center on page boxes at the bottom of the window.
- Click OK.

Headers and footers

To set headers and footers in Excel you have to first go to the Header/Footer tab (Figure 13.6). To do so, either:

- Open the Page Setup window and click on the Header/Footer tab.

Or

- If you are using Excel 2003, click View, Header and Footer.

Once you are in the Header/Footer tab, you'll most likely want to create a custom header or footer, so click on the appropriate button. A window will appear so you can type in the header or footer (Figure 13.7).

Note

If you want to use one of the built-in headers or footers (e.g. Page 1 of 12), instead of clicking on the Custom button, choose an option from one of the combo boxes.

There are three boxes that you can type in. It's fairly self-explanatory. If you want something to appear in the centre, you type it in the Center section box.

Inserting built-in items

If you want to insert special built-in items such as the page number, you can type in its code manually or use one of the buttons in the middle of the window.

The table on page 332 explains what each button does.

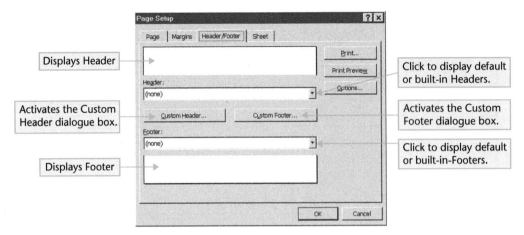

Figure 13.6 *The Page Setup window (Header/Footer tab)*

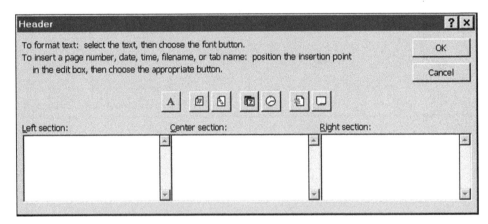

Figure 13.7 *The buttons in the Header dialogue box*

Icon number	Name of icon	Code	Function
A	Font		activates the font dialogue box to select your required font options
	Page number	&[Page]	inserts this code to display the actual page number when a page is printed
	Total pages	&[Pages]	this code represents the total number of pages in a worksheet. For example, if your worksheet contains five pages this code will allow the number 5 to appear on each page when they are printed
	Date	&[Date]	inserts this code to display the current date.
	Time	&[Time]	inserts this code to display the current time
	Filename	Filename	inserts this code to display the filename of the workbook
	Sheet name	&[Tab]	inserts this code to display the name of the sheet

Printing your spreadsheet

When you are ready to print your spreadsheet:

- Click File (or the Microsoft Office button).
- Click Print... The Print Options window (Figure 13.8) will appear.
- Make sure that the settings are to your liking.
- Click the OK button to print the spreadsheet.

Here's an explanation of what each option does.

Print range
Indicate the pages of the document you want to print.

- **All** prints the entire document.
- **Pages** prints only pages you specify. You must enter the page numbers you want.

Print what
The Print what option indicates the portion of the document you want to print.

- <u>Selection</u> prints only the cells and objects selected on the worksheet.
- <u>Active sheet(s)</u> prints each of the selected sheets.
- <u>Entire workbook</u> prints all sheets in the active workbook that contain any data. If a sheet has a print area, only the print area is printed.

Copies
The Copies option specifies the number of copies you want to print.

Collate
The Collate feature organises numbered pages when you print multiple copies of a document. A complete copy of the document is printed before the first page of the next copy is printed.

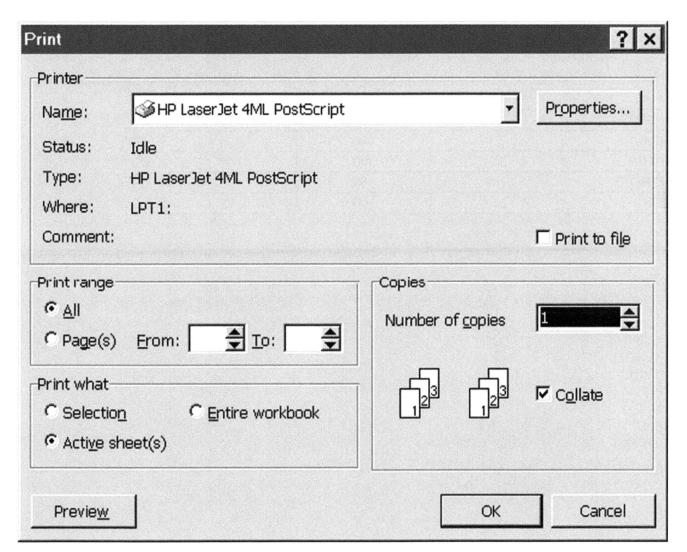

Figure 13.8 *The Print Options window*

Exercise 13a

The data below shows Mrs Wantalot's home budget for the <u>first</u> quarter of the year 2006.

ACCOUNTS	JANUARY	FEBRUARY	MARCH
INCOME			
SALARY	2175	2175	2175
OVERTIME	200	75	155
OTHER	650	514	987
EXPENSES			
FOOD	475	525	500
CLOTHING	300	400	250
ELECTRICITY	50	50	55
TRANSPORT	200	195	229
TELEPHONE	60	60	60
MORTGAGE	675	675	675
SCHOOL	89.60	91.20	67.50
TRAVELLING	500		
MISCELLANEOUS	100	95.50	85.10

1 Create a spreadsheet in Sheet1 to store the budget data, widening columns where necessary.
2 Place <u>all</u> headings in bold.
3 Copy <u>all</u> data from Sheet1 into Sheet2.
4 In Sheet2, change the months to represent the second quarter and change figures as follows:

OVERTIME	100	150	110
OTHER	250	300	420
CLOTHING	500	300	350
TELEPHONE	60	80	100
SCHOOL	120	100	75

5 Copy all data from Sheet2 into Sheet3.
6 In Sheet3, change the months to represent the third quarter and change figures as follows:

OVERTIME	700	500	400
OTHER	550		600
FOOD	275	800	600
CLOTHING	200	30	250
ELECTRICITY	50		55
TRANSPORT	200	30	250
TELEPHONE	60	675	60
MORTGAGE	675	50	675
SCHOOL	100	3000	300
TRAVELLING			
MISCELLANEOUS			

7 Copy all data from Sheet1 into Sheet4.

8 In Sheet4, change the months to represent the fourth quarter and change figures as follows:

OVERTIME	200	300	900
OTHER	400	500	800
FOOD	475	450	700
CLOTHING	200	300	350
ELECTRICITY	50	45	85
TRANSPORT	200	100	250
TELEPHONE	60	60	150
SCHOOL	90	95	100
MISCELLANEOUS	100	100	100

9 Perform these calculations in all sheets:

   a the total income gained for each month
   b the average income gained for each month
   c the total expenses for each month
   d the average expense for each month
   e the savings for each month

10 Format all the figures to show $ and 2 decimal places.
11 Calculate the quarterly totals for each account.
12 Rename sheets as follows:

   Sheet1 to 1st Quarter
   Sheet2 to 2nd Quarter
   Sheet3 to 3rd Quarter
   Sheet4 to 4th Quarter

13 Save the file to the name Budget.

Exercise 13b

1 Retrieve the Books file from your exercise folder.
2 For <u>each</u> year calculate:

   a the total number of loans
   b the average number of loans
   c the maximum and minimum number of loans

3 Format the average number of loans per year to display 0 decimal places.
4 Bold and underline all column headings.
5 Save to a file called Book1.
6 Calculate the total number of loans for <u>each</u> book.
7 Sort the spreadsheet data so that the total number of loans for each book appears in <u>descending</u> order.
8 Centre, bold and underline 'READ-A-BOOK PUBLIC LIBRARY' as a main heading and use a font size of16.
9 Save to a file called Books2.
10 Retrieve the Books1 file and insert the following data for two other books.

BOOK ID	2003	2004	2005	2006
LA1054	110	88	60	75
BL24	25	63	23	65

11 Insert a new column at column A to record the names of the books. Centre the new column heading.

BOOK NAME	BOOK ID
THE GREAT PONDS	QA276
BURIED ALIVE	QA972
CLIMBING THE LADDER	CL419.33
CRAFT FOR KIDS	AC52.1.91
PEOPLE'S WORLD	PP235
BRIGHTER VISIONS	BL908
THE FAIR AND DARK	FD111
AT CROSSROADS	LA1054
A LOOK BEYOND THE CROSS	BL24

12 Delete the statistics for 2003.
13 Save to a file called `Books3`.

Exercise 13c

STOCK NUMBER	BOAT NAME	BOAT LENGTH	COST PRICE	SALE PRICE
0012	FLETCHER	6 METRES	1100	1535
1008	DARY	4 METRES	1260	1604
1003	LAZYE	5 METRES	400	650
0152	SEALADY	6 METRES	7512	8950
1002	PRINCESS	11 METRES	9000	9980
0091	SOVEREIGN	6 METRES	2850	3772
1014	LUGGER	7 METRES	8000	9000

1 Calculate the PROFIT for each boat based on the figures given. The formula is: SALE PRICE – COST PRICE.
2 Calculate the maximum and minimum profit.
3 Format all profit and price figures to display a $ but no decimal places.
4 Arrange the stock numbers in ASCENDING order.
5 Save to a file called `Boat1`.

Modify the spreadsheet as follows:

6 Delete:

 a the columns for PROFIT and COST PRICE
 b the rows showing MINIMUM and MAXIMUM profits.

7 Add a column to the right of SALE PRICE to show the NUMBER OF BOATS SOLD as shown below.

BOAT NAME	NO. BOATS SOLD
FLETCHER	3
DARY	1
LAZYE	6
SEALADY	4
PRINCESS	2
SOVEREIGN	1
LUGGER	1

8 Calculate the revenue gained from the boats sold. The formula is: BOATS SOLD * SALE PRICE. Use the same format as before.
9 Calculate the total number of boats sold.

10 A boat was left out of the spreadsheet by mistake. Insert this boat data between LAZYE and DARY. The information is as follows: 1005 WHALE 9 METRES 995 1225

11 Save to a file called `Boat2`.

12 In an attempt to assess the difference in revenue if a discount was given, insert a row for DISCOUNT at the top of the spreadsheet. The discount is 2.5%.

13 Calculate the POST DISCOUNT REVENUE for each boat. The formula is:
REVENUE – (REVENUE * DISCOUNT)

14 Format the answers to display $ and 2 decimal places.

15 Save as `Boat3`.

Exercise 13d

1 Enter the following information into a spreadsheet beginning at column A, row 1.

GROCERY	WEEK 1	WEEK 2	WEEK 3	WEEK 4	UNIT PRICE
SARDINE	55	66	45	50	0.99
TUNA	40	25	30	35	1.99
KETCHUP	20	15	17	25	3.99
BISCUITS	99	79	89	100	0.64
HORLICKS	10	15	12	16	4.19
MACARONI	35	34	30	32	1.30
BUTTER	15	10	11	16	2.35
CORN FLAKES	21	25	19	20	4.55
HOT DOGS	13	12	14	15	3.65
SALT	12	11	10	10	0.45
SUGAR	35	24	46	49	2.66
RICE	22	23	21	25	5.99

2 Save the file as `Grocery1`.

3 Insert a column after WEEK4 called MONTHLY TOTAL and calculate the total for each item.

4 Insert a column between GROCERY and WEEK1 called UNIT. Enter the units as shown below:

GROCERY	UNIT
SARDINE	TIN
TUNA	TIN
KETCHUP	BOTTLE
BISCUITS	PACK
HORLICKS	BOTTLE
MACARONI	PACK
BUTTER	TUB
CORN FLAKES	BOX
HOT DOGS	PACK
SALT	BOX
SUGAR	PACK
RICE	PACK

5 Resave the file as `Grocery1`.

6 Bold and underline all column headings.

7 Centre the data from column B to F.

8 Change the appearance of the information in column A so it appears in bold and the information in column B so that it appears in italics.

9 In a new column, calculate the total price for each item.

10 Save the file as GROCERY2.

11 Delete the MONTHLY TOTAL and the TOTAL PRICE column.

12 Insert two rows, one between HORLICKS and MACARONI and one between SUGAR and RICE. Complete each new row with data of your own.

13 Delete the record of HOT DOGS.

14 Calculate total prices for each item for each week.

15 Save the file as GROCERY3.

Exercise 13e

1 Create a spreadsheet file with the following data. Begin at cell A5 and use appropriate formats for values. Wrap all two-word headings:

ITEM #	ITEM	BRAND	UNIT PRICE
00310	LOTION	SOFT FEEL	8.99
00105	DEODORANT	SMELL GOOD	7.99
01001	SOAP	BEST BATH	1.99
00311	LOTION	SOFT TOUCH	9.10
00010	TOILET PAPER	SOFT WIPES	0.79
01002	SOAP	LOVERS	1.90
01111	TOOTHPASTE	FRESH CLEAN	4.89
00312	LOTION	SMELL GOOD	9.01
00106	DEODORANT	REACH OUT	7.95
01003	SOAP	FRESHEN	2.15
00011	TOILET PAPER	WIPE OUT	0.69
00400	TOOTHBRUSH	BEST BRUSH	2.10
01004	SOAP	SMELL GOOD	2.05
01112	TOOTHPASTE	BRITE	4.95
00401	TOOTHBRUSH	BRUSH WELL	2.00
00107	DEODORANT	LOVERS	7.76
00402	TOOTHBRUSH	COMPLETE CLEAN	2.05

2 Centre, embolden and underline all column headings and use a font size of 12. This format should be used for all future column headings. Brand names should be in italics. All data in column A should be centred.

3 Use cells at the top of the spreadsheet appropriately to record VAT 15%.

4 Calculate the VAT on each item. The column should be labelled VAT TOTAL.

5 Add a column called NET PRICE and calculate appropriately for each item.

6 Rename the sheet as PRICING.

7 Save as the spreadsheet as Pharmacy.

8 Copy the item numbers, items, brands and net prices from the PRICING sheet to Sheet2. (Sheet2 should be renamed SALES.)

9 In the SALES sheet, add a column called TOTAL SALES and enter the figures in the order given here: 70, 95, 50, 60, 100, 75, 50, 80, 90, 65, 150, 25, 70, 45, 15, 100 and 30.

10 In the SALES sheet, calculate the revenue gained from each item. Use the column name SALES REVENUE.

11 Rename Sheet3 as STOCK.

12 Copy Item #, Item, Brand and Total Sales to the STOCK sheet.

13 In the STOCK sheet, insert a column to the left of TOTAL SALES called TOTAL PURCHASES.

14 Calculate the total purchase if purchases were 5% more than sales.

15 Add a column labelled IN STOCK and calculate, for each item, the total number of items remaining in stock after the sales.

16 In the stock sheet, insert records between:

    a the SMELL GOOD soap and the BRITE toothpaste
    b the SOFT WIPES toilet paper and the LOVERS soap

Also delete the record of:

    a the COMPLETE CLEAN toothbrush
    b the BEST BATH soap
    c the REACH OUT deodorant

17 Resave the file.

Exercise 13f

As administrator of the Garden Hardware Company, you are expected to use the spreadsheet to produce accurate monthly sales statistics for each sales area.

Area	December	Area	January	Area	February
Central	4995.00	Central	5095.00	Central	5196.00
East	6050.00	East	6161.00	East	6272.00
North	3002.00	North	3082.00	North	3163.00
NW	4003.00	NW	4093.00	NW	4184.00
SW	6995.00	SW	7115.00	SW	7236.00
South	7995.00	South	8152.00	South	8256.00
West	2999.00	West	3079.00	West	3160.00

Area	March	Area	April	Area	May
Central	5289.00	Central	5410.00	Central	5505.00
East	6385.00	East	6499.00	East	6614.00
North	3245.00	North	3327.00	North	3410.00
NW	4276.00	NW	4369.00	NW	4462.00
SW	7359.00	SW	7482.00	SW	7607.00
South	8389.00	South	8523.00	South	8658.00
West	3242.00	West	3324.00	West	3407.00

1 Set up a spreadsheet file that shows:

- The monthly sales for each area (the information above)
- The total sales for each month
- The total sales for each area
- The overall total of all areas

2 Bold, centre and italicise as a main heading the two-line title:
The Garden Hardware Company
Sales Figures for December to March 2005
The first line should be a size 14 and the second line 12, with both headings in bold.

3 Bold the months and the areas.
4 Save the file using the name `Sales_Figures_'05`.

5 Two errors occurred in the sales figures for May. Amend the results for South to 8700.00 and West to 3488.00.

6 A local sales tax of 10% has to be paid for all areas. Amend the spreadsheet so that it shows the amount of tax payable for the whole six months.

7 Copy all data used thus far to Sheet2.

8 The sales manager has provided the latest figures for June below. Add these to the current spreadsheet using Sheet2 and recalculate where necessary.

Area	June
Central	5615.00
East	6745.00
North	3478.00
NW	4551.00
SW	7759.00
South	8874.00
West	3517.00

9 To analyse figures for the second quarter only, copy the current spreadsheet to Sheet3 and delete all other columns and rows.

10 From Sheet2, delete the rows containing the main headings.

11 The local sales tax has been reduced to 5% for the quarter under analysis. Update the data to reflect this.

12 Rename Sheet1 as Sales1, Sheet2 as Sales2 and Sheet3 as Sales3.

13 Create a new sheet called SALES BAR which should contain a column graph showing a) the tax and b) the total sales for the six-month period. Use appropriate titles.

14 Resave the file.

Exercise 13g

You are employed at a video shop and your job at the end of the week is to prepare a spreadsheet to report the revenue from rented tapes and the gross wage of the cashier. The following data represents one week's business. From this data, construct a suitable spreadsheet in Sheet1 and perform the tasks that follow:

DATES	DRAMA	COMEDY	ACTION	HORROR
06.08.06	55	89	77	15
06.08.07	79	71	56	26
06.08.08	65	59	79	6
06.08.09	36	37	115	21
06.08.10	87	78	97	15
06.08.11	94	75	101	17
06.08.12	77	81	120	8

1 Comedy tapes are rented at $3.95 per tape, Dramas at $3.75 per tape, Horrors at $3.50 per tape and Actions at $4.00 per tape. Calculate:

    a the daily revenue gained from each type of tape

    b the weekly revenue gained from each type of tape

2 Format <u>all</u> revenue figures to $ and two (2) decimal places.

3 Centre the following heading over the spreadsheet. Place the first line of the heading in bold and at the size of 14. The second line should be underlined.

    BEST SELLER'S VIDEO SHOP
    REVENUE DETAILS FOR WEEK ENDING 12TH AUGUST

4 Place all column headings in italics.
5 Copy all the data from Sheet1 into Sheet2.

Perform questions 6–9 in Sheet2:

6 Delete the data from 06.08.08.
7 Calculate the overall revenue gained each day and the revenue gained from rentals for the entire week.
8 Sort the records so that the total daily revenue figures appear in descending order.
9 Calculate the Gross Wage of the Cashier who is paid $100.00 plus 5% of the total revenue gained from rented tapes.
10 Save the file as `Video1`.
11 Change the fees in Sheet1 as follows: Drama $3.70; Comedy $3.50; Horror $3.25; Action $3.75.
12 Create a bar chart to show the overall daily revenue. Use appropriate titles and show the chart on a separate sheet.
13 In Sheet3, create a listing of the video tapes that are currently available. The information is given below:

TAPE NAME	TAPE TYPE	AMOUNT
SCREAM	HORROR	10
JAWS	THRILLER	5
BOY MEETS WORLD	COMEDY	15
TITANIC	DRAMA	12
THIN BLUE LINE	COMEDY	10
SENSELESS	COMEDY	14
VENGEANCE UNLIMITED	ACTION	11
NEW YORK UNDERCOVER	ACTION	9
THE GAME	HORROR	10
X FILES	THRILLER	8
THE MAN IN THE IRON MASK	DRAMA	11
THE MASK	COMEDY	16
BEYOND ENEMY LINES	ACTION	13
BLADE	ACTION	11
THE THING	HORROR	18
MATRIX	ACTION	11

14 Sort the name of the tape based on the type of tape.
15 Calculate the Total amounts for each type of tape. The fee for thrillers is $3.25.
16 Save the final file as `Video2`.

Exercise 13h

1 Create a spreadsheet to store the data below and save in a file called Chick1.

CUSTOMER	DESCRIPTION	QTY (LBS)	UNIT PRICE
BARBADOS BEACH VILLAGE	WHOLE CHICKEN	50	12.00
COLONY CLUB HOTEL	CHICKEN FEET	42	9.00
TAMARIND COVE HOTEL	WHOLE CHICKEN	35	12.00
A & J DELI	CHICKEN NECKS	45	4.50
GLITTER BAY HOTEL	WHOLE CHICKEN	65	12.00
ROYAL PAVILION	TURKEY BREASTS	100	10.50
THE COACH HOUSE	WHOLE CHICKEN	75	10.50
KINGSBEACH HOTEL	CHICKEN BREASTS	50	10.20
ALMOND BEACH HOTEL	CHICKEN FEET	60	9.00
SANDRIDGE HOTEL	CHICKEN WINGS	45	9.50
EAT & DINE	CHICKEN NECKS	55	4.50
THE CHICKEN HUT	TURKEY BREASTS	85	10.50
EUNETA'S DINER	CHICKEN WINGS	40	9.50
TRACEE'S SNACKETTE	WHOLE CHICKEN	30	12.00
WINGS 'N TINGS	CHICKEN WINGS	150	9.50

2 Sort the customers based on the description in descending order and save as Chick2.
3 Royal Pavilion has cancelled its order. Remove that record.
4 Insert a column at the beginning of the spreadsheet to record a customer ID No for each customer. These numbers should go in the order 0020, 0021, 0022, etc.
5 In a column headed INITIAL PRICE, calculate the total price for each order.
6 Show the minimum, average and maximum figures from these initial prices.
7 Each customer gets a 3% discount. Calculate a) the discount and b) the new prices after the discount has been subtracted. The new prices should appear in a column headed DISCOUNTED PRICE.
8 Format all monetary figures to show the dollar sign and no decimal places.
9 Save the spreadsheet as Chick3.
10 Insert the following record between WINGS 'N TINGS and THE CHICKEN HUT:

00180 MARCIE'S BAR CHICKEN WINGS 90 9.50

11 Centre the following headings at the top of the spreadsheet.

THE MEAT DEPOT
ORDERS FOR OCTOBER 2006

12 Calculate the overall discount for the month of October. The answer should have $ but no decimal places.
13 Make the following amendments:

a Change EUNETA'S DINER to NETA'S DINER.
b Change TAMARIND COVE's order from 35 to 55 and TRACEE'S SNACKETTE from 30 to 70.
c Change COLONY CLUB's order to CHICKEN BREASTS.
d Change the discount to 2%.

14 Create a pie chart, which shows the discount for each customer, using the ID No. Place the chart on a new sheet called PIE1.

15 Save the file as Chick4.

16 Delete PIE1.

17 Create a Bar chart to show the first total price and the new price for each customer:

    a the title of the graph is 'Analysis of Pre & Post Discount Figures'
    b the X-axis title is 'ID No'
    c the Y-axis title is 'Prices'
    d place the chart on a new sheet called GRAPH1.

18 Save the file as Chick5.

Exercise 13i

The information represents data relating to workers at a fast-food restaurant.

NAME	ID NO.	PARISH	GROSS PAY	DEDUCTIONS
BROMES, P	125690	ST MICHAEL	1500	300
WIGGINS, W	478923	CHRIST CHURCH	1100	220
ATKINS, R	897843	ST LUCY	1245	250
WEEKES, I	578847	ST THOMAS	900	180
THOMAS, E	648392	ST LUCY	700	140
BECKLES, Y	574875	CHRIST CHURCH	1300	260
WHITE, B	859357	ST JOHN	1200	240
OLIVER, C	574856	CHRIST CHURCH	1400	280

1 Create a spreadsheet file containing the above information, formatting the GROSS PAY and DEDUCTIONS column to $ and 2 decimal places and placing column headings in bold and italics.

2 Save the file with the filename Food1.

3 Two employees have been left out. Add them at the bottom. They are:

PETERS, Q	784923	ST PHILIP	1500	300
ASHFORD, G	482256	ST THOMAS	1800	360

4 In row 1, add a report title centred over all the columns of information. Underline it and use a font size of 14. The report title should be BETTER FOODS RESTAURANT.

5 Save the file as Food2.

6 Replace the records of the worker whose ID No is 578847 with the following record:

STONE, W	573745	ST PETER	1600	320

7 Delete the record of THOMAS from ST LUCY.

8 Insert a column to the right of the DEDUCTIONS column called NET PAY. In this column, calculate (a) the net pay for each person and (b) the total, average, minimum and maximum GROSS PAY and NET PAY.

9 Save as Food3.

10 Add one record of your choice between the following ID Nos and re-calculate where necessary:

    478923 and 897843   574875 and 859357   784923 and 482256

11 Use proper alignment for all column headings.

12 As it is the Christmas season, management has decided to give employees a token of appreciation for all of their hard work during the year. Add a column called GIFT and assign gifts accordingly. If gross pay is more than $1100.00 the employee will receive a bottle of 'Bailey's Irish Cream'; otherwise the employee will receive a bottle of 'Malibu Coconut Rum'.

13 Create a pie chart to show the NET PAY for each employee.

14 Save as Food4.

Exercise 13j

1 Create the spreadsheet below for L & L ENTERPRISES to record the sales and income of five sale representatives.

NAME	WEEK 1	WEEK 2	WEEK 3	WEEK 4
SHARP	3860	3958	4260	3825
CHILDS	3020	2984	3945	3699
BRODY	4568	3922	3657	4351
HEALY	1923	2956	3754	2744
WEISS	2578	1898	3165	2398

2 Right align all numeric column headings.
3 Centre <u>all</u> the data in column A.
4 Add other columns and/or rows to calculate:

   a the total sales for each sales representative
   b the total sales for each week
   c the average sales for each week
   d the average sales for each sales representative

5 Format <u>all</u> figures to display commas and zero decimal places.
6 Sort the spreadsheet in <u>alphabetical</u> order by name.
7 Save to a file called `Sales1`.
8 Add an additional column to the spreadsheet to record the Base Pay of each sales rep. The Base Pay is as follows:

NAME	BASE PAY
SHARP	500
CHILDS	450
BRODY	575
HEALY	450
WEISS	475

9 Format the Base Pay figures to display $ and zero decimal places.
10 A sales rep earns a 12% commission on his total sales if this total exceeds 15 000. Otherwise, his commission is 9%.
11 Add two columns and calculate the commission and total income for each sales rep where:
COMMISSION = TOTAL SALES * % COMMISSION and TOTAL INCOME = COMMISSION + BASE PAY.
12 Format the total income and commission to display $, comma and two decimal places.
13 Calculate in a new row the highest amount of income paid to a sales rep for the period under analysis. Format to the nearest dollar.
14 Make a bar graph to show the Total Income for each sales rep. The graph should also reflect how much of this total is Base Pay and how much is Commission. Use appropriate legends.

   Title – INCOME ANALYSIS
   X Title – SALES REPS
   Y Title – AMOUNT ($)

15 Centre, underline, bold and italicise the name of the company at the top of the spreadsheet.
16 Arrange the data so that the Total Income is in <u>descending</u> order.
17 Save as `Sales2`.

Exercise 13k

1 Set up the following spreadsheet just as it appears below, changing the width of column A:

MILITARY BOOKS SECTION INVENTORY

TITLE	NO	PRIC	VALUE
VICTORY IN EUROPE	6	10.95	
OVERLOAD	4	12.95	
AIRWARFARE	2	8.95	
MILITARY MOTOR CYCLES	1	12.95	
BRITISH SERVICE HELICOPTERS	3	14.95	
PILLBOXES	5	11.95	
SPITFIRE AT WAR	1	10.95	
VIETNAM	2	12.95	
SEA KING	4	4.95	
SUPER ETENDARD	3	4.75	
F-4 PHANTON II	6	4.75	

2 Find:

    a The total number of books.

    b The total value of each type of book.

    c The total value of all the books in stock.

3 Align and format the data appropriately.

4 Bold and italicise the main heading and all column headings.

5 Save the spreadsheet as `War1`.

6 Insert a column headed BOOK ID in column A to enter the book ID numbers and another headed COPY to the right of the heading TITLE to enter the information for the type of copy.

BOOK ID	TITLE	COPY
001	VICTORY IN EUROPE	HARDBACK
002	OVERLORD	SOFTBACK
003	AIRWARFARE	HARDBACK
004	MILITARY MOTOR CYCLES	HARDBACK
005	BRITISH SERVICE HELICOPTERS	SOFTBACK
006	PILLBOXES	SOFTBACK
007	SPITFIRE AT WAR	HARDBACK
008	VIETNAM	HARDBACK
009	SEA KING	SOFTBACK
010	SUPER ETENDARD	HARDBACK
011	F-4 PHANTON II	HARDBACK

7 Arrange the total value of each book within the type of copy in ascending order.

8 There has been a 5% reduction on all hardback books and a 3% reduction on all softback books. Insert a column headed DISCOUNT PRICE to the right of the NO column and work out the formula for both the hardback and softback books. The discount should be based on the individual prices.

9 Calculate the POST-DISCOUNT VALUE for each type of book.

10 Reveal the formula which was used to calculate the DISCOUNT.

11 Save to a file called `War2`.

Exercise 13l

1   You are employed as a Sales Clerk at the JOY TO THE WORLD Mobile Shopping Centre. Make a spreadsheet, which will keep track of Xmas Orders. Enter the data below, using a format of $ and two decimal places for the COST.

CLIENT #	ORDER 1	ORDER 2	ORDER 3	COST
A-039	393	567	452	59.00
M-539	239	189	102	41.00
A-725	257	200		35.00
R-341	775	348	183	53.65
M-910	158	358	455	89.90
P-394	981	208		47.25
M-032	319	186	128	38.75
M-333	456	235	385	62.00

2   Calculate the NET ORDER (i.e. the total number of orders for each client).
3   Calculate the SUBTOTAL for each client
    (Net Order * Cost).
4   Sales tax is 6%. Handling cost is $8.00.
5   Calculate the TAX AND HANDLING charge for each client. The formula is:
    (Subtotal * Sales Tax) + Handling Cost.
6   Calculate the TOTAL CHARGE for each client.
    Total Charge = SubTotal + Tax and Handling.
7   Format ALL results from the above calculations as $ and zero decimal places.
8   Show the lowest, highest, and average figures for each order.
9   Centre and underline the name of the company at the top of the spreadsheet.
10 Save as Orders1.
11 Change the Sales Tax to 7%, the handling charge to $9.95 and the cost for client # M-910 to $45.78.
12 Delete the record of client # P-394.
13 Sort the records so that the client numbers appear in <u>descending</u> order.
14 Save as Orders2.
15 To the right of $9.95, enter an alternative handling charge as $11.95.
16 To analyse the sales of order 1 only, delete the columns for ORDER 2, ORDER 3 and NET ORDER. Recalculate the SUB-TOTAL for each client: (Order1 * Cost).
17 If a customer buys 319 items or less, the handling charge will be $9.95. If the order is 320 or more then the handling charge will be $11.95. Recalculate the TAX AND HANDLING charge for each customer where:
    TAX AND HANDLING=(SubTotal * Sales Tax) + Handling Cost
    Enter the new formula in the TAX AND HANDLING column. No new column is required for this question.
18 Make a bar graph in a new sheet called COMPARISON which shows the Total Charge for each client. The graph should also reflect how much of this is <u>Tax and Handling</u> and how much is Subtotal. Use appropriate chart and axes titles.
19 Save as Orders3.

Exercise 13m

1   Enter the following information in your spreadsheet and save the file as `Study1`.

NAME	ROOM	COURSE	BOOK	EXAM
Ince Tracey	C	1550.00	65.00	100.00
Jordan Katie	E	1550.00	42.00	76.00
Morris Shelly	A	1400.00	25.00	100.00
Corbin Ryan	C	1000.00	25.00	76.00
Farley Lisa	A	1250.00	42.00	100.00
Walters Rose	A	1550.00	65.00	100.00
Bowen Julia	E	1650.00	85.00	120.00
Allman Trevor	B	1000.00	25.00	76.00
Babb Sheron	B	1550.00	50.00	100.00
Burke Alison	C	1250.00	40.00	100.00
Charles Jeffrey	E	1550.00	65.00	76.00
Bennett Tonya	A	1400.00	20.00	80.00
Downes Jason	E	1550.00	65.00	100.00
Greene Dale	B	1000.00	25.00	76.00
Austin Maria	B	1000.00	42.00	80.00
Fagan Tara	A	1250.00	40.00	120.00
Walcott Lisa	C	1400.00	42.00	100.00
Goring Janelle	E	1000.00	25.00	80.00
Greenidge Eva	A	1250.00	50.00	100.00
King Kaye	B	1400.00	50.00	100.00
Boxill Lucy	E	1550.00	65.00	80.00
Hippolite Sandra	C	250.00	40.00	80.00
Marshall Pamela	A	1500.00	35.00	120.00
Louis Sharon	E	1000.00	25.00	80.00
Howell Delvin	C	1550.00	65.00	100.00
Skeete Sonia	B	1000.00	42.00	80.00
Rollins Wayne	B	1250.00	40.00	100.00
Smith Carol	A	1400.00	50.00	100.00
Joseph Elizabeth	C	1300.00	35.00	75.00
Leacock Kathy	E	1550.00	65.00	120.00

2   Sort the data, using <u>Room</u> as the primary key and Name as the secondary key.
3   Calculate:

   a   The total fee paid by each student.
   b   The total fee for each type of fee per room.
   c   The average fee for each type of fee per room.
   d   The maximum fee for each type of fee per room

4   Add one record in each room, maintaining the sort order.
5   Format all monetary figures to display the dollar sign (no decimal places). This format should be consistent throughout all subsequent spreadsheets.

6   Save the adjusted spreadsheet as Study2.
7   Assuming that the current fees in the spreadsheet were recorded for the year 2000, make a projection for 2001 increasing the course fee by 5%, the book fee by 3% and the exam fee by 1.5%.
8   Calculate the projected totals for each type of fee per room.
9   Create a summary table in a different section of the spreadsheet to display the overall current fees and projected fees for each room. Save as Study3. Note that this summary table should be set up in such a way that if the information changes in the other portion of the spreadsheet, it should automatically update the data in the summary table.
10 Create a graph to compare the current overall fee with the projected overall fee per room. Use appropriate titles and legends. Save the graph as Money.
11 Delete the records of Rose Walters of Room A and Kathy Leacock of Room E and change the percentage increase for course fees to 10%.
12 Retrieve Study1 and perform question 3(a).
13 In the same sheet, copy all the records where the total fee is $1700 or more to a separate section of the spreadsheet. Save as Study4.

Exercise 13n

The data below represents the current subscription fees for computer-oriented magazines.

1   Create an appropriate spreadsheet to store the information shown below, which is to be used for further calculations.

HITECH TECHNOLOGIES CO LTD

NAME OF MAGAZINES ON SUBSCRIPTION	MONTHLY FEES
COMPUTER NEWS	15.00
COMPUTER CATALYST	20.00
HITECH COMPUTERS	25.00
NEW TECHLOOK	12.50
COMPUTER IN TRANSITION	25.00
UPTECH 2000	23.50
COMPUTERING INSIGHTS	15.00
A FORWARD VIEW	13.00

2   Format the Monthly Fees figures to display the dollar sign ($) and two (2) decimal places.
3   Centre, underline, bold and italicise the name of the company at the top of the spreadsheet.
4   Sort the names of the magazines in ascending order.
5   Save as Maga.
6   See the listing of the number of subscribers on a yearly basis at the end of this exercise (on page 349). Three rows below your current spreadsheet, enter the data, centring, bolding and underlining the years.
7   Format the figures of the number of subscribers to display commas but no decimal places.
8   Calculate the total and average number of subscribers for each year.
9   Calculate the total collected each year for each magazine.
10 Delete the record for the magazine called Computers In Transition.
11 Calculate the total fees collected over the period 2002–2006 for each magazine listed and make a pie chart to show these figures. Use a first and second title as listed below:

HITECH TECHNOLOGIES CO LTD
Sub for the period 2002–2006

12 Save the spreadsheet as SUBS.

13 Change the fees for the magazine called UPTECH 2000 from 23.50 to 25.50.

14 Next month is the Annual Award Ceremony. One of the categories for that night will be dealing with the Number Of Subscribers For The Year (2006). You are asked to create a new column titled AWARDS and assign the awards as follows:

15 If the newspaper subscription reached more than 3000 then that Newspaper Company will get a TROPHY, else the Newspaper Company will get a CERTIFICATE.

16 Change the name of the magazine COMPUTERING INSIGHTS to COMPUTER INSIGHTS.

17 Place the headings NAMES OF MAGAZINES ON SUBSCRIPTIONS and MONTHLY SUBS in bold print.

18 List all the records where the monthly subs are greater than 20.00 to another part of the spreadsheet.

19 Save the file as `Zine`.

NO. OF SUBSCRIBERS PER YEAR
NAME OF MAGAZINES ON

SUBSCRIPTION	2002	2003	2004	2005	2006
COMPUTER NEWS	2000	2155	2010	2200	2206
COMPUTER CATALYST	1500	1608	1755	1800	1800
HITECH COMPUTERS	1875	1884	1889	1895	1899
NEW TECHLOOK	2105	1783	1855	1909	1910
COMPUTER IN TRANSITION	3000	2988	3003	2999	3010
UPTECH 2000	3507	3555	3545	3610	3615
COMPUTERING INSIGHTS	2103	2222	2225	2451	2553
A FORWARD VIEW	1950	1999	2002	2121	2130

Microsoft Access

1. Introduction to Microsoft Access

Introduction to Database Management Systems

A Database Management System (DBMS), such as Microsoft Access, is a piece of software specifically designed for working with databases. A **database** is a collection of related data, organised into tables. The DBMS allows you to:

- create and manage tables
- perform queries on data and create additional ones as the need arises
- enforce the integrity of the data
- view reports on the data and create new ones as the need arises

Advantages of DBMSs

DBMSs are specifically designed to work with databases. That is all they do so they are very good at it. Let's compare them to the alternative – storing data in standalone files.

- DBMSs are usually faster. DBMSs index data so that they can quickly search it. Furthermore they can optimise the indexes to speed up the queries you perform most frequently.

- Unlike programs working with standalone files, DBMSs provide a standardised interface for working with tables, queries and reports.
- DBMSs allow users to create tables, queries and reports as the need arises. So for instance, a user can create an ad hoc query. In contrast, when a program works with standalone files, it usually has to be redesigned if the user wants additional reports or queries.

Creating a new database

Unlike other Microsoft Office programs, you can't just open Microsoft Access and start typing. It doesn't automatically create a blank database for you to work with. Instead, you have to create one yourself.

Access 2003

To create a new database in Access 2003:

- Click File, New...
- Click the Blank Database... option from the top of the Task Pane.
- In the dialogue box that appears, go to the location where the new database is to be stored and type the name you want to call it.
- Click the Create button.

Access 2007

In Access 2007 the process is a bit different:

- Click the Microsoft Office button.
- Click New.
- In the Blank Database section at the right of the window, click the folder icon.

Figure 1.1 *Creating a blank database in Access 2007*

- In the dialogue box that appears, type the name of the file and choose the location where it will be stored.
- Change the file type to the 2002–2003 (*.mdb) format.
- Click the OK button.
- Click the Create button.

Note

Access 2007 has made the new (*.accdb) file type its default database format. Unfortunately, previous versions of Access cannot read this format. For that reason, whenever you are creating a new database, change the file type to (*.mdb).

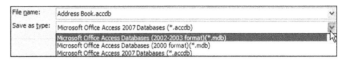

Figure 1.2 *Changing the file type*

Tip

When you first create a database, close the blank table that Access 2007 automatically creates.

The Access 2003 interface

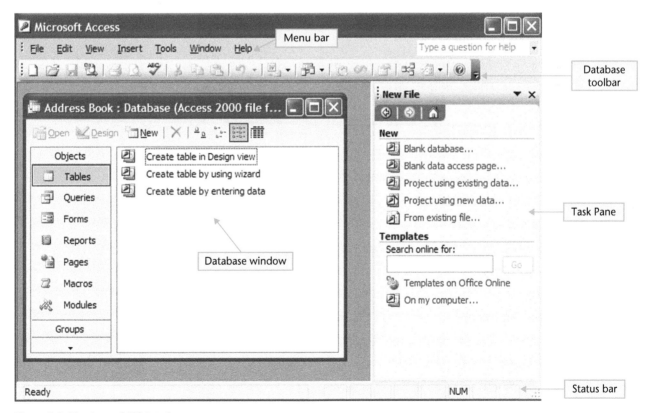

Figure 1.3 *The Access 2003 interface*

The Database window

The heart of Access 2003 is the Database window, where you work with the various types of database objects.

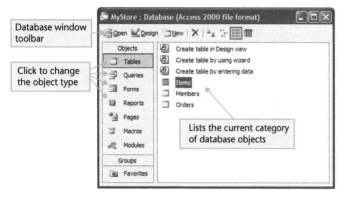

Figure 1.4 *The Database window (Access 2003)*

The Database window only displays one type of object at a time. You use the buttons on the left side of the window to switch to another type of object. The right part of the window shows you a list of the current type of item.

At the top of the window is a toolbar you can use to open, create and edit objects. The following table explains what each toolbar button does.

Button	What it does
Open	open the selected object
Design	allows you to change the design settings of the selected object
New	creates a new object of the current type
X	deletes the currently selected object
	changes the view of the objects to large icons, small icons, list or detail view

The Access 2007 interface

The Access 2007 interface is more complicated than that of Access 2003's.

The Ribbon

The Access 2007 Ribbon is divided into a number of tabs:

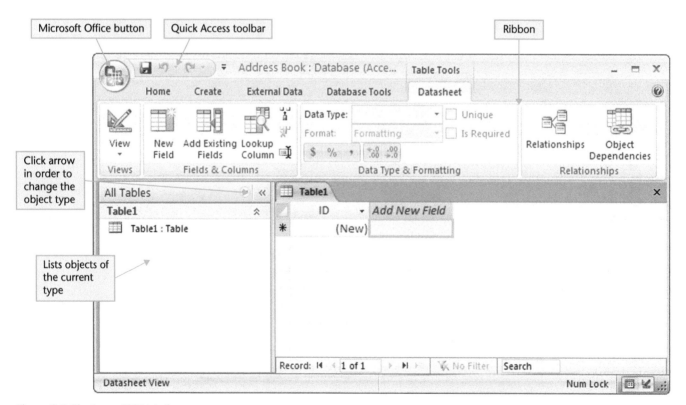

Figure 1.5 *The Access 2007 interface*

Tab	Reasons you'd use it
Home	to sort data; to cut, copy, paste; to delete records
Create	to create tables, queries, forms and reports
External Data	to import data from (or export data to) another office program
Database Tools	to set relationships

You can switch to a tab manually by clicking on it. In some cases Access is smart enough to guess which tab you currently need and automatically switch to it. Each tab of the Ribbon is divided into a number of groups to make it easier for you to find the various options.

The Microsoft Office button

To the top left of the Ribbon is the Microsoft Office button. Clicking this button will display a menu that has the items you'd find in a typical File menu, for example New, Open, Save, Print, Close and Exit.

The Quick Access toolbar

This toolbar contains buttons that allow you to quickly:

- Save changes to the current database object.
- Undo the last thing you did.
- Redo the last thing you undid.

Changing object types

To the left of the Microsoft Access window, there is a list of the objects in the database, organised by type. In Figure 1.5, only the tables are being displayed. To list another type of object:

- Click on the arrow next to the current type of object.
- Switch to another type Figure 1.6.

Tip

I recommend selecting the All Access Objects option (Figure 1.7) since it allows you to see all the different types simultaneously.

Opening an existing database

In order to open an existing database:

- Click File (or the Microsoft Office button).
- Click Open.
- Go to the folder that contains the file, then double-click on the file.

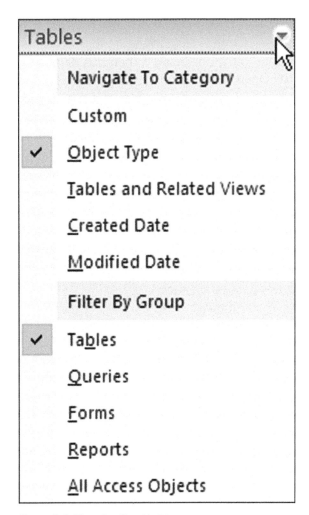

Figure 1.6 *Changing the object type*

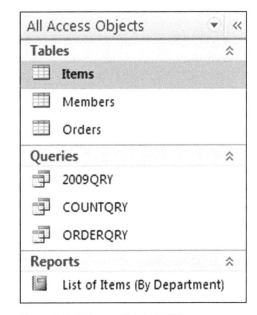

Figure 1.7 *All Access Objects (2007)*

Sometimes when you open a file, Microsoft Access will display a security warning. The appearance of the warning depends on the Access version.

Access 2003

In Access 2003, the security warning will pop up in a window similar to the one below. When this happens, just click the Open button.

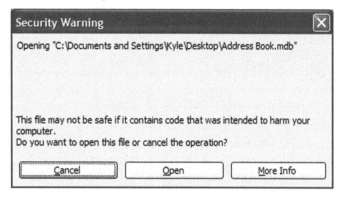

Figure 1.8 *Security warning in Access 2003*

Access 2007

Here's what the security warning looks like in Access 2007. If you get this message, then all action queries (update and delete) in the database will be disabled.

Figure 1.9 *The Access 2007 security warning*

If you get a security warning and want to enable the action queries in the database:

- Click the Options button...
- Click the Enable this content option in the window that pops up.
- Click the OK button.

Once you have enabled the content, the bar with the security warning will disappear.

Figure 1.10 *Enabling content that was disabled by the security warning*

Saving the database

Unlike other Microsoft Office products, Access automatically saves any changes you make to your data. But if you want to save a database object at any time:

- Click File (or the Microsoft Office button).
- Click Save.

Saving an Access 2007 database in another format

Since people using previous versions of Access aren't able to open databases stored in the new (*.accb) format, Access 2007 allows you to save the database using the previous format. To do so:

- Click the Microsoft Office button.
- Point to Save As and, under the section that says 'Save the database in another format', choose the format you want.
- Choose the name of the file and its location.
- Click Save.

Exercise 1a

1 What is a database?
2 What are the advantages of using a DBMS over standalone files?

Exercise 1b

1 Start up Microsoft Access.
2 Make a database called `Videos`.
3 Close Microsoft Access.

2. Table design basics

At the heart of any database are the tables which contain the data. A table is made up columns (also called <u>fields</u>) and rows (also called <u>records</u> or <u>tuples</u>).

The example shown in Figure 2.1 has eight fields: ID, FirstName, LastName, Age, Address, Region, JoinDate and Married.

ID ▾	FirstName ▾	LastName ▾	Age ▾	Address ▾	Region ▾	JoinDate ▾	Married ▾
⊞ HC	Horatio	Caine	48	Somewherein	Miami	2009/01/02	☐
⊞ JA	John	Alleyne	28	Black Rock	St. Michael	2008/12/31	☑
⊞ JB	John	Brown	30	The Pine	St. Michael	2009/01/15	☐
⊞ LC	Lisa	Cuddy	38	Princeton	New Jersey	2008/12/19	☑
⊞ MS	Michael	Scofield	36	Fox River	Illinois	2009/01/01	☐
⊞ TA	Tonya	Alleyne	20	Rock Hall	St. Thomas	2009/02/28	☑
✱							☐

Record: ◄ ◀ 1 of 6 ▶ ▶I ▶⁕ ☒ No Filter Search ◀ ▭▭▭ III ▭▭▭ ▶

Figure 2.1 *A table*

Creating a table

Access provides a variety of ways to create tables, but in this course we'll always create tables using the Design view.

Access 2003
To create a table in Access 2003:

- Switch to the Tables section of the Database window.
- Double-click the <u>Create table in Design view</u> option.

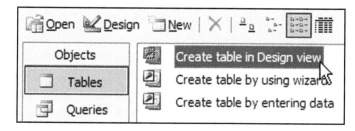

Figure 2.2 *Creating a table in Access 2003.*

Access 2007
In Access 2007, you create a table by going through the Ribbon:

- Click the Create tab of the Ribbon, and then click the Table Design button.

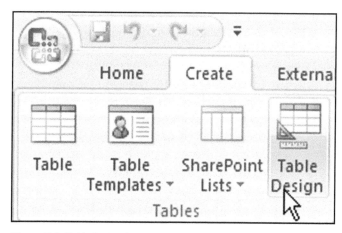

Figure 2.3 *Table Design button (Access 2007)*

The Table Design window

Regardless of what Access version you are using to create the table, the Table Design window will be displayed. It looks complicated, but it helps to think of it as being divided into three main sections:

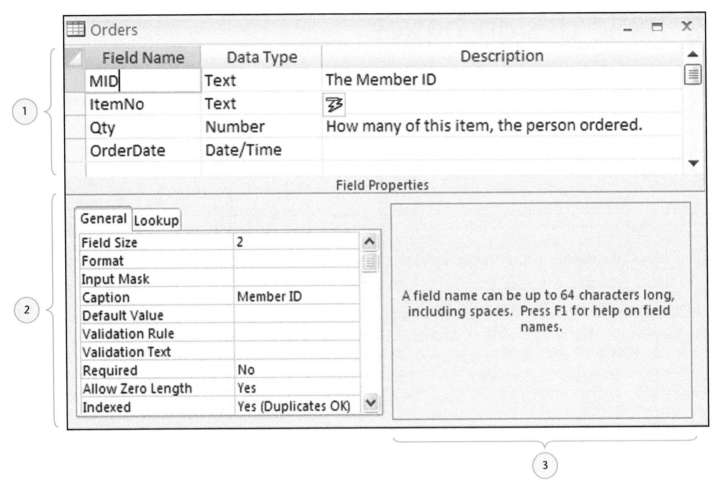

Figure 2.4 *The Table Design window.*

1 a list of the fields, their data types and their descriptions – in Figure 2.4, there are four fields: MID, ItemNo, Qty and OrderDate.

2 the field properties for the <u>currently selected field</u> – in our example, since the MID field is currently selected, the field properties that you see are for that field. If you want to see the settings for another field, you have to click on it.

3 an explanation of what the <u>currently selected field property</u> does – information about the Field Name property is currently being displayed since that is what is currently selected.

Creating fields

Although there are several properties that you <u>could</u> set, the way you typically create a field is:

• Type the field name.
• Choose an <u>appropriate</u> data type.
• Set the field size (if necessary).
• Set the format (if necessary).
• Set the maximum number of decimal places, if necessary.

• If the field is the primary key, right-click on its row and click Primary Key.

Field name

The first thing you have to do is to type in the field name in the next available row. Although field names may be up to 64 characters, most are pretty short. Having spaces in your field names is generally considered to be bad practice, so instead of First Name, say FirstName.

Data type

When you first create a field, it is automatically set to type Text. If your field isn't going to be storing text, you should change this to the <u>appropriate</u> type of data for your field. This is very important for two reasons:

1 This makes sure that the user isn't allowed to enter the wrong type of data. For instance, if you left an age field as type Text, nothing is stopping the user from entering something like 'ABC' or 'hello' for the age.

2 The data type affects what you are able to do with the data. For instance, if the type is <u>Number</u> or <u>Currency</u> you can perform calculations with it.

Choosing the right data type

The following 'cheat sheet' helps you choose the right data type for your field.

The data in your field	Use this type	Example
can only be yes/no or true/false	Yes/No	Married, InStock
are monetary figures	Currency	Price, Cost
are numbers that may be used in calculations or comparisons	Number	Age, Quantity
may contain letters, symbols or punctuation	Text	Address, TelNo
are IDs that may have zeros in front, for example 001 or 002	Text	CustomerID

Field size

If the data type is Text, this is the maximum number of characters that can hold in the field.

If the data type is Number, choose:

- <u>Long Integer</u> if the numbers won't contain decimal points.
- <u>Double</u>, if they <u>will</u> contain decimal points.

Format

This controls the way the information is displayed in the Datasheet view.

If the data type is Date/Time:

- Choose a format from the list.
- Or type yyyy/mm/dd (all lowercase) if you want a four-digit year followed by a two-digit month, followed by a two-digit day.

If the data type is Number:

- Choose fixed if you want a fixed number of decimal places.
- Choose percentage if the number is a percentage.

Other formatting options will be explained in the next chapter.

Decimal places

If the data type is Number or Currency, choose the maximum number of decimal places to be displayed, or leave it as Auto if you want the computer to decide for you.

Saving the table design

To save table design:

- Click the Save icon (the tiny blue disk at the top of the window).
- Type the name you want to give to the table and click OK.

If you haven't created a primary key, Access will ask you to create one. Unless you want Access to create an additional field to be used as the primary key, click No. You will learn more about primary keys shortly.

Closing the Table Design window

To close a table, click on its close button (X) in the top right corner of the Table Design window. If there are any unsaved changes, Access will ask you whether you want to save them.

Renaming a table

To rename a table:

- Go to the list of tables in your database.
- Right-click on the table you want to rename.
- Click Rename.
- Type the new name of the table.
- Press Enter.

Opening the table

In order to open a table that you have created so you can view its contents or enter information, double-click on its name from the list of items in the database.

Exercise 2a

1 Create a database called `Address book`.
2 In that database create a table which stores the following information about each contact:

- first name and last name
- address and parish
- age
- birth-date
- gender
- his or her age
- home and work telephone numbers
- whether or not he or she is married

3 Make sure you use the correct field names and sizes.
4 Save the table as Contacts.

Exercise 2b

1 Create a table called EMPLOYEES which contains the following fields:

- EmployeeID
- FirstName
- LastName
- Salary

2 Make EmployeeID the Primary Key.

3. Additional field properties

In the previous chapter you learned a little about field properties. We will go into more detail in this chapter.

Description

Each field can have a description other than the field name or the caption. The description can be used to provide information about the field. It can be a maximum of 255 characters and is displayed on the Status bar of a form when the field is selected.

Field properties

Each field has a number of properties, which are displayed when the field data type is selected. The properties include the following:

Field size

This is the maximum number of characters that can be entered in a field. For a text field, the default number is 50; however, this number cannot exceed 255. You may set it to the size that best suits the data to be entered in this field. For example, if the longest last name to be entered is 25 characters, you should set the size to 25.

Format

The Format property can be used to create custom formats that change the way numbers, dates, times, and text display and print. Format properties do not change the way the data is stored, only how it is displayed. To change the format of a field, different symbols are entered in the Format text box. Text and Memo data types can use any of four symbols, as shown in the table below.

Symbol	Description	Example
@	a required text character or space	@@@-@@-@@@@ would display 246123457 as 246-12-3457. Nine characters or spaces are required
>	forces all characters to uppercase	> would display SMITH whether you entered SMITH, smith, or Smith
<	forces all characters to lowercase	< would display smith whether you entered SMITH, smith, or Smith
&	an optional text character	@@-@@& would display 12345 as 12-345 and 12.34 as 12-34. Four out of five characters are required and a fifth is optional

Examples of Format settings for different data types are shown in the table below:

Data type	Field size	Decimals	Format
Number	Double	0, 1, 2, etc.	Fixed, Currency
Date			yyyy/mm/dd
Currency		0, 1, 2, etc.	

Input mask

An **Input mask** is a pattern that controls the data that can be entered in a field. It consists of literal characters, which are displayed in the field, and mask characters, which are not. Literal characters are characters such as the parentheses surrounding the area code of a telephone number, or a hyphen used to separate the parts of a telephone number. Mask characters are symbols that control where the data is entered in the field, the type of data that can be entered, whether the data is required or optional, and the number of characters. Their characteristics are summarised in the following table.

Character	What character is accepted/its function	Entry required
0	digit only	yes
9	digit or space	no
#	digit, space, +, −	no
L	letter	yes
?	letter	optional
A	letter or digit	yes
A	letter or digit	optional
&	any character or space	yes
C	any character or space	optional
<	converts characters to lower case	
>	converts characters to upper case	
!	displays from left to right	
\	displays the next character	

Using a space between two quotation marks can create an empty space. An example of the input mask for a telephone number is \ (999") "999\-9999.

Caption

The caption is the label for the field that is displayed on a form. If you do not type in a caption, the default label will be the name of the field. Enter captions in initial caps as this has a tendency to present less eye strain than all caps.

Default value

The Default value is used to specify a value that is automatically entered in a field when a new record is created. This property is commonly used when most or all of the entries in a field will be the same. That default value is then displayed automatically in the field. When a record is added to the table, the user can either accept this value or enter another value. This saves time while entering data. Character default values are enclosed by quotation marks (" ") and date default values by number sign (#).

Examples of default values are:

Value	What is stored in the field
Date ()	The computer system's date
500	500
"Barbados"	Barbados
#01/21/2006#	01/21/2006

Validation rule

When entering data, a check known as a validation check can be performed on the data to ensure that the data is valid. This check is only performed if a validation rule was entered in the table structure. A validity check is set by entering an expression containing the acceptable values. Expressions can be made up of numeric, text or date data, relational operators and/or logical operators (see the table below). The data of the Number data type must not be enclosed in quotation marks, whereas that of the Text data type must be enclosed in quotation marks. The data of the Date/Time field must be enclosed by # signs. When you add a validation rule, you can also add validation text in the validation text property box (see Figure 3.1).

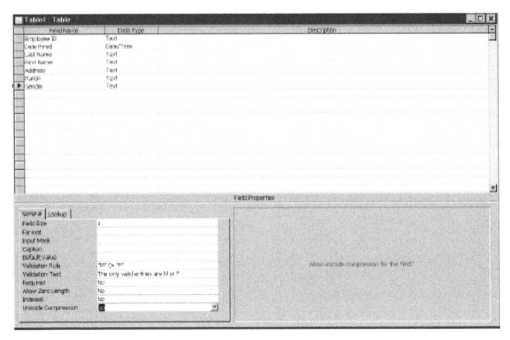

Figure 3.1

Field name	Data type	Expression	Result
Salary	Number	>2000	accepts only salaries that are more than $2000
Gender	Text	"M" or "F"	accepts M or F entries only
Birth Date	Date/Time	>= #1/13/1989# AND<= #12/31/2000#	accepts birth dates that are greater than or equal to 1/13/1989 and less than or equal to 12/31/2000
Result	Text	"PASS" or "FAIL"	accepts only entries with pass or fail

Validation text

The error message that is displayed when the validation rule is broken is called the Validation text. You may create your own error message to notify the user of the problem. Validation text appears in a message box if you attempt to enter invalid information in a text field for which there is a validity check. For example, if you added a validation rule

to a field to only allow the numbers 1 through 10, you might create validation text that would display the message, 'The only valid entries for this field are numbers 1 through 10'. If you do not specify a message, a default error message will be displayed.

Required property

This property could be set to Yes or No. When it is set to Yes, it is necessary for the user to input data in the field. This feature is very useful for ensuring that data is entered in certain fields that are relevant for processing the data. For example, in a payroll system, in order to calculate the gross pay, entering the pay rate is necessary. Omitting this data would result in the gross pay being zero. Hence you would set the Required property to Yes for the pay rate field. Access will not save the record until you type information into this field. You will receive a message indicating that this is a required field.

Allow zero length

Setting this property to Yes allows a zero-length string to be entered in the field. You may only use this option in Text, Memo or Hyperlink data types.

Indexed property

An Indexed property will arrange records to facilitate fast searches of the database. Selecting 'Yes – no duplicates' prohibits duplicate records for this field. Selecting 'Yes – duplicates' allows duplicates.

Exercise 3a

1 Select three of the following data types and state when each should be used in the table structure: Text, Memo, Number, Date/Time, Currency, Yes/ No.
2 List the main components of a table structure and state the functions of each component.
3 What is the purpose of **a)** a caption, **b)** an Input mask and **c)** a Default value?
4 What is the purpose of a Validation rule?
5 Explain the importance of the Required property.
6 Give two examples of Validation rules.
7 What is the purpose of Validation text?
8 What characters are accepted when the following are used in an Input mask: **a)** 0, **b)** 9 and **c)** #?
9 What is the Default value for the computer's system date?

Exercise 3b

1 Create the structure for a customer information table using the field specifications defined below. All table structures for this exercise must be created in the `Videos` database (a blank file is available in the exercise folder).

   a Make the Customer ID field the primary key.
   b Format the Last Name and First Name fields to convert characters to uppercase by using >.
   c Enter Yes in the Required property of the Last Name, First Name and Gender fields.

Table name: Customer				
Field Name	**Data type**	**Size**	**Description**	**Caption**
Customer ID	Text	3	3-digit unique number	Customer ID
Last Name	Text	25	Enter Last Name	Last Name
First Name	Text	15	Enter First Name	First Name
Address	Text	50	Address	Address
Birth Date	Date/Time		Enter yyyy/mm/dd	Date of Birth
Home Tel	Text	14	Home Telephone	Home Telephone
Work Tel	Text	14	Work Telephone	Work Telephone
Email	Text	40	Email Address	Email Address
Gender	Text	1	M or F	Gender
Work Place	Text	40	Place of Employment	Place of Employment

   d Format the Birth Date field yyyy.mm.dd to input the birth dates year, month, and day.
   e Use Input masks for the Home Tel and Work Tel fields. The Input mask should be (999) 999-9999.
   f Format the Gender field to convert the character to uppercase using >.
   g Enter <u>M or F</u> for the Validation rule field of the Gender field.
   h Enter 'The only valid entries are M or F' in the Validation text of the Gender field.
   i Enter Yes in the Required property of the Gender field.
   j Save the table as <u>Customer</u>.

2 Create the Tape, Type and Rental table structures using the field information defined in the tables below.

Table name: Tape.
   a Make the TapeID field the primary key.
   b Enter Yes in the Required property of the Title field.
   c Set the Field Size property of the Mins field to Double, Format to Fixed and Decimals to 0.
   d Set the Cost field Data Type to Currency and Decimals to 2.
   e Set the Field Size property of the Qty field to Double, Format to Fixed and Decimals to 0.
   f Save the table as <u>Tape</u>.

Table Name: Type.
   g Make the Typecode field the primary key.
   h Enter Yes in the Required property of the Description field.
   i Save the table as <u>Type</u>.

Table Name: Rental.

j Enter Yes in the Required property of the Customer ID, TapeID and Date Rented fields.

k Format the Date Rented and Date Due fields yyyy.mm.dd to input the data year, month, and day.

l Set the Rental Fee Field Data Type to Currency and Decimals to 2.

m Save the table as <u>Rental</u>.

Table name: Tape				
Field Name	**Data Type**	**Size**	**Description**	**Caption**
TapeID	Text	6	6-digit unique number	Tape ID
Title	Text	50	Enter Title	Title
Typecode	Text	2	2-digit code	Type Code
Rated	Text	4	Rating	Rated
Mins	Number	Minutes	Minutes	
Cost	Currency	Cost Per Tape	Cost Per Tape	
Qty	Number	Quantity In Stock	Quantity In Stock	

Table name: Type				
Field Name	**Data Type**	**Size**	**Description**	**Caption**
Typecode	Text	2	2-digit unique number	Type Code
Description	Text	25	Enter Title	Description

Table name: Rental				
Field Name	**Data Type**	**Size**	**Description**	**Caption**
Customer ID	Text	3	Enter Customer ID	Customer ID
TapeID	Text	6	Enter the Tape ID	Tape ID
Date Rented	Date/Time		Date Out	Date Rented
Rental Fee	Currency		Rental Fee	Rental Fee
Date Due	Date/Time		Date Due	Date Due

4. Modifying the table design

How to modify your table design

After you have created your table, you might need to go back and make changes. For example, you may want to add a field, or may have discovered that a field size isn't big enough.

If you want to go back to your table design to make changes:

- Right-click on its name in the list of tables.
- Click Design View.

Inserting fields

If you are inserting a field at the bottom of the list, you just click inside the first available row and start typing. If you want to insert a field <u>between</u> existing ones:

- Right-click on the box to the left of an existing field.
- Click Insert Rows.

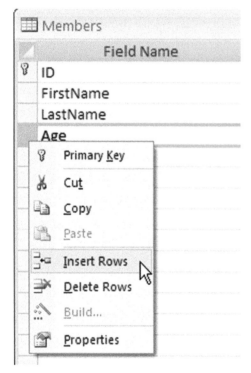

Figure 4.1 *Inserting a field*

Deleting fields

To delete a field:

- Right-click in the row and click Delete.
- Click Yes when the confirmation box pops up.

Changing field properties

You have to be careful when you are changing certain field properties – particularly if the table already contains data. For example, you need to be careful when changing the field size and the data type, because you run the risk of losing data.

Note

If you reduce the size of a field, when you go to save the database Access will warn you that data may be lost, even though that might not be true in your case. If you are confident your field size is big enough, you can ignore the warning.

Exercise 4

After reviewing the table structures for the videos database created in Exercise 3b, it was observed that some changes were needed. You are required to make the changes listed below (a ready-prepared database with the original structure is available in the exercise folder).

1 Change the field size of the e-mail field in the Customer table to 20.
2 Change the Field Name, Caption and Description in the Customer table from 'Work Place' to 'Employer'.
3 Add a field called 'Employer Address' in the Customer table after 'Employer'. Use a suitable Field Size, Caption and Description.
4 Insert a field called 'Date Joined' between 'Gender' and 'Employer' in the Customer table.
5 Format the 'Date Joined' field in the Customer table yyyy.mm.dd to input the dates as year, month, and day.

5. Primary keys

What is a primary key?

Suppose you had the list of bank customers as shown in Table 5.1.

Table 5.1 Customer data

CID	IDNo	FirstName	LastName	Age	Address	Region	Balance
0001	6002110000	Horatio	Caine	49	Somewherein	Miami	$10,000
0002	8001010000	John	Brown	29	Black Rock	St. Michael	$2,000
0003	7712310000	John	Brown	31	The Pine	St. Michael	$2,500
0004	6911110000	Lisa	Cuddy	39	Princeton	New Jersey	$15,000
0005	7205040000	Michael	Scofield	37	Fox River	Illinois	$5,000,000
0006	8804010000	Tonya	Alleyne	21	Rock Hall	St. Thomas	$4,000

If someone asked you for John Brown's balance, your response would probably be 'Which John Brown?' But if someone inquired as to the balance of customer #0002 you'd know exactly who they were referring to. We'd say that the CID (Customer ID) field uniquely identifies the records in the table. That is what a primary key does.

Formally, a **primary key** is 'a field or group of fields that is used to <u>uniquely</u> identify <u>every possible</u> record in a table'. In this table the CID field serves this purpose.

Note

A table can have at most one primary key.

Setting the primary key

In order to set the primary key of a table:

- Open the table's design.
- Select the field(s).
- Right-click on the selected field(s), then click Primary Key.

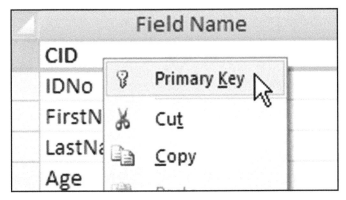

Figure 5.1 *Setting the Primary Key*

Microsoft Access put a tiny yellow key next to the primary key field(s) to distinguish it/them from the rest of the fields. In some texts, the primary key is underlined for this same reason.

Any existing data in the <u>primary key column(s)</u> must meet the following conditions. If it does not, the primary key won't set when you go to save the table design.

- There must be no duplicates.
- There must be no null (i.e.) blank values.

Note

In order to enforce the condition that there be no duplicates, Access will change the Indexed property to 'Yes (No Duplicates)'. Since indexing a field automatically sorts the data by the field, after you set the primary key, the data in the table will be sorted.

Candidate keys

If you look closely at Table 5.1, there were actually two candidates for the role of primary key – CID (the Customer ID) and IDNo (the National Registration Number). A <u>candidate key</u> is a field (or group of fields) that has the properties needed to be a primary key. Out of multiple candidate keys, only one will become the next primary key. The candidate keys that were not chosen are called <u>secondary</u> keys or <u>alternate keys</u>.

Foreign key

A <u>foreign key</u> is a field (or group of fields) in a table that matches the primary key of another table. Suppose our bank had another table used to store the transactions made by its customers (see Table 5.2).

Table 5.2 Transactions table

TID	Date	Customer ID	Amount
90701001	2009/07/01	0002	$1,000
90701002	2009/07/01	0001	−$3,000
90701003	2009/07/01	0003	−$200
90702001	2009/07/02	0004	$1,200
90702002	2009/07/02	0001	−$300
90703001	2009/07/03	0005	$5,000,000

If you look at the data in the Customer ID column, it uses the IDs from the Customer's CID column. So Customer ID is a foreign key since it matches the primary key of the Customer table.

Note

- A foreign key can have the same field name(s) as its corresponding primary key but it doesn't have to.
- A table may contain more than one foreign key.
- A table may contain both a primary key and a foreign key. In Table 5.2, TID is the primary key.

Composite key

A <u>composite key</u> is a primary or candidate key that contains two or more fields. In order to see a case where you'd need a composite key, consider a university that has a table to keep track of when it is offering various courses.

Table 5.3

Course	Semester	Year	Professor	Room
CISC 121	Fall	2009	Lamb	WLH 205
CISC 121	Winter	2010	McCollam	WLH 210
CISC121	Fall	2010	Dawes	WLH 205
CISC124	Fall	2009	McCollam	GOO 510
CISC124	Winter	2010	Lamb	GOO 510

Looking at the data in Table 5.3, you should notice that:

- A course may be offered multiple times a year (in different semesters).
- More than one professor teaches a particular course.

Clearly, you can't uniquely identify a record using one field, or even two. Instead, you have to use <u>three</u> fields. So the primary key is a composite key made up of the Course, Semester and Year fields.

Since composite keys are much more challenging to work with, we won't be placing much emphasis on them in this book.

Exercise 5

1 Explain what the following terms mean:
   a primary key
   b candidate key
   c secondary key
   d foreign key
   e composite key.
2 Why wouldn't you use a person's name as a primary key?
3 Keisha is trying to set the primary key on a table that already contains data. However, Microsoft Access is not allowing her to save the changes to the table design. Give two possible reasons for this.

6. Setting relationships

What is a relationship?

A relationship is a link between two tables that tells the Database Management System (i.e. Access) how they are related.

Let's revisit our bank example from Chapter 5. We had two tables – Customers and Transactions – which are shown below for your convenience.

Table 6.1 Customers

CID	IDNo	FirstName	LastName	Age	Address	Region	Balance
0001	6002110000	Horatio	Caine	49	Somewherein	Miami	$10,000
0002	8001010000	John	Brown	29	Black Rock	St. Michael	$2,000
0003	7712310000	John	Brown	31	The Pine	St. Michael	$2,500
0004	6911110000	Lisa	Cuddy	39	Princeton	New Jersey	$15,000
0005	7205040000	Michael	Scofield	37	Fox River	Illinois	$5,000,000
0006	8804010000	Tonya	Alleyne	21	Rock Hall	St. Thomas	$4,000

Table 6.2 Transactions

TID	Date	Customer ID	Amount
90701001	2009/07/01	0002	$1,000
90701002	2009/07/01	0001	–$3,000
90701003	2009/07/01	0003	–$200
90702001	2009/07/02	0004	$1,200
90702002	2009/07/02	0001	–$300
90703001	2009/07/03	0005	$5,000,000

Suppose the bank manager, looking at the suspicious deposit of five million dollars, wants to find out who customer 0005 is. You'd go in the Customers table, look up the person with CID 0005 and see that it is one Michael Scofield.

But how would Microsoft Access know to do this? It wouldn't unless you set a relationship between the two tables. Otherwise, the computer would think the tables are separate, unrelated entities. But after you set a relationship between the CID field in Customers and the CustomerID field in Transactions, Access will now know how to connect the two tables.

Setting a relationship

When you are setting a relationship between two tables, you have to:

1 Determine which field in each table will take part in the relationship. Make sure that one of the fields is the primary key.

2 Open the Relationships window and add the tables involved in the relationship.
3 Drag from one field to the other in order to set the relationship.
4 Enforce referential integrity (optional but recommended).

In order to see how it works, we'll set a relationship between the Customers table and the Transactions table.

Determining the fields involved

Normally you set the relationship between the primary key in one table and its foreign key in the other table.

Note

You must make sure that at least one of the two fields involved in the relationship is a primary key. Otherwise the relationship won't set.

If the tables already contain data, you can open both tables and see the fields in each table that have similar values. If neither of them is a primary key, you need to make one the primary key.

Tip

If one of the two fields contains duplicates, then the other field is the one that should be set as a primary key.

In our examples, the two fields involved in the relationship will be:

• from Customers – the CID field (which we will refer to as Customers.CID). This field is a primary key

- from Transactions – the CustomerID field
  (i.e. Transactions.CustomerID)

Opening the Relationships window

To open the Relationships window:

- Click Tools, Relationships (in Access 2003 or earlier)
- Click the Database Tools tab of the Ribbon, then click Relationships (in Access 2007 or later).

The first time you go to set relationships, the Show Table window will be displayed (Figure 6.1). Select the tables involved in the relationship, then click Add. Alternatively, you can double-click on them.

When you are finished, click the Close button.

Figure 6.1 *The Show Table window*

After you close the Show Table window, you'll see the Relationships window (Figure 6.2).

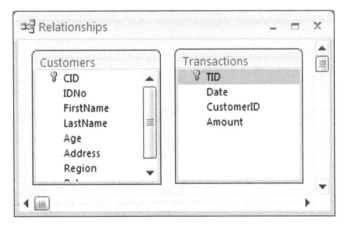

Figure 6.2 *The Relationships window*

Note

Access highlights the primary key field.
In Access 2007, a yellow key is displayed next to the primary key field. In Access 2003 it is bold.

Dragging from one field to the related field

In order to actually set the relationship you have to drag from one field to its related field in the other table. So in this case we drag from Customers.CID to Transactions.CustomerID. When we release the mouse, the Edit Relationships window appears.

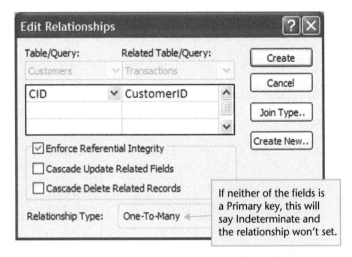

Figure 6.3 *The Edit Relationships window (with Referential Integrity Enforced)*

Enforcing referential integrity

Whenever you set a relationship, you should tick the Enforce Referential Integrity box before you click Create. This will make sure that the user can't put a value in the foreign key field CustomerID that isn't present in the primary key field CID. This prevents the user from entering transactions for customers that don't exist!

Here's what the Relationships window looks like after the relationship is set. The black line represents the relationship.

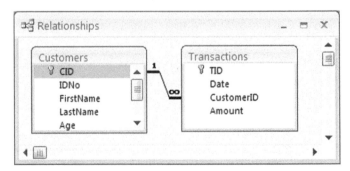

Figure 6.4 *The relationship after it has been set*

Deleting a relationship

In order to delete a relationship:

- Click on the black line that represents the relationship.
- Press the Delete key.
- Click Yes at the confirmation prompt.

Tip

If you accidentally delete the table instead of the relationship you can always use the Show Table window to add it again.

Exercise 6a

1 With respect to databases, what is a relationship?
2 Which of the following is the method used to set a relationship between two tables?
   a Working from the Design view
   b Double-clicking on the fields involved in the relationship
   c Clicking on the fields involved in the relationship
   d Dragging from one field involved in the relationship to the other
3 In the Relationships window, how can you tell which fields are primary keys?
4 If you go to set a relationship and Access lists the relationship type as 'Indeterminate' what is the cause?

Exercise 6b

Open the Videos database and set relationships between four tables.

7. Entering and editing data

The Datasheet View (Figure 7.1) allows you to add and edit information in your table. To open a table:

- Go to the list of tables in the database.
- Double-click on the table you want to open.

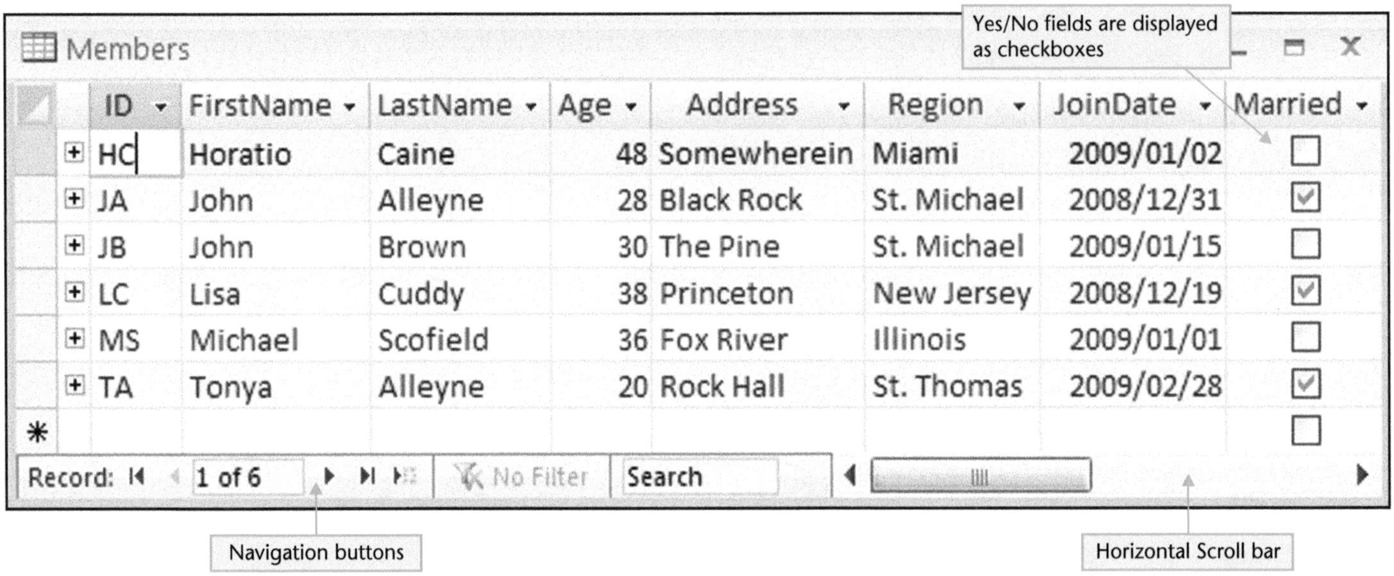

	ID ▾	FirstName ▾	LastName ▾	Age ▾	Address ▾	Region ▾	JoinDate ▾	Married ▾
⊞	HC	Horatio	Caine	48	Somewherein	Miami	2009/01/02	☐
⊞	JA	John	Alleyne	28	Black Rock	St. Michael	2008/12/31	☑
⊞	JB	John	Brown	30	The Pine	St. Michael	2009/01/15	☐
⊞	LC	Lisa	Cuddy	38	Princeton	New Jersey	2008/12/19	☑
⊞	MS	Michael	Scofield	36	Fox River	Illinois	2009/01/01	☐
⊞	TA	Tonya	Alleyne	20	Rock Hall	St. Thomas	2009/02/28	☑
∗								☐

Figure 7.1 *The Datasheet view*

Moving around the datasheet

Since a datasheet is like a giant table, you can click in a particular cell if you want to type new data or edit existing data.

If there is too much information to show on the screen at one time, Access will display one or both scroll bars. You can use the horizontal scroll bar to view additional columns or the vertical scroll bar to view additional rows.

The other ways to move around the datasheet are:

- by using the keyboard shortcuts in the table below
- by using the Navigation buttons

To move to the...	Press the key(s)
next field	Tab
	Enter
	Right Arrow (if the current cell isn't being edited)
previous field	Shift + Tab
	Left Arrow (if the current cell isn't being edited)
last field of a record	End
first field of a record	Home

To move to the...	Press the key(s)
same field in the next record	Down Arrow
same field in the previous record	Up Arrow
last field of the last record	Ctrl + End
first field of the first record	Ctrl + Home
next page of records	Page Down
previous page of records	Page Up

Navigation buttons

At the bottom left of each datasheet are navigation buttons. These allow you to move from one record to the next and even add new records. You can also type the number of a record in the Current Record box and press Enter. The Current Record box also tells you how many records are in your table. In Figure 7.2 there are six records and the current record is #3.

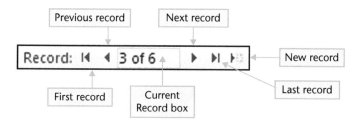

Figure 7.2 *The Navigation buttons*

Editing data

Each cell in the table corresponds to a field in the record. If you click inside the field, the cursor will start flashing inside the field so you can edit its data. Once you start editing a field, Access will display an icon of a pencil to the left of the margin indicating that changes are being made to the record (see Figure 7.3).

	ID ▾	FirstName ▾	LastName ▾	Age ▾
✎ ⊞	HC	Horatio	Caine	49
⊞	JA	John	Alleyne	29
⊞	JB	John	Brown	31
⊞	LC	Lisa	Cuddy	39
⊞	MS	Michael	Scofield	37
⊞	TA	Tonya	Alleyne	21
✱				

Figure 7.3 *Editing a field*

If you are editing a field, but want to revert to what it previously was, press the Esc key. To undo the last change you made to the table, click the undo button.

Adding a new record

Each datasheet has at least one blank row at the bottom. To add a new record just click in the next available row (the one with the *) and start typing. Alternatively, you can click the New Record navigation button.

Deleting a record

To delete a record:

- Right-click on the record.
- Click Delete.
- Click Yes to confirm the deletion.

Saving a record

Microsoft Access automatically saves a record when you go to another one. But if you want to force Access

to save the changes immediately, you can click the Save button.

Widening a column

To change the width of a column:

- Position the cursor over the line to the right of the column.
- Drag the cursor to the right if you want to widen the column. If you want the column to be narrower, drag it to the left.

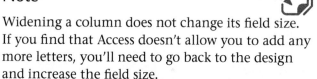

	CID ▾	IDNo ▾	FirstName ▾
	0001	6002110000	Horatio
	0004	6911110000	Lisa
	0005	7205040000	Michael
	0003	7712310000	John
	0002	8001010000	John
	0006	8804010000	Tonya
✱			

Figure 7.4 *Resizing a column*

Note

Widening a column does not change its field size. If you find that Access doesn't allow you to add any more letters, you'll need to go back to the design and increase the field size.

Switching between the Datasheet and Design views

Microsoft Access makes it very easy to switch between the Datasheet and Design views. To do so, just click the appropriate button in the top left corner of the Access window.

Figure 7.5 *Design View button*

Figure 7.6 *Datasheet View button*

Miscellaneous points

Entering dates

Regardless of the date format, you must enter the date either with dashes, for example 2010-01-01, or slashes, for example 2010/01/01. If you try to enter the date with dots, Access will give an error message.

Primary keys

Microsoft Access won't allow you to enter data in a primary key field if:

- you try to leave the field blank
- the data would create a duplicate in the column

Exercise 7a

Data entry is an essential aspect of database management. You should be consistent in how the data is entered. For example, the word Road may be entered as Road, ROAD, Rd. or RD. However, you should decide which of these you are going to use and use it each time.

Perform the following tasks:

1. Open the database Videos.
2. Double-click the Customer table.
3. Enter the following records into the table:

New Customers			
Fields	**Record 1**	**Record 2**	**Record 3**
ID	201	202	203
Last Name	Johnson	Chandler	Banfield
First Name	Michelle	Tyrone	Shirley
Address	Ruby Park, St Philip	Bank Hall, St Michael	71 Long Bay Development, St Philip
Birth Date	1969/02/15	1969/03/05	1970/10/26
Home Tel.	(246) 431-2916	(246) 431-8971	(246) 423-5441
Work Tel.	(246) 433-2196	(246) 422-1119	
Email Add.	michelej@bclub.com	chandler@hotmail.com	sheba@email.com
Gender	F	M	F
Employer	Baker's Night Club	G E Electronics	
Fields	**Record 4**	**Record 5**	**Record 6**
ID	204	205	206
Last Name	Isidore	Johnson	Kellman
First Name	Esther	Angela	Arlene
Address	4 Mt Standfast, St James	Cane Gardens, St Thomas	St Patricks, Christ Church
Birth Date	1968/11/10	1971/12/10	1974/06/10
Home Tel.	(246) 421-1247	(246) 433-9172	(246) 429-2031
Work Tel.	(246) 422-1999	(246) 417-4171	(246) 426-2979
Email Add.		Connell@tsb.bb	sypher@hotmail.com
Gender	F	M	F
Employer	Queen Elizabeth Hospital	Transport Board	KMGP

New Customers			
Fields	**Record 7**	**Record 8**	**Record 9**
ID	207	208	209
Last Name	Payne	Grant	Smith
First Name	Reba	Frederick	Irene
Address	Foster Hall, St George	Grape Hall, St Lucy	Ashton Hall, St Peter
Birth Date	1967/01/03	1962/09/09	1945/07/07
Home Tel.	(246) 423-6823	(246) 417-2280	(246) 433-3302
Work Tel.	(246) 423-9741		
Email Add.	Rebapay@sunbeach.net		storm@hotmail.com
Gender	F	M	F
Employer	Cove Crystal Hotel		
Fields	**Record 10**	**Record 11**	**Record 12**
ID	210	211	212
Last Name	Wickham	Catwell	Greaves
First Name	Thomas	Pauline	Linda
Address	Boscobelle, St Andrew	Braggs Hill, St Joseph	Thompsons Road, St Thomas
Birth Date	1943/04/06	1970/02/02	1972/09/10
Home Tel.	(246) 429-2916	(246) 433-8791	(246) 417-4177
Work Tel.	(246) 422-1231		
Email Add.		catpur@yahoo.com	
Gender	M	F	F
Employer	J G Retirement Home	Caribbean Union	Shoppers Retail Store

Exercise 7b

1 Open the <u>Type</u> table.
2 Enter the following records into the table:

CODE	DESCRIPTION
HO	HORROR
AC	ACTION
WE	WESTERN
DR	DRAMA
SC	SCI FI
AD	ADVENTURE
MU	MUSICAL
MY	MYSTERY
RO	ROMANCE
CL	CLASSIC
MA	MARTIAL ARTS

3 Adjust the column widths appropriately.
4 Open the <u>Tape</u> table.
5 Enter the following records into the table:

TAPE ID	TITLE	TYPE CODE	RATED	MINUTES	COST	QTY
212141	JAWS 2	HO	TVMA	90	7.00	12
633602	ABOVE THE LAW	AC	R	120	7.25	10
151571	THE GOOD, THE BAD & THE UGLY	WE	PG13	75	9.00	15
241251	DIRTY DANCING	DR	PG13	86	6.00	25
120123	THE MATRIX	SC	R	130	12.00	10
421103	JAMES AND THE GIANT PEACH	AD	G	120	10.25	15
307201	DUNGEONS & DRAGONS	AD	PG13	75	8.00	10
102101	DESTINY'S CHILD – ON THE WALL	MU	G	90	9.00	20
521012	YOUNG SHERLOCK HOLMES	MY	R	79	5.25	16
671347	YOU'VE GOT MAIL	RO	G	92	5.25	18
434810	THE TEN COMMANDMENTS	CL	G	210	12.00	22
457482	TAI CHI MASTER	MA	PG13	93	8.25	15

6 Adjust the column widths appropriately.
7 Open the <u>Rental</u> table.
8 Enter the records below.

CUSTOMER ID	TAPE ID	DATE RENTED	RENTAL FEE
201	212141	2006.01.07	2.00
209	457482	2006.01.07	3.25
202	120123	2006.01.08	2.00
201	102101	2006.01.08	3.00
204	421103	2006.01.10	3.25
209	307201	2006.01.11	3.00
201	633602	2006.01.13	2.25
206	671347	2006.01.13	2.25

8. Copying data

In this chapter you will learn how to copy data from one table to the next as well as how to copy data between Microsoft Access and other programs.

Copying/moving data into fields

To copy data into fields:

- Select the data you want to copy.
- Click the Copy icon.
- Click where you want the data to be copied.
- Click the Paste icon.

Note

You can use the same process to move the data. Just click Cut instead of Copy.

Copying an entire table

To copy an entire table:

- Switch to the list of tables.
- Right-click on the name of the table you want to copy.
- Click Copy.
- Right-click anywhere among the list of tables.
- Click Paste.
- Choose the appropriate paste option from the window that pops up.
- Type the name of the destination table.

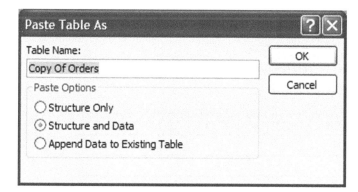

Figure 8.1 *Paste Table options*

Note

The structure of a table is its design so select the second option if you want to copy the table and its data. 'Append' means to 'add'.

Copying an Access table to another program

To copy a Microsoft Access table to another program:

- Switch to the list of tables.
- Right-click on the name of the table you want to copy.
- Click Copy.
- Open the program where you want to copy the table, for example Word or Excel.
- Position the cursor where the table's data should go.
- Click the Paste button in the program.

Creating an Access table using data from an Excel worksheet

Most of the data you work with in Excel is in a tabular form. So it is not surprising that you can create an Access table from an Excel 'table'. You can even use the column headings in the Excel 'table' as the field names in the Access table – provided that none of the column headings begin with a space. Otherwise you will get an error message like the one in Figure 8.2.

To create an Access table using data from an Excel worksheet:

1 Open the spreadsheet in Microsoft Excel.
2 Highlight the data you want imported into Access.
3 Click Copy.
4 Using Microsoft Access, open/create the <u>database</u> that will act as a container for the new table.
5 Ensure you are in the Tables section.
6 Click Paste.
7 If the first row of the data you selected in Excel contains the column headings, click Yes. Otherwise, Access will label the fields in the new table as F1, F2, etc.
8 If you don't want the table to have a name like 'Sheet 1', you will have to rename it:

- Right-click on the name of the newly created table.
- Click Rename.
- Type the new name of the table.
- Press the Enter key.

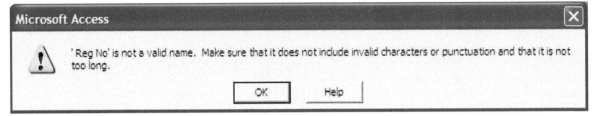

Figure 8.2 *Error message due to an invalid column heading*

Exercise 8a

Some new data has become available and a few changes have to be made to existing tables (available in the Videos database from the exercise folder). These tasks are listed below:

1 Open the <u>Customer</u> table.
2 Enter the new address for Shirley Banfield as 71 Bayfield Development, St Philip.
3 Delete record 12.
4 Enter the following data shown in the table below.

Name	Date Joined	Employer Address
Michelle Johnson	2006.01.05	Rockley, Christ Church
Tyrone Chandler	2006.01.03	Bridgetown, St Michael
Shirley Banfield	2006.01.06	
Esther Isodore	2006.01.05	River Road, St Michael
Angela Johnson	2006.01.03	Roebuck Street, St Michael
Arlene Kellman	2006.01.03	Hastings, Christ Church
Reba Payne	2006.01.03	Hastings, Christ Church
Frederic Grant	2006.01.05	
Irene Smith	2006.01.05	
Thomas Wickham	2006.01.05	Cave Hill, St Michael
Pauline Catwell	2006.01.06	Two Mile Hill, St Michael

5 Close the <u>Customer</u> table.
6 Copy the <u>Tape</u> table structure and data to a new table called <u>Newtape</u>.
7 Enter the following data into the <u>Rental</u> table:

CUSTOMER ID	TAPE ID	DATE RENTED	RENTAL FEE
207	151571	2006.01.07	3.00
210	241251	2006.01.07	2.25
203	521012	2006.01.08	2.00
205	434810	2006.01.09	2.75
208	421103	2006.01.10	3.25
207	307201	2006.01.12	3.00
211	633602	2006.01.15	2.25
211	671347	2006.01.15	2.25

Exercise 8b

Create a blank database called `Importing` and copy the tables from the following Excel worksheets into your database:

1 `Furnt`. Call the new Access table 'Furniture'.
2 `Books`. Rename the new Access table as 'Books'.

9. Sorting and indexing

In Microsoft Access there are two ways to sort data:

- via the Datasheet view
- by indexing it (sorting is a useful side effect of indexing)

Sorting via the Datasheet view

The easiest way to sort the data in a table is to do so via the Datasheet view.

By one field
To sort by one field from inside the Datasheet view:

- Click inside the column for the field you want to sort by.
- Click either the ascending order or descending order button.

By multiple fields
To sort by multiple fields, you use the Advanced Filter/Sort window. Although this window is accessed via the Datasheet view, it is accessed differently depending on whether you are using Access 2003 or 2007.

Access 2003
To open the Advanced Filter/Sort window in Access 2003:

- Make sure you are in the Datasheet view.
- Click Records, Filter, Advanced Filter/Sort...

Access 2007
To open the window in Access 2007:

- Make sure you are in the Datasheet view.
- Switch to the Home tab of the Ribbon.
- Click the Advanced button of the Sort and Filter group.
- Choose the Advanced Filter/Sort option from the list.

Using the Advanced Filter/Sort window
The way you use this window is:

1 Double-click the fields you want to sort by.
2 Choose the sort order for each field.
3 Apply the sort.

Figure 9.1 *Opening the Advanced Filter/Sort window in Access 2007*

Figure 9.2 *Using the Advanced Filter/Sort window*

If you close the window without applying the sort, all your hard work will be in vain. In order to apply the sort:

- In Access 2003, click Records, Apply Filter/Sort.
- In Access 2007, click the Home tab, then click the Toggle Filter button in the Sort and Filter group.

Indexing

Indexing allows Microsoft Access to quickly find information the same way that a book's index helps the reader. This is one reason why Access automatically indexes primary keys – so it can quickly find the record referenced by a foreign key.

At this level, you don't need an in-depth understanding of how indexing works, except for one thing:

When you place an index on a field, you automatically sort the table by that field.

Indexing a field

In order to place an index on a field in a table:

- Open the Design view of the table.
- Select the field.
- Change the Indexed property to either 'Yes (No Duplicates)' or 'Yes (Duplicates OK)'. Unless you have reason to prevent duplicates, choose the latter option.

Note

Microsoft Access automatically indexes fields that end in 'ID' or 'No', for example MemberID.

Exercise 9

1 Open the Videos database.
2 Sort the Customer table by Last Name and First Name.
3 Index the Tape table by the quantity in stock.
4 Sort the NewTape table in descending order by Rated and Title.
5 Index NewType by description.
6 Index the NewRental table by RentalDate and TapeID.

10. Introduction to queries

One of the most powerful (and difficult to master) features of Database Management Systems is the ability to perform queries. You can use queries to:

- display part of a table
- display records that meet certain criteria
- perform calculations
- create/update tables
- delete records

Creating a query

Although there are different ways of creating queries, we'll create queries using the Design view. The way you get to the Query Design view depends on whether you have Access 2003 or 2007, but once you're there the actual process of creating the query is the same.

Access 2003

To get to the Query Design view in Access 2003:

- Switch to the Queries tab of the Database window.
- Double-click on the <u>Create Query in Design View</u> option.

Access 2007

If you want to design a query in Access 2007:

- Switch to the Create tab of the Ribbon.
- Click on the Query Design button.

Figure 10.1 *The Query Design button (Access 2007)*

The Show Table window

When you go to create a query using the Design view, the Show Table window will pop up so you can select the tables you will include in your query design. You can even base your query on another query!

Tip

By default the Show Table shows a list of the tables in your database for you to choose from. If you need to add a query to your design, just click on the Queries tab.

Figure 10.2 *The Show Table window.*

To add a tables or queries, from the Show Table window either:

- Double-click their names in the list.
- Or select their names and click the Add button.

Tip

You can select multiple tables/queries at the same time by using the Shift or Ctrl keys.

When you finish adding the tables/queries you'll be taken to the Query Design View which we'll talk about shortly. But if you ever need to access the Show Table window from this window (perhaps to add some more tables):

- In Access 2003 or earlier: Click Query, Show Table...
- In Access 2007: Make sure you are in the Design tab of the Ribbon and click Show Table.

The Query Design window

The main part of the Query Design view is the Query Design window. This is where you fill in the details that control how your query will work. The process of designing the query normally goes like this:

1. Select the tables/queries that your query needs. You should have done this via the Show Table window.
2. Double-click on the fields that your query will use in order to add them to the Design view.
3. Fill in the field settings as appropriate (e.g. type in any criteria you are going to use, select the sort order, etc.).

The image below shows the two halves of the Query Design window.

By looking at the top half in the example shown in Figure 10.3, you can see that only the Members table has been added to the Query Design. If you wanted to add other tables, you could do so using the Show Table window.

Tip

If you need to remove a table, right-click on its window's title bar and click Remove Table.

The bottom half of the Query Design window is organised like a giant table. Each field that has been added has its own column. Each row corresponds to a particular setting for that field.

Field settings

The following table explains what each field setting is for.

Row	What it is for
Field	This shows the name of the field. Since it is actually a combo box, you can click it and change to another field.
Table	This shows the table that the field belongs to. This is also a combo box.
Sort	By default this is blank, meaning that the field is unsorted. But you can use the combo box to sort it in ascending or descending order.
Criteria	This is where you type the criteria to determine whether a record is shown/affected by the query.
or	You can also type criteria in these rows at the bottom.

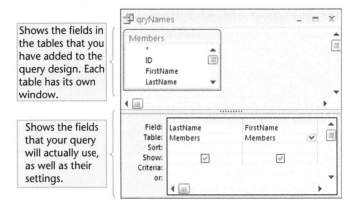

Shows the fields in the tables that you have added to the query design. Each table has its own window.

Shows the fields that your query will actually use, as well as their settings.

Figure 10.3 *The Query Design window.*

Adding fields

If you double-click on a field in the top half of the Query Design window, it will be added to your query. The fields that have been added to the query will be shown in the bottom half of the Query Design window.

Tip

If you want your query to include all the fields in a table, instead of adding them one-by-one, just double-click the asterisk (*).

Removing fields

To remove a field from the query design:

- Select the field by clicking on the horizontal bar at the top of the field. (Make sure that the mouse pointer changes to a black down arrow.) The whole column should become highlighted.
- Press the Delete key.

Field:	FirstName	LastName
Table:	Members	Members
Sort:		
Show:	☑	☑
Criteria:	"John"	

Figure 10.4 *Selecting a field to be deleted.*

Changing a field to something else

Suppose you accidentally added the wrong field. Instead of deleting it and adding the correct one, you can simply change it to the other field. To do so:

- (Optional) Click the arrow next to the name of the table and change it to the correct table.
- Click the arrow next to the name of the field and change it to the correct field.

Repositioning a field

In order to move a field from one position in the design to another:

- Select the field by clicking on the horizontal grey bar at the top of the field.
- Hold down the left mouse button and drag the field to the new position.
- Release the left mouse button.

Note

The heavy black line indicates where the field will go. So in Figure 10.5, the Region field is being moved between the FirstName and LastName fields.

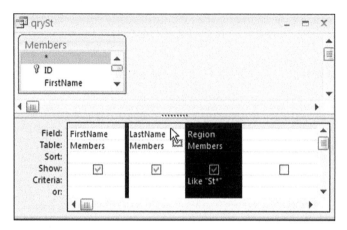

Figure 10.5 *Repositioning a field*

Running a query when you are in the Design view

To run a query, click the red exclamation mark (!) near the top of the Design view.

Switching from the Datasheet view to the Design view

When you run a Select query (which is the default type of query), the query will switch from the Design view to the Datasheet view.

If you need to get back to the Design view, click the Design view button in the top left-hand corner of the window.

Figure 10.6 *The Design view button*

Saving a query

You can save the design of a query at any time by clicking the Save button. As usual, you will be prompted to save any changes when you close the query.

Running a query from outside the Design view

After you have closed the Design view, if you want to run a query:

- Switch to the section that lists all the query objects in your database.
- Double-click on the name of the query.

Exercise 10

1. Open the `Example` database from your exercise folder.
2. Create a new query based on the Customers table.
3. Add the FirstName, Age and Address fields.
4. Remove the Age field from the design.
5. Change the Address field in the design to LastName.
6. Reopen the Show Table window.
7. Add the Transactions table.
8. Add the Date and Amount fields to the query design.
9. Reposition the Date field so that it is now the first field in the design.
10. Run the query.
11. Save the query as My First Query.

11. Basic queries

In this chapter, you'll learn how to create basic queries that display <u>some</u> of the fields or records from a single table.

Displaying selected fields

If you want to list <u>some</u> of the fields in a table, create a query based on that table and add those fields to the design view.

Scenario

* You have a table that stores information about the members of your store (shown below).
* You want to generate a list of the members' names but you aren't interested in the other fields.

Query design

This query, and all other queries in this chapter, is based on the Members table. So when the Show Table window appears, add only this table to your query design.

Since you want to display the names of the members, add both the LastName and FirstName fields to the query design by double-clicking on them. Although you aren't <u>required</u> to put the LastName first, most people follow this convention so we will as well.

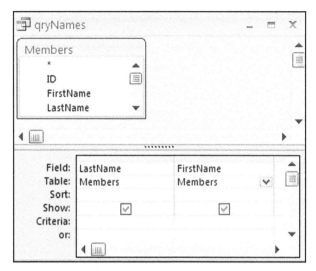

Figure 11.2 *qryNames (Design)*

Results

Figure 11.3 *qryNames (Results)*

Figure 11.1 *Members table*

Sorting

If you need a query's results to be sorted by certain fields, use the Sort row in the query design to set the sort order for those fields. Access will sort by the left-most field that has a sort order, then by the next field with a sort order, and so on.

Scenario

- You want a list of the members sorted in alphabetical order.

Query design

We will base this query on the Members table, but could just as easily base it on the query from the previous example since that also lists the names of the members.

Figure 11.5 *qrySortedNames (Results)*

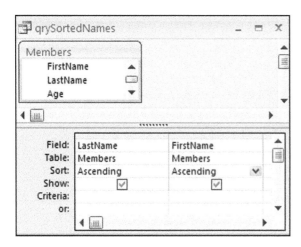

Figure 11.4 *qrySortedNames (Design)*

The records are sorted by LastName, then by FirstName (since LastName is to the left of FirstName).

Tip

Alphabetical order is just another way of saying that the data should be sorted in <u>ascending order</u>.

Results

First the names are sorted in ascending order by the LastName. When you have two people with the same last name (for example Alleyne), their names are then sorted by FirstName.

Placing criteria on a field

If you want to use a field to control which records get displayed:

- Add the field to the Design view (if it isn't there already).
- Type an expression in the Criteria row under that field.
- If you want to hide the field, uncheck its Show box.

Scenario

- You want the first names of the members with the surname Alleyne.
- You don't want to display the surname.

Query design

Since we have to display the <u>first</u> names, we'll add that field to the Design view. Then we'll add LastName and type the word Alleyne as the criteria. <u>The capitalisation does not matter.</u> Lastly, we'll uncheck the Show box for the LastName field since we don't want to display the surnames.

Note

Access automatically places criteria that looks like text, or is placed under text fields, in quotes. You don't have to type the quotes.

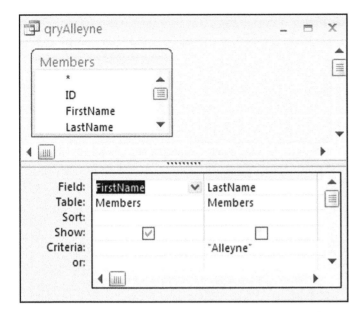

Figure 11.6 *qryAlleyne (Design)*

Results

Figure 11.7 *qryAlleyne (Results)*

Criteria on numbers and currency

Criteria on numbers look pretty much the way you'd expect. The following table shows you different criteria that you could place on the ages of members.

If you want members who are...	Type these criteria under the Age field
28 years old	28
More than 30	> 30
Less than or equal to 25	<=25
Older than 25 and less than 30	> 25 and <30
Between ages 30 and 40	between 30 and 40
Not 30 years old	<> 30

When you are putting criteria on currency fields, remember that monetary figures are really numbers. So if you want all the items that cost more than $9.99 your criteria would be >9.99. <u>If you put the $, Access will misinterpret it as text</u>.

Criteria on dates

The same operators that you use with numbers (for example, >, <= and BETWEEN) can be used with dates. Here are a few examples:

If you want members who joined...	Type these criteria under the JoinDate field
on December 19, 2008	2008/12/19
after January 15, 2009	>2009/01/15
before February 2009	<2009/02/01
in 2009	between 2009/01/01 and 2009/12/31

The one to focus on is the final example. You might be wondering why you couldn't just put 2009 as the criteria. This brings us to an important point – <u>you must use complete dates in your criteria</u>. So you have to think of the criteria in terms of dates like this: 'If someone joined in 2009, they joined between the dates 1st Jan 2009 and 31st Dec 2009'.

Using multiple criteria (AND)

If you have multiple criteria in same row, only the records that meet <u>all</u> those criteria will be displayed.

Scenario

- You want to list all married members who joined before 2009.
- You want to display the following fields: FirstName, LastName, JoinDate, Married.

Query design

The criteria can be broken down into two main parts:

1 Listing the members who joined before 2009. Remembering that we have to put complete dates in criteria, we'll type '<2009/01/01' (without the quotes) as the criteria.

AND

2 Displaying only the ones who are married, i.e. those members whose Married field is set to Yes.

Since the criteria are in the same row, <u>both</u> must be true in order for a record to be displayed.

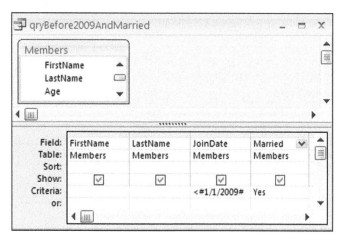

Figure 11.8 *qryBefore2009AndMarried (Design)*

Results

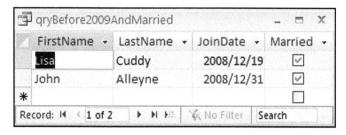

Figure 11.9 *qryBefore2009AndMarried (Results)*

Using multiple criteria (OR)

If you want to display records that match <u>any</u> of a set of criteria, you place the criteria on different rows. For instance, you could place one criterion in the Criteria row, the next in the first Or row, and so on.

When Microsoft Access is determining whether to display a record in the table, it checks to see if it meets the criteria in the Criteria row or any of the Or rows. If the record matches the criteria in <u>any</u> of those rows, it is displayed.

Scenario

• You want to list the members who are married <u>or</u> joined before 2009.

Query design

We have the same two criteria as before but since <u>either</u> can be true, you put them on different rows.

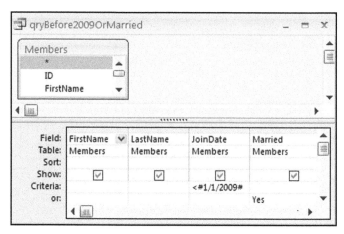

Figure 11.10 *qryBefore2009OrMarried (Design)*

Results

There are now 3 records instead of 2. Although Tonya did not join before 2009, she <u>is</u> married, meaning that one of the conditions is true. So her record is now included.

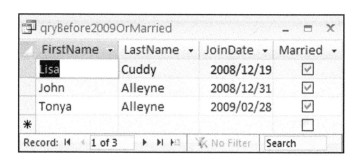

Figure 11.11 *qryBefore2009OrMarried (Results)*

Using * in criteria

The asterisk (*) has a special meaning when you put it in criteria. It acts as a wildcard, which means 'any group of characters or none at all'.

Let's look at an example. Suppose you put the criteria 'sea*' (without the quotes) under a text field. What that means is 'the word 'sea' followed by any group of characters or none at all'. So any of the following would meet the criteria:

• seas
• seaweed
• sea
• sea shells by the sea shore

The following table explains how to use the * wildcard.

Criteria	What it means	Examples
man*	anything that starts with the word 'man'	man, manure, Manchester United
*man	anything that ends with the word 'man'	man, woman
man	anything that contains the word 'man'	man, manager, woman, A Man For All Seasons

Scenario
- You want to list the members who live in a region that starts with 'St'.
- You only want to their names and region.

Query design
We put the criteria St* under the Region field. Access changes this to Like 'St*'.

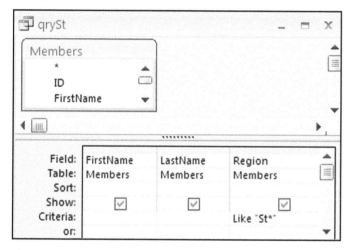

Figure 11.12 *qrySt (Design)*

Note

When you use wildcards in text criteria, Access automatically puts the criteria in quotes and puts the word <u>Like</u> in front.

Results

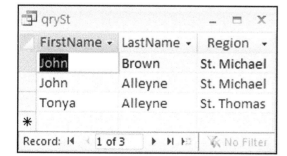

Figure 11.13 *qrySt (Results)*

The queries in Exercises 11a and 11b are to be done using the `Videos` database unless stated otherwise. You can find the database in your exercise folder.

Exercise 11a

Mr Troy is very curious about how the database is going to benefit his video shop and he is requesting a number of printouts of information as follows:

1 Perform a Select query and print the last name, first name, address, home and work telephone numbers for each customer. He would like the information printed with the last names in alphabetical order. Save your query as Customer List.
2 Print out the Tape ID, Title, Rated and Minutes of the Tape table. Print the information with the longest time at the top. Save the query as Tapes.

Exercise 11b

Mr Troy is very pleased with the printouts thus far and is now testing your skills in supplying him with specific information based on given criteria. Please supply him with the necessary printouts from the <u>Customer</u> table for questions 1 to 5 and the <u>Tape</u> table for questions 6 to 10.

1 What is the email address for Tyrone Chandler?
2 What are the names and addresses of female customers?
3 What are the telephone numbers for Thomas Wickham?
4 What are the names and addresses of customers who are older than 40 years of age?
5 What are the names of customers who joined on 3rd January 2006 and those who joined on 5th January 2006? Show the joining date for each customer named.
6 How is the 'Young Sherlock Holmes' tape rated?
7 List all tapes that are rated 'PG13'.
8 List the name and the duration of tapes that run for between 75 and 100 minutes.
9 List the title, type code, rating and minutes for Tape ID 421103 and 457482.
10 List the title of tapes with a type code which begins with 'M'.

12. Multiple-table queries

So far all of our queries have been using one table, but we can just as easily apply the same principles to two or more tables.

In order to create a multiple-table query, the tables must be joined together. If you set relationships between the tables (see Chapter 6), they will be automatically joined when you add them to the Query Design.

Joining tables

Within the Query Design view, you can tell Access to join two tables the same way you'd set a relationship between them – you drag from a field in one table to a similar field in another table. The process is like setting a relationship without enforcing referential integrity.

Scenario

You have three tables (Members, Items and Orders) that are already linked via relationships. Table 12.1 lists the fields in each table.

- You want to do a query that will list the orders made in January 2009.
- You want to display the FirstName, LastName, Description, Qty and OrderDate fields.

Table 12.1 The structures for the three tables

Table	Fields
Members	<u>ID</u>, FirstName, LastName, Age, Address, Region, JoinDate, Married
Items	<u>ItemNo</u>, Department, Brand/Author, Description, Price
Orders	MID, ItemNo, Qty, OrderDate

Query design

Looking at the requirements, we can see that we need to add all three tables to the query design. Because relationships have already been set between the tables, they are already joined. We then add the necessary fields and criteria.

Since the query is to display the January 2009 orders, the OrderDate must be between 1st January 2009 and 31st January 2009. So we put the following criteria under the OrderDate field:

Between 2009/01/01 and 2009/01/31

Access automatically recognises the dates and encloses them in # symbols.

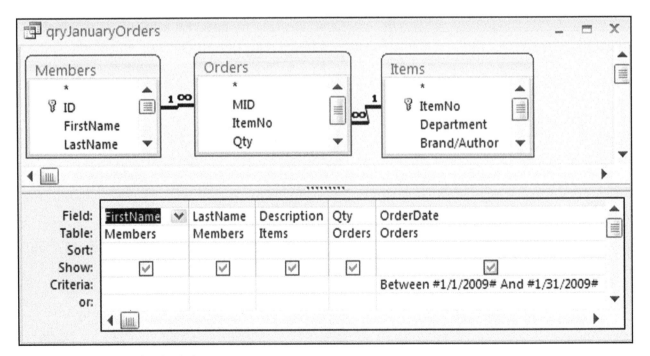

Figure 12.1 *qryJanuaryOrders (Design)*

Results

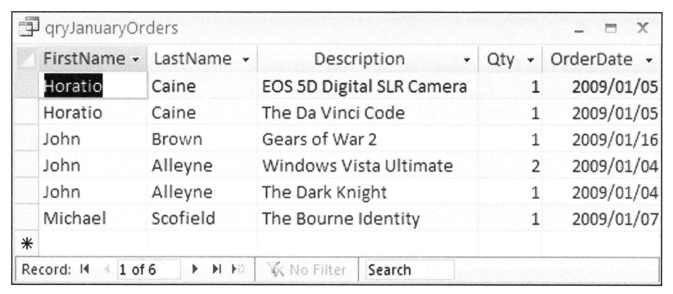

Figure 12.2 *qryJanuaryOrders (Results)*

What happens if the tables aren't joined?

If you have a query with multiple tables, the tables must be joined – either manually or via relationships – so that Microsoft Access can connect the information properly. If you forget to do so, your queries will contain <u>a lot of repeated information</u>.

Figure 12.3 shows the results the query from before would give if the tables were not joined. Actually, it only shows some of the results since there are 540 records in the query.

FirstName	LastName	Description	Qty	OrderDate
Michael	Scofield	The Da Vinci Code	1	2009/01/05
Michael	Scofield	The Da Vinci Code	1	2009/01/05
Michael	Scofield	The Da Vinci Code	1	2009/01/16
Michael	Scofield	The Da Vinci Code	2	2009/01/04
Michael	Scofield	The Da Vinci Code	1	2009/01/04
Michael	Scofield	The Da Vinci Code	1	2009/01/07
Lisa	Cuddy	The Da Vinci Code	1	2009/01/05
Lisa	Cuddy	The Da Vinci Code	1	2009/01/05
Lisa	Cuddy	The Da Vinci Code	1	2009/01/16
Lisa	Cuddy	The Da Vinci Code	2	2009/01/04
Lisa	Cuddy	The Da Vinci Code	1	2009/01/04
Lisa	Cuddy	The Da Vinci Code	1	2009/01/07

Record: 1 of 540   No Filter   Search

Figure 12.3 *qryJanuaryOrders (tables not joined)*

Exercise 12a

Use the Customer, Rental and Tape tables to build queries and generate the necessary information.

1. List all customers in ascending order by last name showing first name, last name, tape ID, title, type code, date rented and rental fee for all action tapes. Name the query Action Tapes.
2. For all tapes rented from 1st January to 10th January 2006, list the name of the customer renting the tape, the tape title and the date rented. Name the query Jan 2006 Services.
3. List all customers who rented tapes from 2006/01/03 and beyond. Show the following fields: first name, last name, tape ID, title and date rented. Name the query New Rentals.

Exercise 12b

Using the same tables, create appropriately named queries for the following:

1. Display the names of all female customers who rented tapes beginning with 'D'.
2. List the rental fees for all tapes with IDs beginning with '2' which were rented by female customers.
3. Display all customers who live in St Michael or St Thomas.
4. Display all the customers whose first names end with 'E'.

13. Calculated fields

When you create a query, you can add calculated fields – fields that were not originally part of a table but instead are calculated using other fields. In order to illustrate the concept, we'll use a table of Items (part of which is shown in Figure 13.1).

Note

Any time you type a field name in an expression you should put it in square brackets [ ]. <u>You shouldn't put anything else besides the field name in square brackets.</u>

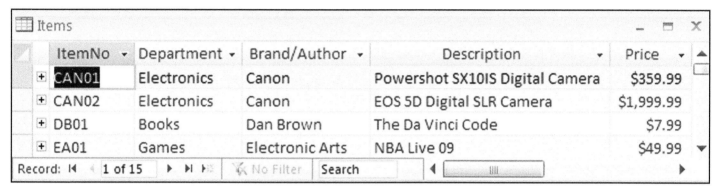

Figure 13.1 *Items table (truncated)*

Creating calculated fields

Let's examine at the process of creating a calculated field by looking at an example.

Scenario

- You want to calculate the Price in BDS dollars by multiplying the Price *$ 1.98.
- This calculated field is to be named BDS.
- You want to show the ItemNo, Price and BDS fields.

Query design

First we add the ItemNo and Price fields by double-clicking on them. However, we can't do that with the BDS field because it doesn't exist yet.

To create the calculated field we have to <u>type</u> an expression in the Field box of the first blank column. The expression has two parts:

1 BDS: (tells Access that we want to name the field 'BDS')
2 [Price] * 1.98 (tells Access how the field is to be calculated).

The second part tells the computer to take the value in the Price field and to multiply it by 1.98. Notice that you don't put in the $.

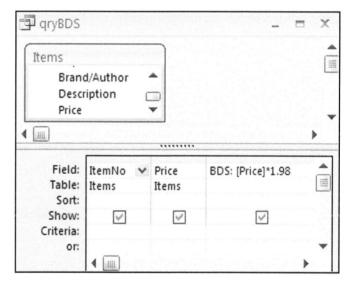

Figure 13.2 *qryBDS (Design)*

Results

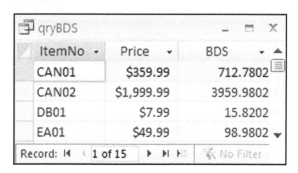

Figure 13.3 *qryBDS (Results)*

Calculating percentages

To calculate a percentage of a field you use a formula similar to this one:

  [fieldname] * percentage / 100

For example, if you want to calculate 2% of a salary you'd use the formula:

  [salary] * 2 / 100

Scenario

- You want a query that shows the ItemNo, Price and two calculated fields: Discount and Discounted Price.
- The Discount is 5% of the Price.

Query design

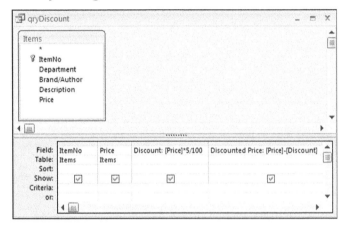

Figure 13.4 *qryDiscount (Design)*

Tip

You could have calculated the Discounted Price without relying on the Discount field by using this formula:

Discounted Price: [Price] – [Price] * 5 / 100.

Results

Figure 13.5 *qryDiscount (Results)*

Parameter errors

When you are working with Queries, Access assumes that anything you put in square brackets is the name of a field. If it does not find any fields (or calculated fields) with that name, it gives an error like the one shown in Figure 13.6.

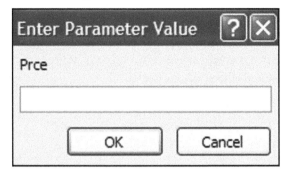

Figure 13.6 *Parameter errors*

In this case, you'd have to correct the part of your formula that says '[Prce]'. The most common causes of parameter errors like this are:

1 misspelling a name, for example typing Prices instead of Price or typing the word Quantity when the field is actually called Qty
2 placing something that you shouldn't in square brackets, for example [Price * 1.98]

14. Summarising data using queries

Queries can also be used to summarise data. For instance, you could use a query to find the total cost of an order. In a case like this, a calculated field (despite its name) would be no help since all it would do is add another column to the data. Instead, you have to use another technique, which will be described shortly.

In this chapter, we will be using the Items table shown in Figure 14.1.

Finding an overall summary

The simplest way to summarise the data in a table is to find the overall total, maximum, average, and so on for a particular column. For example, you could find the total overall Salary in an Employee table.

The general method you'd use is:

- Add the field that you want to summarise to the query design.
- Make sure that the Total row is visible by clicking the Totals button Σ near the top of the window.
- Change the field's Total row setting from 'Group By' to whatever statistic you want to find (for example max, min, average).

Scenario

- You want to find the maximum price in the Items table.

Query design

Since we want to find the maximum price, we add the Price column to the design and turn on the Total row. At first it says 'Group By' but, because it is actually a combo box, we can click it and see what other options are available. We select the Max option.

Figure 14.2 *qryMaxPrice (Design)*

ItemNo	Department	Brand/Author	Description	Price
CAN01	Electronics	Canon	Powershot SX10IS Digital Camera	$359.99
CAN02	Electronics	Canon	EOS 5D Digital SLR Camera	$1,999.99
DB01	Books	Dan Brown	The Da Vinci Code	$7.99
EA01	Games	Electronic Arts	NBA Live 09	$49.99
INT01	Software	Intuit	QuickBooks Pro 2009	$99.95
MIC01	Electronics	Microsoft	Zune MP3 Player	$232.47
MIC02	Software	Microsoft	Windows Vista Ultimate	$238.95
MIC03	Software	Microsoft	Office Home and Student 2007	$79.99
MIC04	Games	Microsoft	Gears of War 2	$53.99
PAR01	DVD	Paramount	Iron Man	$22.99
RL01	Books	Robert Ludlum	The Bourne Identity	$7.99
SAM01	Electronics	Samsung	50-Inch Plasma HDTV	$1,248.02
SON01	Electronics	Sony	Cybershot DSC-T700 Digital Camera	$283.32
SON02	Electronics	Sony	Bravia 52-Inch LCD HDTV	$2,466.49
WB01	DVD	Warner Bros.	The Dark Knight	$20.99

Record: 8 of 15   No Filter   Search

Figure 14.1 *The Items table*

Results

Because we are finding the overall maximum, there will only be one value when you run the query. Notice that Access calls the column MaxOfPrice to indicate what it is doing.

Figure 14.3 *qryMaxPrice (Results)*

Grouping

Suppose instead of finding the <u>overall</u> maximum, we want to divide the Items table into groups and find the maximum for each group. If we grouped by the Department, we'd want something like this:

Department	MaxOfPrice
Books	maximum price for books
DVD	maximum price for DVDs
Electronics	maximum price for electronics
…	…

Scenario

- You want to find the maximum price of each Department in the Items table.

Figure 14.4 *qryMaxDepartmentPrice (Design)*

Query design

This time we have to add two fields – Department and Price. If the Total row is not visible, we display it by clicking the Σ button. We don't have to change anything for the Department column since 'Group By' is the default. However, we have to change the Total setting under the Price to 'Max'.

Results

Figure 14.5 *qryMaxDepartmentPrice (Results)*

Note

When you group by a column, Access automatically sorts by that column.

Exercise 14

Use the `Videos` database to perform the following queries.

1 Calculate the average cost of a tape. Save the query as <u>AvgCost</u>.
2 Use a query called <u>NumInStock</u> to determine the total quantity of tapes in stock.
3 In a single query, calculate the minimum, maximum and average number of minutes per tape. Call the query <u>Minutes</u>.
4 Calculate the average length of a tape for each rating. Call the query <u>LengthPerRating</u>.
5 In a query called <u>MinRatingCost</u>, calculate the minimum cost of a tape for each rating.
6 Use a query called <u>Fees</u> to find the total rental fees paid by each customer. It should also list the customer ID, last name and first name. Rename the SumOfRentalFee field as TotalFee.

15. Make Table and Update queries

So far you have been using the default type of query called the <u>Select Query</u>. In this chapter you will be introduced to two other types of queries:

- <u>Make Table queries</u> – which you can use to generate tables.
- <u>Update queries</u> – which you can use to change values in a table.

Make Table queries

Of the two types Make Table queries are easier, so we'll look at them first. To create a Make Table query:

- Create the query as you normally would.
- Change it to a Make Table query.
- Specify the name of the table that the query is to create.

When you run a Make Table query, instead of displaying the results like a Select query, it will create the table that you specified and put those results in it.

Changing to a Make Table query

Access 2003
In Access 2007 you can change the type of query via the Query menu. So to switch to a Make Table query, just click: Query, Make Table Query...

Access 2007
In Access 2007, you change query type by clicking the appropriate button on the Ribbon's Query Design tab.

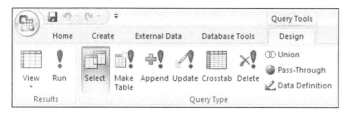

Figure 15.1 *Query Design tab (Access 2007)*

Specifying the destination table
Regardless which version of Access you have, when you switch to a Make Table query a window will popup so that you can type the name of the table that the query is to create.

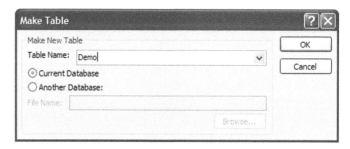

Figure 15.2 *Specifying the destination table*

Why use Update queries?

You might be wondering 'If I want to change a value in a table, why can't I just change it manually?' There certainly is nothing stopping you from changing the values manually and if it is just <u>one</u> value, this might actually be the best option. But what if you tried to change <u>several</u> values manually? You would probably:

- take a long time
- make typographical or random errors in your calculations
- forget to change some of the values

Once you do an Update query correctly, you don't have to worry about <u>any</u> of these things.

Creating an Update query

To create an Update query:

- Create a query using the Design view.
- Add the table you want to update.
- Change the query from a Select query to an Update query.
- Add the field to be updated, and in its <u>Update To</u> row, type either a value or formula that Access will use to update the values in the table.

Switching to an Update query
To switch to an Update query:

- Click Query, Update Query (in Access 2003 or earlier)
- Or Click the Update button of the Design tab of the Ribbon (in Access 2007 or later).

Scenario
- You want to increase all the ages in the Members table by 1.

Query design

Since we want to update the Members table, we add it to the design and change the query to an Update query. Then we add the Age column, because that is what we want to update. But what do we put in its Update To box?

We want the computer to take whatever value is currently in the Age field and add 1 to it. <u>You might think you could put '1' in the Update To row. But all this would do is change all the ages to 1.</u> Instead we use the formula: [Age] + 1

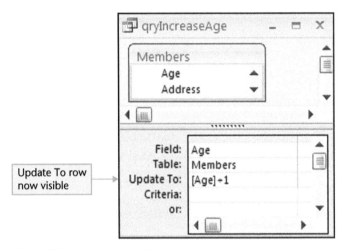

Figure 15.3 *qryIncreaseAge (Design)*

Results

Note

If you got a Security Warning but didn't enable content, you won't be able to run update queries.

When you click the run button (!), you'll get the following confirmation dialogue:

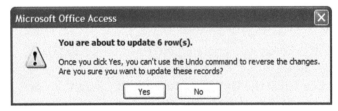

Figure 15.4 *Update Rows confirmation dialogue*

Microsoft Access always tells you how many rows that it is <u>going</u> to update. Clicking Yes will cause Access to actually perform the update.

Note

Since you can't undo an Update query, you should save a copy of the table you're going to update, before you run the query. Make sure you don't run the update query more than once.

In order to see the results of an Update query, you can click the Datasheet icon in the top left of the window.

Here are the results of the query. Note that you'll only see the fields that were updated. Of course, you could also open the table itself to see the changes.

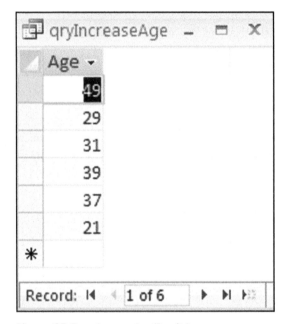

Figure 15.5 *qryIncreaseAge (Results)*

Updating selected records

There are some cases where you want to update <u>some</u> of the records. Fortunately, the procedure is not much different – you only have to add additional fields to set the criteria.

Scenario

- You want to increase the prices of all the games by 5%.

Query design

We want to update the Price column so we add that to the design view and change the Query to an Update Query. Then we put in the formula to increase the price by 5%:

[Price] + [Price] * 5 / 100.

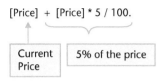

Current Price   5% of the price

But we don't want to change prices for all the items – just the games. So we add the Department field and set its criteria to 'Games'.

Figure 15.6 *qryUpdateGamesPrices (Design)*

Results

When we run the query, Access notifies us that is updating two rows – which is good since there are only two games.

Figure 15.7 *qryUpdateGamesPrices (Results)*

Use the `Videos` database in your exercise folder to perform these queries:

1 All tapes beginning with 'D' should be reduced by $1.50 due to the tapes being outdated. Create (and run) a query called <u>Sale</u> to make this change.
2 Use a query to give all customers with an address containing 'Hall' a 2% discount for each tape rented. Call it <u>New Campaign</u>.
3 Use a query to create a table called <u>Final</u> that calculates the total rental fee for each customer.
4 The table resulting from question 3 should have two fields: Customer ID and SumOfRental Fee. Manually rename the latter field to FeeTotal.
5 Use a selection query to calculate the VAT that each customer in the <u>Final</u> table has to pay. It should display the Customer ID, FeeTotal and VAT fields. Save the query as <u>VAT</u>. (VAT = 15%)
6 Create a query called <u>Total Cost</u> that uses the information in the VAT query to calculate the total cost each customer must pay. (Total Cost = FeeTotal + VAT). It should display the Customer ID, FeeTotal and Total Cost fields.
7 Calculate the total, average, maximum and minimum rental fees in a single query called <u>Statistics</u>.

16. Creating reports

In this chapter, you will learn how to create a report in Microsoft Access. A report is an effective way of presenting data in a printed format. The information in reports can come from tables and queries.

Throughout this chapter you will be creating a report that:

- includes the following fields: FirstName, LastName, Department, Description, Price, Qty
- is grouped by the Department field
- displays the total number of items ordered from each department
- is sorted by Department, then LastName, then FirstName

Figure 16.1 shows how the report that we are creating is supposed to look.

Starting the Report Wizard

In order to create a report, you use the Report Wizard, which takes you through the process of creating a report, step by step. (You can follow the steps using the `MyStore` database provided on the CD in the exercise folder for Chapter 16.)

Access 2003
To start the Report Wizard in Access 2003:

- Switch to the Reports tab of the Database Window.
- Double-click on the <u>Create Report using Wizard</u> option.

Access 2007
If you want to design a query in Access 2007:

- Switch to the Create tab of the Ribbon.
- Click on the Report Wizard button.

Using the Report Wizard

Step 1 – Select the fields you need
The first step is to select the fields you need from the list of tables and queries (Figure 16.2).

- Select the table/query that contains the fields you need.
- Select some of the fields from that table.
- Use the buttons to send across the fields to the list on the right.

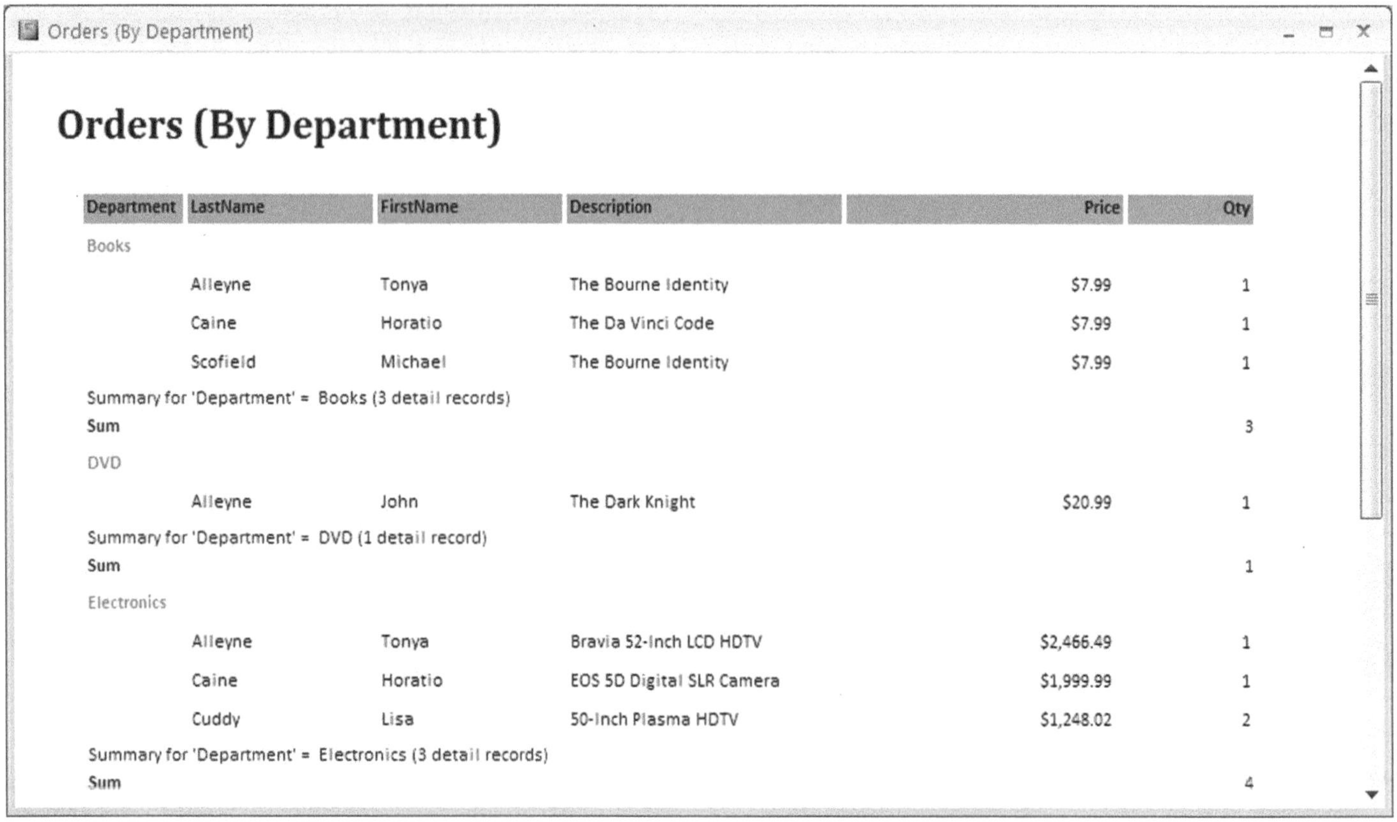

Department	LastName	FirstName	Description	Price	Qty
Books					
	Alleyne	Tonya	The Bourne Identity	$7.99	1
	Caine	Horatio	The Da Vinci Code	$7.99	1
	Scofield	Michael	The Bourne Identity	$7.99	1
Summary for 'Department' = Books (3 detail records)					
Sum					3
DVD					
	Alleyne	John	The Dark Knight	$20.99	1
Summary for 'Department' = DVD (1 detail record)					
Sum					1
Electronics					
	Alleyne	Tonya	Bravia 52-Inch LCD HDTV	$2,466.49	1
	Caine	Horatio	EOS 5D Digital SLR Camera	$1,999.99	1
	Cuddy	Lisa	50-Inch Plasma HDTV	$1,248.02	2
Summary for 'Department' = Electronics (3 detail records)					
Sum					4

Figure 16.1 *Example report*

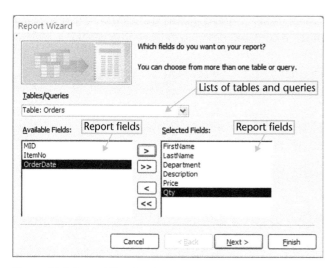

Figure 16.2 *Report Wizard (selecting fields)*

Button	What it does
>	add selected field(s) to the list on the right
>>	add all fields to the list on the right
<	remove selected field from the list on the right
<<	remove all fields from the list on the right

In our example, we want fields from three tables (Members, Items and Orders). We switch to each of these tables and select the fields we need from each.

Note

Some people prefer to create a report query before they start the wizard. In that case you would just select the fields from that query.

Step 2 – Choose how you want to view your data

The next step is to choose how you want to view your data (Figure 16.3):

- Choose a view from the left.
- Look at the preview on the right.

Note

If you have to group later, choose the view that is 'flat' unless there is another view that matches the grouping.

Since we have to group later, we choose the by Items view because that is the one that is 'flat' (i.e. the one with one box).

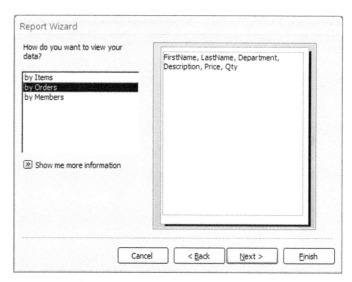

Figure 16.3 *Report Wizard (selecting fields)*

Step 3 – Add grouping levels (if any)

Next, you add any grouping levels. To group by a field:

- Select the field on the left
- Click the > arrow.

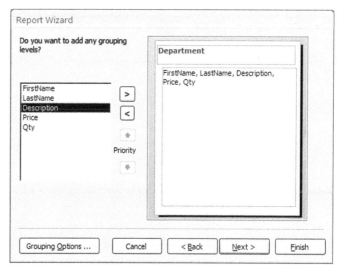

Figure 16.4 *Report Wizard (add grouping levels)*

In our example, we are grouping by the Department field. Notice that in the preview, the other fields are 'under' the Department field.

Step 4 – Sort the records (if necessary)

The next step is to sort the records:

- Add the first field you want to sort by.
- Choose the sort order. The default order is Ascending. If you want to change it to Descending just click the button.
- Repeat as necessary.

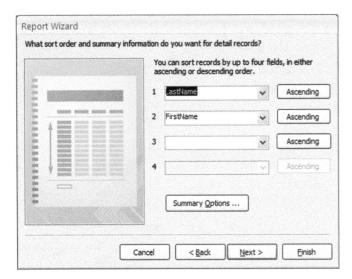

Figure 16.5 *Report Wizard (sort fields)*

Although we want to sort by Department first, Department is not in the list of sort fields. That is because when you group by a field you automatically sort by that field.

Step 5 – Add group summaries (if necessary)

If your report is to include group summaries:

- Click on the Summary Options button.
- Place a tick next to each of the calculations you want to include in your report.
- Click the OK button.

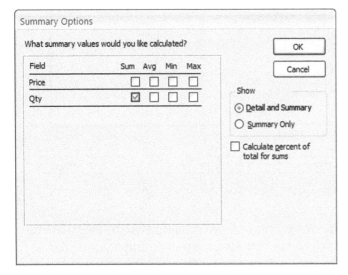

Figure 16.6 *The Summary Options window*

Note

The Summary Options button will only appear if your report is grouped and contains fields that can be calculated (numeric or currency fields).

Our report will contain group summaries since it is required to display 'the total number of items ordered from each department'. We have grouped by Department, so any summary options that we add will be calculated for each department.

Step 6 – Choose report layout and orientation

Choose the layout and orientation you want. The default style is 'Stepped' but it is a matter of preference. If your report contains several columns or has columns that are very wide (like ours) choose the Landscape orientation.

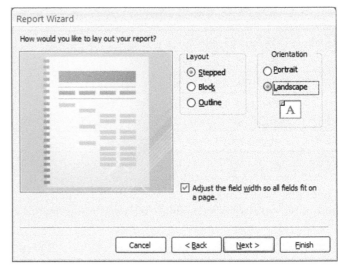

Figure 16.7 *Choose report layout*

Step 7 – Choose report style

Choose the style you want. Again it is a matter of preference.

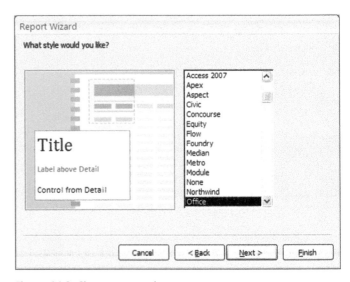

Figure 16.8 *Choose report style*

Step 8 – Choose report title

Type the title you want to give to your report and click OK.

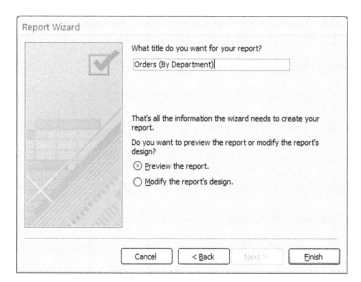

Figure 16.9 *Choose title*

That's it. We're done. If the Preview Report option is selected, you will see what your report looks like. To see what the report in this example looks like, see Figure 16.1.

Exercise 16

Use the `Videos` database to make the following reports.

1 Make a report from the Customer table to print the following information: Customer ID, Last name, First name, Address, Home telephone and Work telephone. The report should be sorted in the Last name and First name fields.
2 Make a report from the Tape table to list the following information: Tape ID, Title, Type code, Rated, Minutes, Cost, Quantity. Sort the report in ascending order.
3 Make a report to show the Customer Name, Date Rented, Title, Type Description and Rental Fee. Group the report by customer. The report title should be 'List of Rentals'. Sort the report in ascending order.

17. Printing

Eventually, after all that hard work creating your database objects such as queries and reports, you are going to want to put them on paper. Fortunately, printing database objects is very straightforward (with the exception of Relationships).

Print Preview

Before you print an item, you should preview it to see how it looks and how many pages it will require. When you want to preview an item, the first thing to do is to select it from the list of objects in the database. Then:

- In Access 2003, click File, Print Preview.
- In Access 2007, click the Microsoft Office button, point at Print then click Print Preview.

When you are finished previewing what the object will look like, you can:

- Click the Close Preview button if you want to exit the Print Preview.
- Click the Page Setup button if you want to change the margins or the orientation.
- Click the Print button if you are ready to print.

Printing tables, queries and reports

You can print an item by clicking the Print button from the Print Preview. Alternatively you can:

- Select the item from the list of objects in the database.
- Click File (or the Microsoft Office button), then Print.
- When the Print dialogue appears, specify which pages to print and how many copies you want.
- Click the OK button to print.

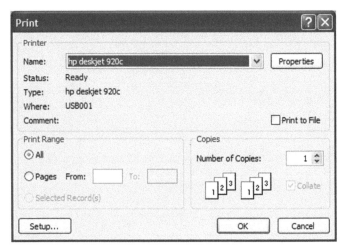

Figure 17.1 *Print dialogue*

Printing relationships

Printing relationships In Microsoft Access is a little trickier than printing other Microsoft Access objects. This is because Access must first create a relationship report and then print <u>that</u>.

Access 2003
In Access 2003:

- Open the Relationships window.
- Click File, Print Relationships… Access will then create the relationship report.
- Click File, Print or click the Print button in the Database toolbar.

Access 2007
To print relationships in Access 2007:

- Open the Relationships window.
- Click the Relationship Report button (Figure 17.2).
- Click the Microsoft Office button then click Print.

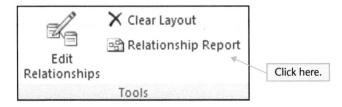

Figure 17.2 *Relationship Report button*

Index